REF

DATE			

Chicago Public Library

REFERENCE

Form 178 rev. 1-94

BAKER & TAYLOR

The Double Eagle Guide to

CAMPING *in*

WESTERN

PARKS *and* FORESTS

VOLUME III
FAR WEST

CALIFORNIA
NEVADA

A DOUBLE EAGLE GUIDE™

DISCOVERY PUBLISHING
BILLINGS, YELLOWSTONE COUNTY, MONTANA USA

The Double Eagle Guide to Camping in Western Parks and Forests
Volume III Far West

PUBLISHED BY
Discovery Publishing
Editorial Offices
Post Office Box 50545
Billings, Montana 59105 USA

Discovery Publishing is an independent, private enterprise. The information contained herein should not be construed as reflecting the publisher's approval of the policies or practices of the public agencies listed.

Information in this book is subject to change without notice.

Cover Photos (clockwise from the top)
Humboldt National Forest, Nevada
Lake Owyhee State Park, Oregon
Memphis Lake State Recreation Area, Nebraska
Big Bend National Park, Texas

Frontispiece: Emerald Bay State Park, California

10 9 8 7 6 5 4 3 2 1

April 1, 1996   7:37 PM Mountain Time

Produced, printed, and bound in the United States of America.

ISBN 0-929760-23-9

TABLE OF CONTENTS

(Continued on the following page)

INTRODUCTION TO THE *Double Eagle*™ SERIES

Whether you're a veteran of many Western camps or are planning your first visit, this series is for you.

In the six volumes of *The Double Eagle Guide to Camping in Western Parks and Forests*, we've described most public campgrounds along or conveniently near the highways and byways of the 17 contiguous Western United States. Also included is basic information about jackcamping and backpacking on the millions of acres of undeveloped public lands in the West. Our goal is to provide you with accurate, detailed, and yet concise, *first-hand* information about literally thousands of camping areas you're most likely to want to know about.

The volumes which comprise the *Double Eagle*™ series constitute a significant departure from the sketchy, plain vanilla approach to campground information provided by other guidebooks. Here, for the first time, is the most *useful* information about the West's most *useable* public camping areas. We've included a broad assortment of campgrounds from which you can choose: From simple, free camps, to sites in deluxe, landscaped surroundings.

The name for this critically acclaimed series was suggested by the celebrated United States twenty-dollar gold piece--most often called the "*Double Eagle*"--the largest and finest denomination of coinage ever issued by the U.S. Mint. The *Double Eagle* has long been associated with the history of the West, as a symbol of traditional Western values, prosperity, and excellence.

So, too, the *Double Eagle*™ series seeks to provide you with information about what are perhaps the finest of all the West's treasures--its public recreational lands owned, operated, and overseen by the citizens of the Western United States.

We hope you'll enjoy reading these pages, and come to use the information in the volumes to enhance your own appreciation for the outstanding camping opportunities available in the West.

Live long and prosper.

Thomas and *Elizabeth Preston*
Publishers

CONVENTIONS USED IN THIS SERIES

The following conventions or standards are used throughout the *Double Eagle*™ series as a means of providing a sense of continuity between one park or forest and other public lands, and between one campground and the next.

State Identifier: The state name and number combination in the upper left corner of each campground description provides an easy means of cross-referencing the written information to the numbered locations on the maps in the Appendix.

Whenever possible, the campgrounds have been arranged in what we have determined to be a reasonable progression, and based on *typical travel patterns* within a region. Generally speaking, a north to south, west to east pattern has been followed. In certain cases, particularly those involving one-way-in, same-way-out roads, we have arranged the camps in the order in which they would be encountered on the way into the area, so the standard plan occasionally may be reversed.

Campground Name: The officially designated name for the campground is listed, followed by the park, forest, or other public recreation area in which it is located.

Location: This section allows you to obtain a quick approximation of a campground's location in relation to nearby major communities.

Access: Our *Accurate Access* system makes extensive use of highway mileposts in order to pinpoint the location of access roads, intersections, and other major terminal points. (Mileposts are about 98 percent reliable--but occasionally they are mowed by a snowplow or an errant motorist, and may be missing; or, worse yet, the mileposts were replaced in the wrong spot!) In some instances, locations are noted primarily utilizing mileages between two or more nearby locations--usually communities, but occasionally key junctions or prominent structures or landmarks.

Since everyone won't be approaching a campground from the same direction, we've provided access information from two, sometimes three, points. In all cases, we've chosen the access points for their likelihood of use. Distances from communities are listed from the approximate **midtown** point, unless otherwise specified. Mileages from Interstate highways and other freeway exits are usually given from the approximate center of the interchange. Mileages from access points have been rounded to the nearest mile, unless the exact mileage is critical. All instructions are given using the current official highway map available free from each state.

Directions are given using a combination of compass and hand headings, i.e., "turn north (left)" or "swing west (right)". This isn't a bonehead navigation system, by any means. When the sun is shining or you're in a region where moss grows on tree trunks, it's easy enough to figure out which way is north. But anyone can become temporarily disoriented on an overcast day or a moonless night while looking for an inconspicuous campground turnoff, or while being buzzed by heavy traffic at a key intersection, so we built this redundancy into the system.

Facilities: The items in this section have been listed in the approximate order in which a visitor might observe them during a typical swing through a campground. Following the total number of individual camp units, items pertinent to the campsites themselves are listed, then information related to 'community' facilities. It has been assumed that each campsite has a picnic table.

Site types: (1) Standard--no hookup; (2) Partial hookup--water, electricity; (3) Full hookup--water, electricity, sewer.

We have extensively employed the use of *general* and *relative* terms in describing the size, separation, and levelness of the campsites ("medium to large", "fairly well separated", "basically level", etc.). Please note that "separation" is a measure of relative privacy and is a composite of both natural visual screens and spacing between campsites. The information is presented as an *estimate* by highly experienced observers. Please allow for variations in perception between yourself and the reporters.

Parking Pads: (1) Straight-ins, (sometimes called "back-ins")-- the most common type, are just that--straight strips angled off the driveway; (2) Pull-throughs--usually the most convenient type for large rv's, they provide an in-one-end-and-out-the-other parking space; pull-throughs may be either arc-shaped and separated from the main driveway by some sort of barrier or 'island' (usually vegetation), or arranged in parallel rows; (3) Pull-offs--essentially just wide spots adjacent to the driveway. Pad lengths have been categorized as: (1) Short-- a single, large vehicle up to about the size of a standard pickup truck; (2) Medium--a single vehicle or combination up to the length of a pickup towing a single-axle trailer; Long--a single vehicle or combo as long as a crew cab pickup towing a double-axle trailer. Normally, any overhang out the back of the pad has been ignored in the estimate, so it might be possible to slip a crew cab pickup hauling a fifth-wheel trailer in tandem with a ski boat into some pads, but we'll leave that to your discretion.

Fire appliances have been categorized in three basic forms: (1) Fireplaces--angular, steel or concrete, ground-level; (2) Fire rings--circular, steel or concrete, ground-level or below ground-level; (3) Barbecue grills--angular steel box, supported by a steel post about 36 inches high. (The trend is toward installing steel fire rings, since they're durable, relatively inexpensive--50 to 80 dollars apiece--and easy to install and maintain. Barbecue grills are often used in areas where ground fires are a problem, as when charcoal-only fires are permitted.)

Toilet facilities have been listed thusly: (1) Restrooms--"modern", i.e., flush toilets and usually a wash basin; (2) Vault facilities--"simple", i.e., outhouses, pit toilets, call them what you like, (a rose by any other name.....).

Campers' supply points have been described at five levels: (1) Camper Supplies--buns, beans and beverages; (2) Gas and Groceries--a 'convenience' stop; (3) Limited--at least one store which approximates a small supermarket, more than one fuel station, a general merchandise store, hardware store, and other basic services; (4) Adequate--more than one supermarket, (including something that resembles an IGA or a Safeway), a choice of fuel brands, and several general and specialty stores and services; (5) Complete--they have a major discount store.

Campground managers, attendants and hosts are not specifically listed since their presence can be expected during the regular camping season in more than 85 percent of the campgrounds listed in this volume.

Activities & Attractions: As is mentioned a number of times throughout this series, the local scenery may be the principal attraction of the campground (and, indeed, may be the *only* one you'll need). Other nearby attractions/activities have been listed if they are low-cost or free, and are available to the general public. An important item: *Swimming and boating areas usually do not have lifeguards.*

Natural Features: Here we've drawn a word picture of the natural environment in and around each campground. Please remember that seasonal, even daily, conditions will affect the appearance of the area. A normally "sparkling stream" can be a muddy torrent for a couple of weeks in late spring; a "deep blue lake" might be a nearly empty hole in a drought year; "lush vegetation" may have lost all its greenery by the time you arrive in late October. Elevations above 500′ are rounded to the nearest 100′; lower elevations are rounded to the nearest 50′. (Some elevations are estimated, but no one should develop a nosebleed or a headache because of a 100′ difference in altitude.)

Season, Fees & Phone: Seasons listed are approximate, since weather conditions, particularly in mountainous/hilly regions, may require adjustments in opening/closing dates. Campground gates are usually unlocked from 6:00 a.m. to 10:00 p.m. Fee information listed here was obtained directly from the responsible agencies just a few hours before press time. Fees should be considered **minimum** fees *per camping vehicle*, since they are always subject to adjustment by agencies or legislatures. Discounts and special passes are usually available for seniors and disabled persons. The listed telephone number can be called to obtain information about current conditions in or near that campground.

Camp Notes: Consider this section to be somewhat more subjective in nature than the others. In order to provide our readers with a well-rounded report, we have listed personal comments related to our field observations. (Our enthusiasm for the West is, at times, unabashedly proclaimed. So if the prose sometimes sounds like a tourist promotion booklet, please bear with us--there's a lot to be enthusiastic about!)

Editorial remarks (Ed.) occasionally have been included.

A Word About Style...

Throughout the *Double Eagle*™ series, we've utilized a free-form writing concept which we call "Notation Format". Complete sentences, phrases, and single words have been incorporated into the camp descriptions as appropriate under the circumstances. We've adopted this style in order to provide our readers with detailed information about each item, while maintaining conciseness, clarity, and conversationality.

A Word About Print...

Another departure from the norm is our use of print sizes which are 10 to 20 percent larger (or more) than ordinary guides. (We also use narrower margins for less paper waste.) It's one thing to read a guidebook in the convenience and comfort of your well-lit living room. It's another matter to peruse the pages while you're bounding and bouncing along in your car or camper as the sun is setting; or by a flickering flashlight inside a breeze-buffeted dome tent. We hope *this* works for you, too.

A Word About Maps...

After extensive tests of the state maps by seasoned campers, both at home and in the field, we decided to localize all of the maps in one place in the book. Campers felt that, since pages must be flipped regardless of where the maps are located, it would be more desirable to have them all in one place. We're confident that you'll also find this to be a convenient feature.

A Word About 'Regs'...

Although this series is about public campgrounds, you'll find comparatively few mentions of rules, regulations, policies, ordinances, statutes, decrees or dictates. Our editorial policy is this: (1) It's the duty of a citizen or a visitor to know his legal responsibilities (and, of course, his corresponding *rights*); (2) Virtually every campground has the appropriate regulations publicly posted for all to study; and (3) If you're reading this *Double Eagle*™ Guide, chances are you're in the upper ten percent of the conscientious citizens of the United States or some other civilized country and you probably don't need to be constantly reminded of these matters.

And a Final Word...

We've tried very, very hard to provide you with accurate information about the West's great camping opportunities But occasionally, things aren't as they're supposed to be .....

If a campground's access, facilities or fees have been recently changed, please let us know. We'll try to pass along the news to other campers.

If the persons in the next campsite keep their generator poppety-popping past midnight so they can cook a turkey in the microwave, blame the bozos, not the book.

If the beasties are a bit bothersome in that beautiful spot down by the bog, note the day's delights and not the difficulties.

Thank you for buying our book. We hope that you'll have many terrific camping trips!

Northern California

Public Campgrounds

The Northern California map is located in the Appendix.

Northern California 1

JED SMITH
Jedediah Smith Redwoods State Park

Location: Northwest corner of California northeast of Crescent City.

Access: From U.S. Highway 199 at milepost 5 (0.7 mile east of the junction of U.S. 199 and California State Highway 197, 9 miles northeast of Crescent City, 77 miles southwest of Grants Pass, Oregon), turn south-west (i.e., right if approaching from Crescent City), to the park entrance station; just inside the entrance jog left for a few yards, then right into the campground.

Facilities: 108 campsites; (hike-bike sites are also available); sites are small to small+, level, with fair to good visual separation; parking pads are packed gravel, primarily short to medium-length straight-ins; adequate space for a medium to large tent in most sites; storage lockers; large fireplaces; firewood is available for gathering on nearby national forest lands, or b-y-o; water at several faucets; restrooms with showers; holding tank disposal station; paved driveways; complete supplies and services are available in Crescent City.

Activities & Attractions: Visitor center and museum featuring exhibits related to local flora and fauna; self-guided nature trail; guided nature walks in summer; swimming area; campfire center for scheduled evening programs; fishing; day use areas.

Natural Features: Located along the banks of the Smith River in a dense forest of lofty redwoods, and an almost uncountable number of other varieties of trees, shrubs, ferns and small plants; campsites are well-shaded/sheltered; some sites are along the riverbank; summers are typically sunny and hot, winters are very rainy; elevation 150'.

Season, Fees & Phone: Open all year; please see Appendix for standard state park fees and reservation information; park office (707) 458-3310 or (707) 464-9533.

Camp Notes: Jedediah Smith, one of the greatest of the Mountain Men, was born in upstate New York in 1799, but he had moved west to join the ranks of the Mountain Men by the time he was 20. Smith's many remarkable journeys included one during which he passed through this region and discovered an overland route from Northern California to the Columbia River. Smith once commented that redwoods were the most noble trees he had ever seen. He probably would be honored knowing a place like this uncommonly beautiful spot, the northernmost of the California state parks, was named after him.

Northern California 2

PANTHER FLAT
Six Rivers National Forest

Location: Northwest corner of California northeast of Crescent City.

Access: From U.S. Highway 199 at milepost 16 +.8 (2 miles east of the Gasquet Ranger Station, 21 miles northeast of Crescent City, 65 miles southeast of Grants Pass, Oregon), turn north and proceed 0.1 mile down into the campground.

Facilities: 41 campsites; sites are medium to large with fairly good separation; parking pads are paved, mostly long, level straight-ins; adequate level space for a large tent in most sites; fireplaces; firewood is available for gathering in the area; water at faucets throughout; vault facilities; holding tank disposal station at a highway rest area, east of here, near milepost 33; gas and groceries at Gasquet, 2 miles west; complete supplies and services are available in Crescent City.

Activities & Attractions: Fishing; day use area; Redwoods National Park is nearby.

Natural Features: Located on a flat overlooking the Middle Fork of the Smith River in the Coast Range; campground vegetation consists of medium to dense, tall conifers and moderately dense underbrush on a thick carpet of forest material; a waterfall tumbles into a deep pool in the river here; the campground is situated about 70 feet above the river level; high, timbered ridges flank the river north and south; hot and dry in summer, very rainy in winter; elevation 500'.

Season, Fees & Phone: Open all year; $7.00; 14 day limit; Gasquet Ranger District (707) 457-3131.

Camp Notes: This campground tends to be a little cooler in summer than the others along this highway. For as close as this is to the temperate Pacific Ocean, it gets surprisingly sizzley in summer. Temps rise to 100° F and beyond quite regularly in these parts.

Northern California 3

GRASSY FLAT
Six Rivers National Forest

Location: Northwest corner of California northeast of Crescent City.

Access: From U.S. Highway 199 near milepost 19 (23 miles northeast of Crescent City, 63 miles southeast of Grants Pass, Oregon), turn south into the campground.

Facilities: 18 campsites; sites are generally medium to large, level, with fair separation; parking pads are gravel, mainly medium-length straight-ins; adequate space for a large tent in most sites; fireplaces; firewood is available for gathering in the area; water at several faucets; vault facilities; paved driveways; gas and groceries at Gasquet, 4 miles west; complete supplies and services are available in Crescent City.

Activities & Attractions: Fishing; Redwoods National Park.

Natural Features: Located on a flat above the Middle Fork of the Smith River; campground vegetation consists primarily of medium-dense conifers and light underbrush; high, timbered mountains border the river north and south; elevation 700'.

Season, Fees & Phone: Mid-May to mid-September; $7.00; 14 day limit; Gasquet Ranger District (707) 457-3131.

Camp Notes: Grassy Flat and its cousin camp, Patrick Creek, are both close to the highway, but the sites at Grassy Flat are perhaps a little farther from the road. Reportedly, there is excellent fishing in this area--for salmon, beginning in November; and for steelhead, starting in January.

Northern California 4

PATRICK CREEK
Six Rivers National Forest

Location: Northwest corner of California northeast of Crescent City.

Access: From U.S. 199 near milepost 22 (opposite a lodge, 26 miles northeast of Crescent City, 60 miles southeast of Grants Pass, Oregon), turn south into the campground.

Facilities: 17 campsites; sites are medium to large, essentially level, with fair separation; parking pads are gravel, mostly medium-length straight-ins; adequate space for large tents; fireplaces; firewood is available for gathering in the area; water at several faucets; restrooms; paved driveways; holding tank disposal station at a highway rest area, east of here, near milepost 33 +.5; gas and groceries at Gasquet, 7 miles west; complete supplies and services are available in Crescent City.

Activities & Attractions: Fishing; Redwoods National Park.

Natural Features: Located on a flat above the Middle Fork of the Smith River; medium-dense conifers and light underbrush provide adequate shade/shelter for most campsites; Patrick Creek enters the river from the north at this point; high, timbered mountains border the river; elevation 800'.

Season, Fees & Phone: May to October; $7.00; 14 day limit; Gasquet Ranger District (707) 457-3131.

Camp Notes: Another small, roadside, forest camp about 2 miles east of Patrick Creek is Cedar Rustic. It has 12 sites, drinking water and vaults, and may be available, subject to use requirements.

Northern California 5

MILL CREEK
Del Norte Coast Redwoods State Park

Location: Northern California Coast south of Crescent City.

Access: From U.S. Highway 101 at milepost 20 +.3 (6 miles south of Crescent City, 15 miles north of Klamath), turn east onto a paved park access road; proceed 1.3 miles to the park entrance station; continue down for 0.9 mile to a "T" intersection; turn left or right to the camp areas.

Facilities: 142 campsites in 2 loops; (several walk-in sites are also available); sites are small+ to medium+, reasonably level, with fairly good to excellent separation; parking pads are hard-surfaced, medium to medium+ straight-ins; tent spots are large and generally private; storage cabinets; fireplaces;

b-y-o firewood; water at several faucets; restrooms with showers; holding tank disposal station; paved driveways; complete supplies and services are available in Crescent City.

Activities & Attractions: Hiking trails include several interconnecting routes around the campground, also Last Chance Trail along an ocean bluff, and Damnation Creek Trail to an ocean beach; (trailheads for the latter 2 trails are near milepost 16, 4 miles south of the campground turnoff); nature trail; guided nature walks and campfire programs in summer; limited trout fishing on Mill Creek.

Natural Features: Located along the banks of Mill Creek in a redwood forest, bordered by steep, forested hills in the Coast Range; dense undergrowth provides excellent privacy for many campsites; some sites are creekside; a profusion of wildflowers is seen in spring; elevation 300'.

Season, Fees & Phone: April to October; please see Appendix for standard California state park fees and reservation information; park office (707) 464-9533.

Camp Notes: The regional climate is typically temperate and foggy, but the campground's microclimate is fairly sunny and warm in summer. Mill Creek is one of the finest camps in the state park system. If the Enchanted Forest had a campground, it might look like this.

Northern California 6

ELK PRAIRIE
Prairie Creek Redwoods State Park

Location: Northern California Coast south of Crescent City.

Access: From U.S. Highway 101 at milepost 127 +.2 (6 miles north of Orick, 14 miles south of Klamath, turn west onto a park access road; proceed 0.15 mile west then south to the entrance station; continue for 0.5 mile to the main campground. **Additional Access** for Gold Bluffs Beach primitive camp: from U.S. 101 near milepost 123 +.8 (3.4 miles south of the main park turnoff), turn west onto Davison Road and proceed 4 miles on a narrow, steep, winding, rough, gravel/dirt road to the Gold Bluffs Beach area; long vehicles or vehicles with trailers aren't allowed on Davison Road).

Facilities: 75 campsites in 3 loops; (hike-bike sites are also available); a dozen sites along the edge of the prairie are medium-sized, level, with nominal separation; remaining sites are level, and vary from small to spacious, with fairly good to very good separation; parking pads are paved, short to medium-length straight-ins; large tent spots; fireplaces or fire rings; firewood is usually for sale, or b-y-o; water at several faucets; restrooms with showers; holding tank disposal station; paved driveways; primitive campsites are also available at Gold Bluffs Beach; gas and groceries in Orick and Klamath.

Activities & Attractions: 70 miles of hiking trails within the park; self-guided nature trail; visitor center with extensive exhibits; campfire circle; guided nature walks and evening programs in summer; stream fishing; day use areas.

Natural Features: Located in a forested area along the edge of a small prairie/meadow; most sites are shaded/sheltered by tall trees and considerable undergrowth providing good separation; some sites are creekside; sites along the edge of the prairie are essentially unsheltered; Gold Bluffs Beach area includes secluded, pleasant Fern Canyon, north of the camping area; elevation 300'.

Season, Fees & Phone: Open all year; please see Appendix for standard California state park fees and reservation information; park office (707) 488-2171.

Camp Notes: Prairie Creek SP is probably best known for its several resident herds of Roosevelt elk. Elk are commonly seen browsing in the meadow near the campground. Although they are often thought of as "tame" elk because they feed in the open, the critters are simply reverting back to their earlier way of life. Like the grizzly, the elk was originally an animal of the plains and open hillsides.

Northern California 7

STONE LAGOON
Humboldt Lagoons State Park

Location: Northern California Coast north of Eureka.

Access: From U.S. Highway 101 at milepost 117 +.3 (17 miles north of Trinidad, 4 miles south of Orick), turn west onto a paved access road and go 0.2 mile down a very steep, narrow road to the beach and the camping area.

Facilities: Primitive camping opportunities ('open camping') are available on this beach; boat-in camps are available on the southwest shore of Stone Lagoon, with access from the visitor center parking lot; (use the sight tubes positioned in the parking lot to locate your landing point).

Activities & Attractions: Beachcombing; seasonally operated visitor center with exhibits and audio-visual programs, 2 miles south on the west side of the highway; motorless boating.

Natural Features: Located on an ocean beach at the north tip of Stone Lagoon; a conifer and brush clad bluff rises behind the beach; sea level.

Season, Fees & Phone: Open all year; please see Appendix for standard California state park fees; park office (707) 488-5435 (seasonally).

Camp Notes: When most of us hear the word "lagoon", we first think of palms, sunshine, sand, and placid waters. Well, with Humboldt Lagoons we've got the sand part right anyway. These lagoons are anything but placid and stagnant. Open to the sea, they're at the mercy of wind and waves, which first build 'barrier beaches' that impound the waters and create the lagoons. Lambasted by really heavy weather and freshwater runoff, the barriers are often breached and their contents spill into the ocean. Then the cycle starts all over again.

DRY LAGOON
Humboldt Lagoons State Park

Location: Northern California Coast north of Eureka.

Access: From U.S. Highway 101 at milepost 114 +.4 (14 miles north of Trinidad, 7 miles south of Orick), turn west onto a paved access road and proceed westerly for 0.5 mile; from this point, the environmental campsites can be reached via a marked trail which goes up a bluff for 200 to 400 yards to the campsites.

Facilities: Environmental (primitive) campsites with tables, fire rings, storage lockers, tent areas, vaults.

Activities & Attractions: Beachcombing on an extensive ocean beach, 0.5 mile west; seasonally operated park visitor center with exhibits and audio-visual programs, 1 mile north on the highway.

Natural Features: Located on a short bluff above a driftwood-strewn beach; the bluff is topped by conifers and shrubs; sea level.

Season, Fees & Phone: Open all year; please see Appendix for standard California state park fees; park phone (707) 488-5435 (seasonally).

Camp Notes: Dry Lagoon's beach is loaded with enormous driftwood logs, witnesses to the ferocity of North Coast weather. But plan to b-y-o firewood or charcoal for your campfire anyway. It would take three years to burn one of those beached behemoths whole--and it would take about the same amount of time to cut one into pieces small enough to dry and burn.

PATRICK'S POINT
Patrick's Point State Park

Location: Northern California Coast north of Eureka.

Access: From U.S. Highway 101 at milepost 106 (15 miles south of Orick, 6 miles north of Trinidad), turn southwest onto Patrick's Point Drive and proceed 0.2 mile; turn west (right) onto the park access road and proceed 0.1 mile to the entrance station; continue a few yards to a fork; turn northwest (right) to Patrick's Point and the Agate Beach camp areas, or south (left) to the camp areas near Abalone Point.

Facilities: 128 campsites in 2 main areas; (hike-bike sites are also available); sites are small to medium-sized, basically level, with nominal to good separation; parking pads are hard-surfaced, mostly short to medium-length straight-ins; ample space for large tents in most sites; storage cabinets; fireplaces or fire rings; firewood is usually for sale, or b-y-o; water at several faucets; restrooms with showers; paved driveways; groceries in Trinidad; gas and groceries in Orick.

Activities & Attractions: Rim Trail follows the coastline for 2 miles from the north to south park boundaries; beachcombing; rock climbing on 'Ceremonial Rock', an ancient sea stack which rises 107 feet above a meadow; guided nature walks and campfire programs in summer; small museum; day use areas.

Natural Features: Located above the ocean in a mixed environment of meadows and forests; most sites are situated on light to moderately forested flats sheltered by tall hardwoods and conifers, plus ferns and other undergrowth; a few sites are on more open, grassy sections; coastal fog and clouds keep the climate cool year 'round; buckets of rain in winter; elevation 200'.

Season, Fees & Phone: Open all year; please see Appendix for standard California state park fees and reservation information; park office (707) 677-3570.

Camp Notes: Patrick's Point is in an ideal location. It has many pleasantly secluded campsites in a forest atmosphere, within an easy walk of stretches of ocean beach and some superb vistas. Woodsmen traditionally refer to the peace and beauty of the outdoors as the "Cathedral in the Pines". Well, Patrick's Point's variation on that theme is "Wedding Rock". The rock is a sea stack which rises nobly above the surf. It was named in 1930 when the park's first ranger and his bride 'tied the knot' on its crest.

BOISE CREEK
Six Rivers National Forest

Location: Northwest California east of Eureka.

Access: From California State Highway 299 at milepost 37 + .2 (1.6 miles west of Willow Creek, 37 miles east of Arcata), turn north into the campground.

Facilities: 17 campsites, including 3 hike-bike sites; sites are mostly medium-sized, with fairly good separation; parking pads are gravel, basically level, short to medium-length straight-ins; tent spots are earth/grass, level and good-sized; fireplaces (many of the old, vertical variety); firewood is available for gathering in the surrounding area; water at a central faucet; vault facilities; paved driveways; limited supplies and services are available in Willow Creek.

Activities & Attractions: Nice view of the canyon and surrounding mountain areas from very near some sites; Berry Summit Vista, about 8 miles west, offers some wide mountain views; quarter-mile trail to the creek.

Natural Features: Located along the south edge of steep and deep Willow Creek Canyon; dense hardwood forest primarily of oak, provides excellent cover and shelter for the sites; forest floor is covered with sparse grass and leaves; Boise Creek flows from the south into Willow Creek near here; elevation 1000'.

Season, Fees & Phone: May to October; $6.00; 14 day limit; Lower Trinity Ranger District, Willow Creek, (916) 629-2118.

Camp Notes: The facilities at Boise are perhaps better for an overnight stop than for a lengthy stay. Be on the alert for the entrance, especially when approaching from the west. If you miss it on the first pass, the traffic may not readily give you a second chance. There's also a designated jackcamping area, East Fork, just off Highway 299 about four miles west of Boise Creek.

TISH TANG
Six Rivers National Forest

Location: Northwest California northeast of Eureka.

Access: From California State Highway 96 at milepost 8 + .1 (8 miles north of Willow Creek, 4 miles south of Hoopa), turn east onto a paved access road which winds 0.5 mile down to the campground.

Facilities: 40 campsites in a single large loop; (a group site is also available); sites are medium to medium+, with mostly good separation; parking pads are gravel, mostly short straight-ins; some pads may require additional leveling; tent spots are mostly level, grassy and good-sized; fireplaces; firewood is available for gathering in the area; water at several faucets; vault facilities; paved driveways; limited supplies and services are available in Willow Creek.

Activities & Attractions: Fishing; river floating; a number of forest roads lead toward the mountains and ridges bordering the valley; Horse Ridge National Recreation Trail provides access to Trinity Mountain.

Natural Features: Located in the Coast Range about 100 yards (depending upon the season and level of the water) from the Trinity River; Tish Tang A Tang Creek flows from the northeast into the Trinity River near here; campground vegetation consists of a fairly dense stand of oaks, manzanita and bushy pines; large open grassy area inside the loop drive; the river can almost be seen through the trees; Trinity Mountain rises to 6300' in a range to the east called Devil's Backbone; elevation 400'.

Season, Fees & Phone: May to November; $6.00; 14 day limit; Lower Trinity Ranger District, Willow Creek, (916) 629-2118.

Camp Notes: Tish Tang Campground is located along the south boundary of the Hoopa Valley Indian Reservation. Sites are far enough from the road so that there would be very little disturbance from traffic noise. It's a pleasant place with river access and some fantastic distant views.

AIKENS CREEK
Six Rivers National Forest

Location: Northwest California east of Eureka.

Access: From California State Highway 96 at milepost 28 +.35 (5 miles north of Weitchpec, 10 miles south of Orleans), turn east onto an access road; proceed 0.3 mile east, south and east to the campground.

Facilities: 27 campsites; sites are medium to medium+, with better than average separation; parking pads are gravel, mostly level straight-ins; good-sized, level, grassy tent spots; fireplaces; firewood is available for gathering in the surrounding area; water at several faucets; restrooms; double holding tank disposal station; paved driveways; gas and groceries at Bluff Creek Station, 1 mile south; minimal supplies and services are available in Orleans.

Activities & Attractions: Fishing, especially from August to November when the salmon are running; several back roads lead from the valley up into ridges and mountains, including the Salmon Summit National Recreational Trail and access to 6957' Salmon Mountain.

Natural Features: Located in the Coast Range on a forested bluff above the west bank of the Klamath River, where Aikens Creek flows from the west into the Klamath River; campground vegetation consist of pine, manzanita, madrone, and some grass and undergrowth; elevation 400'.

Season, Fees & Phone: May to November; $6.00; 14 day limit; Orleans Ranger Dist. (916) 627-3291.

Camp Notes: Really nice camp. At first glance, you may be misled by appearances and miss this campground. It's tucked away in a grove of hardwoods near the riverbank (behind a large dispersed camping area). With an elevation of only 400', this valley maintains a temperate climate. Another area campground is Bluff Creek. Access is west off the highway, 700 yards north of Aikens Creek. Bluff Creek's 11 sites (and a smokehouse) are on a forested flat above the highway.

PEARCH CREEK
Six Rivers National Forest

Location: Northwest California northeast of Eureka.

Access: From California State Highway 96 at milepost 39 +.4 (1 mile northeast of Orleans, 7 miles southwest of Somes Bar), turn southeast onto a paved access road; proceed 0.1 mile to the campground.

Facilities: 11 campsites in a loop and string, with a narrow turnaround at the end; parking pads are gravel, most are straight-ins, some may require minor additional leveling; some good, grassy, mostly level, medium-sized tent spots; fire rings or fireplaces (some of the large, upright variety); firewood is available for gathering in the area; water at several faucets; vault facilities; paved driveways; gas and groceries are available in Orleans.

Activities & Attractions: Fishing (especially during the fall salmon run); access to the Marble Mountain Wilderness from near Somes Bar; super scenery on the drive through this valley.

Natural Features: Located in the Coast Range in the Klamath River Valley; Pearch Creek flows from the south into the Klamath River, across the highway to the north; campground vegetation consists of some fairly tall conifers and oak trees, with lots of leafy brush; some smaller, open grassy areas near some campsites; high, forested ridges rise on both sides of the valley; elevation 400'.

Season, Fees & Phone: Open all year; $6.00; 14 day limit; Orleans Ranger District (916) 627-3291.

Camp Notes: There are two more, fairly remote campgrounds north of Orleans toward the settlement of Happy Camp: Oak Bottom on the Salmon River and Dillon Creek on the Klamath River are especially popular with sportsmen. Oak Bottom is on a side road three miles west of the highwayside community of Somes Bar; Dillon Creek is a roadside campground about 25 miles north of Orleans. Both camps are in Klamath National Forest. This region possesses some of the wildest, most remote, most scenic, most..... Well, you just have to see this beautiful country for yourself.

GRAYS FALLS
Six Rivers National Forest

Location: Northwest California east of Eureka.

Access: From California State Highway 299 at milepost 7 +.6 (13 miles east of Willow Creek, 6 miles east of Salyer, 37 miles west of Weaverville), turn north onto a paved access road; proceed 0.15 mile down to the campground.

Facilities: 33 campsites, including some triple sites; sites are rather narrow but 'deep', with fairly good separation; parking pads are gravel, medium to quite long; all pads are gravel straight-ins, and many may require additional leveling; most tent spots are fairly level, grassy, and adequate for larger tents; fireplaces; firewood is available for gathering in the area; water at several faucets; restrooms; paved driveways; holding tank disposal station at a rest area, 4 miles west on Highway 299; gas and groceries in the hamlets of Burnt Ranch, Salyer and Hawkins Bar; limited supplies and services are available in Willow Creek.

Activities & Attractions: Nature trail; campfire center; river floating, seasonally; nearby forest roads lead to Hennessy Ridge and South Fork of the Trinity River.

Natural Features: Located on a forested slope above the Trinity River in the Coast Range; moderately dense campground vegetation consists of conifers, oaks, madrones, and considerable underbrush; the Trinity River flows through a deep gorge along this stretch; rocky, tree-dotted canyon walls are visible across the gorge to the north and east; elevation 1100'.

Season, Fees & Phone: May to November; $6.00; 14 day limit; Lower Trinity Ranger District, Willow Creek, (916) 629-2118.

Camp Notes: Like most of the campgrounds along Highway 299, Grays Falls was located on whatever wide spot could be found in the canyon. In this case, the wide spot is perhaps a bit more vertical than some of the others. A number of the longer parking pads have a very steep approach 'apron', but once your vehicle makes it up the grade and gets settled in, it levels out tolerably well.

BURNT RANCH
Shasta-Trinity National Forest

Location: Northwest California east of Eureka.

Access: From California State Highway 299 at milepost 10 in the community of Burnt Ranch (16 miles east of Willow Creek, 34 miles west of Weaverville), turn north-east into the upper loop; or continue through the upper loop for 0.2 mile to the lower loop.

Facilities: 15 campsites; sites are small, sloped, with fair separation; parking pads are gravel/dirt, mostly short straight-ins; medium to large tent areas; fireplaces; some firewood is available for gathering in the area; water at faucets; vault facilities; steep, gravel/dirt driveway; gas and groceries in Burnt Ranch.

Activities & Attractions: Burnt Ranch Trail leads 0.75 mile down to the river; fishing.

Natural Features: Located on a slope in an open forest in a deep canyon above the Trinity River in the Coast Range; sites receive light-medium shade from tall conifers and some low hardwoods; elev. 1200'.

Season, Fees & Phone: May to October; $6.00; 14 day limit; Big Bar Ranger District (916) 623-6106.

Camp Notes: Most of the campground is some distance down off the main roadway, and many of the lower sites are in their own little forested 'compartments'. Smaller tents and vehicles will be more likely to find a level spot. This segment of highway is cut into the walls of an impressive canyon.

HAYDEN FLAT
Shasta-Trinity National Forest

Location: Northwest California east of Eureka.

Access: From California State Highway 299 near milepost 20 +.9 (25 miles east of Willow Creek, 1 mile west of Del Loma), turn northeast at 20 +.9 into the main campground, or southwest at 20 +.8 into a secondary section.

Facilities: 35 campsites in 4 loops, including one riverside loop on the south side of the highway; sites are small to medium-sized, with nominal to fair separation; parking pads are gravel, medium-length straight-ins; some pads may require additional leveling; most tent spots are grassy, fairly level, and adequate for large tents; fireplaces; firewood is available for gathering in the surrounding area; water at several faucets; vault facilities; paved driveways; camper supplies in Del Loma; limited supplies in Willow Creek; adequate supplies and services are available in Weaverville, 30 miles southeast.

Activities & Attractions: Fishing; boating and floating; hiking; day use area near the river.

Natural Features: Located on a fairly open forested flat along the Trinity River in the Coast Range; campground vegetation consists of conifers, madrones, tall grass and some undergrowth; forested hills border the grassy valley both to the north and south; two of the trio of loops on the north side of the highway are adjacent to one another, with the third one (farthest from the river) situated up in a draw; elevation 1200'.

Season, Fees & Phone: May to October; $6.00; 14 day limit; Big Bar Ranger District (916) 623-6106.

Camp Notes: Hayden Flat is in a relatively large, open area, as the name somewhat indicates. Just to the west of here, though, the Trinity River flows through a narrow gorge. The highway through these parts is steep and curvy. Watch out for logging trucks which are not inclined to lope along enjoying the scenery like the rest of us.

BIG FLAT
Shasta-Trinity National Forest

Location: Northwest California east of Eureka.

Access: From California State Highway 299 at milepost 31 + .5 (4 miles east of Big Bar, 12 miles west of Junction City), turn north onto a paved access road (Wheel Gulch Road) and continue for 0.1 mile up to the campground.

Facilities: 10 campsites; sites are medium to large, with nominal separation; parking pads are gravel, medium to long straight-ins; some pads may require minor additional leveling; some roomy, fairly level tent spots on a grassy surface; fireplaces and fire rings; firewood is available for gathering in the area; water at several faucets; vault facilities; paved driveways; camper supplies at a store a few yards west, on the highway; adequate supplies and services are available in Weaverville, 20 miles southeast.

Activities & Attractions: Fishing; river floating (access here is rather rocky but much easier than in other, more closed-in sections along the river); trail access to the Salmon-Trinity Alps Primitive Area; scenic drive through the Trinity Valley.

Natural Features: Located on a slightly rolling flat on a bench above the highway and above the river; the campground area is fairly open and grassy, with scattered, tall conifers and some hardwoods through the interior and more trees around the perimeter; forested hills rise immediately to the east and in the distance across the river; elevation 1300'.

Season, Fees & Phone: May to October; $6.00; 14 day limit; Big Bar Ranger District (916) 623-6106.

Camp Notes: Another area campground, Pigeon Point, is located near milepost 36 +.5 on Highway 299. It has 10 sites on a shelf above the Trinity River. A real effort was made to level the sites, and some are virtually cut into the hillside. There is no drinking water at Pigeon Point, but there is a paved foot path leading down to the river.

JUNCTION CITY
Public Lands/BLM Recreation Site

Location: Northwest California west of Redding.

Access: From California State Highway 299 at milepost 42 +.1 (1 mile west of Junction City, 14 miles east of Big Bar, 10 miles northwest of Weaverville), turn east into the campground. (The highway runs north and south following the river in this section.)

Facilities: 23 campsites in 2 loops; sites are small+ to medium-sized, with fair to good separation; parking pads are paved, level, medium to long straight-ins, some are double wide; most sites have level, grassy tent spots adequate for large tents; some framed and gravelled tent pads are provided; fireplaces; b-y-o firewood is recommended; water at several faucets; vault facilities; paved driveways; limited groceries in Junction City; adequate supplies and services are available in Weaverville.

Activities & Attractions: Fishing; access to Salmon-Trinity Alps Primitive Area from near the community of Junction City; the drive along the Trinity River is superscenic.

Natural Features: Located in the Coast Range on a grassy flat above the Trinity River; about half the sites are on fairly open grassy terrain, the other half are in moderately forested surroundings sheltered by short conifers and some hardwoods; wide vistas to the south, west and north; a steep, forested hillside lies behind the campground to the east; elevation 1500'.

Season, Fees & Phone: Open all year; $7.00; 14 day limit; BLM Redding Resource Area Office (916) 224-2100.

Camp Notes: The access to this campground is around a bend in the road and comes up rather suddenly. This is not a run-of-the-mill BLM campground. It's green. It's easily accessible. It has a chain link fence erected to protect its inhabitants from the trucks and other vehicles barreling by on Highway 299. (It's actually a pretty good camp.)

Northern California 19

GRIZZLY CREEK REDWOODS
Grizzly Creek Redwoods State Park

Location: Northwest California southeast of Eureka.

Access: From California State Highway 36 at milepost 17 +.7 (11 miles east of Carlotta, 30 miles west of Mad River), turn south through the park entrance, then swing easterly (left) to the campground.

Facilities: 30 campsites; (environmental-primitive sites are available 3 miles west at Cheatham Grove); sites are small to medium+, level, with fair to very good separation; parking pads are paved short to long straight-ins, some are extra wide; plenty of space for tents in most sites; storage cabinets; fireplaces and fire rings; firewood is usually for sale, or b-y-o; water at several faucets; restrooms with showers; paved driveways; gas and groceries in Carlotta; limited+ supplies and services are available in Fortuna, 20 miles west.

Activities & Attractions: Hiking, including a 1.25-mile trail which is accessible by crossing a 'summer only' bridge to the south bank of the river; self-guided nature trail (0.5 mile) into a grove of virgin redwoods; small visitor center with exhibits; guided nature walks and campfire programs in summer; fishing for trout in summer, upstream from the park (said to be good); fishing for salmon and steelhead in fall (good to very good); designated swimming beach; day use area.

Natural Features: Located on a flat along the north bank of the Van Duzen River in the Van Duzen River Valley; dense vegetation is comprised of huge redwoods mixed with small hardwoods; bordered by timbered hills; Grizzly Creek meets the river at this point; most campsites are in dense shade/shelter, some sites are near fairly open, grassy riverside areas; elevation 400'.

Season, Fees & Phone: Open all year; please see Appendix for standard California state park fees and reservation information; park office (707) 777-3683.

Camp Notes: Grizzly Creek Redwoods was established to set aside virgin groves of redwoods in the Van Duzen River Valley. Ironically, most campsites are within a few yards of the highway and its heavy logging truck traffic. The loggers begin to roll before daybreak and issue graphically audible examples of the expression "a rude awakening" for campers. Sites are still very much in demand during the summer season, though. If Grizzly Creek Redwoods' small campground is full, you might find a rustic campsite available at a Van Duzen County park, locally known as 'Swimmers Delight', located a few miles west on Highway 36.

Northern California 20

ALBEE CREEK
Humboldt Redwoods State Park

Location: Northwest California southeast of Eureka.

Access: From U.S. Highway 101 (*northbound*) near milepost 35 near Dyerville (2.5 miles north of Weott), take the exit signed for "Rockefeller Forest" & "Founders Tree" to a 4-way intersection; turn north (left) and go 0.2 mile across the river bridge, then west through the freeway underpass; from the west side of the freeway, travel south then west on Bull Creek Flats Road for 5.1 miles, then turn north (right) onto a paved access road and go 0.2 mile to the campground. **Alternate Access:** From Highway 101 (*southbound*), take the South Fork/Honeydew Exit (also signed for "Rockefeller Forest", "Founders Tree") to the west side of the freeway and onto Bull Creek Flats Road and continue as above to the campground.

Facilities: 39 campsites; (environmental-primitive campsites are located 0.6 mile southwest); sites are small to small+, with nominal to fairly good separation; parking pads are gravel, short to medium-length straight-ins; most pads will require a little additional leveling; medium to large, sloped areas for tents; storage cabinets; fireplaces; b-y-o firewood is recommended; water at several faucets; restrooms with showers; paved driveways; gas and groceries in Weott.

Activities & Attractions: Largest grove of old growth redwoods in the world at Rockefeller Forest, 3.5 miles east; nature trails at Rockefeller Forest and Founders Grove; tallest tree in the park at Founders Grove.

Natural Features: Located on a slope along the edge of a large clearing/meadow at the confluence of Bull and Albee Creeks; campsites are very lightly to densely shaded/sheltered by redwoods interspersed with slender hardwoods; elevation 300'.

Season, Fees & Phone: May to October; please see Appendix for standard California state park fees and reservation information; park office (707) 946-2311.

Camp Notes: Unlike the other principal campgrounds in the park, Albee Creek has a distant view. Most of the campsites are actually within the forest, but a 30-second walk would put you into the clearing and give you a visual shot up the valley to the nearby mountains. Albee Creek is the most remote of the park's trio of highway-accessible campgrounds, but if it's more solitude you seek, there are also six trail camps for backpackers in the interior of the park. Each small camp has piped water and vaults. Complete directions and the necessary permits can be obtained from the park office next to Burlington Campground.

BURLINGTON
Humboldt Redwoods State Park

Location: Northwest California southeast of Eureka.

Access: From U.S. Highway 101 at milepost 33 +.2 at the Weott Exit, (22 miles north of Garberville, 3 miles south of Dyerville, 25 miles south of Fortuna), turn west onto Newton Road; proceed west 0.2 mile to a "T" intersection; turn south (left) onto Avenue of the Giants (Road 254) and proceed south for 1.5 miles; turn east (left) into the campground.

Facilities: 58 campsites; (hike-bike sites are available 1.7 miles north at the Marin Garden Club Grove, check in at Burlington first); sites are small, level, with minimal separation; parking pads are paved, short straight-ins; tent spots are moderately large; storage cabinets; fire rings; firewood is usually for sale, or b-y-o; water at several faucets; restrooms with showers; holding tank disposal station nearby at Williams Grove; paved driveways; gas and groceries in Weott.

Activities & Attractions: Large visitor center next to the campground; nature walks and other interpretive programs, marathons and campfire programs are scheduled throughout the summer; over 100 miles of hiking and horse trails, including the strenuous Grasshopper Trail which leads to Grasshopper Peak at 3379'; (a detailed brochure/map with contour lines is available).

Natural Features: Located on a forested flat in a narrow valley across the Avenue from the South Fork of the Eel River; the entire valley has huge redwoods towering over a forest floor of hardwoods and ferns; elevation 100'.

Season, Fees & Phone: Open all year; please see Appendix for standard California state park fees and reservation information; park office (707) 946-2311.

Camp Notes: As California's premier sanctuary for *Sequoia sempervirens*, the regal coast redwood, Humboldt Redwoods has an atmosphere--a mystique if you will--that gives it a unique status among the Northern California redwood parks. Very little light filters down through the 'Giants', and the campground generally remains heavily shaded, with a unique atmosphere.

HIDDEN SPRINGS
Humboldt Redwoods State Park

Location: Northwest California southeast of Eureka.

Access: From U.S. Highway 101 at milepost 28 at the Myers Flat Exit, (5 miles south of Weott, 17 miles north of Garberville), from the east side of the freeway, go northeast on Avenue of the Giants for 0.7 mile, then turn north (left) onto the campground access road and proceed 0.1 mile to the campground.

Facilities: 155 campsites in a complex of strings and loops; sites are small to medium-sized, with good to very good separation; parking pads are paved, short to medium-length straight-ins; most pads will require additional leveling; small to medium-sized areas for tents, mostly sloped; fire rings; b-y-o firewood is recommended; restrooms with showers; holding tank disposal station at Williams Grove; paved driveways; camper supplies in Myers Flat.

Activities & Attractions: Trail between Hidden Springs and Williams Redwood Grove; Children's Forest Trail at Williams Grove; fishing; campfire programs; visitor center, near park headquarters, several miles northwest on Avenue of the Giants.

Natural Features: Located on a densely forested hillside above the South Fork of the Eel River; virtually all campsites are surrounded by dense vegetation, primarily tall redwoods, plus some hardwoods and ferns; elevation 450'.

Season, Fees & Phone: April to October; please see Appendix for standard California state park fees and reservation information; park office (707) 946-2311.

Camp Notes: Campsites at Hidden Springs are attractively finished, many with rail fences around the terraced sites and stairs leading to their tables. It appears as if whoever designed this campground considered it a real challenge to build one in this location.

BENBOW LAKE
Benbow Lake State Recreation Area

Location: Northwest California north of Leggett.

Access: From U.S. Highway 101 at milepost 8 +.6 (2 miles south of Garberville, 23 miles north of Leggett), proceed to the east side of the highway, and go east on Lake Benbow Drive for 0.1 mile to a "T" intersection; turn south (right) onto Benbow Drive and proceed 1 mile south and west; turn north (right) onto the campground access road, cross the bridge and continue for 0.25 mile north to the campground entrance.

Facilities: 75 campsites in 2 loops (one on each side of the highway connected by an underpass); sites are medium to large, with fair to good separation; parking pads are hard-surfaced, medium to long, mostly straight-ins, plus a few pull-throughs; tent spots are large, level, many are grassy; storage cabinets; fire rings; b-y-o firewood is recommended; water at several faucets; restrooms with cold showers; paved driveways; limited supplies and services are available in Garberville.

Activities & Attractions: Limited boating (motorless); hiking; guided activities, including nature walks and canoe hikes; campfire programs; designated swimming area; special programs and festivals in summer; large day use area nearby.

Natural Features: Located on a flat along the South Fork of the Eel River; campground vegetation consists of very light to medium-dense Doug firs, redwoods, madrones, oaks and grass; the lake and river valley are flanked by forested hills to the west and tree-dotted slopes to the east; 25-acre Benbow Lake; elevation 400'.

Season, Fees & Phone: April to November (depending on weather); please see Appendix for standard California state park fees and reservation information; phone c/o CDPR Eel River District Office, Weott, (707) 946-2311.

Camp Notes: Here's a novel wrinkle: Benbow Dam is installed across the river each spring to create a summer lake. The impoundment is created just downstream of the day use area. The lake's 25-acres may make it look like a sidewalk puddle compared to some of the whopper ponds in the state. But the recreation area's boundaries encompass about six miles of waterfront property, so there's still plenty of room along the meandering river to wade, splash, stroll or sit.

RICHARDSON GROVE
Richardson Grove State Park

Location: Northwest California north of Leggett.

Access: From U.S. Highway 101 at milepost 1 +.7 (7 miles south of Garberville, 18 miles north of Leggett), turn west into the park, then south (left) to the entrance station; from just inside the entrance, the Huckleberry camp area is to the west (right), the Madrone camp loop is 0.2 mile straight ahead; or turn east (left) from inside the entrance and go under the highway for 0.6 mile (past the day use area) and across the river bridge to the Oak Flat camp area.

Facilities: 169 campsites in 3 loops; (hike-bike sites and a small group camp are also available); sites vary from small to medium-sized, with nominal to good separation; parking pads are paved, short to medium-length, mostly straight-ins; many pads will require additional leveling; medium to large tent spots, may be a bit sloped; storage cabinets; fire rings; b-y-o firewood is recommended; water at several faucets; restrooms with showers; holding tank disposal station; paved driveways; camper supplies at the park store; limited supplies and services are available in Garberville.

Activities & Attractions: Hiking trails; nature trail; visitor center; campfire circle for scheduled interpretive programs in summer; guided walks and other activities in summer; limited fishing (winter steelhead and salmon); designated swimming beach (gravel); day use area.

Natural Features: Located in a forested valley along the South Fork of the Eel River; most campsites are densely forested in a mixture of conifers, including many tall redwoods, and hardwoods; sites in Oak Flat are on a semi-open area just above the riverbank; South Fork flows through a wide riverbed at this point; its size fluctuates considerably from a low level late in summer to great volumes (even flooding) in winter and spring; (the bridge to Oak Flat is removed each autumn); elevation 450'.

Season, Fees & Phone: Open all year (certain loops); please see Appendix for standard California state park fees and reservation information; park office (707) 247-3318.

Camp Notes: The campsites here vary considerably in size and shelter. If circumstances allow, you may want to take a look at all three loops before settling on a site that suits your needs and preferences. The park is named for F.W. Richardson, twenty-fifth governor of California. If you find the "Campground Full" shingle hung out here or at other state parks in the area, you might find a spot at a nearby primitive, wayside camp. Reynolds Wayside Campground is on the west side of U.S. 101, 11 miles south of Richardson Grove. Take the off-ramp for State Highway 271 to reach Reynolds.

STANDISH-HICKEY
Standish-Hickey State Recreation Area

Location: Northwest California south of Garberville.

Access: From U.S. Highway 101 at milepost 93 +.9 (1 mile north of Leggett, 24 miles south of Garberville), turn south to the park entrance station (Highway 101 runs in an east-west direction along this segment); turn left into the Rock Creek area, right into the Hickey area, or proceed 0.5 mile down a steep access road and across the river to the Redwood area.

Facilities: 162 campsites in 3 sections; (a hike-bike site is also available); sites are smallish, with nominal separation; most parking pads are packed gravel, short to short+ straight-ins, some are extra wide; most tent spots are medium-sized; parking pads and tent spots in the Redwood Area are quite small and rather sloped; sites in the Rock Creek and Hickey areas are reasonably level; storage cabinets; fireplaces or fire rings; b-y-o firewood; water at several faucets; restrooms with showers; paved driveways; limited supplies and services are available in Garberville.

Activities & Attractions: Miles of hiking trails; campfire center; ranger-assisted activities; swimmin' holes on the river; kayaking in season; fishing (mostly during winter steelhead and salmon runs).

Natural Features: Located along both banks of the South Fork of the Eel River; South Fork flows through a very narrow, steep-walled, rocky gorge in this section; most campsites are situated on a forested bluff above the north bank of the river; sites in the Redwood area are along the river's south bank; sites receive medium shade/shelter from tall redwoods and other conifers, tall hardwoods and moderate undergrowth; park area is 1012 acres; elevation 800'.

Season, Fees & Phone: Open all year (certain sections); please see Appendix for standard California state park fees and reservation information; park office (707) 925-6482.

Camp Notes: Interestingly, campsites in the Redwood area are accessible only in summer because a temporary bridge across the river must be removed each fall. The natural, 15-feet-deep swimmin' holes scooped into the gravelly riverbed are some of the park's main attractions.

Northern California
North Coast
Please refer to the Northern California map in the Appendix

USAL BEACH
Sinkyone Wilderness State Park

Location: Northwest California north of Fort Bragg.

Access: From California State Highway 1 at milepost 90 +.9 (13.5 miles north of Westport, 14.5 miles southwest of Leggett), head north on Usal Road (Mendocino County Road 431, dirt, rough) for 6 miles to the campground.

Facilities: 15 primitive camp/picnic sites; (9 hike-in trail camps are also available); fire rings; b-y-o firewood; b-y-o drinking water; vault facilities; nearest supplies (gas and groceries) are in Westport.

Activities & Attractions: 17-mile Lost Coast Trail follows the coastline from Usal Beach to Bear Harbor.

Natural Features: Located along a rugged section of the Coast Range; dense forests interspersed with meadows and grassy slopes make up the principal vegetation; elevation 100'.

Season, Fees & Phone: Open all year, subject to weather conditions; please see Appendix for standard California state park fees; phone c/o CDPR Eel River District Office, Weott, (707) 946-2311.

Camp Notes: Even magnificently engineered Highway 1 couldn't penetrate this terrain. This is the last sizable section of coastal wilderness north of San Francisco and it also goes by the name of the "Lost Coast". *Sinkyone* is the name of the Indian tribe which first occupied this territory.

WESTPORT UNION LANDING
Westport Union Landing State Beach

Location: Northern California Coast north of Fort Bragg.

Access: From California State Highway 1 at milepost 80 +.5 (3 miles north of Westport, 19 miles north of Fort Bragg, 24 miles southwest of Leggett), turn west into the park entrance; campsites are located within 1 mile north or south of the entrance.

Facilities: 130 campsites; sites are very small, with zilch to zero separation; parking surfaces are gravel, short straight-ins, or short to medium-length pull-offs; a little additional leveling will be required in many sites; adequate space for a small tent in most sites; fire rings; b-y-o firewood; water at several faucets; vault facilities; paved main driveway; gas and groceries in Westport.

Activities & Attractions: Beach access; surf fishing.

Natural Features: Located on a short, grassy, treeless bluff at the ocean's edge; hills and headlands closely border the beach; sea level.

Season, Fees & Phone: Open all year; please see Appendix for standard California state park fees; phone c/o CDPR Mendocino Coast District Office, Mendocino, (707) 937-5804.

Camp Notes: Campsites in this beach park are situated along the remains of Old Highway 1. The park closely parallels the new highway for nearly two miles. For several bucks you get a parking spot, a table and a fire ring. At this camp strip on the remote North Coast, the favorite campfire song is "It ain't much baby, but it's all we've got". But the views are very good.

MACKERRICHER
MacKerricher State Park

Location: Northern California Coast north of Fort Bragg.

Access: From California State Highway 1 at milepost 64 +.9 (3 miles north of Fort Bragg, 12 miles south of Westport), turn west onto a paved access road and proceed 0.15 mile to the park entrance station; Cleone camping area is just ahead and to the left of the entrance; or jog north (right) for a few yards then turn left and continue west for 0.2 mile to the Pinewood camp area, or 0.5 mile west to the Surfwood camping area.

Facilities: 143 campsites, including 12 walk-in sites, in 3 loops; sites are small to medium-sized, mostly level, with nominal to very good separation; parking pads are short to medium-length, gravel/sand or paved, straight-ins or pull-offs; tent spots are generally large; fireplaces; firewood is usually for sale, or b-y-o; water at several faucets; restrooms with showers; holding tank disposal station; paved driveways; adequate supplies and services are available in Fort Bragg.

Activities & Attractions: Surf fishing and abalone hunting; designated scuba areas; fishing for stocked trout on Lake Cleone; hand-propelled boating and small boat launch on the lake; beach hiking trail; trail around Lake Cleone; seal and whale watching; equestrian trails; guided nature walks and campfire programs in summer; day use area.

Natural Features: Located along the Pacific Ocean just south of Laguna Point; many of the campsites are in dense vegetation of tall conifers and underbrush, other sites are more in the open; Mill Creek flows westward into small, freshwater Lake Cleone and then continues on to the sea; sea level.

Season, Fees & Phone: Open all year; please see Appendix for standard California state park fees and reservation information; phone c/o CDPR Mendocino District Office, Mendocino, (707) 937-5804.

Camp Notes: Most campers probably see only the developed area of the park. (Nothing wrong with that, it's certainly a good one). But there are seven miles of beach and dunes to be explored as well, most of it north of the main park zone where the campgrounds are located. The relatively mild climate (usually cool, sometimes foggy in summer, chilly but not cold, though occasionally rainy in winter), contributes to the excellent camping opportunities during most of the year.

RUSSIAN GULCH
Russian Gulch State Park

Location: Northern California Coast north of Mendocino.

Access: From California State Highway 1 at milepost 53 (2 miles north of Mendocino, 8 miles south of Fort Bragg), turn west and immediately south for 0.1 mile to the park entrance station; go 0.1 mile beyond the entrance to a 4-way intersection; continue south and then east (left, under the highway) for 0.5 mile to the campground.

Facilities: 30 campsites; (a group camp is also available, by reservation); sites are small to small+, basically level, with fair to fairly good separation; parking pads are packed gravel, mostly short straight-ins; most sites are best-suited for small or medium-sized tents; storage cabinets; fire rings; b-y-o firewood; water at several faucets; restrooms with showers; paved driveways; gas and groceries in Mendocino; adequate supplies and services are available in Fort Bragg.

Activities & Attractions: Hiking on about 10 miles of scenic trails in the vicinity, including Falls Loop Trail to a small (35') waterfall, and a beach trail; 3-mile bike trail on an old road; diving for abalone; stream fishing for small rainbow trout; recreation hall; access to a backcountry horse camp.

Natural Features: Located just east of where Russian Gulch meets the Pacific Ocean; campsites are all in a canyon with a dense carpet of ferns topped by fairly dense hardwoods, and conifers including second-growth redwoods; a small, all-season stream flows past many campsites; elevation 100'.

Season, Fees & Phone: Open all year; please see Appendix for standard California state park fees and reservation information; phone c/o CDPR Mendocino District Office, Mendocino, (707) 937-5804.

Camp Notes: Any campground with "Gulch" in its name is sure to bring in a crowd, and this one is no exception. The depth of the gulch itself is emphasized by the arched bridge which links the rims of the chasm high above the beach. From under the shadow of the span, you can hear the surf booming and echoing against the rocky canyon walls and bouncing off the bottom of the bridge. Some yards inland from the edge of the bluff near the park's picnic area you can also hear the whoosh of the waves reverberating inside a wide, ocean blowhole ringed by grass and bushes (and a fence).

VAN DAMME
Van Damme State Park

Location: Northern California Coast south of Mendocino.

Access: From California State Highway 1 at milepost 48 (2.5 miles south of Mendocino, 0.5 mile north of the town of Little River), turn east into the campground.

Facilities: 74 campsites in 2 sections; (10 walk-in sites, a group camp and enroute sites are also available); sites are small to medium-sized, with fair to very good separation; parking pads are packed/oiled gravel, most are short to medium-length straight-ins, plus a few pull-offs; creekside sites are generally level, highland sites tend to be a little sloped; many large tent spots; fire rings; firewood is usually for sale, or b-y-o; water at several faucets; restrooms and showers; holding tank disposal station; paved driveways; gas and groceries in Little River and Mendocino; adequate supplies and services are available in Fort Bragg.

Activities & Attractions: Hiking, including Bog Trail and Fern Canyon Trail; Pygmy Forest Discovery Trail (self-guided nature trail); Van Damme Beach, on a fairly well-sheltered cove, is a designated underwater area; diving for abalone; campfire circle; small interpretive center with sea-related exhibits and audio-visual programs.

Natural Features: Located in and above Fern Canyon near an ocean beach; campsites are located along Little River in the canyon, or in forested areas around a fairly open highland meadow; walk-in sites are tucked away along a forest trail at the east end of the canyon; enroute sites are in the beach parking lot; medium to dense vegetation consists of hardwoods, conifers and large ferns; sea level to 50'.

Season, Fees & Phone: Open all year; please see Appendix for standard California state park fees and reservation information; phone c/o CDPR Mendocino District Office, Mendocino, (707) 937-5804.

Camp Notes: If you're not into abalone hunting or the beach is too populated, you might consider taking a relatively easy, one-way walk through the deep forest. The plan will work if someone can drop you off at the Pygmy Forest parking lot. From there, you can take the main Fern Canyon Trail back to the campground and the beach; or take a shortcut along the old logging road. The trip is 4 to 5 miles, depending upon which route you follow. (A trail map is available at the visitor center.)

MANCHESTER
Manchester State Beach

Location: Northern California Coast south of Mendocino.

Access: From California State Highway 1 at milepost 21 +.4 (1 mile north of Manchester), turn west onto Kinney Road; proceed 0.7 mile, then turn north (right) into the campground.

Facilities: 46 campsites; (hike-bike sites and a reservable group camp are also available); most sites are small to medium-sized, level, with fair separation; parking pads are gravel, short to medium-length, wide straight-ins; adequate space for large tents in most sites; fire rings; b-y-o firewood; water at several faucets; vault facilities; holding tank disposal station; paved driveways; gas and groceries+ in Manchester.

Activities & Attractions: Short trails to the beach; fishing; small campfire circle.

Natural Features: Located on a beachside plain covered with tall grass, dense bushes and some tall evergreens; a dune separates the plain from the beach; Alder Creek and Brush Creek flow through the park, some distance north and south respectfully, of the camp area; sea level.

Season, Fees & Phone: Open all year; please see Appendix for standard California state park fees and reservation information; phone c/o CDPR Mendocino District Office, Mendocino, (707) 937-5804.

Camp Notes: Manchester has a reputation for being one of the best surf fishing beaches on the Mendocino Coast. During the winter rains the park's two creeks are said to be good for steelhead and salmon. The campground is situated roughly midway along the park's four+ miles of beach. This is one of those simple, windswept North Coast beach camps. Likeable.

PAUL M. DIMMICK
Paul M. Dimmick State Wayside

Location: Northwest California southeast of Mendocino.

Access: From California State Highway 128 at milepost 8 (8 miles southeast of the junction of Highway 128 & State Highway 1 near Albion, 21 miles northwest of Boonville) turn south into the campground.

Facilities: 28 campsites; sites are small to medium-sized, respectably level, with fair to fairly good separation; parking pads are dirt/gravel, short to medium-length straight-ins or pull-offs; ample space for large tents; fireplaces or fire rings; b-y-o firewood; water at several faucets; restrooms; paved driveways; gas and groceries in Navarro, 6 miles east.

Activities & Attractions: Fishing.

Natural Features: Located in a redwood forest on a flat along the banks of the Navarro River; elev. 50'.

Season, Fees & Phone: Open all year, subject to weather conditions; (the campground is often flooded in late winter and spring); please see Appendix for standard California state park fees; phone c/o CDPR Mendocino District Office, Mendocino, (707) 937-5804.

Camp Notes: The towering trees and dense foliage create a neat atmosphere for Dimmick's riverside campsites. The only real drawback to staying here in summer might be the heavy daytime traffic; but then again, this *is* a "wayside" campground. It's still a nice spot to spend a night. (We know.)

HENDY WOODS
Hendy Woods State Park

Location: Northwest California southeast of Mendocino.

Access: From California State Highway 128 at milepost 20 +.15 (20 miles southeast of the junction of State Highways 1 & 128 near Albion, 6 miles east of Navarro, 3 miles west of Philo), turn south onto

Philo-Greenwood Road (Mendocino County Road 132) and proceed 0.5 mile; turn east (left) onto a paved park access road and go 0.3 mile to the park entrance station; continue for 0.8 mile, then turn left into the campground.

Facilities: 92 campsites in 2 loops; sites are small+ to generously medium-sized, level, with very good separation; parking pads are paved, medium-length straight-ins; really nice, large tent spots, many on a thick carpet of forest material; fire rings and fireplaces; firewood is usually for sale, or b-y-o; water at several faucets; restrooms with showers; holding tank disposal station; paved driveways; gas and groceries in Philo and Navarro.

Activities & Attractions: Hendy Woods Grove (a stand of old-growth redwoods); hiking trails, including a handicapped-access trail; canoeing and kayaking (late winter and spring); stream fishing; guided nature walks and campfire programs are scheduled in summer; day use area.

Natural Features: Located on a large, densely forested flat along the Navarro River in Anderson Valley; vegetation consists of huge redwoods, ferns, and a good assortment of other small forest plants; elevation 200'.

Season, Fees & Phone: Open all year, subject to weather conditions; (portions of the park tend to flood in late winter and spring); please see Appendix for standard California state park fees and reservation information; phone c/o CDPR Mendocino District Office, Mendocino, (707) 937-5804.

Camp Notes: Hendy Woods is particularly noted for it virgin redwoods groves. They're the last sizable stands in Anderson Valley.

GUALALA POINT
Sonoma County Regional Park

Location: Northern California Coast northwest of Bodega Bay.

Access: From California State Highway 1 at milepost 58 +.3 (0.2 mile south of the Sonoma-Mendocino county line, 2 miles south of Gualala, 10 miles north of Stewarts Point), turn east onto a paved access road; proceed 0.3 mile to the entrance station, then continue for 0.3 mile to the campground.

Facilities: 25 campsites, including 7 walk-ins; sites are small to medium-sized, with very good to excellent separation; parking pads are paved, mostly level, short to medium-length straight-ins; tent spots are very private, many are grassy, and most are level; fire rings; firewood is usually for sale, or b-y-o; water at several faucets; restrooms; holding tank disposal station; narrow, paved driveways; gas and groceries+ are available in Gualala.

Activities & Attractions: Hiking and bicycle paths, including a beach trail; visitor center has interpretive exhibits and natural displays; fishing (especially for steelhead); abalone hunting; beachcombing; nature study; whale watching.

Natural Features: Located along the south bank of the Gualala River just east of where it flows into the Pacific Ocean; the river is very wide, and normally deep and slow-moving through this section; very dense vegetation in the campground consists of a mixture of hardwoods, conifers, ferns and smaller forest plants; sea level.

Season, Fees & Phone: Open all year; $14.00; 14 day limit; park office (707) 785-2377.

Camp Notes: The lush vegetation at Gualala Point provides tunnels of greenery for the roads, trails and campsites. All the sites are really secluded and, as a rule, the campground's atmosphere is serene.

Northern California
North Bay
Please refer to the Northern California map in the Appendix

WOODSIDE
Salt Point State Park

Location: Northern California Coast northwest of Bodega Bay.

Access: From California State Highway 1 at milepost 39 +.8 (7 miles north of the community of Fort Ross, 9 miles south of Stewarts Point), turn east onto the park access road; proceed east for 0.2 mile to the hike-bike camps; or turn south (just past the disposal station, before the hike-bike area) and proceed 0.8 mile to the main camp loops and the walk-in camp.

Facilities: 79 campsites in 2 loops; (10 hike-bike sites and 20 walk-in campsites are also available); sites are medium to large with fair to very good separation; parking pads are paved, medium to long straight-ins; many pads may require additional leveling; most tent spots are large, but may be a bit sloped; storage cabinets; fire rings; firewood is usually for sale, or b-y-o; water at faucets throughout; restrooms; holding tank disposal station; paved driveways; camper supplies in Stewarts Point; gas and groceries+ in Gualala, 20 miles north.

Activities & Attractions: Underwater Reserve; designated scuba and skin diving areas; hiking and equestrian trails including 0.6 mile Gerstle Trail which leads from Woodside down to the ocean beach; (a detailed brochure/map with contour lines is available); whale-watching in winter.

Natural Features: Located on heavily timbered hills above the coastline; tall conifers and hardwoods are the predominant form of vegetation; a considerable quantity of underbrush and some ferns help to provide privacy for the campsites; the walk-in sites are tucked away in the forest; elevation 150'.

Season, Fees & Phone: Open all year; please see Appendix for standard California state park fees and reservation information; park office (707) 847-3221.

Camp Notes: It's not uncommon to find Pacific Blacktail deer wandering through Woodside's campsites. Three miles upcoast from Woodside and on the same side of the highway is Kruse Rhododendron State Reserve. The reserve contains a mixture of second-growth redwoods, Doug firs, oaks, ferns, and thousands of rhododendrons which are at their finest when the pink flowers bloom in spring. The reserve also has five miles of hiking trails which pass through the dense forest and across wooden bridges that span small canyons.

GERSTLE COVE
Salt Point State Park

Location: Northern California Coast northwest of Bodega Bay.

Access: From California State Highway 1 at milepost 39 +.9 (7 miles north of the community of Fort Ross, 9 miles south of Stewarts Point), turn west onto a park access road and proceed 0.15 mile to the campground.

Facilities: 30 campsites; (a group camp is also available, by reservation); sites are small, with nominal to fairly good separation; parking pads are paved, mostly short to short+ straight-ins; some will probably require a little additional leveling; medium to large areas for tents; fire rings; firewood is usually for sale, or b-y-o; water at several faucets; restrooms; holding tank disposal station; paved driveways; camper supplies in Stewarts Point.

Activities & Attractions: Gerstle Cove Marine Reserve; designated scuba and skin diving areas; trails to the beach; hiking/horse trails east of the highway; picnic sites near the beach.

Natural Features: Located on a hillside above the Pacific Ocean; campsites are generally well sheltered by tall conifers; elevation 100'.

Season, Fees & Phone: Open all year; please see Appendix for standard California state park fees and reservation information; park office (707) 847-3221.

Camp Notes: This stretch of the coast is a bit rockier and more heavily forested than many of the other Northern California coastal access points. The campground here is sometimes called "Moonrock". (Also, a 25-site primitive campground with limited availability is located 1.7 miles south of Fort Ross SP, south of Salt Point near mp 31, at the bottom of a ravine off the west side of the highway.)

STILLWATER COVE
Sonoma County Regional Park

Location: Northern California Coast northwest of Bodega Bay.

Access: From California State Highway 1 at milepost 37 (16 miles north of Jenner, 3 miles north of Fort Ross, 11 miles south of Stewart's Point), turn northeast onto a paved park access road; proceed 0.1 mile east and north; turn right into the campground.

Facilities: 23 campsites; sites are smallish, with fairly good separation; parking pads are paved, short to medium-length straight-ins; many pads may require additional leveling; some good tent spots, which may be a bit sloped; fire rings; firewood is usually for sale, or b-y-o; water at faucets throughout; restrooms;

holding tank disposal station; paved driveway; gas and groceries in Fort Ross, and also 1 mile north on Highway 1.

Activities & Attractions: Sandy beach (accessed by a long stairway); skin diving; scuba diving; fishing; hiking, including a nature trail and Stockton Creek (redwood canyon) trail; restored one-room school; Fort Ross State Historic Park, 3 miles south.

Natural Features: Located on a forested bluff, across the highway from well-sheltered Stillwater Cove on the Pacific Coast; Sonoma County's coastline is fairly rugged and densely forested along this stretch; interior of the camping area is somewhat open and grassy; fairly dense vegetation of conifers, hardwoods and considerable underbrush between most campsites; elevation 50'.

Season, Fees & Phone: Open all year; $14.00; 14 day limit; park office (707) 847-3245.

Camp Notes: This campground is decidedly different from those along the Coast to the south of here. Stillwater Cove Regional Park is much more forested and rocky than other, more typically flat, sandy beach parks.

Northern California 38

WRIGHT'S BEACH
Sonoma Coast State Beach

Location: Northern California Coast north of Bodega Bay.

Access: From California State Highway 1 at milepost 16 +.8 (6 miles north of Bodega Bay), turn west onto a park access road and proceed 0.2 mile to the campground.

Facilities: 30 campsites; sites are very small to small, level, with nil to nominal separation; parking pads are sand/gravel, short straight-ins; enough space for small tents in most sites; fire rings; firewood is usually for sale, or b-y-o; water at central faucets; restrooms; paved driveways; gas and groceries in Bodega Bay, or Jenner, 5 miles north.

Activities & Attractions: Beach access.

Natural Features: Located at breaker-level on a sandy beach; bushy trees and shrubs provide some shelter/shade for campsites; closely bordered by a bluff; sea level.

Season, Fees & Phone: Open all year; please see Appendix for standard California state park fees and reservation information; park office (707) 875-3483 or (707) 875-3382.

Camp Notes: This tiny campground is close enough to the ocean to be awash at high tide (almost). (It would be an OK place to stay, provided you're willing to sell off a block of your IBM stock in order to pay the rent. Ed.)

Northern California 39

BODEGA DUNES
Sonoma Coast State Beach

Location: Northern California Coast near Bodega Bay.

Access: From California State Highway 1 at milepost 11 +.7 (1 mile north of the town of Bodega Bay), turn west onto a park access road and proceed 0.4 mile to the entrance station; continue ahead past the entrance for 0.3 mile to the Bodega Dunes main camp loops.

Facilities: 98 campsites; (hike-bike sites are also available); sites are small, level, with nominal to fairly good separation; parking pads are hard-surfaced, mostly short straight-ins; adequate space for medium to large tents in most sites; fire rings; b-y-o firewood; water at several faucets; restrooms with showers; holding tank disposal station; paved driveways; gas and groceries in Bodega Bay.

Activities & Attractions: Trails to the beach and out to Bodega Head from Bodega Dunes; campfire center.

Natural Features: Located in a dunes area on Bodega Bay; campsites are very lightly to lightly shaded but well-sheltered from wind by large, full evergreens and dense, ceiling-height bushes; sea level.

Season, Fees & Phone: Open all year; please see Appendix for standard California state park fees and reservation information; park office (707) 875-3483 or (707) 875-3382.

Camp Notes: Only a few Bodega Dunes campsites overlook the bay, but the sea's edge is only a short walk from any site. There is much more dense, low-level vegetation in this campground than in most other state beach campgrounds on the North Coast. The views from Bodega Head are worth the cost of a long hike or couple of miles' drive off the highway.

DORAN
Sonoma County Regional Park

Location: California Coast north of San Francisco.

Access: From California State Highway 1 at milepost 9 +.1 (1 mile south of the town of Bodega Bay, 21 miles north of Marshall), turn west onto Doran Park Road; proceed 0.2 mile to a fork; bear right onto Doran Beach Road and proceed 0.4 mile to the park entrance station; continue for 0.7 mile to the Shell, Gull and Cove camp loops on the right; or from the entrance, go 1.3 miles to the Jetty camping area.

Facilities: 138 campsites, including 10 walk-in sites, in 5 loops; sites are small to medium-sized, with nominal separation; parking pads are paved, level, short to medium-length straight-ins, some are double wide; good-sized, level, grassy or sandy, unsheltered tent spots; fire rings; firewood is usually for sale, or b-y-o; restrooms with showers at Jetty, vault facilities elsewhere; holding tank disposal station; paved driveways; gas and groceries in Bodega Bay.

Activities & Attractions: Boating; boat launch near the Coast Guard station; fishing; surfing; clamming; nature study of oceanside plants and animals.

Natural Features: Located on a jetty or a peninsula extending into the Pacific Ocean along the south shore of Bodega Harbor; the windswept beach area is sandy, quite flat, and covered with grass, low bushes and a few bushy trees; sea level.

Season, Fees & Phone: Open all year; $14.00; 10 day limit; park office (707) 875-3540.

Camp Notes: Another regional park is located just two miles north of Doran, on the north edge of the town of Bodega Bay. Westside Park has a boat ramp and 47 campsites geared principally toward rv's and vehicles with boat trailers. It's on the Bodega Head side of Bodega Bay and can be accessed from near milepost 11 on California 1.

TOMALES BAY
Tomales Bay State Park

Location: Northern California Coast north of San Francisco.

Access: From California State Highway 1 near milepost 28 +.5 at the south edge of the town of Point Reyes Station, turn west onto Sir Francis Drake Boulevard and travel west and northwest (through the hamlet of Inverness) for 6.5 miles to a fork; take the right fork onto Pierce Point Road and proceed 1.2 miles; turn north (right) onto the park access road for 0.8 mile to the park entrance; continue ahead for 0.7 mile to the camp area in the bluff (upper) park area.

Facilities: 6 hike-bike campsites, drinking water, restrooms, paved parking lot; groceries in Inverness, 4 miles southeast.

Activities & Attractions: Designated swimming/wading areas; 4 sandy beaches (3 beaches are accessible via hiking trails (0.4 mile to 4 miles); day use areas.

Natural Features: Located on Inverness Ridge above Tomales Bay; vegetation consists of stands of medium-tall pines, hardwoods and some dense undergrowth; the park preserves what is said to be one of the finest groves of virgin Bishop pine, a relatively small tree which commonly develops a well-weathered appearance; elevation 100'.

Season, Fees & Phone: Open all year; please see Appendix for standard California state park fees; park office (415) 669-1140.

Camp Notes: Neat little campsites here. Near the campsites are some really dandy picnic sites on a small shelf overlooking Hearts Desire Beach. The views of fjord-like Tomales Bay from within the park are good, but particularly from up here on top. The waters and beaches of the 14-mile-long, mile-wide bay are quite well-sheltered from most heavy weather.

SAMUEL P. TAYLOR
Samuel P. Taylor State Park

Location: Northern California northwest of San Francisco.

Access: From U.S. Highway 101 near San Rafael, take the Sir Francis Drake Boulevard Exit; travel northwest on Sir Francis Drake Boulevard (through the towns of San Anselmo, Fairfax and Lagunitas) for 16 miles; turn south (left) to the Redwood Grove park entrance station and proceed 0.2 mile to the lower camp area or another 0.2 mile to the upper camp loop. **Alternate Access:** From California State Highway 1 in the town of Olema, turn east onto Sir Francis Drake Boulevard and proceed 5.1 miles to the Redwood Grove turnoff and continue as above.

Facilities: 60 campsites, plus enroute sites for self-contained vehicles in the picnic area; (2 group camps and an equestrian camp are also available); lower loop sites are small, level, with nominal separation; parking pads are packed gravel, short straight-ins; small to medium+ tent areas; upper loop sites are small+, with nominal to fairly good separation; parking pads are paved, medium to long straight-ins which might require a little additional leveling; medium to large tent areas; fireplaces or fire rings in the lower loop, barbecue grills and fire rings in the upper loop; b-y-o firewood; water at faucets throughout; restrooms with showers; holding tank disposal station; paved driveways; groceries+, 2 to 3 miles east; adequate supplies and services are available in Fairfax.

Activities & Attractions: Paved bike/horse/hike trail from Redwood Grove to the settlement of Tocoloma, 3 miles west; several additional miles of hike/horse trails; day use area.

Natural Features: Located in a densely forested canyon along and above the banks of Lagunitas Creek (also called Papermill Creek); redwoods tower above hardwoods, bushes and ferns; elevation 150'.

Season, Fees & Phone: Open all year; please see Appendix for standard California state park fees and reservation information; park office (415) 488-9897.

Camp Notes: Near the campground there's a really pretty picnic area on a little shelf above the stream with just enough daylight showing through the redwoods to make a near-perfect spot. The camp areas are trimmed with what must be three miles of rail fence. You couldn't go wrong in any of the campsites, as long as your camping ensemble fits in the available space. The paved path is a real bonus. It's on the opposite side of the stream from the highway. You may still hear the traffic, but it won't be whooshing past your left ear.

PANTOLL
Mount Tamalpais State Park

Location: Northern California northwest of San Francisco.

Access: From California State Highway 1 (northbound) at milepost 3 +.4 (3 miles west of the junction of Highway 1 & U.S. 101 near Mill Valley), head northwest on Panoramic Highway for 5.4 miles to a 3-way junction and the campground. **Alternate Access:** From Highway 1 (southbound) in Stinson Beach, proceed northeast on Panoramic Highway for 3.6 miles to the campground. **Additional Access:** From Stinson Beach, travel southeast on Highway 1 for 0.8 mile to the Steep Ravine camp.

Facilities: 16 park 'n walk campsites, plus approximately 25 enroute sites for self-contained vehicles, and a hike-bike site; park 'n walk sites are small, sloped, with fair separation; parking is in a fairly level, paved lot; tent areas are medium to large and somewhat level; storage cabinets; fireplaces; firewood is usually for sale, or b-y-o; water at several faucets; restrooms. *Additional camping*: Steep Ravine Environmental Campground has 6 primitive campsites and 10 small camping cabins; campsites have a small to medium-sized tent area, table, fireplace and storage locker; cabins have a 'sleeping platform', table, inside wood stove and outdoor fireplace; firewood is available; water at faucets; vault facilities; (2 group camps, and a small backpack camp for individuals and groups are also available, in other areas in the park); complete supplies and services are available in Mill Valley.

Activities & Attractions: More than 50 miles of trails within the park, connecting to a 200-mile system of trails on adjacent public lands; (a detailed brochure/map with contour lines is available); bicycles are allowed on designated fire roads and paved roads; 3 designated hang glider launch points; visitor center at East Peak; "Mountain Theater", with room for about 3,000 individuals.

Natural Features: Located on and around Mount Tamalpais; vegetation consists of dense sections of hardwoods and conifers, open meadows, and brushy hillsides; most campsites (except enroute sites) are well-shaded/sheltered by tall conifers and/or hardwoods; elevation 1100'.

Season, Fees & Phone: Open all year; please see Appendix for standard California state park fees and reservation information; park office (415) 388-2070.

Camp Notes: "Mount Tam" itself is a triple-peaked ridge with a difference of a few feet between its highest points. *Tamalpais* is said to mean "Land of the Tamal (Indians)".

KYEN
Lake Mendocino/Corps of Engineers Park

Location: Northwest California north of San Francisco.

Access: From California State Highway 20 at milepost 35 +.6 (2.3 miles east of the junction of Highway 20 & U.S. Highway 101, 28 miles west of Lakeport), turn south onto Marina Drive; proceed south and west for 0.6 mile to the campground entrance station.

Facilities: 100 campsites in 2 areas; sites are smallish, with nominal to fair separation; some parking pads are paved, some are dirt/gravel, and most are straight-ins; many pads may require additional leveling; mostly large tent spots, but many are sloped; fireplaces; b-y-o firewood is recommended; water at several faucets; restrooms with showers; holding tank disposal station; paved driveways; complete supplies and services are available in Ukiah, 8 miles south.

Activities & Attractions: Boating; boat ramp nearby at Oak Grove; sailing; fishing; swimming at Pomo day use area; 14 miles of hiking trails around the lake; playground; visitor/interpretive center.

Natural Features: Located on the north shore of Lake Mendocino, in the Coast Range; campground vegetation varies considerably--some sites are quite in the open, some are sheltered by tall trees and considerable underbrush; many sites are situated along the lake; the 1800-acre reservoir is located on the East Fork of the Russian River in Coyote Valley; bordered by oak-cloaked hills; elevation 800'.

Season, Fees & Phone: April to September; $10.00-$12.00; 14 day limit; CoE Office (707) 462-7581.

Camp Notes: Another COE campground, Chekaka Campground, is located near the dam, and is accessible from U.S. 101 at milepost 27 +.4, then east on Lake Mendocino Drive. The 23 sites are on a hilltop amid very little vegetation. At Chekaka there are vault facilities, no water, no fee.

BU-SHAY
Lake Mendocino/Corps of Engineers Park

Location: Northwest California north of San Francisco.

Access: From California State Highway 20 at milepost 36 +.6 (3.3 miles east of the junction of Highway 20 & U.S. Highway 101, 27 miles west of Lakeport), turn west onto a paved access road, then go south (under the highway overpass and along the river) for 1.1 miles to the campground entrance; continue for 0.25 mile, then turn right into the campground.

Facilities: 168 campsites in 2 loops; sites are mostly medium-sized, with reasonable separation; parking pads are paved, medium to long straight-ins; some pads may require additional leveling; most sites have excellent, large, grassy tent spots; fireplaces and fire rings; b-y-o firewood is recommended; water at several faucets; restrooms with showers; holding tank disposal station; narrow paved driveways; complete supplies and services are available in Ukiah, 10 miles southwest.

Activities & Attractions: Boating; boat launch nearby at Oak Grove; sailing; fishing for striped bass, largemouth and smallmouth bass, crappie and catfish; swimming at Pomo day use area; 14 miles of hiking trails in the park; playground; visitor center.

Natural Features: Located on the northeast shore of Lake Mendocino in Coyote Valley in the Coast Range; campground vegetation consists predominantly of large oaks and light underbrush on grassy slopes; bordered by hills covered with oaks and madrones; Lake Mendocino is a flood-control and storage reservoir on the East Fork of the Russian River; elevation 800'.

Season, Fees & Phone: April to September; $10.00; 14 day limit; CoE Project Office (707) 462-7581.

Camp Notes: Lake Mendocino is an attractive blue jewel amid rolling golden hills and tree-dotted low mountains. The access is quite convenient, since it's within a few miles of U.S. 101, and a couple hours' drive from San Francisco. Though oaks are the predominant vegetation in this park, the great redwood forests are within a few miles to the west.

BULLFROG POND
Austin Creek State Recreation Area

Location: Northern California northwest of Santa Rosa.

Access: From California State Highway 116 in Guerneville (15 miles northwest of Sebastopol, 14 miles northeast of Jenner), travel north on Armstrong Woods Road for 2.3 miles to the entrance to Armstrong Redwoods State Reserve; continue through the reserve for 0.6 mile; (abandon all hope of turning around past this point--and your trailer, if you have one--anything longer than 20 feet, or with a trailer, is officially barred from making the run to the top); head up a steep, sinuous, single-lane (but paved) track for 2.5 miles to the campground.

Facilities: 24 campsites; (3 trail camps for hikers and equestrians are also available); sites are small to small+, sloped, with minimal to fair separation; parking pads are gravel, short straight-ins; small to large tent areas; storage cabinets; fire rings; b-y-o firewood; water at several faucets; restrooms; paved driveways; adequate supplies and services are available in Guerneville.

Activities & Attractions: Hiking and horse trails (a detailed brochure/map with contour lines is available).

Natural Features: Located on hilly, densely forested terrain; campsites are generally well-sheltered/shaded by hardwoods and conifers, and some sites overlook 2-acre Bullfrog Pond; elev. 1400'.

Season, Fees & Phone: Open all year; please see Appendix for standard California state park fees and reservation information; park office (707) 869-2015.

Camp Notes: It's amazing how totally different this spot is from Armstrong Redwoods, in the valley just below. In the redwood grove you'll pass through on the way up to the campground, it's mild and shadowy and moist; up on top, it's sunshine and blue sky and dry air (May to October, anyway). And the great views are something else! (So is the drive up; we keep some loose change in the ash tray, and about three dollars in dimes and quarters slid out on one of the steeper sections.) To be sure, all of Austin Creek isn't like this. The majority of the park's wild acres lie on the mountainsides and in the valleys flanking Austin Creek and its tributaries. Most of the 20 miles of trails also closely follow the streams.

SPRING LAKE
Sonoma County Regional Park

Location: Northern California in Santa Rosa.

Access: From California State Highway 12 at milepost 18 +.6 on the east side of Santa Rosa, turn south onto Mission Boulevard and go 0.2 mile; swing west (right) onto Montgomery Drive and proceed 0.15 mile; turn south (left) onto Summerfield Road and travel 1 mile; turn east (left) onto Hoen Avenue, go 100 yards, then jog lefterly onto Newanga Avenue and continue east for another 0.6 mile to the park entrance station; from the entrance, a 0.2 mile trip and a quick succession of several turns will get you into the campground.

Facilities: 31 campsites; (a group camp is also available, by reservation); sites are small to medium-sized, tolerably level, with nominal to fairly good separation; parking pads are paved, predominantly medium-length straight-ins; large tent areas, some are a bit sloped; fire rings; b-y-o firewood; water at several faucets; restrooms with showers; holding tank disposal station; paved driveway; complete supplies and services are available in Santa Rosa.

Activities & Attractions: Fishing; limited boating; boat launch; short hiking trail down to the lake; swimming lagoon; day use areas.

Natural Features: Located on a rocky, rolling hilltop above Spring Lake; sites receive light to light-medium shade from large oaks, plus some madrones and conifers on sparse grass; bordered by forested hills and mountains; elevation 200'.

Season, Fees & Phone: Open all year, but open only on weekends and holidays from mid-September to mid-May; $14.00; 14 day limit; reservations accepted, contact the park office (707) 539-8082.

Camp Notes: Good scenery, both near and distant. Glimpses of the lake, through the trees, from some sites. The small lake is dotted with several islands, and a high peak rises to the south.

SUGARLOAF RIDGE
Sugarloaf Ridge State Park

Location: Northwest California east of Santa Rosa.

Access: From California State Highway 12 at milepost 26 +.1 (11 miles east of Santa Rosa, 11 miles north of Sonoma), turn northeast onto Adobe Canyon Road; proceed 3.4 miles on a fairly narrow, winding, steep, paved road to the park entrance station; just beyond the entrance, bear right at the fork to the campground.

Facilities: 50 campsites in a loop and a string; (a large group camp is also available, by reservation); sites are small, with nominal to fair separation; parking pads are gravel, medium to long straight-ins; some pads may require additional leveling; good tent spots in most sites; fire rings; b-y-o firewood; water at several faucets; restrooms; paved driveways; complete supplies and services are available in Santa Rosa.

Activities & Attractions: 25 miles of hiking and equestrian trails within the park connect to miles of trails in nearby Hood Mountain Regional Park; nature trail; (a detailed brochure/trail map with contour lines is available); small visitor center; campfire center; day use area.

Natural Features: Located on the west slope of the Coast Range; an interior large, grassy, open area is ringed by the campsites, large hardwoods and some underbrush; Sugarloaf Ridge itself runs northwest-southeast along the park's southern boundary and tops-out at 1939'; Bald Mountain and Red Mountain rise to 2729' and 2548' at the north end of the park, and Little Bald Mountain rises to 2275' near the southeast corner; elevation 1100'.

Season, Fees & Phone: Open all year; please see Appendix for standard California state park fees and reservation information; park office (707) 833-5712.

Camp Notes: Sugarloaf Ridge seems to be geared especially toward ecology-conscious visitors. Many of the programs and much of the park literature are directed toward appreciating and preserving the natural environment. Sugarloaf Ridge supposedly takes its name from large, solid, conical mounds of sugar which were found in old-time grocery stores. (In summer, it's color and texture also may make it resemble a big hunk of pound cake.)

Northern California 49

BACK RANCH MEADOWS
China Camp State Park

Location: Northern California north of San Francisco.

Access: From U.S. Highway 101 near milepost 12 +.5 on the north end of San Rafael, take the North San Pedro Road Exit and proceed 3 miles east to the park boundary; 0.05 mile inside the boundary, turn south (right) onto a paved access road and proceed 0.4 mile to the campground. **Alternate Access:** From U.S. 101 near milepost 10 +.5 in San Rafael, take the Third Street/Point San Pedro Road Exit and proceed easterly for 4.5 miles to the east park boundary; go north and west for 2.2 miles, then turn south (left) onto the campground access road and continue as above. (Note: the Alternate Access is a 'back door' approach, but it may be a slightly more convenient route if you're coming up '101 from The City.)

Facilities: 30 primitive walk-in campsites (scattered around a wooded hillside, 25 to 100 yards from the parking lot), plus about 20 enroute sites for self-contained vehicles in the paved, level parking lot; water at central faucets; vault facilities; complete supplies and services are available in San Rafael.

Activities & Attractions: Remains of a historic Chinese fishing village; museum; trails into the hills (a large brochure/map with contour lines is available); fishing; small boat launch area.

Natural Features: Located in the hills above a bayside plain above San Francisco Bay; vegetation consists of open grassy/brushy areas, plus a large section of hardwoods; campsites are unshaded to lightly shaded; elevation 100'.

Season, Fees & Phone: Open all year; please see Appendix for standard California state park fees and reservation information; park office (415) 456-0766.

Camp Notes: China Camp was one of the earliest, largest and most productive Chinese fishing villages in California. It was in operation by 1870 and was home to several thousand Chinese immigrants and their descendants who introduced the use of commercial netting to catch bay shrimp off Point San Pedro. The shrimp were then dried and shipped to Chinese people all over the world.

Northern California 50

COLE CREEK & KELSEY CREEK
Clear Lake State Park

Location: Northwest California north of Santa Rosa.

Access: From California State Highway 29 at milepost 34.2 at the east edge of Kelseyville, (9 miles southeast of Lakeport), turn north onto Main Street; follow a well-signed, zigzag route (or just follow the traffic) along Main Street, Gaddy Lane and Soda Bay Road for 4.1 miles to the park; turn north (left onto the park access road and proceed 0.2 mile to the entrance station; go 0.2 mile, then turn left into *Cole*

Creek Campground, or go 0.4 mile past Cole Creek to *Kelsey Creek* Campground, also on the left; (Note: this is the simplest routing of at least 5 accesses from State Highways 29, 175 and 281; they all eventually lead to Soda Bay Road.)

Facilities: *Cole Creek*: 26 campsites; (hike-bike sites are also available); *Kelsey Creek*: 65 campsites; sites in both campgrounds are medium to large, level, with nominal to fair separation; parking pads are paved, medium to medium+ straight-ins; excellent, grassy tent spots; *both camps*: storage cabinets; fireplaces; b-y-o firewood is recommended; water at faucets throughout; restrooms with showers; holding tank disposal station near the visitor center; paved driveways; adequate supplies and services are available in the Kelseyville-Lakeport area.

Activities & Attractions: Boating; boat launch; fishing for largemouth bass, crappie, bluegill and catfish; swimming beach; visitor center; campfire circle; Indian Nature Trail; hiking trails; interpretive programs in summer; large day use area.

Natural Features: Kelsey Creek: located on the south shore of Clear Lake, between the lake and the Kelsey Creek bayou; most sites have lake views; Cole Creek: located along Cole Creek a few hundred yards from the lake shore; large hardwoods provide light to medium shade in both areas, with some open grassy sections in Kelsey Creek; the lake is ringed by wooded hills and mountains; summer temperatures commonly exceed 90° F; elevation 1300'.

Season, Fees & Phone: Open all year; please see Appendix for standard California state park fees and reservation information; park office (707) 279-2267 or (707) 279-8650.

Camp Notes: Clear Lake is the largest natural lake totally within California. Yes, Tahoe is larger; but the key words here are *totally within* California. The lake is popular with picnickers, boaters, campers and mosquitoes.

BAYVIEW
Clear Lake State Park

Location: Northwest California north of Santa Rosa.

Access: From California State Highway 29 at milepost 34.2 at the east edge of Kelseyville, (9 miles southeast of Lakeport), turn north onto Main Street; follow a well-signed, zigzag route (or just follow the traffic) along Main Street, Gaddy Lane and Soda Bay Road for 4.1 miles to the park; turn north (left) onto the park access road and proceed 0.2 mile to the park entrance station; continue for 1.2 miles, (past Cole Creek and Kelsey Creek campgrounds) to *Lower Bayview* Campground or a final 0.6 mile past Lower Bayview to *Upper Bayview* Campground. (Note: this is the simplest routing of at least 5 ways to get here from State Highways 29, 175 and 281; all routes eventually lead to Soda Bay Road.)

Facilities: *Upper and Lower Bayview*: 31 campsites in Lower Bayview and 35 sites in Upper Bayview; sites are mostly medium-sized, with nominal to fair separation; parking pads are paved, short to medium-length straight-ins; many pads may require additional leveling; medium to large tent spots, some may be sloped; storage lockers; fireplaces; b-y-o firewood is recommended; water at faucets throughout; restrooms with showers; holding tank disposal station near the visitor center; paved driveways; adequate supplies and services are available in the Kelseyville-Lakeport area.

Activities & Attractions: Boating; boat launch; fishing for largemouth bass, crappie, bluegill and catfish; swimming beach; visitor center; campfire circle; Indian Nature Trail; hiking trails; interpretive programs in summer; large day use area.

Natural Features: Located on a hill above Soda Bay; large oak trees and sparse grass are the predominant forms of vegetation; some sites have lake views through the trees; the lake is encircled by wooded hills and mountains; elevation 1400'.

Season, Fees & Phone: Open all year; please see Appendix for standard California state park fees and reservation information; park office (707) 279-2267 or (707) 279-8650.

Camp Notes: For such a relatively small park (it covers less than a square mile), this place is loaded with a variety of natural settings and facilities, hence the rather involved descriptions above. Choosing a campsite at Clear Lake is difficult: to camp on top, with more commanding views; or to stay at lake level, closer to the park's activities.

CACHE CREEK CANYON
Yolo County Regional Park

Location: Northwest California northwest of Sacramento.

Access: From California State Highway 16 at milepost 1 +.2 (6 miles north of Rumsey, 8.4 miles south of the junction of California State Highways 16 & 20), turn southwest at "Middle Site" and into the campground.

Facilities: 45 campsites; sites are medium to large, with nominal to fair separation; parking pads are paved, most are quite long, either straight-ins or pull-offs; additional leveling might be necessary; many grassy tent spots, adequate for large tents, some may be a bit sloped; fireplaces and barbecue grills; b-y-o firewood is recommended; restrooms, plus auxiliary vaults; holding tank disposal station; paved driveways; gas and groceries in Guinda, 14 miles south.

Activities & Attractions: Several hiking trails; stream fishing, mostly for catfish and bass; rafting and tubing on Cache Creek; group day use adjacent and at the "Lower (Picnic) Site", 0.6 mile south; pleasant drive on Highway 16 through the canyon.

Natural Features: Located on the east bank of Cache Creek at a bend on the stream in a densely vegetated, narrow, rocky canyon; the campground has mown grass dotted with various types of trees and bushes, including long-needled pines and oaks; mild winter temperatures; elevation 1700'.

Season, Fees & Phone: Open all year; $10.00; Yolo County Parks Department (916) 666-8115.

Camp Notes: Reportedly, this is a very popular place on summer weekends. In order to circumvent the high cost of running electric power lines to the campground, a solar powered system (augmented by diesel) was devised. It's an economical and quiet solution to a common problem.

BOTHE-NAPA VALLEY
Bothe-Napa Valley State Park

Location: Northern California northwest of Napa.

Access: From California State Highways 29/128 at milepost 33 +.5 (3 miles southeast of Calistoga, 4 miles northwest of St. Helena), swing south/west onto the park access road and proceed 0.2 mile to the entrance station and then the visitor center; just past the visitor center, turn west (right) and proceed 0.2 mile to the campground.

Facilities: 50 campsites, including 9 walk-in units; (a group camp is also available); sites are small, with nominal to fairly good separation; parking pads are packed/oiled gravel, short to short+ straight-ins; some pads may require a little additional leveling; small to medium-sized areas for tents; storage cabinets; fire rings or fireplaces; firewood is usually for sale, or b-y-o; water at several faucets; restrooms with showers; adequate supplies and services are available in Calistoga.

Activities & Attractions: 7 miles of hiking trails; history trail to Bale Grist Mill; small (motel-size), creek-fed swimming pool (in the day use area); visitor center with interpretive displays and a 3D map of the region; (a park brochure/map showing contour lines and the locations of many Napa Valley wineries is available); large day use area nearby; Bale Grist Mill State Historic Park, just south of Bothe-Napa Valley, features a fully functioning, water-driven grain mill.

Natural Features: Located on the northwest edge of Napa Valley; campsites are moderately shaded/sheltered by hardwoods and some conifers; bordered by forested hills; elevation 350'.

Season, Fees & Phone: Open all year; (camping is limited to one night only, subject to change); please see Appendix for standard state park fees and reservation information; park office (707) 942-4575.

Camp Notes: The campsites here may a bit small, but the privacy factor is good. Most sites were carefully notched out of the forest, leaving a substantial amount of vegetation between them.

JUNCTION, LIVE OAK, JUNIPER
Mount Diablo State Park

Location: Western California northeast of Oakland.

Access: From Interstate 680 (*northbound*) in Walnut Creek take the Ygnacio Valley Road Exit, travel northeast on Ygnacio Valley Road for 2.2 miles; turn southeast (right) onto Walnut Avenue and go 1.6 miles, then jog right onto Oak Grove for 100 yards, then left onto North Gate Road for 1.7 miles to the northwest park entrance; proceed 4.5 miles to *Junction* Campground, by the park office; continue on the main road for another 2 miles to the Artist Point day use area, then go west (right) for 0.5 mile on a side road to *Live Oak* Campground. From I-680 (*southbound*) in Walnut Creek take the North Main Exit and go south on North Main for 0.6 mile, then turn left onto Ygnacio Valley Road and continue as above.

Alternate Access: From Interstate 680 in Danville at the Diablo Road Exit, head easterly on Diablo Road for 2.9 miles; turn north (left) onto Mount Diablo Scenic Road and proceed 3.7 miles to the south entrance station, then 1.1 miles to the Live Oak turnoff, or an additional 2 miles to Junction.

Additional Access: From Junction, travel northeasterly on the summit road (paved) for 2.5 miles to Juniper Campground. (Note: The north park access road, from Walnut Creek, climbs/descends more gradually and has fewer switchbacks than the south road from Danville.)

Facilities: *Junction*: 6 campsites; *Live Oak*: 18 campsites; *Juniper*: 34 campsites; (4 standard group camps and 2 group horse camps are also available, by reservation); most sites are small to small+, with minimal to nominal separation; parking pads are gravel, mostly short straight-ins, plus some medium+ pull-throughs in Juniper; many pads will require additional leveling; small to medium-sized tent areas; assorted fire appliances; b-y-o firewood; water at faucets; restrooms in Junction and Live Oak, vault facilities in Juniper; complete supplies and services are available in Walnut Creek.

Activities & Attractions: Observation deck at the summit of Mt. Diablo; miles of hiking trails (a detailed brochure/map is available); small interpretive center.

Natural Features: Located on the sides of Mount Diablo; the mountain is cloaked with large, open grassy areas and stands of oaks, plus some junipers and a few tall conifers; most campsites receive very light to light-medium shade; elevation 2300' to 3000'.

Season, Fees & Phone: Open all year, subject to weather conditions; please see Appendix for standard California state park fees and reservation information; park office (415) 837-2525.

Camp Notes: From Mount Diablo's summit you can see about half of California (or so it might seem). Actually, on a clear day you can see portions of nearly two-thirds of the state's 58 counties, or roughly one-fourth of its land area (about 40,000 square miles). To get a good visual effect from this solitary peak, you don't *have* to drive all the way to the top--but just about everyone does. If you're planning on camping at Juniper, the mountaintop will be just "right up the hill" from your campsite.

Northern California
South Bay
Please refer to the Northern California map in the Appendix

HALF MOON BAY
Half Moon Bay State Beach

Location: Central California Coast south of San Francisco.

Access: From California State Highway 1 at milepost 28 +.7 near the south end of the city of Half Moon Bay, turn west onto Kelly Avenue; go 0.65 mile down to the end of Kelly, then hang a short right to the camp area.

Facilities: 50 campsites in a semi-parking lot arrangement; (hike-bike sites, enroute sites, and a primitive group camp in a separate area, are also available); sites are tiny but level; separation--zero; parking slots are paved, mostly short to medium-length straight-ins; small to medium-sized tent spots in some sites, none in others; storage cabinets; barbecue grills or fireplaces; b-y-o firewood; water at central faucets; restrooms; cold outside showers; holding tank disposal station; paved driveways; adequate+ supplies and services are available in Half Moon Bay.

Activities & Attractions: Beach access; day use area.

Natural Features: Located on a wide, sandy beach and on a short bluff at the edge of the beach; vegetation consists of grass and a few trees; bordered by residential and light agricultural zones; coastal hills rise a couple of miles behind the beach; sea level.

Season, Fees & Phone: Open all year; please see Appendix for standard California state park fees and reservation information; park office (415) 726-6238.

Camp Notes: Mark Twain once remarked that the coldest winter he ever experienced was the summer he spent on the San Francisco Peninsula. You don't sun yourself on a beach blanket here--you bundle yourself in it. Not much vegetation, save for worn grass, in this well-used campground. (If the local supermarket parking lot had barbecue grills and a garden hose you could camp there, too. Ed.)

BEN REIS
Butano State Park

Location: Central California coastal area north of Santa Cruz.

Access: From California State Highway 1 at milepost 13 +.7 (14 miles south of Half Moon Bay, 33 miles north of Santa Cruz), turn east onto Pescadero Road and travel 2.5 miles; turn south (right) onto Cloverdale Road and proceed 4.3 miles to Butano Park Road; turn east, (left) and proceed 0.2 mile to the park entrance station; continue for another mile to the campground. **Alternate Access:** From Highway 1 at milepost 5 +.75, turn east onto Gazos Creek Road and proceed 2.1 miles to Cloverdale Road; turn north (left) onto Cloverdale Road and go 1.3 miles to Butano Park Road, and continue as above. (Note: the alternate access is handier if you're coming from Santa Cruz, but it's also more winding.)

Facilities: 35 campsites, including 14 walk-in units located several yards from a parking area; (hike-bike sites are also available; a trail camp can be used, by reservation); sites are medium-sized, with fairly good separation; parking pads are gravel, short to medium-length straight-ins; some pads will require additional leveling; large, basically level, tent areas; fireplaces or fire rings; b-y-o firewood; water at several faucets; restrooms; paved, narrow driveways; limited supplies and services are available in Pescadero, 9 miles northwest.

Activities & Attractions: Several foot trails and fire roads lead 4-5 miles from the campground to the northeast corner of the park; guided nature walks and campfire programs in summer.

Natural Features: Located on the west slopes of the Santa Cruz Mountains, in a very dense forest of redwoods, some oaks, shrubs and ferns; most of this long, narrow park flanks Little Butano Creek, a small, typically seasonal, stream; elevation 250' to 1700'.

Season, Fees & Phone: Open all year; please see Appendix for standard California state park fees and reservation information; park office (408) 338-6132.

Camp Notes: In keeping with the natural theme of the park, the campground provides a very subdued, unembellished, forest environment. Most of the park is deep in the dense woods, but from one trail-accessible high point near the park entrance you can look out to the ocean and Año Nuevo Island.

GRAHAM HILL
Henry Cowell Redwoods State Park

Location: Central California coastal area north of Santa Cruz.

Access: From California State Highway 1 at the Ocean Street-Felton Exit in Santa Cruz at milepost 17 +.3, turn north onto Ocean Street and proceed 0.2 mile; bear right onto Graham Hill Road, go northerly for 3 miles, then turn west (left) onto a park access road for 0.2 mile to the campground entrance station, then a final 0.2 mile to the campground. **Alternate Access:** From the intersection of California State Highway 9 and Graham Hill Road in midtown Felton, travel southeast on Graham Hill Road for 2 miles to the campground access road and continue as above.

Facilities: 113 campsites; (bike sites are also available); sites are medium to medium+ in size, with good separation; parking pads are gravel/dirt, medium-length straight-ins; good to excellent tent-pitching opportunities; at least half of the parking pads and tent areas are essentially level, others are a touch sloped; storage cabinets; fireplaces or fire rings; b-y-o firewood; water at faucets throughout; restrooms with showers; paved driveways; groceries on Graham Hill Road within 2 miles north and south; complete supplies and services are available in Santa Cruz.

Activities & Attractions: Redwood groves; trail from the campground to an observation deck; 15 miles of hiking and horse trails within the park; steelhead and salmon fishing in winter.

Natural Features: Located in the western foothills of the Santa Cruz Mountains; most campsites are well sheltered/shaded; elevation 500'.

Season, Fees & Phone: Open all year; please see Appendix for standard California state park fees and reservation information; park office (408) 335-4598 or campground phone (408) 438-2396.

Camp Notes: Think of the park as being shaped like a drinking gourd. The campground is on the rim of the 'bowl'. Except for service roads and trails, 90 percent of the big dipper is semi-wilderness. Interestingly, in a park known for its great stands of redwoods, the campground's trees are primarily large, full oaks and ponderosa pines. No matter--it's a really nice place.

NEW BRIGHTON
New Brighton State Beach

Location: Central California Coast east of Santa Cruz.

Access: From California State Highway 1 at the Capitola/ Park Avenue Exit near milepost 12 (2 miles east of the Santa Cruz city limits), go southwest on Park Avenue for 0.15 mile; turn southeast (a hairpin left) onto a frontage road for 0.1 mile, then swing sharply right to the park entrance station; at a fork 0.1 mile beyond the entrance, take the left fork for 0.3 mile to the campground.

Facilities: 112 campsites; (hike-bike sites are also available); sites are small+ to medium-sized, level, with minimal to fair separation; parking pads are paved, short+ to medium-length straight-ins; adequate space for medium to large tents in most sites; fire rings; firewood is usually for sale, or b-y-o; water at faucets throughout; restrooms with showers; holding tank disposal station; paved driveways; complete supplies and services are available in Santa Cruz.

Activities & Attractions: Swimming; fishing; steps and trail down to the beach from the blufftop; day use area.

Natural Features: Located in a stand of tall conifers on a bluff above an ocean beach; campsites are lightly to moderately shaded/sheltered; elevation 50'.

Season, Fees & Phone: Open all year; please see Appendix for standard California state park fees and reservation information; park office (408) 475-4850.

Camp Notes: Without knowing that the ocean was at the front door, you might think the campground was in a forest many miles inland. There's tall timber here, and ocean views through the trees from a dozen or so campsites on the edge of a bluff. The beach area is locally known as "China Beach" or "China Cove" in reference to a small village made of scrap lumber and driftwood built by Chinese fishermen in the 1870's and 80's.

SEACLIFF
Seacliff State Beach

Location: Central California Coast east of Santa Cruz.

Access: From California State Highway 1 at Seacliff Beach/Aptos Exit near milepost 10 +.5, turn south-west onto State Park Drive and proceed 0.5 mile to the park entrance station; just past the entrance, swing right and go down to the bottom of the hill, then right again into the campground.

Facilities: 26 campsites with full hookups; sites are very small, level, with nil separation, arranged in a parallel row; parking slots are paved, short to medium+ straight-ins; enough space for a small tent between sites; fire rings; firewood is usually for sale, or b-y-o; water at sites; restrooms with showers; paved driveways; adequate supplies are available in Aptos.

Activities & Attractions: Visitor center with ocean-oriented exhibits; 'wreck' of the *Palo Alto*; fishing; fishing pier; large day use area.

Natural Features: Located on a short shelf just above beach level; a high, wooded bluff forms the backdrop for the campground; sea level.

Season, Fees & Phone: Open all year; please see Appendix for standard California state park fees and reservation information; park office (408) 688-3222.

Camp Notes: The *Palo Alto* was a concrete tanker built during WWI, but the war ended before it sailed. The new ship was sold to a private company which had her towed here. The *Palo Alto* was scuttled at the end of the pier so it would settle onto the sandy bottom. It was completely re-outfitted with a dance floor, a cafe, carny booths and a swimming pool. But the company soon went belly-up, and the ship's fittings were plundered. The 'sunken' ship can be seen from the camp area.

SUNSET
Sunset State Beach

Location: Central California Coast southeast of Santa Cruz.

Access: From California State Highway 1 (southbound) near milepost 8, at the San Andreas Road/Seascape Exit (1 mile east of Aptos), head south on San Andreas Road for 5.2 miles to Sunset Beach Road; turn west onto Sunset Beach Road and proceed 0.8 mile to the park entrance; turn south (left) for 0.7 mile to the campground. **Alternate Access:** From Highway 1 (northbound) at milepost 0.9 (just north of the Santa Cruz-Monterey county line) take the Watsonville/State Highway 129 Exit, go to the west side of the freeway, then north on a frontage road for 0.3 mile to a "T" intersection; turn southwest (left) onto Beach Road and proceed 1.4 miles; turn northwest (right) onto San Andreas Road and travel 2 miles; turn west (left) onto Sunset Beach Road and continue as above.

Facilities: 90 campsites in 3 loops; (hike-bike sites and a medium-sized group camp are also available); sites are small, with minimal to nominal separation; parking pads are paved, mostly short to short+ straight-ins, plus a few pull-offs; many pads will require a little additional leveling; adequate space for large tents in most sites; fire rings; firewood is usually for sale, or b-y-o; water at several faucets; restrooms with showers; paved driveways; complete supplies and services are available in Watsonville.

Activities & Attractions: Beach trails over the dune; campfire center; day use area.

Natural Features: Located on slightly hilly/rolling terrain behind a long dune just east of an ocean beach; vegetation consists of short grass, some small bushes, and large, full conifers that provide a fairly generous amount of shelter/shade in many sites; bordered by farm fields to the east; sea level.

Season, Fees & Phone: Open all year; please see Appendix for standard California state park fees and reservation information; park office (408) 724-1266.

Camp Notes: A dune separates the camp loops from the ocean, so there are no ocean views. Don't let that stop you. The campground is in a very nice "piney" setting. It's one of the nicer-looking state beach camps.

LAGUNA SECA
Monterey County Park

Location: Central California coastal area southeast of Monterey.

Access: From California State Highway 68 at milepost 10 +.9 (7 miles southeast of Monterey, 11 miles southwest of Salinas), turn north onto a steep, winding, paved road and continue for 0.9 mile to the entrance station.

Facilities: 177 campsites, including 110 with partial hookups, in 2 major areas; sites are basically small, with little separation; parking pads are gravel/dirt, mainly short to medium-length straight-ins; most pads will probably require additional leveling; tent-pitching areas are moderately sized, and vary in state of levelness; fire rings; firewood is usually for sale, or b-y-o; water at central faucets and in hookup units; restrooms with showers; holding tank disposal station; paved roadways; complete supplies and services are available in Monterey and Salinas.

Activities & Attractions: Overlooks the Laguna Seca motor sports racetrack; shooting range; nature preserve; sweeping, 360° views from most sites.

Natural Features: Located on a group of hilltops on the west slope of the Coast Range; campground vegetation consists of well-worn grass and some short to medium-height trees; some sites are partially sheltered, most are in the open; surrounded by grass-and-tree-covered hills; elevation 800'.

Season, Fees & Phone: Open all year; $11.00 for a standard site, $16.00 for a partial hookup site; 15 day limit; park office (408) 755-4899.

Camp Notes: If you're a camper and a racing enthusiast, this one's for you. Only a comparatively few world-class courses offer on-premises camping, and this is one of the better ones. Even if you're not a race fan, the magnificent panoramas (especially when the fog either rolls-in or lifts) from this hilltop spot are well worth the stay.

ANDREW MOLERA
Andrew Molera State Park

Location: Central California Coast south of Monterey.

Access: From California State Highway 1 at milepost 51 +.2 (23 miles south of Carmel, 5 miles north of Big Sur), turn west onto a park access road and proceed 0.2 mile to the parking lot; from the lot, trails lead to the campsites.

Facilities: Approximately 50 primitive campsites along the River Trail; drinking water; vault facilities.

Activities & Attractions: 15 miles of hiking trails to the coast, through the river thickets, and into the hills (a detailed brochure/map with contour lines is available); several foot bridges spanning the river are installed in summer.

Natural Features: Located in lowland on the banks of the Big Sur River; vegetation consists of sections of open grass, a considerable quantity of brush and twiggy hardwoods, large hardwoods and conifers; coastal mountains form the backdrop for the campsites; elevation 50'.

Season, Fees & Phone: Open all year; please see Appendix for standard California state park fees; phone c/o Pfeiffer-Big Sur State Park (408) 667-2315.

Camp Notes: Most of the campsites in the 4800-acre park are along the river bottom. One small section of beach is relatively accessible from the parking lot and the campsites. The trail follows the river to its exit at the ocean. The remaining two miles of the park's beach property is awash at high tide.

PFEIFFER BIG SUR
Pfeiffer Big Sur State Park

Location: Central California Coast south of Monterey.

Access: From California State Highway 1 at milepost 46 +.8 in Big Sur (27 miles south of Carmel, 67 miles north of San Simeon), turn east onto the park access road to the entrance station; just beyond the entrance at a fork, take the right fork to the campground.

Facilities: 218 campsites; (hike-bike sites and 2 hike-in group camps are also available); sites are small to small+, level, with separation varying from none to good; parking pads are gravel/dirt, short to medium-length straight-ins; excellent tent-pitching possibilities; fireplaces; b-y-o firewood; water at several faucets; restrooms with showers; holding tank disposal station; paved driveways; small store and laundry in the park; gas and groceries along the highway; nearest source of complete supplies and services is in Monterey.

Activities & Attractions: Nature trails; hiking trails; fishing; ball field; small nature center; campfire center; the 165,000-acre Ventana Wilderness in Los Padres National Forest, lies just east of the park; several small day use areas with shelters.

Natural Features: Located on a large, densely forested flat along the Big Sur River near the west edge of the Santa Lucia Mountains; vegetation consists of a wide variety of hardwoods, conifers (including some 1200-year-old redwoods), brush and ferns; some campsites are in dense forest, others are in more open sections; the campground stretches for a mile along the river; elevation 200'.

Season, Fees & Phone: Open all year; please see Appendix for standard California state park fees and reservation information; park office (408) 667-2315.

Camp Notes: Called *El Pais Grande del Sur* by the Spanish, "The Big Country of the South" is just "Big Sur" to everybody now. The dense, rain forest-like environment along the river makes the campground appear as if it were actually hundreds of miles to the north--in Northwest California, or even Oregon or Washington. Life in Big Sur is a flashback to the 1960's. There probably are more vintage VW bugs and vans, with appropriately attired, suitably hirsute occupants to match, than in any other region in the West, with the possible exception of Boulder, Colorado.

PORTOLA
Portola State Park

Location: Western California southwest of Palo Alto.

Access: From California State Highway 84 (La Honda Road) at milepost 8 +.3 (8 miles east of the junction of Highway 84 & State Highway 1, 7 miles south of the junction of Highway 84 & State Highway 35), turn southwest onto Pescadero Road and proceed 1.1 miles, then pick up Alpine Road and travel another 4 miles; turn south (right) onto Portola Park Road (curvy and very steep on some sections) and proceed 3 miles to the park entrance station; continue for 0.9 mile (past the visitor center) to the campground. **Alternate Access:** From State Highway 35 (Skyline Boulevard) at milepost 3 +.3 (at the junction of Highway 35 & Page Mill Road & Alpine Road), head southwest on Alpine Road for 3.4 miles, then turn south onto Portola Park Road and continue as above.

Facilities: 52 campsites; (a trail camp and a group campground are also available, group area by reservation only); sites are small to small+, with nominal to good separation; parking pads are paved, most are short to medium-length straight-ins; some additional leveling will be required on many pads;

generally small to medium-sized tent areas, many are sloped; storage cabinets; fire rings; firewood is usually for sale, or b-y-o; water at several faucets; restrooms with showers; paved, narrow driveways; limited groceries in La Honda, 9 miles northwest.

Activities & Attractions: Hiking trails (a brochure/map with contour lines and trail profiles is available); Sequoia Nature Trail (0.75 mile loop, trail guide is printed in the park brochure); visitor center; campfire center; several small picnic areas.

Natural Features: Located in a deep, densely forested canyon in the Santa Cruz Mountains; redwoods and other tall conifers are the featured trees, hardwoods and dense undergrowth fill in the remaining available space; Pescadero and Peters Creeks flow through the park; elevation 400'.

Season, Fees & Phone: Open all year; please see Appendix for standard California state park fees and reservation information; park office (415) 948-9098.

Camp Notes: The park's visitor center is reasonably large and looks like it might be a comfortable spot for brief gatherings. It would also be a good spot for leg-stretching during inclement weather. Pescadero Creek is generally an all-year stream (thanks to some springs), and when the water is up during the winter rains, some small (12-16 inch) steelhead and salmon can occasionally be seen making their uphill runs.

BLOOMS CREEK
Big Basin Redwoods State Park

Location: Western California northwest of Santa Cruz.

Access: From California State Highway 236 at milepost 9 or milepost 8 +.7 (0.3 to 0.6 mile south of the park nature center & headquarters, 7.5 miles southwest of the junction of State Highways 236 & 9 at Waterman Gap, 9 miles northwest of Boulder Creek), turn south into either of the 2 sections of the campground.

Special Access Note: for Blooms Creek and the other Big Basin campgrounds following this section: it might help to know that the northeast park boundary crosses the highway near milepost 13, the southeast boundary is near milepost 7 +.5; California 236 is a half loop that connects to State Highway 9 at two points: in the town of Boulder Creek at its south terminus and at Waterman Gap at its north end; Highway 236 follows an east-west line as it passes the campground turnoffs.)

Facilities: 27 campsites in 2 sections; sites are small, with nominal to fair separation; parking pads are gravel, short to medium-length straight-ins; a little additional leveling will be needed on some pads; generally enough space for medium to large tents in most sites; storage lockers; fire rings; firewood is usually for sale or b-y-o; water at several faucets; restrooms with showers; holding tank disposal station; paved driveways; camper supplies at the park store; adequate supplies and services are available in Boulder Creek.

Activities & Attractions: 100 miles of trails for hiking or for hiking & equestrian use; Pine Mountain and Blooms Creek Trails pass by the campground; campfire center near the nature center.

Natural Features: Located on a rolling flat and on sloping terrain in a forested area along Blooms Creek in the Santa Cruz Mountains; sites receive medium to medium-dense shade/shelter from redwoods, plus an abundance of large hardwoods and lower growth; elevation 1000'.

Season, Fees & Phone: Open all year; please see Appendix for standard California state park fees and reservation information; park office (408) 338-6132.

Camp Notes: The forest environment here is hard to top. Sites in the east section of the campground (i.e., #'s 130-156, accessed from mp 8 +.7), are more level and are in slightly nicer local surroundings. About a hundred yards northwest of the turnoff to Blooms Creek is the parking area for the Jay Trail Camp. Jay's half dozen sites are available in a walk-in area northeast of the highway.

HUCKLEBERRY
Big Basin Redwoods State Park

Location: Western California northwest of Santa Cruz.

Access: From California State Highway 236 at milepost 8 +.7 (0.6 mile south of the park nature center & headquarters, 8 miles southwest of the junction of State Highways 236 & 9 at Waterman Gap, 9 miles northwest of Boulder Creek), turn north onto a paved campground access road and go 0.8 up to the hill; turn east (right) for 0.1 mile to the campground.

Facilities: 39 campsites, including about a dozen park 'n walk sites; sites are small, with nominal to fairly good separation; parking pads are gravel, mostly short straight-ins; small to medium-sized tent areas; storage lockers; fire rings; firewood is usually for sale or b-y-o; water at several faucets; restrooms with showers; holding tank disposal station; paved driveways; camper supplies at the park store; adequate supplies and services are available in Boulder Creek.

Activities & Attractions: Many miles of trails; visitor center.

Natural Features: Located in a densely forested, deep and steep region of the Santa Cruz Mountains; sites are on a hillside and are well sheltered/shaded by towering, old growth redwoods, plus large hardwoods and undergrowth; elevation 1100'.

Season, Fees & Phone: Open all year; please see Appendix for standard California state park fees and reservation information; park office (408) 338-6132.

Camp Notes: So you say you don't have enough closet space for a complete tent camping ensemble in your fourth floor flat, or your megamotorhome is in the shop for its annual satellite dish checkup? Big Basin may have just the 'alternative camping' arrangement you need. Huckleberry also has 36 tent cabins for nightly rental. These are small, woodframed jobs with wood siding to about 4' above ground level and all-around window screening. A peaked, open-frame roof is covered by canvas. Each shelter has a couple of bunks with foam pads, a small table and wood stove, plus a parking pad, table and fire ring outside. The canvas roof can be flipped back for sky-watching. A tent cabin cozily sleeps four campers (if they're on really good terms).

WASTAHI
Big Basin Redwoods State Park

Location: Western California northwest of Santa Cruz.

Access: From California State Highway 236 at milepost 8 +.7 (0.6 mile south of the park nature center & headquarters, 8 miles southwest of the junction of State Highways 236 & 9 at Waterman Gap, 9 miles northwest of Boulder Creek), turn north onto a paved campground access road and go 0.9 mile up to the campground.

Facilities: 27 campsites; sites are small, with good separation; parking pads are gravel, short to medium-length straight-ins; many pads will require a little additional leveling; small to medium-sized spots for tents; fire rings; holding tank disposal station nearby; paved driveways; firewood is usually for sale or b-y-o; water at several faucets; restrooms with showers; paved driveway; holding tank disposal station nearby; camper supplies at the park store; adequate supplies and services are available in Boulder Creek.

Activities & Attractions: 100 miles of trails for hikers, or for hikers & horsers; nature center.

Natural Features: Located on a hillside in a densely forested region of the Santa Cruz Mountains; sites are well sheltered/shaded by old growth redwoods, large hardwoods and dense lower growth; elevation 1100'.

Season, Fees & Phone: Open all year; please see Appendix for standard California state park fees and reservation information; park office (408) 338-6132.

Camp Notes: Big Basin has more miles of trails that just about anyone could walk in a good part of a lifetime. One of them is the Sequoia Trail that passes alongside the campground. Using this route, together with other connecting park trails and the park map/brochure, will allow you to take a couple of easy loop trips that begin and end at your campsite.

SEMPERVIRENS
Big Basin Redwoods State Park

Location: Western California northwest of Santa Cruz.

Access: From California State Highway 236 at milepost 8 +.45 (0.8 mile south of the park nature center & headquarters, 8 miles southwest of the junction of State Highways 236 & 9 at Waterman Gap, 8.5 miles northwest of Boulder Creek), turn north or south into the camp loops.

Facilities: 45 campsites; sites are small, essentially level, with nominal to fair separation; parking pads are gravel, short to medium-length straight-ins; medium-sized tent areas; fire rings; firewood is usually for sale, or b-y-o; water at several faucets; restrooms with showers; paved driveways; camper supplies at the park store; adequate supplies and services are available in Boulder Creek.

Activities & Attractions: Hiking and horse trails; nature center.

Natural Features: Located on a rolling flat along or near Blooms Creek in the Santa Cruz Mountains; sites are moderately sheltered by lofty redwoods, plus medium-dense hardwoods for lower cover; elevation 1000'.

Season, Fees & Phone: Open all year (subject to need); please see Appendix for standard California state park fees and reservation information; park office (408) 338-6132.

Camp Notes: In addition to this and the other three individual campgrounds described above, Big Basin also has two group camps (available by rez). Sequoia Group camp is about a half mile off the main highway via a side road from near the nature center (but actually close to the highway as the crow flies); Sky Meadow Group Camp is back in the boonies about two miles from civilization. For an excellent perspective of the countryside encompassed by the triad of state parks in this region--Big Basin Redwoods, Portola, and Castle Rock--take a good look at the large, 3D map in the nature center.

HENRY W. COE
Henry W. Coe State Park

Location: Western California southeast of San Jose.

Access: From U.S. Highway 101 in Morgan Hill, take the East Dunne Avenue Exit and travel east on Dunne Avenue for 12 miles to the park boundary, then another 0.5 mile to the ranch yard and park headquarters, and a final 0.3 mile to the campground. (Note: the trip up from the freeway involves going up and over a couple of hills on a paved, narrow, often steep road with a fair number of switchbacks and other tight turns; the route is straightforward as long as you watch the road signs while passing through the subdivisions leaving Morgan Hill; if you cross a major bridge high above a reservoir 4 miles out, you're on the right road.)

Facilities: 20 camp/picnic sites; (about the same number of individual backpacking sites, and 11 backpacking group camps, are also available; no fires in the backcountry); sites are small to small+, with nominal separation; parking pads are gravel/earth, short to medium-length straight-ins; most pads will require a bit of additional leveling; large areas for tents; small ramadas (sun shelters) for about half of the sites; fireplaces; b-y-o firewood; water at central faucets; vault facilities; gravel driveways; complete supplies and services are available in Morgan Hill.

Activities & Attractions: Hiking and horse trails; (detailed maps are available in the museum); small museum with ranch life exhibits; barn, stables, sheds with antique farm equipment; possible fishing for small trout in streams at lower elevations.

Natural Features: Located high in the Diablo Range on a ridgetop overlooking a series of mountains and canyons; main campground vegetation consists of scattered, large hardwoods on a grassy surface; vegetation in the backcountry is mostly oak woodland with ponderosa pine forest on the western ridges, plus large grasslands and oak savannah; nearly all rain falls November through March; the park is noted for it's dazzling wildflower blooms; total park area is 67,000 acres, including a 22,000-acre wilderness; main campground elevation 2400'.

Season, Fees & Phone: Open all year; please see Appendix for standard California state park fees; park office (408) 779-2728.

Camp Notes: California's second-largest state park originally was called Pine Ridge Ranch, started in the mid-1800's by Henry Coe. Most people who come here do so to hike and camp, and occasionally they catch a glimpse of a mountain lion, a bobcat or an eagle. The grizzly which once roamed California is gone, but if the Silvertip ever did come back, this is the kind of country he would come back to first.

LAKEVIEW
Coyote Lake/Santa Clara County Park

Location: West-central California southeast of San Jose.

Access: From U.S. Highway 101 in Gilroy, at the exit for Santa Clara County Road G9 and for California Highway 152 to Watsonville, turn east onto Leavesley Road (Road G9); proceed east for 1.8 miles to New Avenue; turn north (left) onto New Avenue, continue for 0.6 mile to Roop Road; turn east (right, onto Roop), and follow Roop Road northeasterly for 3 miles (steep and winding in sections) to Coyote Lake Road; turn northwest (left) onto Coyote Lake Road and continue for a final 0.9 mile to the park entrance and the campground.

Facilities: 75 campsites in a single, large, complex loop; sites are medium-sized or better, with minimal separation; parking pads are paved, medium to long straight-ins; most pads will probably require some additional leveling; spacious, grassy, slightly sloped tent spots; fireplaces; b-y-o firewood; water at several faucets; restrooms; paved driveway; complete supplies and services are available in Gilroy.

Activities & Attractions: Boating; boat launch; fishing; many sites have a lake view.

Natural Features: Located on a slightly sloping flat at the southwest corner of Coyote Lake; campground vegetation consists of more than a score of large oak trees on a grassy surface; at least half of the sites have some shelter/shade; the lake is bordered by tree-dotted hills; elevation 800'.

Season, Fees & Phone: Open all year; $8.00; 14 day limit; park office (408) 842-7800.

Camp Notes: Subjectively speaking, it's worth traveling a few miles off the freeway to get here. Even in August, the surroundings are quite pleasantly green and gold, (though the lake may be low by summer's end). While you're in the neighborhood, say "Hi" to the folks in Gilroy (which lays claim to being "The Garlic Capital of the World").

FREMONT PEAK
Fremont Peak State Park

Location: Western California south of San Jose.

Access: From California State Highway 156 at milepost 3 in the city of San Juan Bautista (3 miles south of the junction of Highway 156 & U.S. Highway 101 northeast Salinas), turn west onto Salinas Road/San Juan Canyon Road/San Benito County Road G1 and go 0.3 mile, then take a quick left-right jog and stay on San Juan Canyon Road/G1; travel southerly for 10.5 miles to the park boundary; continue ahead on the main park road for another 0.5 mile to the campground, on the right, or for a final 0.1 mile to the trailhead parking lot. (Note: the road is paved all the way to the park, but the last 5 miles are very steep and curvy.)

Facilities: 17 primitive campsites; (several group camps and a horse camp are also available); sites vary from small to large, with nominal to good separation; parking pads are sandy gravel, short to medium-length straight-ins; some additional leveling may be needed; large tent areas; fire rings; b-y-o firewood; water at several faucets (b-y-o extra water 'just in case'); vault facilities; hard-surfaced driveways; limited supplies and services are available in San Juan Bautista.

Activities & Attractions: Trail to the summit of 3169' Fremont Peak; nature trail.

Natural Features: Located on grassy slopes dotted with hardwoods and some conifers; (but the mountainsides below the park look like a battalion of berserk bulldozers once played a frenzied game of tic-tac-toe across their mid-sections); elevation 3100'.

Season, Fees & Phone: Open all year; please see Appendix for standard California state park fees and reservation information; phone c/o CDPR Gavilan District Office, San Juan Bautista, (408) 623-4255.

Camp Notes: Fremont Peak was called "Gavilan Peak" (from the Spanish word for "Hawk") in early California. In March of 1846, Captain John Charles Fremont of the U.S. Army Corps of Engineers was conducting his third exploration of California. His presence with an armed force in a settled area was unsettling to the Mexican authorities and they ordered him out. Instead, Fremont and his troops ascended Gavilan Peak and built a log fort. A sapling was cut for a flagpole and on March 6th, Fremont raised a United States flag--the first American flag to fly over California. Meanwhile, the Mexican forces were mobilized down in San Juan Bautista. Before any shots were traded, though, the flagpole blew down on the afternoon of March 9th. Fremont took this as a bad sign, and moved on toward the San Joaquin Valley. An American-Mexican confrontation was avoided, for the time being anyway, and Gavilan Peak once again became the meeting place of the hawks.

CHAPARRAL
Pinnacles National Monument

Location: Western California south of Salinas.

Access: From U.S. Highway 101 near milepost 61 at the exit for Soledad/California State Highway 146 (25 miles south of Salinas, 19 miles north of King City), proceed northeasterly on Highway 146 for 1 mile into Soledad; then head southeast (watch for the signs), continuing on Highway 146 for 13 miles as the road gradually winds northeasterly to the Chaparral Ranger Station and the campground, just beyond. (Note: the last half-dozen miles are steep and curvy and are "not recommended for cars with trailers".)

Facilities: 18 park 'n walk or walk-in campsites; (group camping is also available, by reservation only); sites are small to medium-sized, fairly level, with nominal separation; parking is in a paved lot; small to medium-sized areas for tents on a sandy surface; b-y-o shade; barbecue grills; charcoal fires only; water at central faucets; restrooms; paved driveway; adequate supplies and services are available in Soledad.

Activities & Attractions: Foot trails cross rugged hills to the visitor center at Bear Gulch and to other areas on the east side of the park (about a two-hour trip).

Natural Features: Located on hilly terrain in the Gabilan Range; sites are unshaded to lightly shaded by a few large hardwoods on a surface of crunchgrass and brush; the Pinnacles are the eroded, last remnants of an ancient volcano; very rugged surroundings, including spired and cragged rock formations; elevation 1400'.

Season, Fees & Phone: Open all year; camping limited to Monday through Thursday only (i.e., no weekend camping), February to June; $10.00; park headquarters (408) 389-4485.

Camp Notes: The twisty road up to the park is more suitable for Volvos and 'Vettes than for Winnebagos and other wonder wagons. Ditto the campground. February to Memorial Day is the busiest time here. If you're looking for an uncrowded midsummer camp when all of the waterfront campgrounds are overflowing, you might consider Chaparral. Summer daytime temps often reach 100° F, but nighttime lows can dip deeply into the 40's. It may be h-o-t, but you'll probably have only the rangers and the rattlers for company.

Northern California
Northern Inland
Please refer to the Northern California map in the Appendix

Northern California 73

O'NEILL CREEK
Klamath National Forest

Location: Northern California west of Yreka.

Access: From California State Highway 96 at milepost 65 +.4 (3 miles west of Hamburg, 25 miles east of Happy Camp, 22 miles west of Klamath River), turn south onto a paved, winding access road and proceed 0.1 mile to the campground.

Facilities: 19 campsites in 2 loops; sites are medium to large, with fair to very good separation; parking pads are packed gravel, medium-length straight-ins; medium to large areas for tents; tent spaces and parking pads are reasonably level, considering the terrain; assorted fire appliances; water at central faucets; vault facilities; paved driveways; gas and groceries in Hamburg.

Activities & Attractions: Hiking trail; fishing.

Natural Features: Located in a valley on a forested hillside above the Klamath River in the Coast Range; sites are well-sheltered by tall conifers and some low hardwoods; elevation 1500'.

Season, Fees & Phone: May to October; $6.00; 14 day limit; Oak Knoll Ranger District, Klamath River, (916) 465-2241.

Camp Notes: If a more isolated campsite is your preference, you might look into O'Neill Creek Campground. Even though the terrain is tilted, there are some excellent, spacious sites here. The river is on the north side of the highway and is within a few minutes' walk of the campsites. Camping would be a pleasure in this region no matter what the facilities were like, though. The Klamath River Highway ('96) passes through some of the best country in the West.

Northern California 74

SARAH TOTTEN
Klamath National Forest

Location: Northern California west of Yreka.

Access: From California State Highway 96 at milepost 69 +.9 or milepost 70 (1.5 miles east of Hamburg, 29 miles east of Happy Camp, 6 miles west of Horse Creek, 17 miles west of Klamath River), turn north into the campground. (There are two entrances for the 2 sections.)

Facilities: 19 campsites in 2 loops; sites are rather small, with fairly good separation; parking pads are gravel, mostly level, short to medium-length straight-ins; tent spots tend to be large, and a bit sloped; barbecue grills; firewood is available for gathering in the area; water at faucets; vault facilities; paved gravel driveways; gas and groceries in Hamburg.

Activities & Attractions: Fishing; floating; the Klamath River is considered a Wild and Scenic River through this section; great scenery along Highway 96 through the canyon.

Natural Features: Located on the east slope of the Coast Range on the south bank of the Klamath River; campground vegetation consists primarily of thin to moderately dense tall pines, some second growth timber, low bushes, and tall grass; the canyon widens here just enough to allow room for a neat little riverside campground; low, timber-covered canyon walls line both sides of the river; elevation 1600'.

Season, Fees & Phone: Open all year, with limited services October to May; $6.00; 14 day limit; Oak Knoll Ranger District, Klamath River, (916) 465-2241.

Camp Notes: There are some nice little campsites tucked away among the trees here, and even a few streamside sites. Campsites in the east section are a bit more open and roomier than those in the west section. The Klamath is a member in good standing of the Wild and Scenic River System.

TREE OF HEAVEN
Klamath National Forest

Location: Northern California north of Yreka.

Access: From California State Highway 96 at milepost 99 +.1 (12 miles east of Klamath River, 13 miles north of Yreka), turn south onto a paved, steep access road; proceed down for 0.3 mile to the campground.

Facilities: 21 campsites in 2 loops; sites vary in size, with nominal to fair separation; parking pads are gravel, level, short to medium-length straight-ins; most sites have excellent tent spots; assorted fire appliances; b-y-o firewood is recommended; water at several faucets; vault facilities; paved driveways; gas and groceries in Klamath River; adequate supplies and services are available in Yreka.

Activities & Attractions: River access at a small, hand-launch ramp; floating the Wild and Scenic Klamath River; the drive along the river is also quite scenic; most sites have a river view.

Natural Features: Located between the Coast Range and the Cascade Range along the bank of the Klamath River; sites are on a grassy, tree-covered flat along this swiftly flowing river; the Tree of Heaven and other planted hardwoods and big, bushy pines shelter the campground; tree-dotted hills border the canyon; summer temperatures reach or exceed 100° F; elevation 2100'.

Season, Fees & Phone: Open all year, with limited services October to April; $7.00; 14 day limit; Oak Knoll Ranger District, Klamath River, (916) 465-2241.

Camp Notes: Tree of Heaven, a native of China, commonly came west with resourceful pioneers. Many settlers planted this variety because its rapid growth and coarse foliage made the Tree of Heaven excellent for shade and windbreaks. Prime examples of the large hardwood flourish in the camp area. They help make Tree of Heaven a topnotch forest campground.

TANNERY GULCH
Whiskeytown-Shasta-Trinity National Recreation Area

Location: Northwest California west of Redding.

Access: From California State Highway 3 at milepost 42 +.6 (11 miles north of Weaverville, 18 miles south of Trinity Center), turn east onto a paved access road; proceed 1.1 miles to the campground.

Facilities: 84 campsites in 4 loops; sites are mostly medium-sized, with fair separation; parking pads are paved, medium to long straight-ins; many pads may require some additional leveling; medium to large, reasonably level, tent areas; fireplaces and fire rings; firewood is usually available for gathering in the area; water at several faucets; restrooms, plus auxiliary vaults; paved driveways; adequate supplies and services are available in Weaverville.

Activities & Attractions: Boating; sailing; small boat ramp; fishing (the lake holds the California record for largest smallmouth bass); designated swimming beach; amphitheater; ranger-guided activities; Trail of the Trees Nature Trail; very scenic drive along the lakeshore.

Natural Features: Located in the Coast Range on a a forested slope along the southwest shore of Clair Engle Lake (also known as Trinity Lake); vegetation in the campground is mostly tall conifers, some second growth, and sparse grass; a number of sites have lake views through the trees; the 20-mile-long lake is surrounded by intensely green forested hills and mountains; elevation 2400'.

Season, Fees & Phone: May to October; $9.00 for a standard site, $15.00 for a multiple site; 14 day limit; Weaverville Ranger District (916) 623-2121.

Camp Notes: Tannery Gulch is one of the most popular campgrounds on this lake for at least two reasons: it has the closest and most convenient access from major population centers; and it has a sizeable boat launch.

STONEY POINT
Whiskeytown-Shasta-Trinity National Recreation Area

Location: Northwest California west of Redding.

Access: From California State Highway 3 at milepost 44 +.3 (13 miles north of Weaverville, 17 miles south of Trinity Center), turn southeast into the campground parking lot.

Facilities: 22 park 'n walk or walk-in campsites; sites are small to medium-sized, with fair separation; parking is available in a roadside lot; small to medium-sized areas for tents; fireplaces; some firewood is available for gathering in the area if you range out a bit; water at several faucets; (water may not be available, so b-y-o to be sure); restrooms and vaults; adequate supplies and services are available in Weaverville.

Activities & Attractions: Fishing and boating; Stoney Creek swim area is a mile east.

Natural Features: Located on a point of land at the southwest end of Clair Engle Lake in the Coast Range; sites are on a short hilltop and on a forested slope above the tip of a big bay; elevation 2500'.

Season, Fees & Phone: Open all year, with limited services October to April; $7.00; (no water, no fee); 14 day limit; Weaverville Ranger District (916) 623-2121.

Camp Notes: This is a year 'round favorite of tent campers, in part because fishing is good in the vicinity of nearby Stuart Point. Campsites are quite well sheltered by fairly dense forest, and a bunch of 'em have lake views. The sites are stretched out along the point in a pattern that resembles a string with a balloon at the end. Some sites are only a few yards from the parking lot, others are a few hundred yards from the road.

MINERSVILLE
Whiskeytown-Shasta-Trinity National Recreation Area

Location: Northwest California west of Redding.

Access: From California State Highway 3 at milepost 47 +.3 (16 miles north of Weaverville, 14 miles south of Trinity Center), turn southeast onto a paved, steep and winding access road; proceed 0.85 mile down to the campground.

Facilities: 21 campsites, including many park 'n walk sites, in 2 loops; sites are fairly small, with nominal to good separation; some parking pads are gravel, smallish straight-ins, many of which may require additional leveling; adequate spots for medium to large tents, but they may be a bit sloped; parking lot for park 'n walk sites; fireplaces; firewood is usually available for gathering in the vicinity; water at several faucets; restrooms; paved driveways; adequate supplies and services in Weaverville.

Activities & Attractions: Boating (boat ramp); fishing; lake trail; superscenic drive along the lakeshore.

Natural Features: Located on the northwest shore of Clair Engle Lake (Trinity Lake) on the east side of the Coast Range; campsites are on a short 'shelf' above the lake itself; campground vegetation is fairly dense with tall conifers, cedars, oaks, tall grass and some underbrush; the lake has 145 miles of shoreline; elevation 2500'.

Season, Fees & Phone: Open all year, with limited services November to April; $8.00-$14.00; 14 day limit; Weaverville Ranger District (916) 623-2121.

Camp Notes: Sites along the shoreline have a great view of this beautiful mountain lake and the forested peaks beyond it to the east.

HAYWARD FLAT
Whiskeytown-Shasta-Trinity National Recreation Area

Location: Northwest California west of Redding.

Access: From California State Highway 3 at milepost 50 +.6 (19 miles north of Weaverville, 11 miles south of Trinity Center), turn southeast onto a paved, steep and winding access road; proceed 2.15 miles to the entrance station; camp loops are right and left of the entrance.

Facilities: 98 campsites in 5 loops; sites are mostly average-sized, with fair separation; parking pads are paved, short to long straight-ins; many pads may require substantial additional leveling; some large tent spots, but most are a bit sloped; fire rings and fireplaces; firewood is usually available for gathering in the vicinity; water at several faucets; restrooms; paved driveways; adequate supplies and services are available in Weaverville.

Activities & Attractions: Beach; good views of forested ridges to the east, across the North Lake area; campfire center; nearest boat ramp is at Bowerman, about 10 miles by road, or about a mile across the North Lake 'arm' by boat.

Natural Features: Located on a sloping flat along the north shore of Clair Engle Lake (Trinity Lake) in the Coast Range; campground vegetation consists mainly of tall pines and very little grass or underbrush; many of the sites have been notched out of a hillside; views of the lake through the trees from some sites; elevation 2400'.

Season, Fees & Phone: May to September; $9.00 for a standard site, $16.00 for a multiple site; 14 day limit; Weaverville Ranger District (916) 623-2121.

Camp Notes: The soil in the camp area is an extraordinary reddish-orange color that contrasts strikingly with the deep green of the forest. The absence of a boat ramp or dock at this campground is an important factor for boaters. (You might want to put in at another facility and perhaps just spend your landlocked hours here.) It's an important factor to non-boaters, also. (You'll know that most boaters will be someplace else on a perfect boating weekend.)

ALPINE VIEW
Whiskeytown-Shasta-Trinity National Recreation Area

Location: Northwest Cailfornia west of Redding.

Access: From California State Highway 3 at milepost 53 +.7 (22 miles north of Weaverville, 8 miles south of Trinity Center), turn southeast onto Covington Road; proceed south for 2.7 miles (most of the road is paved); turn right into the campground.

Facilities: 67 campsites in 3 loops; sites are small to medium-sized, with some separation; parking pads are gravel, short to medium-length straight-ins; virtually all parking pads will require additional leveling; tent spots have been leveled in a number of sites, but they may still tend to be a bit sloped; fireplaces and fire rings; firewood is usually available for gathering in the area; water at several faucets; restrooms; paved driveways; gas and groceries in Trinity Center; adequate supplies and services are available in Weaverville.

Activities & Attractions: Boating (a major public boat ramp is located nearby at Bowerman); sailing; fishing; reportedly very good waterskiing in the North Lake Area; nature trail.

Natural Features: Located in the Coast Range on Clair Engle Lake (Trinity Lake); campground vegetation consists of tall conifers, sparse grass and some second growth timber on unusual, reddish earth; views from most sites of forested ridges across the lake to the west; the North Lake Area extends beyond the campground toward the north; elevation 2400'.

Season, Fees & Phone: May to September (subject to needs and funds); $8.00; 14 day limit; Weaverville Ranger District (916) 623-2131.

Camp Notes: Overall, there's a relatively quiet atmosphere at Alpine View. Deer are commonly seen wandering through the camp. Parking pads are remarkably level, considering the slope. In this fairly well protected 'arm' of the lake, a number of boaters in lakeside sites can have their boat tied up to within a few yards of their tents.

PREACHER MEADOW
Shasta-Trinity National Forest

Location: Northwest California west of Redding.

Access: From California State Highway 3 at milepost 58 +.3 (27 miles north of Weaverville, 3 miles south of Trinity Center), turn southwest onto a paved access road; proceed 0.4 mile to the campground.

Facilities: 45 campsites in 2 loops; sites are medium to large, with mostly good separation; parking pads are gravel, medium to long straight-ins; some pads may require additional leveling; sites are roomy enough for large tents, though some are a bit sloped; chimneyed fireplaces; firewood is available for gathering in the area; water at several faucets; (drinking water may not be available, b-y-o just in case); vault facilities; paved driveways; gas and groceries in Trinity Center; adequate supplies and services are available in Weaverville.

Activities & Attractions: Trails to Granite Lake and the Trinity-Alps Primitive Area; stream and lake fishing; boating on the lake (nearest boat ramp is south of Trinity Center); museum in Trinity Center; scenic drive along Highway 3.

Natural Features: Located on a gentle to moderate slope along Swift Creek, just west of Clair Engle Lake (Trinity Lake), in the Coast Range; campground vegetation consists of tall pines, cedars, fairly dense second growth timber and sparse grass; elevation 2900'.

Season, Fees & Phone: May to October; $5.00; 14 day limit; Weaverville R.D. (916) 623-2131.

Camp Notes: It appears Preacher Meadow is a little known and seldom crowded forest camp. Sites here are roomy, private and the atmosphere is quiet and peaceful. If having a lakeside site is not imperative, this slightly off-the-beaten-path campground should be seriously considered for a base of operations. Nearby recreational opportunities are numerous. Though not actually visible from most sites, the rocky-topped peaks of the Trinity Alps are to the west. They can be glimpsed from points along Highway 3.

DOUGLAS CITY
Public Lands/BLM Recreation Site

Location: Northwest California west of Redding.

Access: From California State Highway 299 at milepost 57 +.9 (6 miles south of Weaverville, 36 miles west of Redding), turn west onto Steiner Flat Road; follow a well-signed route through Douglas City for 0.5 mile and turn south (left) onto a paved campground access road; proceed 0.25 mile down to the campground.

Facilities: 19 campsites; sites are mostly medium-sized, with fairly good to very good separation; parking pads are paved, level, medium to long straight-ins; some very nice, level, roomy tent spots; fireplaces; some firewood is usually available for gathering in the area; water at several faucets; flush & vault facilities; paved driveways; gas and groceries in Douglas City; adequate supplies and services are available in Weaverville.

Activities & Attractions: Fishing; floating; beach access; Clair Engle Lake (Trinity Lake) and Lewiston Lake are both within an hour's drive.

Natural Features: Located along the bank of the Trinity River in a deep valley in the Coast Range; campsites are all on a narrow flat within a few yards of the riverbank; tall pines, cedars and considerable underbrush provide very good shelter/separation for the sites; views of the river and surrounding green hills and mountains from many sites; elevation 1600'.

Season, Fees & Phone: May to October; $8.00; 14 day limit; BLM Redding Resource Area Office (916) 224-2100.

Camp Notes: This is not your typical BLM campground. It's one of their super specials. It has water, lots of trees, and, as a bonus, it's just a (paved) mile off the main thoroughfare. Another local, smaller, BLM campground is accessible from Highway 299 at milepost 61. Turn north onto Steel Bridge Road and proceed down into the valley to Steel Bridge Campground. Steel Bridge has a half dozen sites and vaults near the Trinity River.

OAK BOTTOM
Whiskeytown-Shasta-Trinity National Recreation Area

Location: Northwest California west of Redding.

Access: From California State Highway 299 at milepost 11 +.4 (10 miles west of Redding, 25 miles east of Douglas City), turn southeast onto the Oak Bottom access road; proceed 1.1 miles to the entrance station; turn north (left) into the rv lot, or south (right) into the tent area.

Facilities: 100 tent campsites and 50 rv sites; spaces in the rv lot are paved, mostly level, with zilch separation, adequate for long vehicles; tent sites are all park 'n walk units, small, with nominal separation; tent spots are a bit sloped, and most are on bare earth; fireplaces; b-y-o firewood is recommended; restrooms; (freshwater rinse showers are available near the swimming beach); holding tank disposal station in the rv lot; paved driveways; complete supplies and services are available in Redding.

Activities & Attractions: Boating; boat launch; marina near the rv lot; sailing; fishing for trout and salmon; swimming; gold-panning; hiking and jogging trails; ranger-guided interpretive activities; visitor center, 5 miles east; Shasta State Historic Park, 7 miles east.

Natural Features: Located on the northwest shore of Whiskeytown Lake on the east edge of the Coast Range; tent sites are situated on a series of small hills overlooking the lake; tent campground vegetation consists of a variety of scattered trees and small bushes; a number of sites have views of the lake through the trees; tall peaks of the Trinity Mountains rise to the west; the lake is virtually surrounded by green hills and mountains; elevation 1200'.

Season, Fees & Phone: Open all year, with limited services September to May; $9.00 for an rv spot, $11.00 for a tent site; 14 day limit; please see Appendix for reservation information; Whiskeytown Unit Headquarters (916) 241-6584.

Camp Notes: Lots of people come to Whiskeytown for water recreation, and, possibly, because of its colorful history. Unlike the other three lakes that make up this national rec area, Whiskeytown is maintained at a stable level in summer. Also unlike the other units in the nra operated by the Forest Service, this one is run by the National Park Service. You can tell.

CASTLE CRAGS
Castle Crags State Park

Location: North-central California north of Redding.

Access: From Interstate 5 near milepost 63 +.5 (6 miles south of Dunsmuir, 50 miles north of Redding), turn west onto Castle Creek Road; proceed 0.3 mile and turn north (right) to the park entrance station; turn east (right) and proceed 0.7 mile to the campground loops.

Facilities: 64 campsites in 3 loops; (3 environmental camps and enroute/overflow sites are also available); sites are small to medium-sized, with fair to fairly good separation; parking pads are paved, short to medium-length straight-ins; many pads will require a strong dose of additional leveling; tent spots are mostly sloped; large, stone fireplaces; firewood is usually for sale, or b-y-o; water at several faucets; restrooms with showers; paved driveways; gas and groceries at the freeway interchange.

Activities & Attractions: Terrific views from the vista point; 18 miles of hiking and equestrian trails, including 7 miles of the Pacific Crest Trail along the base of the Crags; self-guided nature trail; guided nature walks; campfire center for scheduled summer evening programs; trout fishing on the river (said to be good); swimming/wading in the river and in Castle Creek.

Natural Features: Located between the Coast Range and the Cascades a few miles north of the Sacramento Valley, at the base of an unusual geological feature, Castle Crags; another prominent volcanic feature, Mt. Shasta, is clearly visible from points in the park; the Sacramento River flows through a canyon and is within a short walk of most campsites; tall pines, oaks and light underbrush predominate; elevation 2500'.

Season, Fees & Phone: Open all year; please see Appendix for standard California state park fees and reservation information; park office (916) 235-2684.

Camp Notes: On a reasonably clear day, not only are the comely Castle Crags visible from the vista point, but 14,100' Mount Shasta can be viewed in all its glory from the same advantageous perch hundreds of feet above the canyon floor at the vista point. It's possible to take a walk up to the viewpoint from the camp loops.

SIMS FLAT
Shasta-Trinity National Forest

Location: North-central California north of Redding.

Access: From Interstate 5 near milepost 57 +.4 (13 miles south of Dunsmuir, 42 miles north of Redding), turn east onto Sims Road; proceed east and south for 0.7 mile down a paved access road to the campground.

Facilities: 20 campsites; sites are medium-sized to spacious, with fair to excellent separation; parking pads are gravel, level, medium to long straight-ins; some excellent tent spots; barbecue grills and fire rings; firewood is available for gathering in the area; water at several faucets; restrooms, plus auxiliary vaults; paved driveways; gas and groceries in Dunsmuir.

Activities & Attractions: Fishing; foot path along the riverbank; old suspension bridge over the river; scenic views; the very popular Shasta Lake recreation area is located about 15 miles south; Castle Crags State Park is about 7 miles north.

Natural Features: Located between the Coast Range and the Cascades on a semi-open forested flat along the Sacramento River; campground vegetation is a mixture of tall pines, oaks, hardwoods and some undergrowth; Mount Shasta is a prominent feature visible from the riverbank and from the bridge over the river; elevation 1600'.

Season, Fees & Phone: May to September; $8.00; 14 day limit; Mt. Shasta R.D. (916) 926-4511.

Camp Notes: Sims Flat is a fairly nice facility with private sites in a quiet pastoral setting. Even though the railroad line runs along the opposite bank of the river, there's rarely a disturbance. Another area campground, Pollard Flat, is a good quick stop, as it is located right off Interstate 5 at about milepost 50 +.4. It too is a forested camp along the Sacramento River.

LAKESHORE EAST
Whiskeytown-Shasta-Trinity National Recreation Area

Location: North-central California north of Redding.

Access: From Interstate 5 near milepost 41, at the Lakeshore Drive-Antlers Road Exit, (26 miles north of Redding, 29 miles south of Dunsmuir), turn west, then south onto Lakeshore Drive; proceed 1.2 miles; turn east (left) into the main campground; or continue for another 100 yards, then turn left into the tent area.

Facilities: 23 campsites, including 9 park 'n walk tent sites; sites are small to medium-sized, with mostly average separation; parking pads are gravel/dirt, short to medium-length straight-ins; pads may require a little additional leveling; most sites will accommodate large tents; small parking area for the tent section; barbecue grills or fire rings; some firewood is usually available for gathering in the area; water at several faucets; restrooms; paved driveways; gas and groceries at the Lakeshore exit; complete supplies and services are available in Redding.

Activities & Attractions: Boating; fishing.

Natural Features: Located between the Coast Range and the Cascade Range toward the north end of Shasta Lake; campground vegetation consists of moderately dense stands of tall pines, hardwoods, manzanita and a variety of berry bushes; some lake views through the trees; when it's full, Shasta Lake covers nearly 30,000 acres (about 45 square miles) and there are 370 miles of shoreline; elevation 1100'.

Season, Fees & Phone: $9.00; May to September; 14 day limit; Forest Service Information Center (916) 275-1587.

Camp Notes: Lakeshore-Lakehead is a fairly popular resort area. Business establishments are open year round, but the most popular season is spring and early summer. To accommodate extra campers on holidays, an additional dozen sites may be available at Lakeshore West, across the road from the primary Lakeshore camp.

ANTLERS
Whiskeytown-Shasta-Trinity National Recreation Area

Location: North-central California north of Redding.

Access: From Interstate 5 at milepost 41, at the Lakeshore Drive-Antlers Road Exit, (26 miles north of Redding, 29 miles south of Dunmuir), turn south onto Antlers Road (parallels the Interstate on the east); proceed south, east and north for 0.7 mile; turn east (right) into the campground.

Facilities: 59 campsites, including 18 multiple-occupancy units, in 2 loops, plus overflow sites; sites are medium to large with good to excellent separation; parking pads are level, paved, medium to long straight-ins; some excellent tent spots; fire rings; firewood is usually available for gathering in the surrounding area; water at several faucets; restrooms (H) with auxiliary vaults; gas and groceries at the Lakeshore exit; complete supplies and services are available in Redding.

Activities & Attractions: Boating; boat launch nearby; fishing; amphitheater for scheduled interpretive programs; many remote areas of Shasta Lake are accessible only by boat.

Natural Features: Located between the Coast Range and the Cascade Range near the north end of Shasta Lake, on the Sacramento River Arm; the lake was created in 1948 by the damming of the Sacramento, McCloud, and Pit Rivers; moderately dense forest of tall pines, oak and manzanita; elevation 1100'.

Season, Fees & Phone: Open all year, with limited services in winter; $9.00 for a single site, $12.00 for a multiple site; 14 day limit; Forest Service Information Center (916) 275-1587.

Camp Notes: When all factors are considered, Antlers is perhaps one of the best public campgrounds in this area. Sites here are comfortable and private, a boat ramp is nearby for lake access, commercial outlets for basic supplies are within a few miles, and access from I-5 is quite easy. Because of the possibilities of deep drawdown in order to fulfill Shasta's irrigation and electrical power responsibilities, best times of the year for taking full advantage of its recreational opportunities are spring and early summer. If you're planning on boating, particularly in the upper reaches of the lake, it might be helpful to request a 'tide table' from the information center.

Northern California 88

OAK GROVE
Whiskeytown-Shasta-Trinity National Recreation Area

Location: North-central California north of Redding.

Access: From Interstate 5 near milepost 37 at the Salt Creek Road-Gilman Road Exit (20 miles north of Redding, 40 miles south of the town of Mt. Shasta), go to the west side of the freeway to Salt Creek Road (parallels the highway as a west frontage road); turn west onto Conflict Point Road; proceed 1.15 miles, then turn north (right) into the campground. (Note: northbound traffic must exit toward the east and pass under the Interstate to Salt Creek Road.)

Facilities: 43 campsites; sites are small to a generous medium size, with average to good separation; parking pads are gravel/dirt, short to medium-length straight-ins; many pads may require additional leveling; some excellent tent spots, a few may be a bit sloped; chimneyed fireplaces; some firewood is usually available for gathering in the area; water at several faucets; restrooms; paved driveways; gas and groceries in Salt Creek; complete supplies and services are available in Redding.

Activities & Attractions: Nearby boating and fishing; scenic views.

Natural Features: Located between the Coast Range and the Cascades near the north shore of Salt Creek Inlet toward the north end of Shasta Lake; sites are situated on a slope with spreading oak trees, sparse grass and moderate underbrush as the predominant campground vegetation; the impounding of 3 major Northern California Rivers has created a reservoir with 370 miles of shoreline; elevation 1100'.

Season, Fees & Phone: May to September; $7.00; 14 day limit; Forest Service Information Center (916) 275-1587.

Camp Notes: Near Oak Grove is Nelson Point, a neat little campground 0.7 mile west of I-5 on Conflict Point Road. It has 8 small sites with a great view of the inlet and surrounding green hills. Note that the Shasta Unit (as well as the Trinity Unit) of the merged, tri-unit national recreation area is on national forest lands and managed by the USDA Forest Service. The Whiskeytown Unit is controlled by the National Park Service.

Northern California 89

JONES VALLEY
Whiskeytown-Shasta-Trinity National Recreation Area

Location: North-central California northeast of Redding.

Access: From Interstate 5 (southbound) near milepost 24 (8 miles north of Redding), take the Mountain Gate/Wonderland Boulevard Exit and go to the east side of the freeway; pick up Old Oregon Trail and proceed southeast for 3 miles to a "T"; turn northeast (left) onto Bear Mountain Road and travel 6.7 miles to a fork; take an easy right onto Jones Valley Road and continue easterly for 0.4 mile; turn south (right, just after a sharpish curve) into the *Upper Jones Valley* unit; or continue for another 0.1 mile, then hang a left into the *Lower Jones Valley* unit. **Alternate Access:** From Interstate 5 (northbound), near milepost 19 (3 miles north of Redding), take the Oasis Road Exit; go to the east side of the freeway and travel northeast on Oasis Road, which shortly becomes Old Oregon Trail, for 3.5 miles; then pick up Bear Mountain Road and continue as above. (Note: Old Oregon Trail is a half loop that connects to I-5 at the 2 exits; all roads are paved.)

Facilities: *Upper* unit: 13 campsites; *Lower* unit: 14 campsites; *both units*: sites are very small to small, with fair separation; parking pads are gravel, short to medium-length straight-ins; most pads will require a little additional leveling; small to medium+, somewhat sloped, tent areas; fire rings; b-y-o firewood is suggested; water at several faucets; vault facilities; paved driveways; gas and groceries on Bear Valley Road; complete supplies and services are available in Redding.

Activities & Attractions: Fishing for bass, catfish, panfish, trout and salmon; boating; boat launch nearby; hiking trail along/above the shore; major Forest Service Information Center at the Mountain Gate Exit off I-5.

Natural Features: Located on hillsides above an arm of Shasta Lake, a major irrigation water reservoir on the Sacramento River and its tributaries; sites are lightly shaded by oaks and other hardwoods, plus some tall conifers; elevation 1100'.

Season, Fees & Phone: Open all year, with limited services in winter; $7.00; 14 day limit; Forest Service Information Center (916) 275-1587.

Camp Notes: Many campsites have been cut into the moderately steep slopes here. In addition to the Jones Valley standard campgrounds, primitive camping is also available in the nearby Jones Inlet shoreline area. 'Shoreline' may be a bit of a misnomer. Depending upon the time of year and what kind of year it is, the reservoir may be drawn down hundreds of feet below the "full" mark to irrigate the farmlands of the vast, fertile Great Central Valley. Your 'shoreline' camp could thus be 200 yards or 2000 yards from the water's edge.

WOODSON BRIDGE
Woodson Bridge State Recreation Area

Location: North-central California south of Red Bluff.

Access: From Interstate 5 near milepost 7 +.5 at the South Avenue Exit on the south edge of Corning (17 miles south of Red Bluff), travel east on South Avenue for 4.3 miles, then pick up Tehama County Road A9 and continue easterly for another 1.8 miles; turn north (left) onto the park access road and proceed 0.25 mile, then go east (right) for 0.2 mile to the campground. **Alternate Access:** From California State Highway 99 at milepost 4 +.5 (23 miles southeast of Red Bluff, 18 miles northwest of Chico), turn southwest onto Tehama County Road A9 and proceed 3.2 miles to the park turnoff and continue as above.

Facilities: 46 campsites; sites are small+ to medium-sized, most are level, with fair to very good separation; most parking pads are paved, medium to long straight-ins, plus a few pull-offs; plenty of tent space; fire rings and barbecue grills; b-y-o firewood; water at central faucets; restrooms with showers; holding tank disposal station; paved driveways; adequate supplies and services are available in Corning.

Activities & Attractions: Fishing; limited floating/canoeing; nature trail.

Natural Features: Located on a large flat along the east bank of the Sacramento River; vegetation consists of very tall valley oaks and other hardwoods, sections of dense undergrowth, areas of mown grass and tracts of waist-high grass; surrounded by orchards; the Coast Range can be seen in the west and the foothills of the Sierra can be glimpsed to the east; elevation 200'.

Season, Fees & Phone: Open all year; please see Appendix for reservation information, park entry and campground fees; park office (916) 839-2112.

Camp Notes: In summer, this would be the place for a large, airy tent and a gallon of 'deet'. There is a generous amount of grass and shade here. But possibly only a bull rider, a bungee jumper, or a native of Louisiana would really *want* to spend a midsummer night in this scenic sauna. It can become more than a bit still and steamy along the densely vegetated riverbank after sundown. The locals make good-natured wise cracks about "attack formations" formed by "mosquito squadrons".

BUCKHORN
Black Butte Lake/Corps of Engineers Park

Location: North-central California northwest of Sacramento.

Access: From Interstate 5 at the northernmost of the two Orland exits (signed for Highway 32), turn west onto Newville Road (Road 200); head northwest for 12 miles (past the park HQ and around the north end of the lake) to Buckhorn Road; turn east (left) onto Buckhorn Road for a final mile to the campground.

Facilities: 65 campsites in 4 loops; (a couple dozen primitive sites and a group camp area are also available); sites vary from small+ to large, with nominal separation; parking pads are paved, medium to long straight-ins, plus a few super-long pull-throughs; many pads will require a little additional leveling;

large tent areas, most are fairly level; barbecue grills; b-y-o firewood; water at several faucets; restrooms with showers; holding tank disposal station; paved driveways; gas and groceries on Road 200, near the freeway, and in Orland.

Season, Fees & Phone: Open all year; $12.00 for a standard site, $6.00 for a primitive site; 14 day limit; CoE Project Office (916) 865-4781.

Natural Features: Located on a rolling hill on a point on the northwest shore of Black Butte Lake; campground vegetation consists of short grass and large oaks; majority of the sites have some shade/shelter; many deer often pass through the campground on their way to get a sip at the lake, particularly in summer; surrounded by grassland, hills and buttes; the Coast Range lies several miles to the west; elevation 500'.

Activities & Attractions: Boating; boat launches; fishing for bass, crappie and Florida bluegill; Buckhorn Interpretive Trail (a good guide booklet is available from the park office); playground.

Camp Notes: This campground is a winner! The facilities are excellent and the views are terrific. It's a real deal. The park's other campground, Orland Buttes, has similar facilities, the views are also good, but Buckhorn is still a bit nicer.

ORLAND BUTTE
Black Butte Lake/Corps of Engineers Park

Location: North-central California northwest of Sacramento.

Access: From Interstate 5 at the northernmost of the two Orland exits (signed for Highway 32), turn west onto Newville Road (Road 200); travel northwest for 9 miles; turn south (left) onto County Road 206, proceed 3 miles, then turn westerly (right) onto the campground access road for 0.8 mile to the campground.

Facilities: 30 campsites; (a group camp area is also available); sites are small+ to medium in size, with nominal separation; parking pads are paved, medium to long straight-ins, plus a few long pull-throughs; a little additional leveling may be needed on many pads; large tent areas; barbecue grills; b-y-o firewood; water at several faucets; restrooms with showers; holding tank disposal station; paved driveways; gas and groceries on Road 200, near the freeway, and in Orland.

Activities & Attractions: Boating; boat launch; fishing for bass, crappie and Florida bluegill; Big Oak Nature Trail, at the south tip of the lake (a nice guide booklet is available from the park office); playground; day use area.

Natural Features: Located on a rolling hill above the southeast shore of Black Butte Lake, a flood control impoundment on Stony Creek; large oaks provide some shade for most sites; surrounded by grassland, hills and buttes; the Coast Range lies several miles to the west; elevation 500'

Season, Fees & Phone: May to October; $12.00; 14 day limit; CoE Project Office (916) 865-4781.

Camp Notes: You really couldn't go wrong at either of this lake's two campgrounds. The so-called "Florida bluegill" is a prolific, good-sized, scrappy critter that's one of the most popular fish on the lake. In spring, it is caught in tremedous numbers.

COLUSA-SACRAMENTO RIVER
Colusa-Sacramento River State Recreation Area

Location: North-central California northwest of Sacramento.

Access: From the junction of California State Highways 20 & 45 in midtown Colusa, proceed northeast on Levee Road for 0.2 mile to the park entrance, and the camping area, just beyond. (Note: from Interstate 5, take the Colusa-Clear Lake Exit, then drive east on State Highway 20 for 8.6 miles to Colusa.)

Facilities: 22 campsites; sites are small, level, with minimal separation; parking pads are paved, short to medium-length straight-ins, some are extra wide; large, grassy tent areas; storage cabinets; barbecue grills; firewood is usually for sale, or b-y-o; water at central faucets; restrooms with showers; paved driveways; limited supplies and services are available in Colusa.

Activities & Attractions: Trail to a river beach; fishing for a variety of fish, depending upon the season, including salmon, trout, striped bass, shad; fishing from a boat is recommended; boat launch; state park day use area and Colusa Levee Scenic Park are adjacent.

Natural Features: Located on the west bank of the Sacramento River in the great Sacramento Valley; vegetation consists of several acres of watered and mown lawns, and hardwoods which provide some shade/shelter in most campsites; lots of large trees in the surrounding area; elevation 50'.

Season, Fees & Phone: Open all year; please see Appendix for standard California state park fees and reservation information; park office (916) 458-4927

Camp Notes: This place is a dump! Or, rather, it was when the state acquired the first of several pieces of property on the edge of Colusa and turned it into a park. They've really performed a beautiful job of landscaping this former riverfront junkyard. The campground is located between the entrance station and the day use facility, so thru traffic may be a minor concern. In summer, bring the skeeter stuff, 'cause the wee beasties might bug you at times.

FOWLERS
Shasta-Trinity National Forest

Location: Northeast California southeast of Weed.

Access: From California State Highway 89 at milepost 19 (5 miles east of McCloud, 43 miles northwest of the junction of State Highways 89 & 299 near Burney), turn south onto a paved access road and go 0.65 mile to a fork; take the left fork, continuing on the paved road another 0.25 mile to the campground.

Facilities: 39 campsites in 2 loops; sites are medium to large, with fair to good separation; parking pads are gravel, medium-length straight-ins, and some may need a little additional leveling; large, framed-and-gravelled tent pads; paved path from parking pad to table area in most units; fire rings; some firewood is available for gathering in the area; water at several faucets; vault facilities; paved driveways; limited supplies and services are available in McCloud.

Activities & Attractions: Trail to Lower Falls and Middle Falls; fishing.

Natural Features: Located on a light to moderately forested flat along the north bank of the McCloud River; campground vegetation consists of tall conifers and light underbrush; several sites have river views; fairly low, timbered terrain in the surrounding area; elevation 3600'.

Season, Fees & Phone: May to November; $8.00; 14 day limit; McCloud R.D (916) 964-2184.

Camp Notes: There are some excellent, unobstructed views of Mount Shasta from this general area, though not from the campground proper. Fowlers is one of the better campgrounds in this region. While there aren't any glimpses of magnificent Mount Shasta from the campground proper, spectacular, unrestricted views can be had just a short distance from here.

CATTLE CAMP & ALGOMA
Shasta-Trinity National Forest

Location: Northeast California southeast of Weed.

Access: From California State Highway 89 near milepost 14 (10 miles east of McCloud, 38 miles northwest of the junction of State Highways 89 & 299 near Burney), turn south onto a gravel access road and go 0.4 mile, then turn east (left) into *Cattle Camp*; or near milepost 11 (3 miles east of the turnoff to Cattle Camp), turn south onto Stouts Meadow Road (paved) and proceed 0.8 mile to *Algoma* Campground.

Facilities: *Cattle Camp*: approximately 10 campsites, plus enough room for a half dozen jackcampers; sites are large, level with nominal separation; parking surfaces are dirt/gravel, long straight-ins; plenty of space for tents; *Algoma*: approximaely 8 campsites; sites are medium+, reasonably level, with fair separation; parking pads are gravel, medium-length straight-ins; adequate space for a large tent in most sites; *both camps*: fire rings; some firewood is available for gathering in the area; no drinking water; vault facilities; gravel/dirt driveways; limited supplies and services are available in McCloud.

Activities & Attractions: Fishing.

Natural Features: Located on a large, level flat in a stand of very tall, moderately dense timber a short distance from the north bank of the McCloud River (Cattle Camp); located on a rolling flat in a moderately dense conifer forest along the bank of the McCloud River (Algoma); Cattle Camp elevation 3600', Algoma elevation 3800'.

Season, Fees & Phone: May to November; no fee (subject to change); 14 day limit; McCloud Ranger District (916) 964-2184.

Camp Notes: There's lots of room around here, especially in Cattle Camp, although it tends to be very dusty during dry spells. Official literature tactfully encourages jackcamping ("dispersed camping") in this region if the local established campgrounds are "too crowded and confining". Either method of camping would be pleasurable in this gentle locale.

McArthur-Burney Falls
McArthur-Burney Falls Memorial State Park

Location: Northeast California northeast of Redding.

Access: From California State Highway 89 at milepost 27 +.55 (5.8 miles north of the junction of State Highways 89 & 299 near Burney, 52 miles southeast of the junction of Highway 89 & Interstate 5 near Dunsmuir), turn north-west onto a paved park access road and proceed 0.1 mile to the park entrance station; continue ahead for 0.1 mile past the entrance to the camping areas.

Facilities: 118 campsites in 2 sections; (a small environmental-walk-in camp is also available); overall, sites are medium to large, essentially level, with fair to good separation; parking pads are paved or earth/gravel, short to medium-length straight-ins, many pads are extra wide; large tent areas; storage lockers; fireplaces or fire rings; b-y-o firewood; water at several faucets; restrooms with showers; holding tank disposal station; paved driveways; gas and groceries 1 mile south.

Activities & Attractions: Hiking trails, including a 1-mile Falls Trail and a 1.5-mile Rim Trail from the falls/camping area to Lake Britton; amphitheater for evening campfire programs; museum; fishing for warm water species, boating, boat launch and sandy beach at Lake Britton; good to excellent trout fishing on local streams, especially wide, deep, fast, beautiful (and world-famous) Hat Creek.

Natural Features: Located on a large, forested flat along the rim of Burney Creek Gorge, at the southern end of the Cascade Range; Burney Falls is within the gorge; campsites are sheltered/shaded by moderately dense, tall conifers and some smaller hardwoods; elevation 3000'.

Season, Fees & Phone: Open all year; please see Appendix for standard California state park fees and reservation information; park office (916) 335-2777.

Camp Notes: A fascinating feature of the falls, which is the focal point of the park, is that its water supply originates in an aquifer (underground lake), and the falls flows all year, even when the creek is bone dry a half-mile upstream. Lake Britton shouldn't be overlooked. It's a fairly nice-looking, 4000-acre reservoir on the Pit River. No wonder this is a popular park--there's elbow room here. Because it is some distance from Northern California's major metro areas, and because of its cool (but relatively dry) weather during much of the year, the park doesn't see a lot of use except in summer. Both spring and fall are superb times to visit here.

Indian Well
Lava Beds National Monument

Location: Northeast California northwest of Alturas.

Access: From California State Highway 139 at milepost 27 +.9 (28 miles northwest of the intersection of Highways 139 and 299 near Canby, 28 miles southeast of the California-Oregon border), turn westerly onto County Road 97/Forest Road 97 (paved) and proceed 2.5 miles; turn north onto Lava Beds National Monument Road/Forest Road 10 (paved), and travel 14 miles to the campground turnoff (opposite the visitor center); turn north (right) onto a paved access road and continue for 0.4 mile to the campground. **Alternate Access:** From California State Highway 139 at a point 2 miles northwest of Newell, 7 miles southeast of the California-Oregon border, head south, west, then south again on Forest Road 10 (paved) for 21 miles to the campground turnoff and continue as above. (Note: the *Access* is best if you're northbound on '139 from Alturus and other points south; the *Alternate Access* works well if you're inbound from Oregon and also like roundabout, but scenic, drives.)

Facilities: 42 campsites; sites are about average in size, with little to some separation; parking pads are paved, mostly level, short to medium-length straight-ins or pull-offs; tent areas are small to medium sized, and somewhat level; fireplaces, plus many barbecue grills; b-y-o firewood; water at several faucets; restrooms; paved driveways; gas and groceries are available on County Road 97.

Activities & Attractions: Lava cave exploration, either self-guided or ranger-guided; outdoor nature walks; amphitheater for evening programs.

Natural Features: Located on a slightly sloping, rocky sage flat (or is it a mostly flat, rocky, sage slope?); a sparse population of junipers provides some shade/shelter in many sites; lava flow areas lies to the north and west; the campground overlooks a vast valley/basin to the northeast; the region is dotted with cinder cones; elevation 4500'.

Season, Fees & Phone: Open all year, with limited services mid-September to May; $7.00; 14 day limit; park headquarters (916) 667-2282.

Camp Notes: This is an intriguing, off-the-beaten-path park. The regional landscape isn't quite as starkly forbidding as the name suggests, (but close). The campground rarely fills. Bring warm clothing, even in midsummer.

HOWARDS GULCH
Modoc National Forest

Location: Northeast California west of Alturas.

Access: From California State Highway 139 at milepost 6+.3 (6 miles northwest of the junction of State Highways 139 & 299 southwest of Canby, 50 miles southeast of the California-Oregon border), turn west onto a paved access road and proceed 0.3 mile to the campground.

Facilities: 11 campsites; sites are small to medium-sized, mostly level, with nominal to good separation; parking pads are gravel, short to medium-length straight-ins; good tent-pitching areas; fireplaces; some firewood is available for gathering in the surrounding area; water at central faucets; (note: the water supply is unpredictable, so b-y-o water is recommended); vault facilities; paved driveway; gas and groceries in Canby, 7 miles; adequate+ supplies and services are available in Alturas.

Activities & Attractions: Convenient access.

Natural Features: Located on a flat around the base of a small hill, adjacent to a meadow; campground vegetation consists of a mixture of light to medium-dense, tall conifers and small hardwoods; partially forested hills and low ridges lie in the surrounding area; elevation 4700'.

Season, Fees & Phone: May to October; no fee (subject to change); 14 day limit; Devil's Garden Ranger District, Canby, (916) 233-4611.

Camp Notes: Campgrounds are few and far between in the northeast region. And this spot, although it's not a fantastic campground with lots of activities in a spectacular setting, certainly merits consideration if you're in the neighborhood and want a very pleasant, economical campsite. Lava Beds National Monument is about a 45-minute drive northwest of here, and Howards Gulch could serve as a simple, green alternative to the somewhat open, dry surroundings there.

CEDAR PASS & STOUGH
Modoc National Forest

Location: Northeast corner of California northeast of Alturas.

Access: From California State Highway 299 at milepost 49 +.5, turn south onto a gravel access road into *Cedar Pass* Campground; or at milepost 52 +.25, turn north onto a gravel access road and proceed 0.75 mile to *Stough*. (Note: the campground turnoffs are approximately 1.5 miles west and east, respectively, of the summit of Cedar Pass; the pass is 11 miles east of the junction of Highway 299 and U.S. Highway 395 north of Alturas).

Facilities: *Cedar Pass*: aproximately 12 campsites; *Stough*: 9 campsites; *both camps*: sites are small to medium-sized, with fair to good separation; parking areas are small, dirt straight-ins or pull-offs; tent space varies from small to large; sites are somewhat less than level at Cedar Pass, and passable at Stough; maneuvering larger vehicles and trailers may be difficult in both campgrounds, particularly in Stough; fireplaces; firewood is available for gathering in the area; water at central faucets; (note: the water supplies may be unreliable, b-y-o is recommended); vault facilities; pack-it-in/pack-it-out trash removal system; gravel/dirt driveways; adequate+ supplies and services are available in Alturas.

Activities & Attractions: Fishing (reportedly good) for small trout on local streams.

Natural Features: Located in moderately dense, tall timber in the Warner Mountains; a small stream, Thomas Creek, flows westward through Cedar Pass past Cedar Pass Campground; Stough is adjacent to a tiny reservoir and meadow; the summit of the pass itself is at 6305'; elevation 5900' at Cedar Pass, 6200' at Stough.

Season, Fees & Phone: May to October; no fee (subject to change); 14 day limit; Warner Mountain Ranger District, Cedarville, (916) 279-6116.

Camp Notes: Although these camps have minimal facilities, their surroundings are pleasant enough, and they possess an atmosphere of accessible remoteness. They provide easy, highwayside stops. The national forest is named for the Modoc Indians, who were early residents of northeast California and south-central Oregon.

RUSH CREEK
Modoc National Forest

Location: Northeast California southwest of Alturas.

Access: From California State Highway 299 at milepost 8 +.35 (8 miles north of the Modoc-Lassen county line, 7 miles north of Adin, 15 miles south of Canby), turn southwest onto County Road 198 (paved) for 0.15 mile; then turn northeast (left) onto a reddish gravel road (Rush Creek Drive) and proceed 0.55 mile to the Lower unit, or an additional 1.6 miles to the Upper unit.

Facilities: 13 campsites in the Upper unit, 10 sites, including 5 walk-ins, in the Lower unit; sites are small to medium-sized, with fair to good separation; parking pads are gravel, short to medium-length straight-ins; some pads may require a little additional leveling; good tent spots, but some in the Upper section may be a little sloped; fire rings and barbecue grills; firewood is available for gathering; water at several faucets; vault facilities; gravel driveways; gas and groceries in Canby; gas, and grocerie+ in Adin.

Activities & Attractions: Fishing in the lower creek area.

Natural Features: Located along the north bank of Rush Creek at the northern end of Big Valley; the Upper unit is on a hillside; the Lower unit is on a flat, and the walk-ins are scattered along the south bank, across a foot bridge; campground vegetation consists of light to moderately dense, tall pines mixed with small hardwoods, particularly in the Lower unit; low, partially timbered ridges rise in the surrounding area; elevation 4400' and 5200'.

Season, Fees & Phone: May to October; no fee (subject to change); 14 day limit; Big Valley Ranger District, Adin, (916) 233-4611.

Camp Notes: This is a classic little forest camp--tall timber, a small creek that tumbles down over the rocks, and just far enough off the highway to offer both tranquility and convenience. Subjectively speaking, the Upper section is nicer, but either area is worth considering for a stop. Hopefully, this will continue to be one of the best buys in California camping.

WILLOW CREEK
Modoc National Forest

Location: Northeast California between Susanville and Alturas.

Access: From California State Highway 139 at milepost 52 +.5 (14 miles south of Adin, 54 miles southwest of Alturas, 53 miles north of Susanville), turn east into the campground.

Facilities: 8 campsites; sites are medium to large, level, with adequate separation; parking pads are medium to long straight-ins; large, grassy tent areas; fire rings and barbecue grills; some firewood is available for gathering in the vicinity; water at several faucets; vault facilities; paved driveway, with a turnaround at the south end; gas and groceries+ are available in Adin.

Activities & Attractions: Possible fishing for small trout; a footbridge crosses the creek to an adjacent day use area; a rail fence adds a finishing touch to the recreation area.

Natural Features: Located on a roadside flat bordered by lightly forested, low hills and ridges; vegetation consists of short, bushy pines, a few tall conifers, willows, and scrub oak; Willow Creek flows along the north edge of the campground; elevation 5200'.

Season, Fees & Phone: May to October; no fee (subject to change); 14 day limit; Big Valley Ranger District, Adin, (916) 233-4611.

Camp Notes: Since the highway passes through comparatively gentle, easy-peddling terrain, the campground often provides a rewarding stop for bicycle campers. Even though the campsites are only a few yards off the road, nighttime traffic isn't objectionable because there isn't much of it. The stream may hold some promise for fishing, since it typically flows quite freely and deeply, even toward summer's end. Even if you're not planning to camp, the day use area would provide an exceptionally pleasant place for a roadside stop.

NORTH EAGLE LAKE
Public Lands/BLM Recreation Site

Location: Northeast California north of Susanville.

Access: From California State Highway 139 at milepost 30 +.85 (31 miles north of Susanville, 36 miles south of Adin), turn west onto Eagle Lake Road/Lassen County Road A1 (paved); proceed west for 0.5 mile, then turn north onto the campground access road for 0.15 mile to the campground. (Alternate access is available from the national forest recreation areas at the south end of the lake by traveling north on Eagle Lake Road along the west shore to the campground turnoff.)

Facilities: 20 campsites; sites are medium to large, with minimal to nominal separation; parking pads are gravel, mostly long, pull-throughs; a little additional leveling will be required on most pads; tent areas are large, some are level; fireplaces and barbecue grills; b-y-o firewood; water at faucets throughout; vault facilities; holding tank disposal station; gravel driveways; nearest reliable sources of supplies and services (adequate+) are in Susanville.

Activities & Attractions: Fishing for Eagle Lake trout, a subspecies of rainbow trout adapted to the alkaline water of the lake; boating.

Natural Features: Located on a grass/sage slope at the north end of Eagle Lake, second-largest natural lake lying entirely within the state; a number of medium-height pines dot the slope and provide some shade/shelter in most sites; timbered hills and mountains surround the lake; elevation 5200'.

Season, Fees & Phone: May to October; $6.00; 14 day limit; BLM Susanville Office (916) 257-0456.

Camp Notes: This campground is quite a surprise. Although it is about a third of a mile from the lake shore, the slightly elevated location provides some excellent lake/mountain views from a number of sites, and from the general campground area. (The price is reasonable compared to the assessment at the national forest camps at the other end of the lake. Ed.)

EAGLE
Lassen National Forest

Location: Northeast California northwest of Susanville.

Access: From California State Highway 36 at milepost 21 (3 miles west of Susanville, 2.8 miles east of the junction of State Highways 36 & 44), turn north onto Eagle Lake Road/Lassen County Road A1 (paved) and proceed 13.4 miles to an intersection right by the California Department of Forestry fire station; turn east (right) onto a paved road (Road 231) and continue for 0.75 mile to the campground entrance. (Access is also possible from the north, around the west side of Eagle Lake, from California State Highway 139.)

Facilities: 50 campsites; sites are small to medium+ in size, level, with minimal separation; parking pads are paved, medium to long straight-ins; excellent tent spots; gathering of firewood prior to arrival from local forest lands, or b-y-o is recommended; water at several faucets; restrooms; holding tank disposal station 1 mile west at Merrill Campground; paved driveways; security patrols; camper supplies at the marina, 0.5 mile east; adequate+ supplies and services are available in Susanville.

Activities & Attractions: Boating; boat launch; marina nearby; fishing for the elusive Eagle Lake trout.

Natural Features: Located on a flat near the south shore of Eagle Lake; campground vegetation consists primarily of medium-dense, very tall conifers on a surface of grass and evergreen needles; forested hills and low mountains surround the lake; elevation 5100'.

Season, Fees & Phone: May to October; $12.00-$16.00; 14 day limit; Eagle Lake Ranger District, Susanville, (916) 257-2151.

Camp Notes: If this campground is full (likely), camping may be available at Christie Campground, 4 miles northwest, or at 20-site Aspen Grove Campground, 0.3 mile east.

MERRILL
Lassen National Forest

Location: Northeast California northwest of Susanville.

Access: From California State Highway 36 at milepost 21 (3 miles west of Susanville, 2.8 miles east of the intersection of State Highways 36 and 44), turn north onto Eagle Lake Road/Lassen County Road A1 (paved) and travel 14.3 miles to milepost 14 +.3; turn northeast (right) into the campground.

Facilities: 182 campsites in 5 loops; sites are small to average in size, essentially level, with minimal separation; parking pads are earth/gravel, medium-length straight-ins; some pads may require additional leveling; medium to large tent areas; fire rings; some firewood may be available for gathering in the surrounding area; gathering firewood prior to arrrival, or b-y-o, is suggested; water at several faucets; restrooms; holding tank disposal station; paved driveways; security patrols; camper supplies at the marina, 2 miles east; adequate+ supplies and services are available in Susanville.

Activities & Attractions: Boating; fishing for Eagle Lake trout; amphitheater.

Natural Features: Located on the south shore of Eagle Lake; campground vegetation primarily consists of grass, and medium-dense, very tall conifers; the lake is surrounded by forested hills and low mountains; elevation 5100'.

Season, Fees & Phone: May to October; $12.00-$16.00; 14 day limit; Eagle Lake Ranger District, Susanville, (916) 257-2151.

Camp Notes: This campground might almost remind you of many oceanside campgrounds. Most of the sites are tucked in among the trees, but there is a line of sites situated along an open, grass and gravel beach. (They really pack 'em in at this one, folks. For the price of admission, maybe they also host an afternoon hospitality hour. Ed.)

CHRISTIE
Lassen National Forest

Location: Northeast California northwest of Susanville.

Access: From California State Highway 36 at milepost 21 (3 miles west of Susanville, 2.8 miles east of the junction of State Highways 36 and 44), turn north onto Eagle Lake Road/Lassen County Road A1 (paved) and proceed 16.5 miles to the campground (at milepost 16 +.5). (Access is also possible from the north, from California State Highway 139, via Eagle Lake Road.)

Facilities: 69 campsites in 3 loops; sites are medium-sized, level, with some separation; parking pads are paved, medium to long straight-ins or pull-throughs; large tent areas; fire rings; some firewood may be available for gathering in the surrounding area; gathering firewood prior to arrival, or b-y-o, is suggested; water at several faucets; restrooms; holding tank disposal station at Merrill Campground, 2 miles southeast; paved driveways; camper supplies at the marina, 3 miles east; adequate+ supplies and services are available in Susanville.

Activities & Attractions: Boating; fishing; activities such as junior ranger programs may be scheduled.

Natural Features: Located on the southwest shore of Eagle Lake; campground vegetation consists of medium-dense, medium to tall conifers on a needle-covered, reddish earth, forest floor; forested hills and low mountains surround the lake; elevation 5100'.

Season, Fees & Phone: May to October; $11.00-$15.00; 14 day limit; Eagle Lake Ranger District, Susanville, (916) 257-2151.

Camp Notes: A few campsites have views of the lake through the forest, but it's only a short walk from any of the sites to the shoreline. It costs a bit less to camp at Christie than at the other forest camps near here. According to the campground host at another campground, the differential is because Christie is "hotter".

BRIDGE
Lassen National Forest

Location: Northeast California north of Lassen Volcanic National Park.

Access: From California State Highway 89 at milepost 4 (4 miles north of the junction of State Highways 89 & 44 near Old Station, 19 miles north of Lassen Park, 18 miles south of the junction of State Highways 89 & 299 near Burney), turn west into the campground.

Facilities: 25 campsites; sites are medium to large, essentially level, with fair to very good separation; parking pads are paved, medium to long straight-ins, plus a couple of pull-throughs; large tent areas; fire rings and barbecue grills; some firewood is available for gathering in the area; gathering firewood on nearby forest lands prior to arrival, or b-y-o, is suggested; water at several faucets; vault facilities; paved driveways; gas and groceries are available 5 miles south.

Activities & Attractions: Hat Creek Trail; trout fishing; self-guided exploration of Subway Cave, 4 miles south (free).

Natural Features: Located on a slightly rolling flat along Hat Creek; campground vegetation consists primarily of medium-dense, tall conifers, plus small timber and small hardwoods; surrounding terrain is comprised of partially timbered hills and low mountains; excellent views of distant Mount Shasta from near the campground; situated on a major lava bed; elevation 4000'.

Season, Fees & Phone: May to October; $9.00; 14 day limit; Hat Creek Ranger District, Fall River Mills, (916) 336-5521.

Camp Notes: As it flows past this campground, Hat Creek is a beautiful, deep, clear, swiftly moving stream in summer. In terms of environment, Bridge is probably near the top of the list of campgrounds along this highway. Two very small campgrounds either side of Bridge--Rocky, 0.75 mile south, and Honn, 5 miles north--serve primarily as simple fishing camps with no water, tight quarters, and a 'fiver' for a fee.

CAVE
Lassen National Forest

Location: Northeast California north of Lassen Volcanic National Park.

Access: From California State Highway 89 at a point 0.3 mile north of the junction of State Highways 89 & 44 near Old Station (15 miles north of Lassen Park, 22 miles south of the junction of State Highways 89 & 299 near Burney), turn west into the campground.

Facilities: 46 campsites in 2 areas; sites are small to medium-sized, basically level, with fair to good separation; parking pads are paved, medium to long, straight-ins; excellent tent-pitching opportunities; fire rings and barbecue grills; gathering firewood on nearby forest lands prior to arrival, or b-y-o, is recommended; water at several faucets; restrooms; paved driveways; gas and groceries are available less than a mile south.

Activities & Attractions: Self-guided venturing into Subway Cave, located across the highway from the campground (free); trout fishing on Hat Creek; handicapped-access fishing platform; foot bridge across the creek.

Natural Features: Located in a valley on a flat between the highway and Hat Creek; light to medium-dense, tall conifers provide adequate shelter/shade for most campsites; surrounding terrain is comprised of partially timbered hills and low mountains; situated on a major lava bed; elevation 4200'.

Season, Fees & Phone: May to October; $9.00; 14 day limit; Hat Creek Ranger District, Fall River Mills, (916) 336-5521.

Camp Notes: The campground is larger than it looks from the entrance. It might pay to thoroughly check it out before checking-in, since the limits extend to nearly 0.4 mile south of the gate. Also worth checking-out is Subway Cave, a lava tube with a trail about a third of a mile long. (Parents and kids have a particularly good time exploring the tunnel--especially when the leader douses the flashlight!)

HAT CREEK
Lassen National Forest

Location: Northeast California north of Lassen Volcanic National Park.

Access: From California State Highway 89 at milepost 61 +.1 (1.4 miles south of the junction of State Highways 89 & 44 near Old Station, 14 miles north of Lassen National Park), turn west into the campground.

Facilities: 55 campsites; sites are medium-sized, with minimal to fair separation; parking pads are paved, medium-length, reasonably level, straight-ins; good tent areas; fire rings, plus some barbecue grills; limited firewood is available for gathering in the general vicinity; firewood-gathering prior to arrival, or b-y-o, is suggested; water at several faucets; restrooms, plus auxiliary vaults; holding tank disposal station at a day use facility across the highway; paved driveways; gas and groceries within 1.5 miles, north and south.

Activities & Attractions: Trout fishing; handicapped access fishing platform; foot bridge across the creek; Spatter Cone Nature Trail (1.5 miles) passes volcanic features; Subway Cave, (national forest site, no charge) 2 miles north.

Natural Features: Located on a sloping, rolling flat in light forest of short to medium-tall pines; the campground area is dotted with lava rock; Hat Creek flows along the western perimeter of the campground; low, partially timbered hills lie in the surrounding area; elevation 4400'.

Season, Fees & Phone: May to October; $9.00; 14 day limit; Hat Creek Ranger District, Fall River Mills, (916) 336-5521.

Camp Notes: Excellent access to campground's namesake, a world famous trout stream. This area is believed to be the origin of a massive lava flow that spread northward through Hat Creek Valley for more than 20 miles. The fiery event took place in geologically modern times, less than two millenia ago.

BIG PINE
Lassen National Forest

Location: Northeast California north of Lassen Volcanic National Park.

Access: From California State Highway 89 at milepost 58 +.1 (4 miles south of the junction of State Highways 89 & 44 near Old Station, 12 miles north of Lassen Park), turn east onto a gravel access road and proceed 0.5 mile, then turn onto a paved driveway into the campground.

Facilities: 19 campsites; sites are medium-sized, with minimal to fair separation; parking pads are paved, short to medium-length straight-ins; most pads will probably require some additional leveling; ample space for large tents in most sites; fire rings and barbecue grills; some firewood is available for gathering in the area; water at hand pumps; vault facilities; paved driveway; gas and groceries 2 miles north.

Activities & Attractions: Forest atmosphere; good fishing on the lower, full-flowing section of Hat Creek, north of here.

Natural Features: Located on a forested, gently sloping flat; sites receive light to light-medium shade/shelter from tall pines on a thick carpet of pine needles and some tall grass; the upper, considerably shallower section of Hat Creek flows past the campground; bordered by timbered hills; elevation 4600'.

Season, Fees & Phone: May to October; $7.00; 14 day limit; Hat Creek Ranger District, Fall River Mills, (916) 336-5521.

Camp Notes: If all of the big highwayside camps along the fishable segments of Hat Creek are busy, check out Big Pine. Good camping here.

MANZANITA LAKE
Lassen Volcanic National Park

Location: Northeast California at the northwest corner of Lassen Volcanic National Park.

Access: From California State Highway 89 (the main park road) at a point 0.55 mile from the northwest entrance station and 29 miles from the southwest entrance station, turn south onto a paved access road and proceed 0.45 mile to the campground.

Facilities: 181 campsites in 4 loops; sites are small to medium in size, with fair to good separation; parking pads are gravel/sand, mostly short to medium-length straight-ins or pull-throughs; many pads may require some additional leveling; tent areas are generally medium-sized, but many are large, and most are tolerably level; fire rings; firewood is usually for sale, or b-y-o; water at several faucets; restrooms; holding tank disposal station; paved driveways; ranger station; gas, groceries, ice and showers are available at nearby stores.

Activities & Attractions: Several trails; amphitheater for evening campfire programs; limited boating.

Natural Features: Located on the slightly sloping shore of Manzanita Lake, (but no lake views from campsites); campground vegetation consists primarily of light to medium-dense, tall conifers and manzanitas; a good-sized stream flows near the campground area; bordered by high mountains; elevation 5900'.

Season, Fees & Phone: Late-May to mid-September; $10.00; 14 day limit; park headquarters (916) 595-4444.

Camp Notes: You'll find some good shots of Lassen Peak from the campground area. Many campsites are actually quite spacious (by national park standards). The other camp in the park's northwest corner, Crags Campground, five miles northeast and just off the main park road, is open during peak periods.

SUMMIT LAKE
Lassen Volcanic National Park

Location: Northeast California near the center of Lassen Volcanic National Park.

Access: From California State Highway 89 (the main park road) at a point 12.5 miles southeast of the northwest entrance station and 16 miles northeast of the southwest entrance station, turn east into the North or South units, 0.15 mile apart.

Facilities: 49 campsites in the North unit and 52 campsites in the South unit; sites are rather small, with minimal to fair separation; parking pads are paved, short to medium-length straight-ins or pull-throughs; adequate space for a medium-sized tent in most sites; fire rings; b-y-o firewood; water at several faucets; restrooms in the North unit, vault facilities in the South unit; gas and groceries are available at Manzanita Lake, 12 miles northwest.

Activities & Attractions: Trails; motorless boating; amphitheater; picnicking area on the lakeshore.

Natural Features: Located on slightly hilly terrain near the north and south shores of small Summit Lake in the Cascade Range; campground vegetation consists of light to medium-dense conifers, and very little grass or underbrush; timbered hills and mountains in the surrounding area; elevation 6800'.

Season, Fees & Phone: Late-May to mid-September; $10.00 in the North unit, $8.00 in the South unit; 14 day limit; park headquarters (916) 595-4444.

Camp Notes: Some campsites have lake views, a few more in the North unit than in the South unit. But the view from the south end may be a little more interesting. It probably would be a good idea to check both sides before settling in. Because of its popularity (it's a nice lake), the campground is a bit frayed around the edges.

SOUTHWEST
Lassen Volcanic National Park

Location: Northeast California at the southwest corner of Lassen Volcanic National Park.

Access: From California State Highway 89 (the main park road) at a point 0.1 mile north of the park's southwest entrance station and 30 miles south of the northwest entrance station, turn east into the campground.

Facilities: 21 park 'n walk campsites; sites are small, with nominal to fair separation; enough space for a small tent on a sloped surface; paved parking is available nearby; paved walkways to the sites from the parking area; water at central faucets; restrooms; gas and groceries in Mineral, 10 miles south.

Activities & Attractions: Good views of Lassen Peak and its surroundings.

Natural Features: Located on a boulder-strewn hillside above a ravine near the southern tip of the Cascade Range; sites are lightly sheltered/shaded by tall conifers; elevation 6000'.

Season, Fees & Phone: Late-May to mid-September; $8.00; 14 day limit; park headquarters (916) 595-4444.

Camp Notes: For a campsite with fewer neighbors than you'll have in the other campgrounds along the park's main road, check out this one if you're a tent camper. Southwest has also been known as Sulphur Works, after a local geological feature. Good mountain views here. In addition to the campgrounds along the main park road two other park camps are available in the boonies. Juniper Lake ($6.00) in the southeast corner of the park, and Warner Valley ($8.00) in the south-central area, are small tent camps accessed from State Highway 89 in Chester. From Chester head north for 13 miles on Juniper Lake Road, or 17 miles via Chester-Warner Valley Road, respectively, to the small, primitive campgrounds.

BATTLE CREEK
Lassen National Forest

Location: Northeast California southwest of Lassen Volcanic National Park.

Access: From California State Highway 36 at milepost 81 +.4 (at the west end of the Battle Creek bridge, 2 miles west of Mineral, 41 miles east of Red Bluff), turn south onto a paved access road and continue for 0.2 mile to the campground.

Facilities: 50 campsites; sites are small to medium in size, essentially level, with nominal to fair separation; parking pads are paved, medium-length straight-ins; good to excellent tent spaces; fire rings; some firewood is available for gathering in the area; water at several faucets; restrooms, plus auxiliary vault facilities; paved driveways; gas, groceries and laundromat are available in Mineral.

Activities & Attractions: Possible fishing for small trout on the creek.

Natural Features: Located on slightly rolling terrain on the edge of a large park (meadow); campground vegetation consists of light to moderately dense, very tall conifers, a few patches of grass, and very little underbrush; Battle Creek flows nearby; small, forested hills are in the area close to the campground; elevation 4800'.

Season, Fees & Phone: May to October; $7.00; 14 day limit; Almanor Ranger District, Chester, (916) 258-2141.

Camp Notes: Scenario: You're headed for Lassen National Park on a summer weekend and are running a little late. A campsite is available here. Grab it, and start out fresh in the a.m. Seriously, park officials indicate that Lassen's major, full service campgrounds (Manzanita and Summit Lake) fill up on Thursday, Friday, and Saturday nights--and typically are at 80 percent of capacity on other nights. The main campgrounds in Lassen are quite good (both have lake shore property). Battle Creek's surroundings are less grand and a little more subdued, though it's still a very good second choice.

GURNSEY CREEK
Lassen National Forest

Location: Northeast California south of Lassen Volcanic National Park.

Access: From California State Highways 36/89 at milepost 97 +.5 for Highway 36 (10 miles east of the junction of Highways 36 & 89 near Mineral, 14 miles west of the junction of Highways 36 & 89 near Chester, or 2.5 miles west of the junction of Highways 36/89 & State Highway 32), turn north into the campground.

Facilities: 30 campsites; (a large, group area is also available); sites are medium to large, with fair to very good separation; parking pads are gravel, medium-length straight-ins, some of which may need a bit of additional leveling; excellent, mostly level, tent spaces; fireplaces or fire rings; firewood is available for gathering in the surrounding area; water at several faucets; vault facilities; paved driveways; not much in the way of supplies in these parts: gas, groceries and laundromat are available in Mineral.

Activities & Attractions: Pleasant, forest setting; located just a few miles from Lassen Volcanic National Park.

Natural Features: Located on a slightly rolling flat along Gurnsey Creek; campground vegetation consists of moderately dense to quite dense, tall conifers on a thick carpet of fallen needles; mountainous, heavily timbered terrain in the surrounding area; elevation 5000'.

Season, Fees & Phone: May to October; $7.00; 14 day limit; Almanor Ranger District, Chester, (916) 258-2141.

Camp Notes: This is a highwayside campground, but only a comparatively few sites would really be bothered by traffic noise. The rest of the campsites should enjoy the tranquility of the very pleasant, deep forest setting. Subjectively, it's one of the nicest campgrounds in this area. It would serve as an excellent alternative to the campgrounds in Lassen Park. (In several respects, it is preferable to the park's campgrounds.)

ELAM CREEK
Lassen National Forest

Location: Northeast California south of Lassen Volcanic National Park.

Access: From California State Highway 32 at milepost 21 +.5 (3 miles south of the junction of Highway 32 with State Highways 36/89, 36 miles north of Forest Ranch, 49 miles north of Chico), turn west (just south of the national forest information station) into the campground.

Facilities: 15 campsites; sites are small, tolerably level, and closely spaced; parking pads are gravel, mostly short to medium-length straight-ins; small to medium-sized tent areas; fireplaces or fire rings;

firewood is available for gathering in the area; water at a hand pump; vault facilities; paved driveway; camper supplies just west of the junction of Highway 32 & Highways 36/89.

Activities & Attractions: Fishing for small trout.

Natural Features: Located on a gently sloping flat at the confluence of Elam Creek and Deer Creek; sites receive light shade from tall conifers and hardwoods; Deer Creek, the principal stream, continues southwest through a canyon; closely bordered by forested hills; elevation 4600'.

Season, Fees & Phone: May to October; $7.00; 14 day limit; Almanor Ranger District, Chester, (916) 258-2141.

Camp Notes: Because of its streamside setting, Elam Creek is a favorite spot even though it offers no frills camping. Most sites are creekside or in view of the stream.

Northern California 116

POTATO PATCH
Lassen National Forest

Location: Northeast California south of Lassen Volcanic National Park.

Access: From California State Highway 32 at milepost 14 +.8 (10 miles south of the junction of Highway 32 with State Highways 36/89, 29 miles north of Forest Ranch, 42 miles north of Chico), turn east into the campground.

Facilities: 32 campsites; sites are small to medium-sized, with fair to very good visual separation; parking pads are hard-surfaced, medium-length, basically level, straight-ins; adequate space for at least a medium-sized tent in most sites; fireplaces or fire rings; firewood is available for gathering in the area; water at several faucets; vault facilities; paved driveways; camper supplies just west of the junction of Highway 32 & Highways 36/89.

Activities & Attractions: Fishing; small, national forest visitor information station, 7 miles north.

Natural Features: Located in a narrow canyon on a slightly sloping flat above Deer Creek; campground vegetation consists of moderately dense, tall conifers, oaks, and other smaller hardwoods and bushes; most sites are quite well sheltered/shaded; timbered ridges border the canyon; elevation 3400'.

Season, Fees & Phone: May to October; $7.00; 14 day limit; Almanor Ranger District, Chester, (916) 258-2141.

Camp Notes: If you stay at Potato Patch, or are just passing by, take a look at the campground map. Perhaps the name was suggested by the layout of the place--the shape might remind you of a huge, sprouting, California spud. Or maybe.....

Northern California 117

ALMANOR
Lassen National Forest

Location: Northeast California southeast of Lassen Volcanic National Park.

Access: From California State Highway 89 at milepost 36 +.7 (10 miles southeast of Chester, 17 miles northwest of Greenville, directly opposite the Almanor Rest Area), turn north onto a paved access road and proceed 0.75 mile to the South unit, or 0.1 mile farther to the North unit.

Facilities: 52 campsites in the South unit, 49 campsites in the North unit; sites are medium to large, with fair to good separation; parking pads are paved or gravel, short to long straight-ins; most pads are level or nearly so; good to excellent tent-pitching possibilities; fire rings; some firewood is available for gathering in the vicinity; water at several faucets; vault facilities; paved driveways; gas and groceries in Almanor, 0.5 mile, or Canyon Dam, 7 miles southeast; limited to adequate supplies and services are available in Chester or Greenville.

Activities & Attractions: Fishing; boating; boat launch; amphitheater.

Natural Features: Located on level to slightly rolling terrain within walking distance of the southwest shore of Lake Almanor; campground vegetation consists of tall grass, tall pines and light underbrush; some sites are in the open, others are sheltered; the lake area is surrounded by forested hills and mountains; elevation 4500'.

Season, Fees & Phone: May to October; $8.00; 14 day limit; Almanor Ranger District, Chester, (916) 258-2141.

Camp Notes: Ahhh, this is a nice place to camp. A little busy, perhaps, but still nice. The campground covers a huge area. Although there are beaten paths throughout the camp, it's satisfying to just wander through the tall grass. Incidentally, the softly aristocratic name for the lake was derived from the names of <u>Ali</u>ce <u>Martha</u> and <u>Elea</u>nor <u>Earl</u>, the daughters of Guy Earl, an early pioneer.

BIDWELL CANYON
Lake Oroville State Recreation Area

Location: Northeast California east of Oroville.

Access: From California State Highway 162 at milepost 22 +.85 (8 miles east of the junction of State Highways 162 & 70 in Oroville), turn north onto Kelly Ridge Road (paved); proceed north for 1.6 miles; at a fork in the road, take the right fork and continue east and north for 0.5 mile to the entrance station; camp loops are within a mile of the entrance; (Highway 162 is an extension of Olive Highway in Oroville.)

Facilities: 75 campsites with full-hookups in 2 loops; (primitive and boat-in camps are also available, at scattered spots around the lake shore); sites are small to small+, with nominal separation; parking pads are paved, medium to long straight-ins; many pads will require additional leveling; tent spots are mostly small and many are sloped; fire rings; firewood is usually for sale, or b-y-o; water at sites; restrooms with showers; paved driveways; gas and groceries at the marina; complete supplies and services are available in Oroville.

Activities & Attractions: Boating; boat launch; fishing; nearby visitor center has interpretive displays and presentations, and a 47' observation tower for views of the lake; community center (available to groups by reservation).

Natural Features: Located in the western foothills of the Sierra Nevada on a hill above the south shore of Lake Oroville; the campground's lightly wooded slopes are dotted with manzanitas, oaks, pines and planted hardwoods; wooded/grassy hills surround the lake; elevation 1100'.

Season, Fees & Phone: Open all year; please see Appendix for standard California state park fees and reservation information; park office (916) 538-2200 or (916) 538-2218.

Camp Notes: Considering the slope of this hillside, most of the campsites are well leveled. Although there are spots for tents here, the campground clearly is more suitable for rv's. Nearby Loafer Creek Campground has a lot of nice sites better-suited to tenters. Bidwell Canyon is named for General John Bidwell of Chico, a pioneering agriculturalist and politician in the late 1800's. Bidwell's title stemmed from his appointment as a brigadier general in the California Militia by Governor Leland Stanford.

LOAFER CREEK
Lake Oroville State Recreation Area

Location: Northeast California north of Sacramento.

Access: From California State Highway 162 at milepost 24 +.5 (10 miles east of the junction of California State Highways 70 and 162 in Oroville), turn north onto a paved park access road; proceed north for 0.2 mile to the entrance station; continue for 0.7 mile (down) and turn east (right) into the campground; (Highway 162 is an extension of Olive Highway in Oroville.)

Facilities: 137 campsites in 2 loops; (6 small or medium-sized group camp areas are also available); sites are medium to medium+ in size, with fairly good to very good separation; parking pads are paved, mostly level, medium to medium+ straight-ins or pull-throughs; some tent spots may be sloped, but most are excellent; fire rings or fireplaces; firewood is usually for sale, or b-y-o; (only driftwood may be gathered); water at several faucets; restrooms with showers; holding tank disposal station; paved driveways; complete supplies and services are available in Oroville.

Activities & Attractions: Boating; boat launch; fishing mostly for rainbow trout, largemouth and smallmouth bass, catfish; designated swimming beach; interpretive trail; scheduled interpretive programs in summer; large day use area.

Natural Features: Located in the foothills of the Sierra Nevada on an oak-covered hill overlooking the south shore of Lake Oroville; the campground is shaded/sheltered by a fairly dense mixture of oaks, conifers, manzanitas, with a few open grassy areas; elevation 1000'.

Season, Fees & Phone: May to October; please see Appendix for standard California state park fees and reservation information; park office (916) 538-2200; Loafer Creek phone (916) 538-2217 (seasonally).

Camp Notes: The best seasons to enjoy the recreational opportunities at Lake Oroville are spring and early summer. Like many large reservoirs, the water level typically drops considerably later in the year. There are many pleasant, private campsites at Loafer Creek, (known locally as Coyote Campground in order to distinguish it from the group camp areas).

GANSNER BAR
Plumas National Forest

Location: Northeast California northeast of Oroville.

Access: From California State Highway 70 at milepost 16 + .6 (just east of a bridge across the North Fork of the Feather River, 50 miles northeast of Oroville, 18 miles northwest of Quincy), turn north onto Caribou Road (hard-surfaced); proceed north for 0.5 mile; turn west (left) into the campground.

Facilities: 14 campsites; sites are medium to large, level, with fair to good separation; parking pads are paved, medium to medium+, mostly straight-ins; some large, grassy tent spots; large stone fireplaces, fire rings, and barbecue grills; some firewood is available for gathering in the area; water at several faucets; restrooms; holding tank disposal station at North Fork Campground, 2 miles north; paved driveways; adjacent to a Forest Service fire station; camper supplies in Belden, 2 miles west; adequate supplies and services are available in Quincy.

Activities & Attractions: Fishing (reportedly very good); hiking; nature exhibits; picnic area; access to the Pacific Crest Trail from near Belden; Bucks Lake Wilderness to the south.

Natural Features: Located in the Sierra Nevada on a narrow flat along the North Fork of the Feather River; the campground has considerable hardwood vegetation along the river and more open tree-dotted grassy areas in the infield closer to the roadway; steep, conifer-and-oak-cloaked rocky ridges border the canyon; elevation 2300'.

Season, Fees & Phone: April to late October; $8.00; 14 day limit; Quincy R.D. (916) 283-0555.

Camp Notes: Gansner Bar was named for a local ore-producing gravel bar, not, as some campers have suggested, after a local business establishment.

NORTH FORK
Plumas National Forest

Location: Northeast California northeast of Oroville.

Access: From California State Highway 70 at milepost 16 + .6 (just east of a bridge that spans the North Fork of the Feather River, 50 miles northeast of Oroville, 18 miles northwest of Quincy), turn north onto Caribou Road (hard-surfaced); go north for 2.2 miles; turn west (left) into the campground.

Facilities: 20 campsites; sites are small to medium-sized, with fair separation; parking pads are paved, level, short to medium, and mostly straight-ins; some really fine, level tent spots; fire rings, barbecue grills, and some large stone fireplaces; limited firewood is available for gathering in the vicinity; water at several faucets; restrooms; holding tank disposal station; paved driveways; camper supplies in Belden, 2 miles west; adequate supplies and services are available in Quincy.

Activities & Attractions: Fishing (reportedly very good); hiking; access to the Pacific Crest Trail from near Belden; Caribou Road follows the river north past the campground to the old mining community of Caribou and to Butt Valley Reservoir.

Natural Features: Located along the North Fork of the Feather River in a canyon on the west slope of the Sierra Nevada; campground vegetation consists of medium-height conifers and hardwoods, undergrowth and sparse grass; forested, rocky canyon walls closely flank the river; elevation 2300'.

Season, Fees & Phone: May to October; $8.00; 14 day limit; Quincy Ranger District (916) 283-0555.

Camp Notes: The North Fork is a fairly deep and swiftly flowing stream. Most sites in the river's namesake camp are streamside or very near the stream.

QUEEN LILY
Plumas National Forest

Location: Northeast California northeast of Oroville.

70

Access: From California State Highway 70 at milepost 16 +.6 (just east of a bridge across the North Fork of the Feather River, 50 miles northeast of Oroville, 18 miles northwest of Quincy), turn north onto Caribou Road (hard-surfaced); travel north for 2.5 miles; turn west (left) into the campground.

Facilities: 12 campsites; sites are small to medium-sized, level, with good separation; parking pads are paved, nearly all are medium-length straight-ins, plus a couple of longer pads; small to medium-sized areas for tents; fire rings; some firewood may be available for gathering in the area; water at several faucets; restrooms; paved driveway; holding tank disposal station at North Fork Campground (listed above); camper supplies in Belden, 2 miles west; adequate supplies and services are available in Quincy.

Activities & Attractions: Fishing; Caribou Road continues northward into mountain country at 4,000' to 5,000'.

Natural Features: Located in a canyon on the east bank of the North Fork of the Feather River; sites are well-shaded/sheltered mostly by dense hardwoods; bordered heavily timbered, steep canyon walls; elevation 2300'.

Season, Fees & Phone: May to October; $8.00; 14 day limit; Quincy Ranger District (916) 283-0555.

Camp Notes: Many of Queen Lily's sites are tucked away in fairly dense vegetation along the river.

HALLSTED
Plumas National Forest

Location: Northeast California northeast of Sacramento.

Access: From California State Highway 70 at milepost 26 +.5 (12 miles east of Belden, 18 miles northwest of Quincy), turn south onto a paved access road; proceed south 0.1 mile, then turn east (left) into the campground.

Facilities: 20 campsites in a loop and a string; sites are medium to large, with average to very good separation; parking pads are basically paved, level, medium to long straight-ins; some excellent tent spots-large and level with a forest material base; assorted fire facilities; firewood is available for gathering in the surrounding area; water at several faucets; restrooms; paved driveways; camper supplies in Twain, 1 mile east; adequate supplies and services are available in Quincy.

Activities & Attractions: Fishing; scenic drive along Highway 70, through what some sources refer to as "Serpentine Canyon"; Bucks Lake Wilderness is to the southwest; 2 high mountain lakes in the vicinity, Snake Lake and Silver Lake, are accessible by backroads from Quincy.

Natural Features: Located on a forested flat above the East Branch of the North Fork of the Feather River in the Sierra Nevada; campground vegetation consists of oaks and tall pines over a forest floor of pine needles; though there are no river views, the river is just a few yards through the trees from any site; elevation 2400'.

Season, Fees & Phone: May to October; $8.00; 14 day limit; Quincy Ranger District (916) 283-0555.

Camp Notes: Enough distance, vegetation and hills are between the sites at Hallsted and the highway, so that very little traffic noise should be heard in the campground.

JACKSON CREEK
Plumas National Forest

Location: Northeast California northeast of Oroville.

Access: From California State Highways 70/89 at milepost 60 +.5 (7 miles northwest of Blairsden, 15 miles southeast of Quincy), turn northeasterly (i.e., sharply right if approaching from Blairsden), then almost immediately turn sharply right again, and proceed 0.25 mile to the campground.

Facilities: 15 campsites; sites are small+ to medium-sized, somewhat sloped, with fair separation; parking pads are paved, short to medium-length straight-ins; small to medium-sized spots for tents in most sites; fire rings and barbecue grills; firewood is available for gathering in the area; water at several faucets; restrooms; gas and groceries+ in Blairsden; adequate supplies and services are available in Quincy.

Activities & Attractions: Fishing; numerous back roads and some hiking trails in the general vicinity.

Natural Features: Located on a forested slope in the Sierra Nevada where Jackson Creek meets the Middle Fork of the Feather River; campsites receive medium shelter/shade from tall conifers above a ground cover of short grass and some small bushes; densely forested hills and ridges surround the area; elevation 4500'.

Season, Fees & Phone: May to October; $8.00; 14 day limit; Beckwourth Ranger District, Mohawk, (916) 836-2572.

Camp Notes: This is a good highway camp. The Middle Fork of the Feather River is classified as a "Wild", "Scenic" or "Recreational" River along its various segments in this region.

UPPER JAMISON
Plumas-Eureka State Park

Location: Northeast California northeast of Oroville.

Access: From California State Highway 89 at milepost 7 +.8 (0.9 mile south of the junction of State Highways 89 & 70 at Blairsden, 8 miles north of the Plumas-Sierra county line), turn west onto Plumas County Road A14 (paved) and travel westerly for 5.2 miles (to a point just beyond the Jamison Creek picnic area and the museum); continue south/southwest on a paved park road (narrow with pullouts) for an additional 1.2 miles, then turn east (sharply left, at the end of the road) into the Campground.

Facilities: 70 campsites; sites are small to medium-sized, with good to very good separation; parking pads are paved, short to medium-length straight-ins; some pads may require a little additional leveling; generally enough space for small to medium-sized tents in most sites (some will take larger canvas); storage cabinets (bear boxes); fireplaces; some firewood may be available for gathering on surrounding national forest lands, b-y-o to be sure; water at several faucets; restrooms with showers; paved driveways; gas and groceries+ in Blairsden.

Activities & Attractions: Museum with displays relating to mining and early pioneer life; hiking trails; nature trail; stream fishing for small trout; campfire center; the park surrounds the old mining town of Johnsville, which includes a partially restored stamp mill.

Natural Features: Located on gently rolling and sloping terrain along Jamison Creek in the Sierra Nevada; campsites are in a super dense forest of conifers and some low hardwoods; elevation 4000'.

Season, Fees & Phone: May to October; please see Appendix for standard California state park fees and reservation information; park office (916) 836-2380.

Camp Notes: Although it's many miles from the coast, this campground might remind you very much of Redwood Country. It's just *that* kind of place--towering trees, tranquility, environmental orientation, and so forth. The campsites are surprisingly private (compared to most state parks). Although some are relatively closely spaced, you'll still see only two or three of your neighbors at any one time. If you spend a night here, it might rapidly become one of your favorite camps in the California state park system.

GRIZZLY
Plumas National Forest

Location: North-eastern California northwest of Reno, Nevada.

Access: From California State Highway 70 at milepost 78 +.8 (3 miles east of Portola, 2 miles west of Beckwourth), travel north on Grizzly Road (paved) for 6.5 miles; turn west (left) into the campground. (Alternate access note: Lake Davis can also be reached via a paved road from West Street in midtown Portola; the access is a bit longer and slightly more complicated than the principal Access above.)

Facilities: 55 campsites in 2 loops; sites are medium to medium+ in size, with fair to good separation; parking pads are paved, mostly medium to long straight-ins; most pads will require a little additional leveling; large, somewhat sloped tent spots; fireplaces and fire rings; some gatherable firewood is available in the general area; water at several faucets; restrooms; paved driveways; holding tank disposal station nearby on Grizzly Road; camper supplies near the dam; limited+ supplies and services are available in Portola.

Activities & Attractions: Fishing for several varieties of trout; boating; three boat launches along the lake's east shore.

Natural Features: Located on a slope above the southeast shore of Lake Davis; sites receive moderate shade/shelter from tall conifers above flowering plants, tall grass and a thick coating of pine needles; some sites are near the lake shore; the lake is bordered by well-timbered hills and low mountains; elevation 5900'.

Season, Fees & Phone: May to October; $12.00; 14 day limit; Beckwourth Ranger District, Mohawk, (916) 836-2575.

Camp Notes: If you consider site size and levelness to be important campsite characteristics, you need travel no farther up the road than Grizzly. Even though the lake really isn't within view of most sites, there are nonetheless some excellent camp spots here. The forest floor in the camp area, especially in the draws and coulees, is liberally coated with leafy flowering plants of an uncommon variety.

GRASSHOPPER FLAT
Plumas National Forest

Location: North-eastern California northwest of Reno, Nevada.

Access: From California State Highway 70 at milepost 78 + .8 (3 miles east of Portola, 2 miles west of Beckwourth), head north on Grizzly Road (paved) for 7 miles; turn west (left) into the campground.

Facilities: 70 campsites in 3 loops; sites are small+ to medium-sized, with nominal to fair separation; parking pads are paved, mostly medium-length straight-ins; majority of pads will require a little additional leveling; large, generally sloped tent spots; fireplaces and fire rings; some firewood is available for gathering in the general vicinity; water at several faucets; restrooms; paved driveways; holding tank disposal station nearby on Grizzly Road; camper supplies near the dam; limited+ supplies and services are available in Portola.

Activities & Attractions: Fishing for native and stocked trout, including a rainbow-kamloops crossbreed; also bass and catfish; boating; three boat launches along the lake's east shore.

Natural Features: Located on a rolling slope above the southeast shore of Lake Davis; sites are moderately sheltered by tall, slim conifers above patches of tall grass and a thick carpet of pine needles; some sites are near the lake shore; the lake is encircled by forested hills and mountains; elevation 5900'.

Season, Fees & Phone: May to October; $12.00; 14 day limit; Beckwourth Ranger District, Mohawk, (916) 836-2575.

Camp Notes: Campsites in the uppermost loop (i.e., those closest to the entrance) are farthest from the lake but are also the most level in the place. Following Grizzly Road up the east shore of the lake for another three miles will take you to Lightening Tree Campground, a rustic area for self-contained camping.

CHILCOOT
Plumas National Forest

Location: North-eastern California northwest of Reno, Nevada.

Access: From the junction of California State Highways 70 & 284 in the town of Chilcoot (near Highway 70 milepost 94), travel north on Highway 284 for 5.5 miles; turn west (left) onto a paved access road for 0.05 mile to the campground.

Facilities: 35 campsites; sites are small to medium+ in size, level, with fair to very good separation; parking pads are gravel, mostly short to medium-length straight-ins, plus a couple of pull-throughs; adequate space for tents; fireplaces and fire rings; b-y-o firewood is recommended; water at faucets throughout; restrooms; paved driveways; holding tank disposal station in the Cottonwood Springs area, 3 miles north; gas and groceries in Chilcoot.

Activities & Attractions: Stream fishing; fishing, boating, boat launch on Frenchman Lake, 3 miles north.

Natural Features: Located on a flat along Little Last Chance Creek in the Sierra Nevada; sites receive light-medium to fairly dense shade/shelter from a mixture of conifers and hardwoods; the road passes through a small, scenic canyon just north of the campground; elevation 5300'.

Season, Fees & Phone: May to October; $11.00; 14 day limit; Milford Ranger District (916) 253-2223.

Camp Notes: A really nice campground. Many dandy sites here. If you're coming to this region from the Bay Area or the Sacramento Valley and have only a standard weekend to spare, you're best approach might be via I-80 to Reno, then north on four-lane U.S. 395 to its junction with California 70, then west a few miles to the town of Chilcoot. The two-lane state highways that wind and climb eastward through the Sierra may follow more scenic routes, but the time and fuel you'll save using the non-stop I-80 approach may justify that choice.

FRENCHMAN
Plumas National Forest

Location: North-eastern California northwest of Reno, Nevada.

Access: From the junction of California State Highways 70 & 284 in the town of Chilcoot, travel north on Highway 284 for 8 miles to the dam; turn east (right) continuing on a paved local road for 0.3 mile; turn north (left) onto a steep paved access road and go down 0.05 mile, then swing west (left) into the campground. (Watch carefully for the last turn into the campground, especially at night, because the boat ramp is.....well, you probably get the picture.)

Facilities: 36 campsites in a loop and a string; (Cottonwood Springs Group Camp, near the dam, is also available); sites are medium to medium+ in size, with fair separation; parking pads are paved, medium to long, mostly straight-ins, plus some pull-offs and pull-throughs; additional leveling will be needed on most pads; large, sloped, tent areas; fireplaces; b-y-o firewood is recommended; water at faucets throughout; vault facilities; paved driveways; holding tank disposal station in the Cottonwood Springs area west of the dam; gas and groceries in Chilcoot.

Activities & Attractions: Fishing for stocked rainbow, brook and kamloops trout; boating; boat launch; hiking trail.

Natural Features: Located on a steep, forested slope a couple hundred yards above the south shore of Frenchman Lake; tall conifers above a ground cover of sage and tall grass provide medium shade/shelter for the campsites; the lake is bordered by lightly forested hills; elevation 5600'.

Season, Fees & Phone: May to October; $11.00; 14 day limit; Milford Ranger District (916) 253-2223.

Camp Notes: Whoever named the lake's natural features (perhaps it was the "Frenchman"?) may have had fishing on his mind when he handed out the 'handles'. Included on the list of notable spots along the shoreline are Nightcrawler Bay, Lunker Point, and Salmon Egg Shoal. (The origin of "Snallygaster Point" is uncertain.)

SPRING CREEK
Plumas National Forest

Location: North-eastern California northwest of Reno, Nevada.

Access: From the junction of California State Highways 70 & 284 in the town of Chilcoot, travel north on Highway 284 for 8 miles to the dam; turn east (right) continuing on a paved local road for another mile, then turn north (left) onto a paved access road and proceed 0.1 mile down into the campground.

Facilities: 35 campsites in 2 loops; sites are medium-sized, with nominal to fair separation; parking pads are paved, mostly medium to long straight-ins, plus a couple of pull-offs; most pads will require a little additional leveling; large, generally sloped tent areas; fireplaces; b-y-o firewood is recommended; water at several faucets; vault facilities; paved driveways; gas and groceries in Chilcoot.

Activities & Attractions: Fishing; boating; boat launch nearby; lake trail.

Natural Features: Located on a steep slope above the south tip of Frenchman Lake; sites receive light-medium shade from tall conifers above some sagebrush; Spring Creek enters the lake at this spot; the lake is bordered by lightly forested hills; elevation 5600'.

Season, Fees & Phone: May to October; $11.00; 14 day limit; Milford Ranger District (916) 253-2223.

Camp Notes: Nearly all sites here have lake views: either full views or views through the trees. Considering the slope, the parking, table and tent areas have been reasonably well leveled. A very pleasantly scenic lake.

BIG COVE
Plumas National Forest

Location: North-eastern California northwest of Reno, Nevada.

Access: From the junction of California State Highways 70 & 284 in the town of Chilcoot, travel north on Highway 284 for 8 miles to the dam; turn east (right), continuing on a paved road for another 1.8 miles, then swing sharply north (left) for a final 0.5 mile; turn northwest (left) into the campground.

Facilities: 38 campsites in 2 loops; sites are medium to medium+, level or nearly so, with zip to fair separation; parking pads are paved, short to medium-length straight-ins or pull-throughs; medium to large areas for tents; fireplaces; b-y-o firewood is recommended; water at several faucets; restrooms; paved driveways; gas and groceries in Chilcoot.

Activities & Attractions: Fishing for rainbow, brook and kamloops trout; boating; boat launch nearby.

Natural Features: Located near the shore of a cove at the southeast end of Frenchman Lake (Reservoir) on the east slope of the Sierra Nevada; sites are on a sage flat dotted with some conifers; bordered by lightly timbered hills; elevation 5600'.

Season, Fees & Phone: May to October; $11.00; 14 day limit; Milford Ranger District (916) 253-2223.

Camp Notes: There are a dozen nice sites along the edge of a low bluff about 20 feet above the lake shore. If you need a level site, this camp would probably be your best choice of the trio of campgrounds on Frenchman Lake. The relatively small lake (1600 acres) has 21 miles of shoreline, courtesy of numerous bays, inlets and coves.

Northern California Special Section

THE GOLD CAMPS OF '49
Tahoe National Forest

The area in and around Nevada City and the Yuba River Valley is popular not only for recreation but for its historical significance. The territory is rich in ghost towns, old diggings, and stories of gold miners who came here to seek their fortunes. Adventurers still flock to the area to try their luck at finding the precious metal. The information for "The Gold Camps of '49" has been listed in an abbreviated form because so much of the information is repetitive. Unless otherwise noted, *all have the following features in common*:

Common Elements of the Gold Camps:

Location: Northeast California northeast of Sacramento. (Of the 12 campgrounds listed here, 11 of them are in Sierra County, and 1 is in Yuba County.)

Access: From California State Highway 49 from a point 20 miles north of Nevada City to a point 11.5 miles west of Sierraville; all campgrounds are along or near California State Highway 49.

Sources of Supplies: Limited to adequate supplies and services are available in Nevada City and Truckee; gas & groceries are available in North San Juan (3 miles south of the Nevada/Yuba county line); Downieville (Sierra milepost 16.7); Sierra City (Sierra milepost 28.9); and Sierraville (6 miles east of Sierra County milepost 47.5).

Season & Phone: Generally, the campgrounds are available May to September; 14 day limit of stay; Downieville Ranger District (916) 288-3231.

Natural Features: In general, the campgrounds are situated along or near the North Yuba River in a forested canyon bordered by timbered ridges.

Activities & Attractions: Fishing; hiking; Wild Plum Loop Trail provides access to the Pacific Crest Trail; Kentucky Park Mine and Museum east of Sierra City; gold dredging or panning.

"There's gold in them thar hills!"

Northern California 132

SCHOOLHOUSE

Access: From milepost 3 +.65 (Yuba County), turn west onto Marysville Road (E20); proceed 3.25 miles; turn north (right) onto a paved access road and proceed 0.15 mile to the campground.

Facilities: 67 campsites; sites are small to medium-sized, and most are well separated; pads are paved, mostly short straight-ins; some pads may require additional leveling; some sites have large tent areas; fireplaces and fire rings; firewood is available for gathering in the area; water at several faucets; restrooms, plus auxilary vaults; paved driveways; $8.00.

Natural Features: Located on a rolling, forested hilltop above Bullards Bar Reservoir (on the North Yuba River); elevation 2200'.

Camp Notes: This is the most easily accessible of five campgrounds situated along the shore of Bullards Bar Reservoir. The season usually extends from April to October.

Northern California 133

FIDDLE CREEK

Access: From milepost 4 +.9, turn south and immediately west into the campground.

Facilities: 13 campsites; sites are small, with very little separation; dirt parking pads; no room for trailers or large camping vehicles; fireplaces; limited firewood is available for gathering in the area; no drinking water; vault facilities; hard-surfaced driveway; $8.00.

Natural Features: Located on a flat along the river; elevation 2200'.

Camp Notes: This is a miners' and fishermen's "tent city". Gold dredging is permitted under certain conditions.

Northern California 134

INDIAN VALLEY

Access: From milepost 5 +.35, turn south onto a paved access road; proceed 0.15 mile to the campground.

Facilities: 17 campsites; sites are small to medium in size, with nominal to fair separation; parking pads are gravel/dirt, level, short to medium-length straight-ins; some good tent spots; fireplaces and fire rings; firewood is available for gathering in the vicinity; water at several faucets; vault facilities; paved driveways; $8.00.

Natural Features: Located on a rocky flat along the river; elevation 2200'.

Camp Notes: There are many riverside sites where you can toss a line out into one of the rocky river's deep pools where some good-sized trout lurk. These rather small sites are commonly jammed to capacity.

Northern California 135

RAMSHORN

Access: From milepost 10 +.8, turn north into the lower loop of the campground; proceed 0.25 mile east and up to the upper loop.

Facilities: 16 campsites in 2 loops; sites are small to medium-sized, with very little separation; parking pads are dirt, fairly level, short to medium-length straight-ins; some tent spots are adequate for large tents; fireplaces; firewood is available for gathering in the vicinity; water at several faucets; vault facilities; gravel/dirt driveways; $8.00.

Natural Features: Located just across and above the highway from the river; some tall pines, cedars and open grassy areas in the campground; elevation 2600'.

Camp Notes: The upper loop is not recommended for trailers since it's tight, and there's no turnaround. Some sites, though very close to the highway, have nice views across the river and up the canyon.

Northern California 136

UNION FLAT

Access: From milepost 22 +.65, turn south into the campground.

Facilities: 14 campsites; sites are small and close together, for the most part; parking pads are gravel/dirt, short to medium-length straight-ins; some pads may require additional leveling; some tent spots are spacious enough for large tents; fireplaces; firewood is available for gathering in the vicinity; water at several faucets; vault facilities; gravel driveways; $8.00.

Natural Features: Located on a hilly riverbank; elevation 3400'.

Camp Notes: This is another popular gold dredging camp. Because most sites are streamside or nearly streamside, the campground is often filled to capacity.

LOGANVILLE

Access: From milepost 27 +.1, turn south, then bear left for 0.1 mile to the upper loop; or bear right and proceed 0.2 mile to the lower loop.

Facilities: 18 campsites in 2 loops; sites in the lower loop are a bit roomier than the small sites in the upper loop; separation ranges from fair to good; parking pads are dirt, fairly level, short to medium-length straight-ins; some tent spots are adequate for large tents; fire rings; firewood is available for gathering in the area; water at central faucets; vault facilities; dirt driveway; $8.00.

Natural Features: Located on a forested hilltop (upper loop); or on a forested flat a few yards from the river (lower loop); elevation 3800'.

Camp Notes: There are no river views from the sites, but unlike most other campgrounds in this area, there is a moderate amount of privacy provided by the fairly tall, dense conifers.

WILD PLUM

Access: From milepost 29 +.8, turn south onto Wild Plum Road; bear right; proceed 1.35 miles (paved for 0.6 mile), and over a 1-lane bridge to the campground's lower section; upper section is 0.1 mile farther.

Facilities: 47 campsites in 3 loops; sites are small to medium in size, with nominal to average separation; parking pads are gravel/dirt, short to medium-length straight-ins; some pads may require additional leveling; some tent spots are a bit sloped or rocky; fire rings and fireplaces; firewood is available for gathering in the area; water at several faucets; vault facilities; gravel/dirt driveways; $8.00.

Natural Features: Located along Haypress Creek; 2 loops are on a boulder-strewn, forested flat along the creek; the third loop is above the creek on a forested bluff; elevation 4400'.

Camp Notes: Some sites in the lower loop are creekside and some in the upper loop have a view of the creek through the trees. Sites at Wild Plum are away from the mainstream of activity, so the atmosphere is somewhat more relaxed.

SARDINE

Access: From milepost 34 +.3, turn northwest onto Gold Lake Road (signed for "Sierra Buttes Recreation Area"), drive 1.4 miles; turn southwest (left) and go 0.5 mile down to the campground.

Facilities: 29 campsites; sites are small to medium-sized, with fair separation for most sites; parking pads are mostly small to medium-length straight-ins; some good tent spots; fireplaces; some firewood may be available for gathering, but b-y-o is recommended; water at several faucets; vault facilities; June to October; $8.00.

Natural Features: Located on a sage slope with tall forested peaks and the Sierra Buttes visible from nearby; elevation 5800'.

Camp Notes: Because of nearby boating and swimming areas, Sardine Campground tends to become packed during much of the summer. (The name then befits the camping circumstances.) Jackcamping isn't permitted around here.

SALMON CREEK

Access: From milepost 34 +.3, turn northwest onto Gold Lake Highway (signed for "Sierra Buttes Recreation Area"), proceed 1.6 miles; turn southwest (left) into the campground.

Facilities: 33 campsites in 2 loops connected by a string; sites are mostly medium-sized, with nominal to fair separation; parking pads are hard-surfaced/gravel, short to medium-length straight-ins; some pads may require additional leveling; some good tent spots; fireplaces; firewood is usually available for gathering in the vicinity; water at several faucets; vault facilities; hard-surfaced driveways; June to October; $8.00.

Natural Features: Located on a sage and grass flat along Salmon Creek; more vegetation in sites along the creek and less vegetation (mostly sage) in sites out in the open; elevation 5800'.

Camp Notes: The vistas from here are much more expansive than the views from down in the Yuba River Canyon along the highway. To the west, Sierra Buttes are prominent amid forested hills and mountains. There are a dozen small mountain lakes within a dozen miles of Salmon Creek Campground. Virtually all of them are easily accessible.

Northern California 141

SIERRA

Access: From milepost 36 +.5, turn south into the campground.

Facilities: 16 campsites; sites are fairly good-sized, with average or better separation; parking pads are gravel, medium to long straight-ins; some pads may require additional leveling; some spacious tent spots; fireplaces; firewood is available for gathering in the area; no drinking water; vault facilities; gravel driveways; $6.00.

Natural Features: Located on a forested slope along Sierra Creek; elevation 5600'.

Camp Notes: There are some vast scenic views from along the highway in this area.

Northern California 142

CHAPMAN CREEK

Access: From milepost 37 +.3, turn north into the campground.

Facilities: 29 campsites; sites are large, with good separation; parking pads are gravel, medium to long straight-ins; large mostly level, tent spots; fireplaces; firewood is available for gathering in the area; no drinking water; vault facilities; paved driveways; $8.00.

Natural Features: Located on a rolling flat; lightly forested with very tall timber and large grassy areas; elevation 6000'.

Camp Notes: This is a really nice camp--with some of the most spacious and private sites along this stretch. If you can bring your own drinking water, you're all set.

Northern California 143

YUBA PASS

Access: From milepost 40 +.88, turn south and proceed 0.1 mile to the campground.

Facilities: 20 campsites; most sites are large, with fair to good separation; parking pads are gravel, fairly level, medium to long straight-ins; some very good tent spots; fire rings and fireplaces; firewood is available for gathering in the area; no drinking water; vault facilities; gravel driveways; $8.00.

Natural Features: Located in a semi-open forest setting very near the summit of Yuba Pass; elevation 6700'.

Camp Notes: This campground is just over the rise from some steep grades on the slopes bordering the great Sierra Valley. Because it's far from the mainstream of activity along the Yuba River, Yuba Pass Campground is seldom filled to capacity.

Northern California 144

COTTONWOOD & COLD CREEK
Tahoe National Forest

Location: North-east California north of Truckee.

Access: From California State Highway 89 at milepost 10 +.6 (4.5 miles south of Sierraville, 20 miles north of Truckee), turn east into Cottonwood Campground; or at milepost 10 +.25, turn west into Cold Creek Campground.

Facilities: *Cottonwood*: 49 campsites in 2 loops; *Cold Creek*: 13 campsites; *both camps*: most sites are large, with fairly good separation; parking pads are paved, generally level, short to medium+ straight-ins; level, grassy tent spots, some will accommodate medium to large tents comfortably; fire rings and fireplaces; firewood is available for gathering in the area; water at several faucets; vault facilities; paved driveways; camper supplies in Sierraville; adequate supplies and services are available in Truckee.

Activities & Attractions: Fishing; Cottonwood Creek Botanical Trail is a half-mile-long self guiding nature trail which identifies the local trees and plants.

Natural Features: Located in the Sierra Nevada at the south edge of the Sierra Valley; forested surroundings include firs, pines, cedars, cottonwoods, aspens and willows; most sites have very good shelter provided by trees and brush; Cottonwood Creek and Cold Creek flow through their respective campground areas; several small bridges span the creeks; elevation 5800'.

Season, Fees & Phone: May to October; $8.00; 14 day limit; Sierraville Ranger District (916) 994-3401.

Camp Notes: Cold Creek Campground is a bit more open than Cottonwood Campground. Sites at Cold Creek are also a little closer to the highway than those at Cottonwood. There are some excellent panoramic views of the immense Sierra Valley from nearby on Highway 89.

Northern California 145

LITTLE TRUCKEE
Tahoe National Forest

Location: North-east California north of Truckee.

Access: From California State Highway 89 at milepost 3 +.6 for Upper Little Truckee and milepost 3 +.2 for Lower Little Truckee (8 miles south of Sierraville, 17 miles north of Truckee), turn west into the campground units.

Facilities: 26 campsites in the Upper unit and 15 campsites in the Lower unit; sites are fairly small, with nominal to average separation; parking pads are gravel/dirt, level, short to medium-length, mostly pull-offs; good, level tent spots, some will accommodate large tents; fire rings; limited firewood is available for gathering in the area; water at several faucets; vault facilities; gravel driveways; camper supplies in Sierraville, adequate supplies and services are available in Truckee.

Activities & Attractions: Fishing; several lakes, including Independence Lake, Webber Lake and Jackson Meadow Reservoir, are accessible by back roads which lead west from about milepost 6 on Highway 89; the scenic drive along Highway 89 is impressive; elevation 6100'.

Natural Features: Located in the Sierra Nevada south of the expansive Sierra Valley; campsites are situated on a sagebrush flat next to the river; some sites are streamside; campground vegetation consists of fairly typical riverside brush, a few medium-sized conifers, sagebrush and some grass; the Little Truckee River flows past the campgrounds on its way south to join the Truckee River; elevation 5600'.

Season, Fees & Phone: June to October; $8.00; 14 day limit; Sierraville Ranger District (916) 994-3401.

Camp Notes: Upper Little Truckee and Lower Little Truckee are basically just 2 loops of the same campground. Campsites at both are rather close to the highway, but the preoccupied, resident camper-fishermen don't seem to be deterred by that potential distraction.

Northern California 146

PROSSER
Tahoe National Forest

Location: North-east California north of Truckee.

Access: From California State Highway 89 at milepost 4 +.2 (3 miles north of Truckee, 22 miles south of Sierraville), turn east onto a paved access road; proceed 1.5 miles east (past a left turnoff to the Lakeside dispersed camping area); turn left into the campground.

Facilities: 29 campsites; sites are medium to large, with basically fair separation; parking pads are rocky gravel, generally level, medium-length straight-ins; some sites are roomy enough to accommodate large tents; fire rings and barbecue grills; a limited amount of firewood is available for gathering in the area, b-y-o is recommended; water at several faucets; vault facilities; paved/gravel driveways; adequate supplies and services are available in Truckee.

Activities & Attractions: Boating; boat ramp nearby; fishing; 1 mile south, off Highway 89, is the Donner Camp historic site with an interpretive trail and picnic facilities; back roads interconnect Prosser Reservoir with nearby Boca and Stampede Reservoirs.

Natural Features: Located in the Sierra Nevada on the west shore peninsula of Prosser Reservoir; campsites are all situated on a flat-topped hill above the lake; sparse grass, sagebrush and bushy pines are the predominant forms of vegetation in the campground; a number of sites are in an open area in the interior of the camp area; elevation 5300'.

Season, Fees & Phone: June to October; $9.00; 14 day limit; Truckee Ranger District (916) 587-3558.

Camp Notes: There are some nice views of the lake, surrounding timbered ridges, and forested mountains through the trees from a number of the Prosser Campground sites. The level of the reservoir can vary considerably from season to season and year to year.

MALAKOFF DIGGINS
Malakoff Diggins State Historic Park

Location: East-central California northeast of Sacramento.

Access: From California State Highway 49 at a point 0.4 mile northwest of the junction of Highway 49 & State Highway 20 at the north end of Nevada City, (0.2 mile west of the USDA Forest Service headquarters complex), turn north onto North Bloomfield Road and proceed 0.6 mile north, then bear northeast (right) onto North Bloomfield-Graniteville Road and travel another 14 miles to the park visitor center and the campground just beyond.

Alternate Access: From State Highway 49 at a point 11 miles northwest of Nevada City, head northeast on Tyler-Foote Crossing Road and proceed 8 miles to a point just past the settlement of North Columbia; turn east (right) onto Lake City Road and proceed 6 miles to the visitor center and thence the campground. (Note: both routes involve a half-dozen miles of gravel travel as they approach the park; the *Alternate Access* is suggested for single vehicles larger than a crew cab pickup or for any vehicles with trailers; you'll pass The Diggins on the way to the visitor center.)

Facilities: 30 campsites; (a group camp is also available, by reservation); sites are small, with minimal separation; parking pads are mostly short straight-ins; additional leveling may be required; small to medium-sized tent areas; storage cabinets; water at central faucets; restrooms, plus auxiliary vault facilities; paved driveways; adequate supplies and services are available in Nevada City.

Activities & Attractions: Location of an hydraulic mining operation of the mid 1800's; museum with mining exhibits and a film about hydraulic mining; historic buildings.

Natural Features: Located in the high foothills on the west slope of the Sierra Nevada; bordered by meadows and conifer-dotted hills; elevation 3000'.

Season, Fees & Phone: April to November (subject to weather conditions); please see Appendix for standard California state park fees and reservation information; park office (916) 265-2740.

Camp Notes: Malakoff Diggins SP focuses on the hydraulic mining methods employed by gold miners in the late 1800's. Water cannons, charged by an ingenious system of gravity-fed pressure-boosting plumbing, blasted gold-bearing gravel from the hillsides. The ore was then washed down into giant sluice boxes for separation. Hydraulic mining used incredible quantities of water and did an incredible amount of damage to the local landscape. Nature has reclaimed a portion of The Diggins.

Northern California
North Central Inland
Please refer to the Northern California map in the Appendix

BRANNAN ISLAND
Brannan Island State Recreation Area

Location: West-central California southwest of Sacramento.

Access: From California State Highway 160 at milepost 7 +.3 (14 miles northwest of Antioch, 3.4 miles south of the junction of Highway 160 and State Highway 12), turn east and proceed 0.1 mile to the park entrance station; continue for 0.1 mile and turn south (right) into the camping area.

Facilities: 102 campsites in 2 loops; (32 slips in the Delta Vista area on Three-Mile Slough are available for overnight on-boat camping or adjacent walk-in camping; also, 6 primitive small group areas are available by reservation); sites are fairly spacious, level, with reasonable separation for most sites; parking pads are paved, short to long straight-ins, some are double wide; very nice large, grassy, tent spots; storage cabinets; fireplaces and fire rings; firewood is usually for sale, or b-y-o; water at each site; restrooms; holding tank disposal station; paved driveways; adequate+ supplies and services are available in Antioch.

Activities & Attractions: Boating; sailing; large boat launch, boat-in camping slips; fishing for striped bass, black bass, sturgeon, catfish and panfish; swimming beach nearby on Seven Mile Slough; campfire circle; visitor center with interpretive displays; recreational vehicle rally site; large day use area.

Natural Features: Located on the Sacramento-San Joaquin Delta between the main channel of the Sacramento River and backwaters known as Three Mile Slough and Seven Mile Slough; waves of green and golden grass are dotted with a wide variety of large hardwoods and evergreens throughout the camp area; from a knoll nearby, the river and delta are visible; typically breezy, with mild temperatures year round; elevation 25'.

Season, Fees & Phone: Open all year; please see Appendix for standard California state park fees and reservation information; park office (916) 777-6671.

Camp Notes: The Delta provides a thousand miles of opportunities for water-oriented recreation. If you have a boat, you can also explore nearby Franks Tract State Recreation Area, 5 miles southeast of Brannan Island. Franks Tract encompasses about 3500 acres, though all but 300 of them are under water. The lake there was created when a levee burst and the island was flooded. The area is said to have exceptionally productive fishing waters.

DURHAM FERRY
Durham Ferry State Recreation Area

Location: Central California west of Modesto.

Access: From Interstate 5 at the California State Highway 33 Exit (5 miles south of the junction of Interstates 5 & 205 east of Tracy, 6 miles north of the junction of Interstates 5 & 580 southeast of Tracy), proceed southeast on State Highway 33 for 1.3 miles; turn east (left) onto Durham Ferry Road and travel 3 miles, then the road becomes Airport Way; continue northeasterly on Airport Way for 1.7 miles; turn northwest (left) onto a paved park access road and proceed 0.5 mile to the park entrance station; continue ahead for 0.6 mile to the campground.

Facilities: 60 campsites, some with electrical hookups; sites are small, level, with minimal separation; parking pads are gravel, short to short+ straight-ins, some are extra wide; adequate space for small tents on designated areas; small ramadas (sun shelters) over table areas; fire rings and/or barbecue grills; a limited amount of firewood may be available for gathering in the general vicinity, b-y-o to be sure; water at several faucets; restrooms with showers; holding tank disposal station; gravel driveways; gas and groceries 2 miles southwest.

Activities & Attractions: Equestrian area; archery range; limited fishing.

Natural Features: Located on a riverside plain near the east bank of the San Joaquin River, a mile downstream of the confluence of the San Joaquin & Stanislaus Rivers; vegetation consists of large, open grassy areas dotted with a few trees, plus stands of hardwoods along the river; elevation 30'.

Season, Fees & Phone: Open all year; park entry fee $2.00 ($3.00 weekends/holidays); standard site $7.00, hookup site $9.00, pet $1.00, $3-$4 for extra vehicles (subject to change); campsite reservations accepted (see phone, below); operated by San Joaquin County; County of San Joaquin Department of Parks & Recreation, Stockton, (209) 953-8800.

Camp Notes: The developed areas of the park are protected from flooding by a high dike along the river, so there aren't any easy river views. From the campground, a short scramble up and over the embankment and through the woods will take you to the San Joaquin. The 'ridgetop' trail along the dike is often used by hikers.

CASWELL
Caswell Memorial State Park

Location: Central California northwest of Modesto.

Access: From California State Highway 99 at the Ripon Exit (10 miles northwest of Modesto) go west into midtown Ripon and travel west on Main Street through downtown; at the west edge of town, Main Street becomes West Ripon Road; continue on West Ripon Road for another 2 miles (a total of 3.3 miles from '99); turn south (left) onto Austin Road and proceed 2.8 miles to the park entrance station; just past the entrance, turn east (left) into the campground.

Facilities: 66 campsites; (a group camp is also available, by reservation); sites are small to medium-sized, reasonably level, with fair to excellent separation; parking pads are paved, very short straight-ins, some are extra wide; enough space for small to medium-sized tents in most sites, large in some; storage cabinets; fire rings; b-y-o firewood; water at several faucets; restrooms with showers; paved driveways; adequate supplies and services are available in Ripon.

Activities & Attractions: Fishing for bass, catfish, bluegill; seasonal rafting/floating; designated wading beach; nature trail; great blue heron rookery (available for field study at a distance); campfire center; annual Tule Fog Fete in February.

Natural Features: Located along the north bank of the Stanislaus River; the campground is within a woodland consisting mostly of tall valley oaks and very dense undercover; bordered by farmland which includes hundreds of acres of orchards; elevation 40'.

Season, Fees & Phone: Open all year; please see Appendix for standard California state park fees and reservation information; park office (209) 599-3810.

Camp Notes: The Central Valley's legendary winter ground cloud is celebrated during the park's annual Fog Fete--a contest to decide which cook has the tastiest or thickest pea soup. The one-day fest (for the benefit of the Great Valley Museum) draws quite a crowd. In summer, the woods are as thick and green as the pea soup they brew up in the winter.

GEORGE J. HATFIELD
George J. Hatfield State Recreation Area

Location: Central California northwest of Merced.

Access: From Interstate 5 near milepost 5 + .5 at the Stuhr Road/Newman Exit (5.5 miles north of the junction of I-5 & State Highway 140 west of Gustine) travel east on Stuhr Road/Stanislaus County Road J18 for 4.8 miles; cross over State Highway 33 and continue east on Stuhr Road for another 1.9 miles to a "T" intersection; turn northeast (left) onto Hills Ferry Road and proceed northeast for 2 miles, then bear north onto Kelly Road and go 0.1 mile, then swing east (right) to the park entrance station; just beyond the entrance at a fork, bear left for a few yards to another fork, then bear right to the main camping area.

Alternate Access: From California State Highway 165 near milepost 30 at the south end of the Merced River bridge (8 miles south of Turlock, 3 miles south of Hilmar, 2 miles north of Stevinson), turn west onto River Road/Merced County Road J18 and travel westerly (the road makes several sharp turns) for 7.1 miles to a 3-way intersection just west of another Merced River bridge (locally called the Stevinson Bridge); turn north (right) onto Kelly Road and continue as above. (It's great sport trying to find this park after dark. Ed.)

Facilities: Approximately 12 park 'n walk campsites; (a group camp is also available, by reservation); sites are small, level, with nominal separation; parking areas are paved, short straight-ins or pull-offs; ample space for large tents; storage cabinets; fireplaces; b-y-o firewood; water at several faucets; restrooms; paved driveways; limited+ supplies and services are available in Hilmar.

Activities & Attractions: Fishing for warm water species, plus some salmon seasonally; limited floating/rafting; campfire center; interpretive displays about Indians and acorns, and about mosquitos; day use area.

Natural Features: Located in the San Joaquin Valley on a large flat on the north bank of the Merced River just upstream of the confluence of the Merced and San Joaquin Rivers; campground vegetation consists of a large, open grassy section plus stands of large oaks; elevation 60'.

Season, Fees & Phone: Open all year; please see Appendix for standard California state park fees and reservation information; park office (209) 632-1852.

Camp Notes: Former California Lieutenant Governor and State Senator George Hatfield provided the land for this recreation area. The park's real estate includes 1¼ miles of river frontage and several sandy beaches. Finding this place in the dark without directions can be a real adventure. (We know).

McCONNELL
McConnell State Recreation Area

Location: Central California southeast of Modesto.

Access: From California State Highway 99 at the Delhi Exit at milepost 34 + .4 (20 miles southeast of Modesto, 19 miles northwest of Merced), turn east off the freeway, then south onto Vincent Road; proceed 0.3 mile, then turn east (left) onto El Capitan; travel 3.1 miles on El Capitan, then turn south (right) onto Pepper Street; drive south 1 mile on Pepper to Second Avenue South; turn east (left) onto Second, proceed 0.5 mile, then the road curves to the right and becomes McConnell Road (just a little farther and you've got it made); continue for 0.1 mile to the park entrance, and a final 0.15 mile to the campground. (Whew.)

Facilities: 17 campsites, plus a small overflow area; (a group camp is also available); sites are large, level, and fairly well separated; parking pads are paved, short, extra-wide straight-ins or long pull-offs; very nice, spacious tent spots; storage cabinets; fireplaces; firewood is usually for sale, or b-y-o; water at faucets throughout; restrooms with showers; paved driveways; limited supplies and services are available in Delhi.

Activities & Attractions: Limited fishing for bass, perch, catfish on the river; campfire center for weekend evening programs in summer; day use area.

Natural Features: Located on a wooded flat along the bank of the Merced River in the San Joaquin Valley; fully developed hardwoods on watered and mown lawns provide light-medium to medium-dense shade for most campsites; elevation 100'.

Season, Fees & Phone: Open all year; please see Appendix for standard California state park fees and reservation information; park office (209) 394-7755.

Camp Notes: McConnell was the first state park unit established in the fertile San Joaquin Valley. The park is surrounded by nut farms. It's really an attractive little place.

Northern California 153

BEAL'S POINT
Folsom Lake State Recreation Area

Location: East-central California northeast of Sacramento.

Access: From U.S. Highway 50 near milepost 15 +.7 at the Hazel Avenue/Sacramento County Highway E3 Exit southwest of Folsom, travel north on Hazel Avenue for 2.4 miles; turn east (right) onto Madison Avenue and proceed 2 miles, then pick up Greenback Lane and continue east for another mile to a 3-way intersection at Greenback Lane and Folsom-Auburn Road; turn north (left) onto Folsom-Auburn Road and proceed 2.6 miles; turn east (right) onto the park access road and go 0.2 mile to the park entrance station; continue ahead for 0.1 mile to the campground.

(*Access* Note: if you're southwestbound on U.S. 50 from Placerville, you could take the Scott Road/Bidwell Road Exit near milepost 22 east of Folsom for 5 miles into Folsom on Scott Road; then you'll have to pick your way through downtown Folsom and north across the American River bridge in order to get northbound onto Folsom-Auburn Road).

Alternate Access: From Interstate 80 at the Greenback Lane/Elkhorn Boulevard/Sacramento County Highway E14 Exit (13 miles northeast of Sacramento, 4 miles southwest of Roseville) travel east on Greenback Lane/E14 for 8 miles to the intersection of Greenback Lane & Folsom-Auburn Road and continue as above.

Facilities: 49 campsites, including a number of park 'n walk sites; sites are small to medium-sized, with nominal to fairly good separation; parking surfaces are paved, short to short+ straight-ins, some are double-wide and some will require a little additional leveling; adequate space for mostly small to medium-sized tents; fire rings; b-y-o firewood; water at several faucets; restrooms with showers; paved driveway; adequate+ supplies and services are available in the Folsom area.

Activities & Attractions: Large, sandy swimming beach nearby; boating; boat launch; American River Bikeway begins near here and ends at Old Town Sacramento, 32.8 miles downstream; large day use area.

Natural Features: Located a few hundred yards west of the shore of Folsom Lake near the western foothills of the Sierra Nevada; the campground is on and around a grassy, lightly forested knoll; elevation 450'.

Season, Fees & Phone: April to October; please see Appendix for standard California state park fees and reservation information; park office (916) 988-0205.

Camp Notes: No campfire sing-along at Folsom Lake would be complete without a soulful rendition of the ol' Country favorite "Folsom Prison Blues". (The slammer that's the song's namesake is near the lake's south shore.)

Northern California 154

NEGRO BAR
Folsom Lake State Recreation Area

Location: East-central California northeast of Sacramento.

Access: From U.S. Highway 50 near milepost 15 +.7 at the Hazel Avenue/Sacramento County Highway E3 Exit southwest of Folsom, travel north on Hazel Avenue for 2.4 miles; turn east (right) onto Madison Avenue and proceed 2 miles, then pick up Greenback Lane and continue east for another 0.7 mile; turn south (right) onto the park access road and go 0.1 mile to the park entrance station; continue ahead (easterly) for 0.4 mile to the main section of the campground.

(*Access* Note: if you're southwestbound on U.S. 50 from Placerville, you could take the Scott Road/Bidwell Road Exit near milepost 22 east of Folsom, then 5 miles into Folsom on Scott Road; wind through downtown Folsom and north across the American River bridge to Greenback Lane; go west on Greenback Lane for 0.3 mile to the park turnoff.

Alternate Access: From Interstate 80 at the Greenback Lane/Elkhorn Boulevard/Sacramento County Highway E14 Exit (13 miles northeast of Sacramento, 4 miles southwest of Roseville) travel east on Greenback Lane/E14 for 8 miles to the park turnoff and continue as above.

Facilities: 20 campsites, including a half-dozen park 'n walk units; (3 group camps are also available); most sites are along the perimeter of the parking lot and are very small to small, level, with nil separation; parking slots are paved, level, short, wide straight-ins; generally small tent areas; fire rings; b-y-o firewood; water at central faucets; restrooms; holding tank disposal station; paved driveways; adequate+ supplies and services are available in the Folsom area.

Activities & Attractions: Large, sandy swimming beach; boating; boat launch; American River Bikeway; equestrian trail, equestrian staging area and parking lot; hiking trail; guided tours of the historic Folsom Powerhouse; large day use area.

Natural Features: Located along the north shore of Lake Natoma, a long, slender, secondary impoundment on the American River downstream of the main dam on Folsom Lake; most campsites receive light to light-medium shade from large hardwoods; elevation 250'.

Season, Fees & Phone: Open all year; please see Appendix for standard California state park fees and reservation information; park office (916) 988-0205.

Camp Notes: When the water level on the main lake is just on the high side of dry, (e.g. at the end of summer in a rain-short year), you may find the environment in the Negro Bar section of the park to be a little more to your liking. Lake Natoma essentially is kept at a constant level.

ACORN
New Hogan Lake/Corps of Engineers Park

Location: Central California southeast of Sacramento.

Access: From California State Highway 26 at milepost 6 (30 miles east of Stockton, 0.4 mile south of Valley Springs at the junction of California State Highways 12 & 26), turn east onto Hogan Dam Road; proceed east-southeast for 1.1 miles to a fork; bear left and continue east for 1.3 miles to the campground.

Facilities: 122 campsites; sites are medium to medium+, with fair separation; parking pads are paved, medium to long, mostly straight-ins and pull-offs, plus a few pull-throughs; many pads may require additional leveling; large, grassy tent spots, some may be a bit sloped; fire rings and barbecue grills; b-y-o firewood; water at several faucets; restrooms with showers; holding tank disposal station; paved driveways; gas and groceries in Valley Springs; complete supplies and services are available in Stockton.

Activities & Attractions: Boating; fishing; swimming (seasonally good at nearby Wrinkle Cove); nature trail and equestrian trail nearby along the Calaveras River at Monte Vista Recreation Area.

Natural Features: Located in the western Sierra Nevada foothills on the north shore of New Hogan Lake, an 8-mile-long flood-control and irrigation reservoir on the Calaveras River; campsites are on rolling, grassy, oak-dotted hills overlooking the lake and the surrounding forested mountains; elev. 700'.

Season, Fees & Phone: Open all year; $12.00; 14 day limit; CoE Project Office (209) 772-1343.

Camp Notes: In addition to the nice sites at Acorn Campground, there are 53 popular, less developed units at the adjacent Oak Knoll Campground. New Hogan Lake boasts a distinguished neighbor: the nearby town of Angels Camp hosts an Annual Frog Jumping Contest, made famous by Mark Twain's "Celebrated Jumping Frog of Calaveras County."

TURLOCK LAKE
Turlock Lake State Recreation Area

Location: East-central California east of Modesto.

Access: From California State Highway 132 at milepost 35+.9 (10 miles west of La Grange, 8 miles east of Waterford, 21 miles east of Modesto), turn south onto Roberts Ferry Road; proceed 1.1 miles to a "T" intersection; turn east (left) onto Lake Road and go 2.2 miles (past the day use turnoff) to the campground access road; turn north (left), and go down 0.2 mile to the campground.

Facilities: 67 campsites; sites are small to medium-sized, level, with fair to very good separation; parking pads are gravel, short to medium-length, mostly extra-wide straight-ins; excellent, large tent spots; storage cabinets; fireplaces or fire rings; b-y-o firewood; water at faucets throughout; restrooms with showers; paved driveways; minimal supplies at a small store, 2 miles west; limited to adequate supplies and services are available in Waterford.

Activities & Attractions: Swimming beach on a small cove; fishing for catfish, bass, crappie, bluegill and rainbow trout in both the lake and the river; boating, boat launch and docks on the lake; short nature trail; artesian well; campfire circle; marina; day use areas nearby.

Natural Features: Located on bottomland along the south bank of the Tuolumne River north of Turlock Lake; large hardwoods, mown grass, berry bushes, wildflowers and other dense vegetation fills the campground; surrounding terrain is comprised of mostly treeless, rolling grassland and farmland; lake surface area varies from 1800 acres to 3500 acres, depending upon precip and drawdown; elevation 250'.

Season, Fees & Phone: Open all year; please see Appendix for standard California state park fees and reservation information; park office (209) 874-2008.

Camp Notes: When you consider the nearly treeless surrounding terrain, this riverside campground is a lush, green surprise. Here's another oddity--the lake is above the level of the river, rather than being a mainstream impoundment, as you might expect. Diversion canals running parallel to the river feed and drain the shallow, upper basin in which the lake sits. Fishing is said to be good on either the lake or the river, but knowledgeable locals admit to heading directly for a streamside fishing spot when motorized traffic picks up on the lake.

HORSESHOE BEND
Merced Irrigation District Recreation Area

Location: East-central California east of Modesto.

Access: From California State Highway 132 at milepost 15 (4 miles west of Coulterville, 20 miles east of LaGrange), turn south onto a paved road and go 0.1 mile; turn right at a "T' intersection and continue for 0.3 mile to the recreation area entrance; the campground is 0.15 mile beyond the entrance station.

Facilities: 90 campsites, including 15 with partial hookups and several walk-in sites; sites are medium-sized, with some spacing but little visual separation; parking pads are gravel/paved, short to medium-length, wide straight-ins or pull-offs; large tent areas; some sites have small ramadas (sun shelters); storage lockers; barbecue grills; charcoal fires only; water at several faucets; restrooms with showers; paved driveways; limited supplies and services are available in Coulterville.

Activities & Attractions: Boating; boat launch (extra fee); fishing.

Natural Features: Located on a low hill at the north end of Lake McClure, an impoundment formed by Exchequer Dam on the Merced River; campground vegetation consists of a variety of large hardwoods and tall pines, plus some sections of watered, mown grass; most sites have some shade/shelter; the lake is encircled by dark green hills and low mountains; elevation 900'.

Season, Fees & Phone: Open all year; $11.00 for a standard site, $15.00 for a hookup site; rservations accepted, contact the Parks Administration Hq (800) 468-8889 or (209) 378-2521.

Camp Notes: This is one of those pleasant, unassuming places that reportedly almost always has room for a late arrival. When the lake's water level is close to normal, some sites would have a lakeshore view. The walk-in/tent sites are in a nice, separate section in a grove of trees.

AUBURN
Auburn State Recreation Area

Location: East-central California east of Sacramento.

Access: From Interstate 80 near milepost 17+.4 in Auburn, take the Grass Valley/Placerville Exit for California State Highway 49; travel southeasterly on Highway 49 through downtown Auburn for 1.6 miles, then swing north (left) to the park office (see below); or continue southeasterly for another 1.5 miles to the junction of Highway 49 and Foresthill Road at the river; from this point you can begin your exploration of the recreation area (see below) and your quest for a campsite. (Note: you can avoid Auburn's CBD by taking the Foresthill/Auburn Ravine Road Exit, 2 miles northeast of the Auburn Exit, if you'd prefer to go directly to the center of the park and right into the thick of it, so to speak.).

Facilities: 5 medium-sized, primitive, walk-in, or boat-in campgrounds, most with vault facilities but no drinking water, throughout the recreation area; gravel/dirt roads serve most camps; boat-in camp is on Lake Clementine; some campsites along the river trail are also available; adequate supplies and services are available in Auburn.

Activities & Attractions: More than 50 miles of hiking, equestrian and mountain bike trails; fishing; boating; boat launch at the dam on Lake Clementine.

Natural Features: Located in the forested foothills of the Sierra Nevada bordering the American River Canyon/Gorge, and along the North and Middle Forks of the American River; Lake Clementine backs up for several miles behind the dam on the North Fork; vegetation consists of a mixture of oaks and other hardwoods, pines and junipers; elevation 600' to 2800'.

Season, Fees & Phone: Open all year; please see Appendix for standard California state park fees; park office (916) 885-4527.

Camp Notes: Auburn is a roughcut rec area, albeit a large and popular one. Your best bet is to stop by the park office just east of Auburn in order to get your bearings, a detailed park map, and the current 'regs' for camping in the 20-mile-long, 5-mile-wide, 42,000-acre recreation area.

WHITE CLOUD
Tahoe National Forest

Location: Northeast California northeast of Sacramento.

Access: From California State Highway 20 at milepost 29 +.6 (10.5 miles east of Nevada City, 17 miles west of Interstate 80 at Yuba Gap, 41 miles west of Truckee), turn south and proceed a few yards west into the campground.

Facilities: 46 campsites in 2 loops; sites are medium to large, with good separation; parking pads are paved, medium to long straight-ins, and some may require minor additional leveling; some excellent tent spots on a forest floor of evergreen needles and leaves; fire rings and some large, stone fireplaces; firewood is available for gathering in the area; water at several faucets; restrooms, plus auxilary vault facilities; paved driveways; adequate supplies and services are available in Nevada City.

Activities & Attractions: Pleasant drive through the Sierra along Highway 20; Vista Point at about milepost 31 on Highway 20 of the South Yuba River Valley to the north; fishing on nearby mountain lakes, including Scotts Flat Reservoir; Malakoff Diggins State Historical Park, 16 miles northeast of Nevada City; Rock Creek Nature Study Area, 5 miles west then north on Rock Creek Road; gold panning on the South Yuba River near Washington.

Natural Features: Located on the west slope of the Sierra Nevada; campground vegetation consists of a quite dense stand of very tall cedars and other conifers, considerable underbrush and second growth timber; elevation 4200'.

Season, Fees & Phone: May to October; $9.00; 14 day limit; Nevada City R. D. (916) 265-4538.

Camp Notes: White Cloud is a neat, forested camp within a two-hour drive of Sacramento. The nearby community of Nevada City is a bustling center of activity for many amateur mining buffs.

SKILLMAN
Tahoe National Forest

Location: Northeast California northeast of Sacramento.

Access: From California State Highway 20 at milepost 32 +.75 (13.5 miles east of Nevada City, 14 miles west of Interstate 80 at Yuba City, 38 miles west of Truckee), turn south, then east (left), and proceed 0.2 miles (gravel) into the campground.

Facilities: Group camping for 30 to 60 campers; parking areas are gravel, medium to long straight-ins or pull-throughs; good to excellent tent spots, though some may be a bit sloped; fireplaces and fire rings; firewood is available for gathering in the area; water at several faucets; vault facilities; gravel driveways; adequate supplies and services are available in Nevada City.

Activities & Attractions: Scenic drive along Highway 20, especially near milepost 31 where there is a vast view of the South Yuba River Valley; gold panning nearby at Keleher Picnic Area, upriver from Washington; fishing on the South Yuba River and at nearby mountain lakes, including Fuller Lake.

Natural Features: Located on a slightly rolling, forested flat in the Sierra Nevada; campground vegetation consists of very tall cedars and pines, with light underbrush; elevation 4400'.

Season, Fees & Phone: May to September; $30.00-$60.00; 14 day limit; Nevada City Ranger District (916) 265-4538.

Camp Notes: The lofty evergreens which shelter the campground are sometimes referred to as "incense cedar" because of their pungent aroma. Campers who've stayed here say the May wildflowers are a wonderful site. (This former individual-site campground was changed to a group-use area; we retained the info here since it's a nice spot and may be useful to those of you with lots of friends.)

Northern California 161

INDIAN SPRINGS
Tahoe National Forest

Location: North-east California east of Truckee.

Access: From Interstate 80 at milepost 62 at the Eagle Lakes Exit (22 miles west of Truckee, 80 miles northeast of Sacramento), turn north onto Carlyle Road; proceed 0.5 mile north and west (the road parallels the Interstate); turn south (left) into the campground.

Facilities: 35 campsites, including 7 walk-in tent sites; sites are small to large, with nominal to good separation; parking pads are paved, medium to long straight-ins; many pads may require additional leveling; medium to large areas for tents; fireplaces and fire rings; b-y-o firewood is recommended; water at faucets; vault facilities; paved driveways; camper supplies in Cisco Grove, 3 miles east; adequate supplies and services are available in Truckee.

Activities & Attractions: The most obvious 'attraction' at this campground is its closeness to Interstate 80 and the railroad line; some nice scenic areas along the South Fork of the Yuba River; fishing.

Natural Features: Located in the Sierra Nevada along the rocky, sloped north bank of the South Fork of the Yuba River; moderately heavy timber in the campground area provides some shade/shelter; Eagle Lakes are accessible a few miles to the north; elevation 5600'.

Season, Fees & Phone: June to October; $9.00; 14 day limit; Nevada City R.D. (916) 265-4538.

Camp Notes: Depending upon whether your site is right under the Interstate, or a few yards away to the north, this can be a tolerable place to crash for the night. Indian Springs was probably a really neat campground before the Interstate was built and acquired such a tremendous volume of traffic.

Northern California 162

BIG BEND
Tahoe National Forest

Location: North-east California east of Truckee.

Access: From Interstate 80 (eastbound) at milepost 64 +.5 at the Big Bend Exit (82 miles east of Sacramento, 20 miles west of Truckee), turn south and east onto Hampshire Rocks Road; proceed 0.25 mile; turn north (left) onto the campground access road and go across the bridge to the campground. **Alternate Access:** From Interstate 80 (westbound) at milepost 66 +.2 at the Rainbow Road Exit (84 miles east of Sacramento, 18 miles west of Truckee), turn south and west onto Hampshire Rocks Road; proceed west for 1.5 miles; turn north and continue as above.

Facilities: 15 campsites; sites are small to average in size, with nominal to fair separation; parking pads are sand/dirt, short to medium-length straight-ins, some pads may require additional leveling; some fairly nice spots for large tents; fire rings and barbecue grills; b-y-o firewood is recommended; water at faucets; vault facilities; paved driveways; ranger station is just across the bridge; camper supplies nearby on Hampshire Rocks Road; adequate supplies and services are available in Truckee.

Activities & Attractions: Fishing; visitor information center at the ranger station; trail to high mountain lakes nearby.

Natural Features: Located in a canyon along the north bank of the South Fork of the Yuba River in the Sierra Nevada; campground vegetation consists of very tall pines with a little underbrush; the river is relatively wide and slow-moving at this point; elevation 5900'.

Season, Fees & Phone: June to October; $9.00; 14 day limit; Nevada City R. D. (916) 265-4538.

Camp Notes: This was once probably a peaceful and popular stop for the adventurers who came over Donner Pass. Imagine what this spot would have been like about 1844, when it was used as a stopover on the overland emigrant trail.

HAMPSHIRE ROCKS
Tahoe National Forest

Location: North-east California east of Truckee.

Access: From Interstate 80 at milepost 66 + .25 at the Rainbow Road Exit (16 miles west of Truckee, 86 miles east of Sacramento), turn south, then west onto Hampshire Rocks Road and proceed 100 yards; turn north (right) into the campground.

Facilities: 31 campsites in a loop and a string; sites are small to large, with fair to good separation; parking pads are sandy gravel or hard surfaced, level, short to medium-length straight-ins; some level, grassy tent spots, adequate for large tents; fireplaces; b-y-o firewood is recommended; water at several faucets; vault facilities; paved driveways; camper supplies nearby on Hampshire Rocks Road; adequate supplies and services are available in Truckee.

Activities & Attractions: Fishing; hiking access to high elevation lakes nearby; good base camp for exploration of the Sierra.

Natural Features: Located in the Sierra Nevada along the boulder-laden South Fork of the Yuba River; a considerable amount of vegetation shelters the campground area, including very tall conifers and hardwoods, abundant bushes and tall grass; several sites are riverside; the rocky canyon walls rise abruptly along this section of the river; elevation 5800'.

Season, Fees & Phone: June to October; $9.00; 14 day limit; Nevada City R.D. (916) 265-4538.

Camp Notes: There is a line of vegetation here which fairly well camouflages the super highway, so this is perhaps the best of the three Interstate-convenient campgrounds in this area. The trio of camps in this vicinity (Hampshire Rocks, Big Bend, Indian Springs) along with Mormon Island SRA in south-central Nebraska, comprise the only public campgrounds within earshot of Interstate 80 in the West.

DONNER MEMORIAL
Donner Memorial State Park

Location: Eastern California west of Reno, Nevada.

Access: From Interstate 80 near milepost 13 at the Donner Lake/Donner State Park Exit, 1 mile west of Truckee, from the south side of the freeway proceed west on Donner Pass Road (Old Highway 40) for 0.3 mile; turn south (left) into the park entrance and a "T" intersection; go west (right) to the 3 camping sections, all within 0.8 mile south and west of the entrance.

Facilities: 154 campsites in 3 loops; sites are small to medium-sized, with nominal to fair separation; parking pads are sand/gravel, short to medium-length straight-ins; some pads may require a little additional leveling; most tent spots are reasonably level and will accommodate good-sized tents; storage lockers; fireplaces and fire rings; firewood may be available for gathering on national forest land in the vicinity, or b-y-o; water at several faucets; restrooms with showers; paved driveways; adequate supplies and services are available in Truckee.

Activities & Attractions: Swimming/wading; short hiking trails; nature trail; (guide pamphlet available); campfire center for scheduled programs in summer; guided nature walks; the park's Emigrant Trail Museum has information about building the railroad through Donner Pass, and about the Donner party's winter in the Sierra, including a slide presentation; boating; public boat launch at the northwest corner of the lake; lake and stream fishing (reportedly fair) for stocked trout and kokanee salmon; large day use area.

Natural Features: Located in the Sierra Nevada along the northeast shore of Donner Lake in an open, conifer forest; tall pines, scattered underbrush and sparse grass are the predominant forms of vegetation; elevation 6000'.

Season, Fees & Phone: May to October; please see Appendix for standard California state park fees and reservation information; park office (916) 587-3841.

Camp Notes: Of all the Sierra's lakes, Donner Lake's beauty may be second only to Lake Tahoe's. Many travelers would say that, in some ways, it's the other way around.

GOOSE MEADOW
Tahoe National Forest

Location: Eastern California south of Truckee.

Access: From California State Highway 89 at milepost 17 + .6 (4 miles south of Truckee, 9 miles north of Tahoe City), turn east and proceed 100 yards to the campground.

Facilities: 25 campsites; sites are medium to large, with fair separation; parking pads are gravel/dirt, medium to long straight-ins, some are double-wide; some pads may require a little additional leveling; some nice large tent spots; barbecue grills and fire rings; firewood is available for gathering in the area; no drinking water; vault facilities; gravel driveways; adequate supplies and services are available in Truckee.

Activities & Attractions: Fishing; river floating nearby; several backroads in the area for mountain exploration; Lake Tahoe, 9 miles south, offers boating, sailing and related recreational activities.

Natural Features: Located in the Sierra Nevada along the west bank of the Truckee River in a fairly narrow segment of Truckee Canyon; campground vegetation consists of tall conifers, light underbrush and some grass; a large meadow borders the camp area on the north; elevation 5800'.

Season, Fees & Phone: July to September; $8.00; 14 day limit; Truckee Ranger Dist. (916) 587-3558.

Camp Notes: All things considered, Goose Meadow *may* be the best of the three campgrounds on this stretch of Highway 89. Granite Flat, at milepost 20 + .7, has room for about six dozen camping outfits, drinking water, vaults, a handicapped-access fishing platform, and a ten-buck fee. And then there's also Silver Creek, described below.

SILVER CREEK
Tahoe National Forest

Location: Eastern California south of Truckee.

Access: From California State Highway 89 at milepost 15 (7 miles south of Truckee, 6 miles north of Tahoe City), turn east and into the campground.

Facilities: 32 campsites in 2 loops; sites are small+, level, with minimal separation; parking pads are dirt/gravel, mostly medium-length straight-ins, plus a few longer pull-throughs; medium to large areas for tents; fire rings and barbecue grills; some firewood is available for gathering in the general vicinity, b-y-o to be sure; water at a hand pump; vault facilities; paved driveway; adequate supplies and services are available in Truckee.

Activities & Attractions: Fishing; river floating downstream of here; Deer Creek Trailhead.

Natural Features: Located in a canyon on a large, moderately timbered flat at the confluence of the Truckee River and Silver Creek in the Sierra Nevada; sites are moderately shaded by tall conifers; the canyon is bordered by forested hills; elevation 5900'.

Season, Fees & Phone: May to October; $8.00; 14 day limit; Truckee Ranger Dist. (916) 587-3558.

Camp Notes: Good river access here.

TAHOE
Tahoe State Recreation Area

Location: Eastern California on the west shore of Lake Tahoe.

Access: From California State Highway 28 at milepost 0 + .7 on the northeast edge of Tahoe City (0.7 mile northeast of the junction of Highway 28 & State Highway 89, 10 miles southwest of the California-Nevada border), turn southeast into the park entrance and the campground.

Facilities: 39 campsites; sites are generally small, with nominal separation; most parking pads are gravel, short straight-ins; some pads may require a bit additional leveling; most tent spots are grassy and roomy enough for large tents; storage cabinets; fire rings and barbecue grills; b-y-o firewood; water at several faucets; restrooms with showers; paved driveways; limited+ supplies and services are available in Tahoe City.

Activities & Attractions: Boating; sailing; (boat ramp at Lake Forest, 2 miles east); fishing; fishing pier; floating on the Truckee River, nearby.

Natural Features: Located on a short bluff above the west shore of Lake Tahoe in the Sierra Nevada; sites receive light to light-medium shade/shelter from short to very tall conifers and light underbrush on a surface of sparse grass; elevation 6300'.

Season, Fees & Phone: May to September; please see Appendix for standard California state park fees and reservation information; park office (916) 583-3074 or (916) 525-7982.

Camp Notes: The setting for this park--on a grassy, tree-dotted bluff overlooking a beautiful mountain lake--is ideal. Most of the sites, however, are within a few yards of a very busy highway. Lake access is limited because of a residential strip between the park and the lake shore. But there are some views of the lake through the trees. Lake Tahoe's deepest hole, sounded at 1645 feet, is six miles east-southeast of this park, in the north third of the lake. The lake's other stats: 12 miles wide, 22 miles long, 19.6 square miles/122,600 acres in area, with 72 miles of shoreline.

Northern California 168

WILLIAM KENT
Lake Tahoe Basin Management Unit

Location: Eastern California on the west shore of Lake Tahoe.

Access: From California State Highway 89 at milepost 6 +.3 (6.3 miles north of the El Dorado-Placer county line, 2.2 miles south of Tahoe City, 16 miles south of Truckee), turn west into the campground.

Facilities: 95 campsites in a complex loop; sites are small to medium-sized, with nominal separation; parking pads are paved, short to medium-length straight-ins; some pads may require additional leveling; most sites have good tent spots for medium-sized tents, but many are a bit sloped; fireplaces; b-y-o firewood is recommended; water at several faucets; restrooms; paved driveways; limited+ supplies and services are available in Tahoe City.

Activities & Attractions: Beach (a few yards east); swimming; boating; (boat launch at Meeks Bay); fishing; great scenic drive along Lake Tahoe's shore.

Natural Features: Located in the Sierra Nevada just across the highway from the west shore of Lake Tahoe; campground vegetation consists mainly of tall conifers, very little underbrush, and a small, open, interior grassy area; the property along the perimeter of the camping area is entirely privately owned; elevation 6300'.

Season, Fees & Phone: May to October; $12.00; 7 day limit; Lake Tahoe Basin Management Unit, South Lake Tahoe, (916) 573-2600 or (916) 544-5994.

Camp Notes: The west shore of Lake Tahoe is a highly developed area with numereous resorts, commercial establishments and summer homes. The campgrounds along the shore of the lake are commonly filled early in the day during most of the summer. Kaspian Campground, 2 miles south and managed by the same agency, offers sites principally for hikers/bikers.

Northern California 169

GENERAL CREEK
Sugar Pine Point State Park

Location: Eastern California on the west shore of Lake Tahoe.

Access: From California State Highway 89 near milepost 26 (1 mile south of the El Dorado/Placer County line, 2 miles south of Tahoma, 18 miles north of South Lake Tahoe), turn east to the day use area and the visitor center; or near milepost 26 +.5, turn west onto the campground access road and proceed 0.1 mile to the entrance station, then continue for 0.2 mile to the camping area.

Facilities: 175 campsites in 4 loops; (group camps are also available, by reservation); sites are small to medium-sized, essentially level, with nominal to fairly good separation; many units are situated in clusters; parking pads are hard-surfaced, short to medium+ straight-ins; tent spots vary from small to large; assorted fire appliances; firewood is usually for sale, or b-y-o; storage cabinets; water at several faucets; restrooms with showers; (showers available in summer only); holding tank disposal station; paved driveways; groceries in Tahoma; adequate+ supplies and services are available in South Lake Tahoe.

Activities & Attractions: Fishing; fishing pier; day use area has a half-mile-long sandy beach; hiking trails; nature trail; amphitheater; visitor center; early settler's cabin.

Natural Features: Located in the Sierra Nevada, along and above the west shore of Lake Tahoe, where General Creek flows into the lake; vegetation consists of tall conifers, a small amount of underbrush, and some new growth timber; elevation 6300'.

Season, Fees & Phone: Open all year, with limited services September to May; please see Appendix for standard California state park fees and reservation information; park office (916) 525-7982.

Camp Notes: General Creek is named for "General" William Phipps, a Kentuckian who was one of the first permanent residents of the area. Phipps filed a homestead claim on the Point in 1860, and his second cabin is still standing near the lakeshore. Sugar Pine Point is the only state park on Lake Tahoe with winter camping. Winter campers can expect to find deep snow pack, frequent snow storms, and nighttime lows near zero. However, it should also be noted that seeing Lake Tahoe and its snow-cloaked mountains in the crisp, clear, cold air following a frontal passage is one of the outdoors' most memorable occasions.

MEEKS BAY
Lake Tahoe Basin Management Unit

Location: Eastern California on the west shore of Lake Tahoe.

Access: From California State Highway 89 at milepost 24 +.8 (16 miles north of the South Lake Tahoe area, 2.4 miles south of the El Dorado-Placer County line), turn east into the campground.

Facilities: 40 campsites in 4 loops; sites are small to average-sized, with little to fair separation; parking pads are paved, level, short to medium-length straight-ins; tent spots are quite level and large enough to accommodate good-sized tents; fire rings and barbecue grills; b-y-o firewood is recommended; water at several faucets; restrooms; paved driveways; camper supplies nearby; adequate+ supplies and services are available in the South Lake Tahoe area.

Activities & Attractions: Boating; sailing; fishing; swimming; (Meeks Bay Beach and boat ramp are a few yards beyond the camping area).

Natural Features: Located in the Sierra Nevada on Meeks Bay along the west shore of Lake Tahoe; campground vegetation consists of sparse grass and underbrush, and some tall conifers; limited views through the trees of the lake; elevation 6300'.

Season, Fees & Phone: May to October; $12.00; 7 day limit; Lake Tahoe Basin Management Unit, South Lake Tahoe, (916) 573-2600 or (916) 544-5994.

Camp Notes: Meeks Bay has one of the few public boat launches along the west shore of Lake Tahoe. All campsites at Meeks Bay are quite close to the highway. The Lake Tahoe Basin Management Unit operates several public campgrounds in the area. It's a special division of the Forest Service that manages public lands on three national forests around Lake Tahoe. The sub-agency was set up to provide a unified approach to management of Tahoe's exceptionally important natural resources.

D.L. BLISS
D.L. Bliss State Park

Location: Eastern California on the west shore of Lake Tahoe.

Access: From California State Highway 89 at milepost 19 +.5 (7 miles south of the El Dorado/Placer county line, 11 miles north of the South Lake Tahoe area), turn northeast onto the park access road; proceed 1 mile down a curvy, narrow roadway to the park entrance station; campsites are in 3 sections within 1.3 miles of the entrance station. (Note: there is limited maneuvering room in the park; only very short trailers are welcome.)

Facilities: 168 campsites in 3 sections; (a group camp is also available, by reservation); most sites are small, quite sloped, with fair to good separation; parking areas are mostly dirt, short to short+ straight-ins; many pads will require additional leveling; fairly good sized, sloped tent spots; storage cabinets; assorted fire appliances; b-y-o firewood; water at several faucets; restrooms with showers; paved driveways; adequate+ supplies and services are available in South Lake Tahoe.

Activities & Attractions: Swimming beach in the day use area; hiking trails, including the Lighthouse Trail to an old lighthouse and a trail to nearby Emerald Bay State Park; Balancing Rock Nature Trail; campfire center; day use area.

Natural Features: Located above the west shore of Lake Tahoe just north of Emerald Bay; campsites are all situated on a forested slope; vegetation consists of light to medium-dense, tall conifers, including gnarled and stunted sugar pines, and a considerable amount of undergrowth; some campsites are near the lake shore; elevation 6400'.

Season, Fees & Phone: May to September; please see Appendix for standard California state park fees and reservation information; park office (916) 525-7277.

Camp Notes: D.L. Bliss has what is considered to be one of the two best beaches on the lake. The area is named for a lumberman whose family donated the original tract for the park. This may be one of the very few state parks in the Lake Tahoe area where a campsite might be available late in the day during the week without a reservation.

EAGLE POINT
Emerald Bay State Park

Location: Eastern California on the west shore of Lake Tahoe.

Access: From California State Highway 89 at milepost 15 +.3 (7 miles northwest of the South Lake Tahoe area, 12 miles south of the El Dorado/Placer county line), turn northeast into the park; proceed 0.1 mile to the entrance station; continue ahead for 0.4 mile to the upper camp area or another 0.8 mile to the lower camp area.

Facilities: 100 campsites; (20 primitive, walk-in or boat-in campsites on the middle north-west shore of the bay are also available); sites are small to small+, with minimal to nominal separation; parking pads are mostly short straight-ins, and many will require additional leveling; some pads are hard-surfaced, others are gravel/sand; tent spots are small to medium-sized and may be a bit sloped or rocky; storage cabinets; fire rings and barbecue grills; b-y-o firewood is recommended; water at several faucets; restrooms with showers; paved driveways; gas and groceries on Highway 89, 4 miles south; adequate+ supplies and services are available in the South Lake Tahoe area.

Activities & Attractions: Trail to the beach from the lower camp loop; boating; sailing; dock and mooring buoys at the boat-in camp; (public boat launch in Camp Richardson, 5 miles southeast); shoreline fishing for small trout; boat fishing for Mackinaw trout and kokanee salmon; campfire center; guided tours of Vikingsholm, a 38-room castle built in 1929; Rubicon Trail leads 3.5 miles from near Vikingsholm to D.L. Bliss State Park.

Natural Features: Located around Emerald Bay on the southwest shore of Lake Tahoe; upper campsites are on a forested slope; lower sites are situated out on tree-dotted Eagle Point; vegetation includes tall conifers, moderate underbrush and sparse grass; Lake Tahoe's only isle, Fannette Island, lies near the southwest tip of the bay; elevation 6400'.

Season, Fees & Phone: June to September; please see Appendix for standard California state park fees and reservation information; park office (916) 541-3030.

Camp Notes: Emerald Bay is shaped like an elongated 'U' with a narrow harbor entrance. The half-mile wide, 1.5-mile long bay is one of the most sheltered spots on the lake. This part of Lake Tahoe's shoreline is indeed naturally beautiful. That was recognized when it was designated a National Natural Landmark. The Indians called Tahoe "Lake of the Sky", and someone has yet to improve on that title.

EL DORADO
South Lake Tahoe City Park

Location: Eastern California on the south shore of Lake Tahoe.

Access: From the intersection of U.S. Highway 50 & Rufus Allen Boulevard in midtown South Lake Tahoe, (2 miles west of the California-Nevada border), turn south onto Rufus Allen Boulevard; proceed 0.1 mile, then turn west (right) into the campground.

Facilities: 170 campsites in 7 loops; most sites are small, with very little separation; parking pads are sandy, level, short to medium+ straight-ins; tent spots are level and will accommodate large tents easily; barbecue grills; b-y-o firewood is recommended; water at several faucets; restrooms with showers; holding tank disposal station; paved driveways; adequate+ supplies and services are available within a few blocks.

Activities & Attractions: Boating; boat launch across the highway from the park; sailing; fishing; swimming on a lakeside swimming beach, and also a city-operated pool in the adjacent recreation complex; playground; bike trail.

Natural Features: Located on a forested flat across the highway from El Dorado Beach on the south shore of Lake Tahoe; tall conifers, plus sparse grass and underbrush, are the predominant vegetation in the campground; adjacent is a large lawn area; elevation 6300'.

Season, Fees & Phone: May to September; $17.00; 15 day limit; reservations available, contact the City Parks Office (916) 573-2059.

Camp Notes: This would be a convenient place to park for an urban stay. The facility offers the necessary amenities and is conveniently close to the beach and to beautiful Lake Tahoe. (The Nevada casinos are also close at hand. Ed.)

SLY PARK
Eldorado Irrigation District County Park

Location: East-central California east of Sacramento.

Access: From U.S. Highway 50 at milepost 31 +.3 (13 miles east of Placerville, 50 miles southwest of South Lake Tahoe), turn south onto Sly Park Road (Road E16); proceed 0.3 mile to a fork in the road; bear left and continue for 3.8 miles (the road is steep and curvy, but paved); turn east (left) to the park entrance station and the campground.

Facilities: 155 campsites in 8 loops; sites are small to medium-sized, with nominal to fair separation; parking pads are gravel/dirt, short to long, mostly straight-ins, plus a few pull-throughs; many pads will require additional leveling; medium to large areas for tents, though many tent spots are sloped; fire rings and barbecue grills; firewood is usually available for gathering early in the season, b-y-o to be sure; water at several faucets; vault facilities; paved/gravel driveways; camper supplies at a small store near the entrance; adequate supplies and services are available in Placerville.

Activities & Attractions: Boating; fishing; boat ramp nearby (extra charge); swimming; day use area; hiking trails, including Hilltop Lake Trail and Southshore Trail; Miwok Nature Trail; equestrian trails along the south shore.

Natural Features: Located on a bluff above Jenkinson Lake in the foothills of the Sierra Nevada; most camp loops are sheltered by tall pines, cedars, sequoias, and a little underbrush; easternmost sites are more forested; forested peaks are visible across the lake to the south; elevation 3500'.

Season, Fees & Phone: Open all year (weather permitting); $10.00; 14 day limit; (916) 644-2545.

Camp Notes: The level of the lake fluctuates considerably from season to season. Camping and other types of recreation are at their best in spring and early summer.

CHINA FLAT
Eldorado National Forest

Location: East-central California east of Sacramento.

Access: From U.S. Highway 50 at milepost 49 in the community of Kyburz (31 miles east of Placerville, 32 miles southwest of South Lake Tahoe), turn south onto Silver Fork Road; proceed south and east and up this curvy, paved road for 2.4 miles; turn west (right) into the campground.

Facilities: 23 campsites, including 6 walk-in sites, in 2 sections; (several small-group sites are also available); sites are small to large, with little to fair separation; some parking pads are paved, long and very level; other pads are earth/gravel, short and sloped; all pads are straight-ins; tent spots vary from small to fairly spacious; walk-in sites are situated on a grassy bluff and are reached by a footbridge across the Silver Fork; fire rings and barbecue grills; firewood is available for gathering in the area; water at several faucets; vault facilities; hard surfaced or gravel driveway sections; complete supplies and services are available in Placerville and South Lake Tahoe.

Activities & Attractions: Stream fishing; day use area; superscenic drive to the campground; a cross-country road leads southeast from here toward Silver Fork Campground and California State Highway 88.

Natural Features: Located on the west slope of the Sierra Nevada along both banks of the Silver Fork of the American River; the campground is situated in an open forest setting with tall timber towering over many of the sites; elevation 4800'.

Season, Fees & Phone: May to September; $8.00; 14 day limit; Placerville Ranger District (916) 644-2324.

Camp Notes: The parking at China Flat for walk-ins and day trippers is rather tight. Overall, though, China Flat is a somewhat more secluded (and peaceful) campground than the more easily accessible Sand Flat, located nearby, along U.S. 50, 2 miles west of Kyburz. San Flat Has 29 sites and a fee that matches China Flat's.

INDIAN GRINDING ROCK
Indian Grinding Rock State Historic Park

Location: East-central California east of Sacramento.

Access: From California State Highway 88 at milepost 23 + .4 (in the small community of Pine Grove, 9 miles east of Jackson, 3.4 miles west of the junction of State Highways 88 & 26), turn north onto Pine Grove-Volcano Road (paved); proceed 1.3 miles northeast, then turn west (left) into the park; continue for 0.1 mile, and turn north (right) into the campground.

Facilities: 21 campsites; (environmental-primitive sites with shelters are also available); sites are small to medium-sized, with generally good separation; parking pads are gravel, medium-length, mostly straight-ins, plus a few pull-throughs; some additional leveling may be necessary in many sites; good, private tent spots, adequate for medium to large tents; fire rings, plus a few barbecue grills; b-y-o firewood; storage cabinets; water at several faucets; restrooms; paved driveway; gas and groceries in Pine Grove; limited supplies and services are available in Jackson.

Activities & Attractions: Reconstructed Indian village with petroglyphs, displays and exhibits; interpretive programs; nature trail; museum with exhibits and Indian crafts demonstrations.

Natural Features: Located on a forested slope in the western foothills of the Sierra Nevada; tall conifers, oaks, and a considerable amount of underbrush provide ample shelter and also separate most of the campsites nicely; the park has some open meadows as well; elevation 2400'.

Season, Fees & Phone: Open all year; please see Appendix for standard California state park fees and reservation information; park office (209) 296-7488.

Camp Notes: The principal 'grinding rock' is a massive limestone table measuring about 25 yards by 60 yards. The slab is punctuated with nearly 1200 small holes, so-called "mortar cups", which were worn into the soft stone by enthusiastic Miwok Indians grinding acorns and other seeds to make hot cereal or cake flour. The rock also is randomly marked with more than 350 petroglyphs. Within the reconstructed village are small, bark teepees used as family residences and a *hun'ge* or roundhouse, a domed, multi-sided, wooden structure used as a community center.

SOUTH SHORE
Eldorado National Forest

Location: East-central California east of Sacramento.

Access: From California State Highway 88 at milepost 51 + .6 (38 miles east of Jackson, 15 miles west of Kit Carson), turn south onto a steep, winding, paved access road; proceed 2 miles to a fork; take the right fork and continue for 1.3 miles (over the causeway); turn right into the campground.

Facilities: 22 campsites, including a few double-occupancy units, in a loop and a string; most sites are medium-sized, with fair to fairly good separation; parking pads are gravel/dirt, mostly medium-length straight-ins; a few pads are pull-offs or double-sized straight-ins; many pads may require additional leveling; fairly good-sized tent spots on bare earth with a bit of worn grass; fireplaces, plus a few barbecue grills; a limited amount of firewood is available for gathering, b-y-o is suggested; water at several faucets; vault facilities; narrow, paved/gravel driveway; camper supplies at a resort on the north shore of the lake; limited supplies and services are available in Jackson.

Activities & Attractions: Access to the lake is across the roadway; boating; small public boat launch 1 mile west; fishing.

Natural Features: Located in the Sierra Nevada on a steepish hillside above the boulder-strewn south shore of Lower Bear River Reservoir; tall conifers and light underbrush are the predominant vegetation in the campground; some views through the trees of the lake; elevation 5900'.

Season, Fees & Phone: May to September; $9.00; Amador Ranger District, Pioneer, (209) 295-4251.

Camp Notes: Though there is limited access to the lake itself, the campground and other recreational facilities are popular and well-used. The lake, though not 'natural', is picturesque and in a lovely setting.

SILVER LAKE
Eldorado National Forest

Location: East-central California east of Sacramento.

Access: From California State Highway 88 at milepost 66 +.6 (52 miles east of Jackson, 19 miles west of Pickett's Junction), turn southeast into the East (main) section of the campground, or northwest into the West section.

Facilities: 92 campsites in basically 2 sections; sites vary in size from small to medium, with fair to very good separation; most parking pads are gravel, short to medium-length straight-ins; many pads may require additional leveling; most tent spots are medium-sized and rather sloped; fireplaces or fire rings; limited firewood is available for gathering in the area; water at several faucets; vault facilities; narrow, mostly paved, driveways; camper supplies at a small store at Kit Carson (a resort area on Silver Lake); limited supplies and services are available in Jackson, 53 miles west.

Activities & Attractions: Boating and fishing on Silver Lake; a number of 4wd trails and foot trails nearby, including Silver Lake Trail; great scenery along the very steep and curvy Highway 88.

Natural Features: Located in the Sierra Nevada near Silver Lake's north shore; campsites are sheltered/shaded by very tall conifers and very little underbrush; a number of sites have huge boulders for separation; some sites are near Oyster Lake (a small pond), or Oyster Creek; elevation 7200'.

Season, Fees & Phone: May to September; $9.00; 14 day limit; Amador Ranger District, Pioneer, (209) 295-4251.

Camp Notes: None of the sites at Silver Lake are situated lakeside, or have a lake view. Sites at Silver Lake West, north of the highway, are perhaps a bit less worn and a little better separated than those at Silver Lake East.

KIRKWOOD LAKE
Eldorado National Forest

Location: East-central California east of Sacramento.

Access: From California State Highway 88 at milepost 70 +.65 (57 miles east of Jackson, 7 miles west of Carson Pass, 14 miles west of Pickett's Junction on California State Highway 89), turn north onto a one-lane, paved, twisty access road (trailers are not recommended); proceed 0.5 mile to the campground.

Facilities: 12 campsites; sites are small, with nominal to fair separation; parking pads are gravel, short straight-ins, and most are tolerably level; spots for tents are typically small and rocky; fire rings and/or barbecue grills; a limited quantity of firewood is available for gathering in the area; water at several faucets; vault facilities; narrow, gravel driveway; camper supplies at a resort near milepost 71 +.3 on Highway 88; limited supplies and services are available in Jackson.

Activities & Attractions: Fishing; motorless boating; swimming; nearby Caples Lake (off Highway 88 at milepost 71 +.4) has a boat ramp.

Natural Features: Located in the Sierra Nevada on the west shore of tiny, but beautiful, Kirkwood Lake; campground vegetation consists of a few medium height conifers and some underbrush; large boulders separate many of the sites, and the lake itself is boulder-dotted; elevation 7600'.

Season, Fees & Phone: June to September; $8.00; 14 day limit; Amador Ranger District, Pioneer, (209) 295-4251.

Camp Notes: Though the campsites and parking spaces at Kirkwood are very small, the campground and lake areas are superscenic. Partly because there are a number of vacation homes in the area, Kirkwood Lake tends to be rather congested on summer weekends.

CAPLES LAKE
Eldorado National Forest

Location: East-central California east of Sacramento.

95

Access: From California State Highway 88 at milepost 1 +.1 (in Alpine County) (60 miles east of Jackson, 5 miles west of Carson Pass, 12 miles west of Pickett's Junction), turn north into the campground.

Facilities: 39 campsites in 2 loops and a connecting string; sites are small to medium-sized, with average separation; parking pads are paved, mostly medium-length straight-ins; some additional leveling may be required; some fairly good-sized tent spots, but many are rather small and rocky; fireplaces or fire rings; firewood is usually for sale, or b-y-o; water at several faucets; vault facilities; paved driveways; camper supplies at a small resort nearby; limited supplies and services are available in Jackson.

Activities & Attractions: Boating, boat launch and fishing on Caples Lake; hiking trails in the vicinity; the drive along Highway 88 offers some super scenery.

Natural Features: Located high in the Sierra Nevada across the highway from the north shore of Caples Lake; short to medium-height conifers and moderate underbrush are interspersed with large boulders in the campground area; a steep rock ridge borders the camping area on both sides; a small creek flows near a few of the sites; elevation 7800'.

Season, Fees & Phone: May to September; $9.00; 14 day limit; Amador Ranger District, Pioneer, (209) 295-4251.

Camp Notes: Caples Lake is a beautiful mountain lake in a sub-alpine setting just below the tree line. There is lake access within a short walk of any of the campsites. Unfortunately, some of these sites are rather close to the highway. But let's look at the bright side. A few of the roadside sites also have lake views through the trees.

WOODS LAKE
Eldorado National Forest

Location: East-central California east of Sacramento.

Access: From California State Highway 88 at milepost 3.3 (in Alpine County, 62 miles east of Jackson, 2.7 miles west of Carson Pass), turn southeast onto a paved access road; proceed 0.8 mile to a fork in the road; take the right fork and continue south for 0.4 mile to the campground.

Facilities: 35 campsites; sites are small, with nominal to fair separation; parking pads are paved, short to medium-length straight-ins; some pads are double-wide; many pads will require considerable additional leveling; many tent spots are yards from their parking pads, and are also somewhat rocky; fire rings and barbecue grills; firewood is usually available for gathering in the area; water at several faucets; vault facilities; paved driveway; camper supplies at a small store, 3 miles west; limited supplies and services are available in Jackson.

Activities & Attractions: Hiking; Lost Cabin Mine Trail; access to the Pacific Crest Trail; trailhead for Mokelumne Wilderness; fishing; motorless boating.

Natural Features: Located high in the Sierra Nevada just a few yards north of Woods Lake; campground vegetation consists of fairly tall conifers and light underbrush; sites are located around a rocky hill; large boulders provide separation for some sites; several small ponds are in the campground area; a small creek flows near some sites and northwest into Caples Lake; elevation 8200'.

Season, Fees & Phone: June to September; $8.00; 14 day limit; Amador Ranger District, Pioneer, (209) 295-4251.

Camp Notes: Many campers have discovered that this region of the Sierra is beautiful and easily accessible. You may prefer a visit toward the beginning or end of the season, when there's less traffic. The Woods Lake vicinity is often populated with campers who are taking advantage of a 'dispersed camping' invitation.

KIT CARSON
Toiyabe National Forest

Location: Eastern California east of Sacramento and southwest of Carson City, Nevada.

Access: From California State Highway 88 at milepost 14 +.8 (9 miles east of Carson Pass, 1.3 miles east of Picketts Junction, 6.7 miles west of Woodfords), turn north onto a paved access road; proceed 0.1 mile up to the campground.

Facilities: 12 campsites in 2 loops; sites are medium-sized and fairly well separated; parking pads are paved, short to medium-length straight-ins, and many will require additional leveling; tent spaces are better for small to medium-sized tents; fireplaces; firewood is available for gathering in the area; vault facilities; paved driveways; camper supplies at a small store nearby on Highway 88; adequate supplies and services are available in South Lake Tahoe, 20 (steep) miles north.

Activities & Attractions: Stream fishing; superscenic drive along Highways 88 and 89, including some especially vast views from the summit of Carson Pass, 9 miles west of here; the extremely popular and attractive Lake Tahoe recreation area is about 20 miles north.

Natural Features: Located on tilted terrain on the east slope of the Sierra Nevada slightly above the West Fork of the Carson River; campground vegetation consists of fairly dense stands of conifers and aspens, and moderate underbrush; elevation 6700'.

Season, Fees & Phone: June to October; $7.00; 14 day limit; Carson Ranger District, Carson City NV, (702) 882-2766 (office) or (702) 882-9211 (recorded information).

Camp Notes: Kit Carson is quite a pleasant campground just a short drive from the Lake Tahoe area. The creek can be heard from most sites. Other small campgrounds along the piece of highway between Picketts Junction and Woodfords are Snowshoe Springs at mp 15 +.4 and Crystal Springs at mp 18 +.4.

INDIAN CREEK
Public Lands/BLM Recreation Site

Location: Eastern California south of Carson City, Nevada.

Access: From California State Highways 89/4 at milepost 17 +.5 (2.7 miles north of Markleeville, 3.8 miles south of Woodfords), turn east onto Airport Road; proceed east and north for 3.6 miles on a winding, paved road to the campground.

Facilities: 38 campsites in 2 loops; sites are average or better in size, with fairly good separation; parking pads are paved, mostly straight-ins, and some are spacious enough to accommodate very long rv's; many pads may require additional leveling; a number of sites have large, framed-and-gravelled tent pads; barbecue grills and/or fire rings; firewood is available for gathering in the area; water at several faucets; restrooms; holding tank disposal station; paved driveways; gas and groceries+ in Markleeville; complete supplies and services are available in Carson City, 30 miles north.

Activities & Attractions: Boating; fishing; hiking, including trails to Summit Lake and Curtz Lake; Alpine County Airport is just east of the reservoir so 'fly-in camping' is popular here.

Natural Features: Located in a basin surrounded by sage hills and tall mountain peaks, near 160-acre Indian Creek Reservoir; tall conifers, sagebrush and sparse underbrush in the campground; elev. 6000'.

Season, Fees & Phone: May to October; $8.00; 14 day limit; Bureau of Land Management Office, Carson City NV, (702) 882-1631.

Camp Notes: The slopes of the surrounding basin are rather treeless, but the campground itself is nicely forested. Campsites designated for tents are closer to the lake than those in the trailer loop. Some sites have lake views through the trees.

TURTLE ROCK
Alpine County Park

Location: Eastern California south of Carson City, Nevada.

Access: From California State Highways 89/4 at milepost 17 +.3 (2.5 miles north of Markleeville, 4 miles south of Woodfords), turn west onto a paved access road and proceed 0.4 mile to the campground.

Facilities: 29 campsites; sites are mostly medium-sized, with fair separation; parking pads are paved, short to long straight-ins, and some are double-wide; many pads may require additional leveling; level, grassy tent spots will accommodate medium to large tents; barbecue grills and fire rings; some firewood could be gathered in the outlying area, but b-y-o is recommended; water at faucets throughout; restrooms; paved driveways; gas and groceries+ are available in Markleeville.

Activities & Attractions: Stream fishing; Grover Hot Springs State Park is 6 miles to the west; Indian Creek Reservoir is 5 miles to the east.

Natural Features: Located in a valley east of the Sierra Nevada along Millberry Creek, which flows south into the East Fork of the Carson River; sites are situated in an open forest with tall conifers and some underbrush on a pine needle forest floor; a meadow borders the campground perimeter; elevation 5900'.

Season, Fees & Phone: May to September; $7.00; Alpine County Public Works Dept. (916) 694-2225.

Camp Notes: Turtle Rock Campground is located in a lovely section of a valley just east of some of the most beautiful mountains in California. However, you may witness some burn scars in other parts of the valley, especially if you approach from the north.

GROVER HOT SPRINGS
Grover Hot Springs State Park

Location: Eastern California south of Carson City, Nevada.

Access: From California State Highways 89 & 4 at milepost 14 +.8 in midtown Markleeville, turn west onto Montgomery Street which becomes Hot Springs Road; proceed 3.5 miles; turn north (right) to the park entrance station; continue for 0.2 mile to the "Quaking Aspen" camp loop or another 0.2 mile to the "Toiyabe" camp section.

Facilities: 76 campsites in 2 sections; sites are medium to medium+, with minimal to fair separation; parking pads are paved, short to medium-length, most are straight-ins, many pads may require additional leveling; tent spots are on grass or pine needle surfaces, some are sloped, many are spacious enough for large tents; storage lockers; fireplaces; firewood is usually for sale, or b-y-o; water at several faucets; restrooms with showers; paved driveways; gas and groceries+ are available in Markleeville.

Activities & Attractions: Hot springs pools; nature trail; 3 hiking trails; stream fishing for small trout (stocked periodically as stream conditions permit); amphitheater for scheduled programs in summer; Nordic skiing; day use area.

Natural Features: Located in a valley on the east side of the Sierra Nevada, with mountains rising sharply on 3 sides; grassy slopes and meadows are interspersed with stands of aspens and conifers; elevation 5800'.

Season, Fees & Phone: Standard campground is open May to October; camping is available in the picnic area, with limited services, during the winter; please see Appendix for standard California state park fees and reservation information; extra fee for pool use; park office (916) 694-2248.

Camp Notes: Grover's mineral-rich waters leave the ground at 148°, but the temps in the water of the park's two pools run 102° to 105°. Unlike the water of most hot springs, the sulphur content of the water here is quite low. Many people believe that these waters, which percolate up from thousands of feet below the surface, are good for just about whatever ails you. You don't have to come here to use the pools, though. The alpine scenery is worth camping here.

NORTH GROVE
Calaveras Big Trees State Park

Location: East-central California northeast of Stockton.

Access: From California State Highway 4 at milepost 44 +.4 (23 miles east of Angels Camp, 27 miles southwest of Lake Alpine), turn south for 0.1 mile to the park entrance station; just past the entrance, turn right into the campground.

Facilities: 74 campsites; (a group camp area is also available nearby, by reservation); sites are small to medium-sized, with minimal to fair separation; parking pads are reasonably level, dirt/gravel straight-ins, plus a few pull-throughs; medium to large tent areas; some designated tent sites; fireplaces; firewood is usually for sale, or b-y-o; water at several faucets; restrooms with showers; paved driveways; holding tank disposal station; adequate supplies and services are available in Arnold, 3 miles west.

Activities & Attractions: Self-guided nature trail through North Grove; special Three Senses Trail; several other, longer hiking trails through the park (a detailed brochure/map with contour lines is available); visitor center; rustic community building; campfire circle; several day use areas in the park.

Natural Features: Located in and around a large meadow surrounded by very tall conifers on the west slope of the Sierra Nevada; North Grove, adjacent to the campground, holds about 150 giant sequoias; elevation 4700'.

Season, Fees & Phone: Open all year, subject to brief closures during periods of heavy snow, with limited services October to May; please see Appendix for standard California state park fees and reservation information; park office (209) 795-2334.

Camp Notes: When these forest giants were first glimpsed by early settlers, the discovery set off a global rush to see the "Big Trees of Calaveras County". It also touched off a rash of commercial ventures which exploited the trees in standard nineteenth century fashion. North Grove, right along the main highway, contains the most heavily promoted of the Calaveras trees. Suddenly encountering these lofty leviathans while merely driving past the park is startling. *Sequoiadendron giganteum* is the largest (though not quite the tallest) of the three species of redwoods left on the planet.

OAK HOLLOW
Calaveras Big Trees State Park

Location: East-central California northeast of Stockton.

Access: From California State Highway 4 at milepost 44 +.4 (23 miles east of Angels Camp, 27 miles southwest of Lake Alpine), turn south for 0.1 mile to the park entrance station; continue on the main park road for 3.8 miles to the campground turnoff, then another 0.5 mile to the campground.

Facilities: 55 campsites; (3 environmental camp areas are located within several miles north and south of Oak Hollow); sites are small to medium-sized, with minimal to fair separation; parking pads are dirt/gravel, mostly short straight-ins, plus some extra-wide straight-ins and a few medium-length pull-offs; medium to large tent areas; fireplaces; firewood is usually for sale, or b-y-o; water at several faucets; restrooms with showers; paved driveways; holding tank disposal station at North Grove; adequate supplies and services are available in Arnold, 3 miles west of the park entrance.

Activities & Attractions: Loop trail through a section of South Grove; several other, longer hiking trails through the park visitor center; campfire circle; trout fishing on the Stanislaus River; several day use areas.

Natural Features: Located on hilly terrain in a stand of oaks within a conifer forest on the west slope of the Sierra Nevada; South Grove Natural Preserve protects a primeval sequoia forest; the North Fork of the Stanislaus River flows through the center of the park; elevation 4400'.

Season, Fees & Phone: May to October; please see Appendix for standard California state park fees and reservation information; park office (209) 795-2334.

Camp Notes: South Grove, accessible only on foot, lies on the secluded slopes along Beaver Creek at the far southeast corner of the park. It can be reached relatively easily via a one-mile foot trail from the trailhead several miles south of Oak Hollow.

BIG MEADOW
Stanislaus National Forest

Location: East-central California northeast of Stockton.

Access: From California State Highway 4 at milepost 61 +.5 (8 miles west of Lake Alpine, 44 miles southwest of the junction of State Highways 4 & 89 south of Markleeville, 40 miles east of Angels Camp), turn south into the campground.

Facilities: 69 campsites; (an adjacent group campground is also available); sites are medium to medium+, with fair to very good separation; overall, sites are quite level, although one section is somewhat sloped; parking pads are gravel or hard surfaced, medium-length straight-ins; adequate space for a large tent in most sites; fireplaces or fire rings; firewood is available for gathering in the area; water at several faucets; vault facilities; paved driveways; gas and camper supplies are available in the Bear Valley and Lake Alpine areas several miles east.

Activities & Attractions: Views of Hells Kitchen and the valley.

Natural Features: Located on a forested flat, on the edge of a rocky, timber-topped canyon named Hells Kitchen, in the Sierra Nevada; campground vegetation consists mostly of short grass and short to medium-height conifers; the North Fork of the Stanislaus River flows through the valley about a mile south; elevation 6500'.

Season, Fees & Phone: May to October; $7.00; 14 day limit; Calaveras Ranger District, Hathaway Pines, (209) 795-1381.

Camp Notes: This is the first of a number of national forest campgrounds as you travel east on Highway 4. (The majority of visitors approach this area from the west.) The next campground is Silvertip, 7 miles east, on the south side of the highway. Silvertip also has a forested environment, 24 sites, drinking water, restrooms, and a fee that surpasses Big Meadow's by several bucks. It's near the popular Lake Alpine area. Silvertip has some valley views, but the panoramas available from in and around Big Meadow are somewhat more impressive.

LAKE ALPINE
Stanislaus National Forest

Location: Eastern California northeast of Stockton and south of Lake Tahoe.

Access: From California State Highway 4 at the east end of Lake Alpine near milepost 4 (4 miles east of the Alpine-Calaveras county line, 49 miles northeast of Angels Camp, 28 miles southwest of the junction of State Highways 4 & 89 south of Markleeville), turn south and continue a short 0.1 mile to the campground.

Facilities: 25 campsites; sites are small to medium in size, with nominal separation; parking pads are paved, mostly level, short to medium-length straight-ins; medium to large, level tent spots; fireplaces; firewood is available for gathering in the vicinity; water at several faucets; restrooms; paved driveways; gas, general store, laundromat and showers at a lodge, 0.2 mile east.

Activities & Attractions: Fishing; boating; boat launch nearby.

Natural Features: Located on the gently sloping west shore of Lake Alpine in Bear Valley in the Sierra Nevada; a light to medium dense forest of tall conifers provides adequate shelter/shade in most campsites; the lake is surrounded by low, heavily timbered ridges and hills; elevation 7400'.

Season, Fees & Phone: June to October; $11.00; 14 day limit; Calaveras Ranger District, Hathaway Pines, (209) 795-1381.

Camp Notes: This is an interesting location. The classic, High Sierra panoramas are absent. Instead, the terrain immediately around the lake is more, well, call it 'gentle', rather than 'grand'. Lake Alpine Campground is also known as just "Alpine" Campground. If this campground is filled (which it typically is on summer weekends), there are other waterfront options in the vicinity, including two campgrounds on the east shore of Lake Alpine. Also, a small camp at Mosquito Lakes, 7 miles east, has good fishing. And Pacific Valley, 9 miles east, and 0.4 mile off the south side of the highway, is in a pretty meadow along Pacific Creek. No drinking water or fee at the latter two.

PINE MARTEN
Stanislaus National Forest

Location: Eastern California northeast of Stockton and south of Lake Tahoe.

Access: From California State Highway 4 at the east end of Lake Alpine near milepost 5 (5 miles east of the Alpine-Calaveras county line, 27 miles southwest of the junction of State Highways 4 & 89 south of Markleeville, 50 miles northeast of Angels Camp), turn south onto the campground access road and proceed 0.2 mile; turn right and go 0.1 mile to the campground.

Facilities: 32 campsites; sites are small to medium-sized, closely spaced, but with some visual separation; most parking pads are gravel/paved, short to medium-length straight-ins; medium to large tent areas; about half of the sites are reasonably level, remainder are slightly sloped; fireplaces or fire rings; firewood is available for gathering in the area; water at several faucets; restrooms; paved driveways; gas, general store, laundromat and showers at a lodge, 1 mile west.

Activities & Attractions: Fishing; trails to the lake.

Natural Features: Located on a rolling flat at the east end of Lake Alpine in the Sierra Nevada; sites are well-shaded/sheltered by tall conifers; elevation 7400'.

Season, Fees & Phone: June to October; $11.00; Calaveras Ranger District, Hathaway Pines, (209) 795-1381.

Camp Notes: A glimpse of the lake through the forest can be had from a few sites here. There is also a small, no fee, backpackers campground near here, a few yards off the highway.

SILVER VALLEY
Stanislaus National Forest

Location: Eastern California northeast of Stockton and south of Lake Tahoe.

Access: From California State Highway 4 at the east end of Lake Alpine near milepost 5 (5 miles east of the Alpine-Calaveras county line, 27 miles southwest of the junction of State Highways 4 & 89 south of

Markleeville, 50 miles northeast of Angels Camp), turn south onto the campground access road and proceed 0.4 mile (past Pine Marten Campground) to the campground.

Facilities: 21 campsites; sites are small to medium-sized, with fair separation; parking pads are gravel/paved, mostly short to medium-length straight-ins; additional leveling may be needed on many pads; enough space for medium to large tents in most sites, but areas are generally a bit sloped; fireplaces or fire rings; firewood is available for gathering in the area; water at several faucets; restrooms; paved driveways; gas, general store, laundromat and showers at a lodge, 1 mile west.

Activities & Attractions: Fishing; limited boating; trails to the lake; Highland Creek Trailhead.

Natural Features: Located on a slight to moderate slope above the east end of Lake Alpine in the Sierra Nevada; a medium to dense forest of tall conifers provides ample shelter for campsites; elevation 7400'.

Season, Fees & Phone: June to October; $11.00; Calaveras Ranger District, Hathaway Pines, (209) 795-1381.

Camp Notes: Trout fishing is said to be reasonably good on the lake. Alpine is also becoming a popular lake with windsurfers and other small-boat sailors.

SILVER CREEK
Toiyabe National Forest

Location: Eastern California northeast of Stockton and south of Lake Tahoe.

Access: From California State Highway 4 at milepost 24 +.4 (8 miles southwest of the junction of State Highways 4 & 89 south of Markleeville, 69 miles northeast of Angels Camp), turn north or south into either of the 2 campground loops.

Facilities: 22 campsites in 2 loops; sites are about average in size, with minimal to fairly good visual separation; parking pads are mostly paved straight-ins, plus a few longer pull-throughs; some additional leveling may be necessary on many pads; medium to large, slightly sloped tent areas; fire rings; firewood is available for gathering in the area; water at several faucets; vault facilities; paved driveways; gas and groceries+ are available in Markleeville, 12 miles north.

Activities & Attractions: Scenic views; stream fishing.

Natural Features: Located along Silver Creek, high on the east slope of the Sierra Nevada; campground vegetation is primarily mixed, tall conifers and tall grass; lofty, rugged, gray peaks and timbered slopes surround the campground; elevation 6800'.

Season, Fees & Phone: June to October; $7.00; 14 day limit; Carson Ranger District, Carson City NV, (702) 882-2766 (office) or (702) 882-9211 (recorded information).

Camp Notes: This is a dandy spot. There's a lot of scenery in the Sierra, and some of the best is around here. It's not the easiest roadside campground to reach, particularly from the west. Highway signs advise against trailer-towing west of here through the Ebbetts Pass area. There are several miles of steep, sharp switchbacks and very narrow roads that start (or end) near the campground. (They must have used a helicopter to haul the asphalt.) But, wow! The near-wilderness environment in this region is really something.

BOOTLEG
Toiyabe National Forest

Location: Eastern California north of Bridgeport and Southeast of Lake Tahoe.

Access: From U.S. Highway 395 at milepost 98 +.6 (9 miles south of Walker, 21 miles north of Bridgeport), turn west into the campground; the first sites are near the highway, but most are farther up the hill.

Facilities: 63 campsites in 2 loops; sites are medium-sized, with nominal separation; parking pads are paved, medium to long straight-ins, pull-offs or pull-throughs; most pads have been reasonably well leveled, considering the terrain; tent areas are mostly medium-sized and sloped; barbecue grills; some firewood is available for gathering in the area, b-y-o is suggested; water at several faucets; restrooms; paved driveways; gas and groceries+ are available in Walker.

Activities & Attractions: Stream fishing for trout.

Natural Features: Located on a moderately steep, forested hillside in a small canyon on the east slope of the Sierra Nevada; light to moderately dense, tall conifers provide adequate shelter/shade in most sites;

ridges covered with timber and sage border the canyon; the Walker River flows through the canyon, but is not in view of the campground; elevation 6700'.

Season, Fees & Phone: Late-May to late-September; $7.00; 14 day limit; Bridgeport Ranger District (619) 932-7070.

Camp Notes: Bootleg was apparently designed from the ground up with rv's in mind, judging from the long, paved, curbed parking pads. The tent spots aren't the largest or most level around, although they do have a good surface of conifer needles. However, small or possibly medium-sized, self-standing tents could easily be pitched on the large, fairly level parking pads.

Northern California 194

CHRIS FLAT
Toiyabe National Forest

Location: Eastern California north of Bridgeport and southeast of Lake Tahoe.

Access: From U.S. Highway 395 at milepost 97 +.2 (10 miles south of Walker, 20 miles north of Bridgeport), turn east into the campground.

Facilities: 15 campsites in 2 loops; sites are small to medium-sized, level, with good visual separation; parking pads are paved, medium to long straight-ins; medium to large tent areas; fireplaces; limited firewood is available for gathering in the area, b-y-o is suggested; water at a central faucet; vault facilities; paved driveways; gas and groceries+ are available in Walker.

Activities & Attractions: Trout fishing.

Natural Features: Located on a flat along the west bank of the Walker River at the base of the east slope of the Sierra Nevada; campground vegetation consists mostly of short willows and pines; sage-covered ridges dotted with timber border the river on the east and west; many sites are unsheltered except for small bushes and trees; elevation 6600'.

Season, Fees & Phone: May to October; $7.00; 14 day limit; Bridgeport Ranger Dist. (619) 932-7070.

Camp Notes: There are two other easily accessible Toiyabe camping areas southwest of here, on California State Highway 108. Sonora Bridge Campground is on a gravel road just off the south side of Highway 108 at a point 1.5 miles west of the U.S. 395 & Highway 108 junction south of Chris Flat. To the west of Sonora Bridge is Leavitt Meadows, along the south side of the highway, 7 miles from the junction. Leavitt Meadows appears to be used principally as a fishing camp. An added feature is its location near the U.S. Marine Corps Mountain Warfare Training Center. Leathernecks occasionally can be seen rappeling off the vertical property near the campground.

Northern California 195

HONEYMOON FLAT
Toiyabe National Forest

Location: Eastern California southwest of Bridgeport.

Access: From U.S. Highway 395 at milepost 76 +.8 at the northwest corner of Bridgeport, turn south onto Kirkwood Street/Twin Lakes Road (paved) and drive south and southwest for 8 miles; turn east or west into the camp loops.

Facilities: 47 campsites in 2 loops; sites are very small to small+, generally level, with minimal separation; parking pads are gravel, short to long straight-ins; tent space varies from small to large; fireplaces or fire rings; b-y-o firewood; water at several faucets; vault facilities; gravel driveways; laundry and showers at local resorts; adequate supplies and services are available in Bridgeport.

Activities & Attractions: Fishing.

Natural Features: Located along the banks of Robinson Creek on a sage flat in a valley below the east slope of the Sierra Nevada; some sites are unsheltered, most are in among medium-dense conifers and very dense hardwoods; elevation 7000'.

Season, Fees & Phone: May to late-October; $7.00; 14 day limit; Bridgeport Ranger District (619) 932-7070.

Camp Notes: You can see the entire valley and the striking peaks beyond from many of the campsites. For an off-pavement camp in this vicinity, you might check Buckeye Campground. The turnoff from Twin Lakes Road is a mile northeast of Honeymoon Flat, then it's northerly up a gravel road for three miles. Buckeye has over 60 small campsites, water and vaults near the confluence of two streams.

ROBINSON CREEK
Toiyabe National Forest

Location: Eastern California southwest of Bridgeport.

Access: From U.S. Highway 395 at milepost 76 +.8 at t he northwest corner of Bridgeport, turn south onto Kirkwood Street/Twin Lakes Road (paved) and drive south and southwest for 9 miles; turn east (left) onto a paved access road and go 0.05 mile to the campground.

Facilities: 54 campsites, including several park 'n walk sites, in 2 loops; sites are small to small+, with nominal separation; parking pads are hard surfaced, mostly level, short to medium-length straight-ins; small to medium-sized spots for tents; fire rings; b-y-o firewood; water at several faucets; vault facilities; paved driveways; laundry and showers at local resorts; adequate supplies and services are available in Bridgeport.

Activities & Attractions: Trout fishing; fishing and boating on nearby Twin Lakes; paved paths pass through the campground.

Natural Features: Located along the bank of Robinson Creek in a valley on the east side of the Sierra Nevada; sites receive very light to light-medium shade from rows of tall conifers; adjacent to a meadow, a sage plain, and rocky hill, with high peaks in the distance; elevation 7000'.

Season, Fees & Phone: May to October; $8.00; 14 day limit; Bridgeport Ranger Dist. (619) 932-7070.

Camp Notes: Robinson Creek is a nice stream that offers fairly good fishing for small trout. The campground offers excellent views of big Sierra scenery.

PAHA
Toiyabe National Forest

Location: Eastern California southwest of Bridgeport.

Access: From U.S. Highway 395 at milepost 76 +.8 in Bridgeport, turn south onto Kirkwood Street/Twin Lakes Road (paved); head south and southwest for 9 miles; turn easterly (left) onto a paved access road and proceed 0.1 mile to the campground.

Facilities: 22 campsites in 2 loops; sites are small+ to medium-sized, with minimal to nominal separation; parking pads are paved, short to medium-length straight-ins; a touch of additional leveling might be needed in some sites; medium-sized, fairly level tent areas; fire rings; b-y-o firewood; water at several faucets; vault facilities; paved driveway; laundry and showers at local resorts; adequate supplies and services are available in Bridgeport.

Activities & Attractions: Stream fishing; boating and fishing on Twin Lakes, a mile southwest.

Natural Features: Located along Robinson Creek in a valley below the the east slope of the Sierra Nevada; streamside sites are in a stand of conifers and receive light to medium shade; a few sites are along the edge of the timber adjacent to a sage flat and are unshaded or very lightly shaded; elev. 7000'.

Season, Fees & Phone: May to October; $8.00; 14 day limit; Bridgeport Ranger District (619) 932-7070.

Camp Notes: Like the other four campgrounds in this area, most campsites in Paha are along the stream.

LOWER TWIN LAKES & SAWMILL
Toiyabe National Forest

Location: Eastern California southwest of Bridgeport.

Access: From U.S. Highway 395 at milepost 76 +.8 in Bridgeport, turn south onto Kirkwood Street/Twin Lakes Road (paved) and travel south and southwest for 10 miles; about 100 yards before reaching the lake (just past a resort) turn easterly (left) onto a gravel access road and proceed 0.15 mile; turn left and go 200 yards to *Sawmill* Campground; or continue for another 0.1 mile to *Lower Twin Lakes* Campground.

Facilities: *Twin Lakes*: 17 campsites in 2 loops; sites are small to medium-sized, basically level, closely spaced, with fair visual separation; parking pads are gravel, medium-length straight-ins; *Sawmill*: 8

campsites; sites are quite small and closely spaced; parking pads are gravel, short straight-ins; *both camps*: medium to large tent areas; fire rings or fireplaces; b-y-o firewood; water at faucets; vault facilities; gravel driveways; laundry and showers at local resorts; adequate supplies and services are available in Bridgeport.

Activities & Attractions: Boating; fishing on the lake and on the stream; hiking trails.

Natural Features: Located in a valley near the northeast tip of Lower Twin Lakes just above the lakes' outlet stream, Robinson Creek; tall conifers and some short aspens provide moderate shelter/shade for most campsites; bordered by sage slopes and a sage flat, with views of the high peaks of the Sierra Nevada in the distance; elevation 7000'.

Season, Fees & Phone: May to October; $9.00 in Lower Twin Lakes, $6.00 in Sawmill; 14 day limit; Bridgeport Ranger District (619) 932-7070.

Camp Notes: Lower Twin Lakes has some very nice streamside sites in one loop. Sawmill is off the principal gravel road, so drive-by traffic is minimized.

MEADOWVIEW
Stanislaus National Forest

Location: Eastern California east of Stockton.

Access: From California State Highway 108 at milepost 30 +.2 (30 miles northeast of Sonora, 51 miles west of the junction of Highway 108 & U.S. 395), turn east (i.e., an easy right turn off the highway if eastbound) onto Pinecrest Lake Road (paved) and proceed 0.35 mile; turn right onto Dodge Ridge Road (paved) and continue for 0.2 mile to a final right turn into the campground.

Facilities: 100 campsites in what amounts to 3 loops; (nearby Pioneer Trails Group Campground is also available, by reservation); sites are small to medium-sized, with nominal separation; parking pads are paved, medium-length straight-ins, and about half will require a little additional leveling; tent areas are large and somewhat level; fireplaces in most sites, plus some barbecue grills; firewood is available for gathering in the vicinity; water at several faucets; restrooms; holding tank disposal station on Highway 108, 0.3 mile west of the Pinecrest Lake Road turnoff; paved driveways; ranger station nearby; small store at Pinecrest Lake; complete supplies and services are available in Sonora.

Activities & Attractions: Shadow of the Mi-Wok Interpretive Trail near the ranger station; Pinecrest Lake, with boating, fishing, and designated swimming beach, 1 mile east.

Natural Features: Located on a moderately timbered, rolling flat on the west slope of the Sierra Nevada; vegetation consists of tall conifers, plus some new growth timber and a small amount of underbrush, on a thick carpet of conifer needles; elevation 5500'.

Season, Fees & Phone: May to October; $9.00; 14 day limit; Summit Ranger District, Pinecrest, (209) 965-3434.

Camp Notes: Undoubtedly, many campers treat Meadowview as a Plan B option to the campground at Pinecrest Lake. (See description below.) But Meadowview, although not in the center of activity, has its advantages--and the greatest one may be that it's *not* in the center of activity. Both camps are normally filled on summer weekends.

PINECREST
Stanislaus National Forest

Location: Eastern California east of Stockton.

Access: From California State Highway 108 at milepost 30 +.2 (30 miles east of Sonora, 51 miles west of U.S. 395), turn east (i.e., an easy right turn off the highway if eastbound) onto Pinecrest Lake Road (paved) and proceed 0.6 mile; turn right, into the campground.

Facilities: 200 campsites in 5 loops; sites are average-sized, mostly level, with minimal to fair separation; parking pads are paved, medium to long straight-ins; large tent spots in most units; fireplaces; firewood is available for gathering in the general vicinity; gathering firewood on national forest lands prior to arrival is recommended; water at several faucets; restrooms; holding tank disposal station on Highway 108, 0.3 mile west of the Pinecrest Lake Road turnoff; paved driveways; ranger station, 0.7 mile; small store nearby; complete supplies and services are available in Sonora.

Activities & Attractions: Boating; boat launch and dock; fishing; designated swimming area with sand/pebble beach; amphitheater; large, very popular lakeside day use area.

Natural Features: Located on a timbered flat a few yards from the southwest shore of Pinecrest Lake, on the west slope of the Sierra Nevada; campground vegetation consists of light to medium-dense tall conifers, plus some second growth timber and a small amount of undercover; elevation 5600'.

Season, Fees & Phone: May to October; $12.00; 14 day limit; Summit Ranger District, Pinecrest, (209) 965-3434.

Camp Notes: At recent prices, a campsite here is one of the more expensive pieces of national forest real estate in California. Although the lake is certainly beautiful, and the camp spots nice, it might be worth considering staying in one of the many other, less expensive, campgrounds along this highway. (Pocket the difference, and spend it on that Alaska trip. Ed.)

BOULDER FLAT
Stanislaus National Forest

Location: East-central California east of Stockton.

Access: From California State Highway 108 at milepost 50 +.3 (20 miles east of Pinecrest, 31 miles west of the junction of Highway 108 & U.S. Highway 395), turn north into the campground.

Facilities: 20 campsites; sites are small to medium in size, mostly level, with little separation; parking pads are gravel, short to medium-length straight-ins; large, fairly level tent areas; fireplaces; firewood is available for gathering in the area; water at faucets; (water availability is subject to change, b-y-o to be sure); vault facilities; paved driveway; gas and camper supplies 3 miles east; complete supplies and services are available in Sonora, 50 miles southwest.

Activities & Attractions: Fishing for weekly stocked hybrid trout.

Natural Features: Located on a boulder-strewn flat (appropriately) above the Middle Fork of the Stanislaus River in the Sierra Nevada; a number of tall conifers provide some shelter/shade within the campground; bordered by light to medium-dense forest; high, partly timbered peaks are visible to the north and east, across the river; elevation 5700'.

Season, Fees & Phone: May to October; $6.00; 14 day limit; Summit Ranger District, Pinecrest, (209) 965-3434.

Camp Notes: This may not be the greatest in terms of facilities, but the river/mountain views are some of the best of the campgrounds along this highway. There are several other roadside campgrounds both east and west of here. Three to the west, toward Sonora, merit consideration: Cascade Creek, 7 sites, near mile 40; Mill Creek, 10 sites, near mile 43; and Niagara Creek, 9 sites, near mile 44. They all have tables, fireplaces and vaults, but none has drinking water. However, all three are at least a little farther off the highway than most of the other campgrounds along this route. Next door to Boulder Flat, a half mile east, is Brightman Flat, with more shelter than Boulder Flat. No fee is charged at any of the waterless camping areas (with the cautionary "subject to change", of course).

DARDANELLE
Stanislaus National Forest

Location: Eastern California east of Stockton.

Access: From California State Highway 108 at milepost 52 +.9 (23 miles east of Pinecrest, 28 miles west of U.S. 395), turn north into the campground.

Facilities: 28 campsites, including several walk-ins; sites are small to medium-sized, mostly level, with some separation; parking pads are paved, short to medium-length straight-ins, and some are extra wide; large tent areas; fire rings; firewood is available for gathering in the area; water at several faucets; vault facilities; paved driveways; gas and camper supplies at a store just across the highway; complete supplies and services are available in Sonora, 53 miles southwest.

Activities & Attractions: Fishing for stocked trout; Columns of the Giants geological site, 2 miles east.

Natural Features: Located on a light to moderately forested, slightly rolling flat along the bank of the Middle Fork of the Stanislaus River in the Sierra Nevada; a high, timbered ridge lies to the south; high, partially timbered mountains rise to the north; elevation 5800'.

Season, Fees & Phone: May to October; $7.00; 14 day limit; Summit Ranger District, Pinecrest, (209) 965-3434.

Camp Notes: Another forest campground near here that has some possibilities is Pidgeon Flat, 1.7 miles east. It has a half-dozen walk-in sites right along the riverbank. The highway is rather close, but the rushing river should drown out most of the traffic noise. (Oops, pun unintended.) Farther east, near mp 55, is Eureka Valley Campground. It has 22 sites, hand pumps and vaults on a large, dirt flat in an almost open-camping arrangement. Beautiful country around here--it really is.

BAKER
Stanislaus National Forest

Location: Eastern California east of Stockton.

Access: From California State Highway 108 at milepost 58 (28 miles east of Pinecrest, 22 miles west of the junction of Highway 108 & U.S. Highway 395), turn south into the campground.

Facilities: 44 campsites, including several double-occupancy units; sites are small to medium-sized, basically level, with fair separation; parking pads are sand/gravel, primarily short to medium-length straight-ins, plus a few long pull-throughs; nice, large tent areas; fireplaces; firewood is available for gathering in the general vicinity; water at several faucets; vault facilities; paved driveways; gas and camper supplies at stores at Kennedy Meadow, 1 mile south, and on the highway, 5 miles west; complete supplies and services are available in Sonora.

Activities & Attractions: Fishing for stocked, hybrid trout; Columns of the Giants geological site, 4 miles west.

Natural Features: Located on a rolling flat in a canyon along the bank of the Middle Fork of the Stanislaus River in the central Sierra Nevada; several sites are riverside or have river views; campground vegetation consists of light to medium-dense conifers, some new-growth timber, and grass; high, rocky, timbered ridges border the canyon; elevation 6300'.

Season, Fees & Phone: May to October; $7.00; 14 day limit; Summit Ranger District, Pinecrest, (209) 965-3434.

Camp Notes: This is one of the nicer campgrounds along this route. Several sites are in the very good to excellent category. Highway signs indicate that trailers are not advised between here and the other side of Sonora Pass, near the junction of Highway 108 with U.S. 395. The advice is quite sound. The road is very steep and winding. But the country through which it passes is truly splendid.

HODGDON MEADOW
Yosemite National Park

Location: Eastern California in western Yosemite National Park.

Access: From California State Highway 120/Big Oak Flat Road at a point 100 yards southeast of the Big Oak Flat Entrance Station of Yosemite National Park (8 miles northwest of Crane Flat Junction, 28 miles east of the town of Big Oak Flat), turn north onto a paved campground access road and proceed 0.5 mile, then swing right into the campground.

Facilities: 105 campsites, including many park 'n walk sites; (several small group sites are also available); sites are small, generally a little sloped, closely spaced, with nominal to fair visual separation; parking surfaces are sandy gravel/earth, primarily short straight-ins, plus some medium+ pull-throughs; medium to large areas for tents; storage lockers (bear boxes); fireplaces; b-y-o firewood is recommended; water at central faucets; restrooms; paved driveways; limited supplies and services are available in Yosemite Village.

Activities & Attractions: Forest setting.

Natural Features: Located on a rolling slope in the Sierra Nevada; campsites are lightly to moderately sheltered/shaded by tall conifers above an 'open' forest floor with some low hardwoods that provide limited visual separation; a meadow is a short distance east of the campground; elevation 4900'.

Season, Fees & Phone: March to October; $12.00; 14 day limit; reservations mandatory June-October; please see Appendix for additional reservation information; park information (209) 372-0265 (live) or (209) 372-0264 (comprehensive recorded message).

Camp Notes: Although there are a couple dozen sites which can accommodate small motorhomes and short trailer combinations, Hodgdon Meadow is really a 'tent campers' special'. A number of park 'n walk campsites are on small 'shelves' below their parking spaces. Pleasant atmosphere here.

CRANE FLAT
Yosemite National Park

Location: Eastern California in western Yosemite National Park.

Access: From Big Oak Flat Road (California State Highway 120) at a point 0.15 mile west of the junction of Big Oak Flat Road & Tioga Pass Road (8 miles east of the Big Oak Flat entrance, 16 miles west of Yosemite Village and 32 miles west of the Tioga Pass entrance), turn south onto the paved campground access road and proceed 0.15 mile to the campground entrance.

Facilities: 165 campsites in 5 loops; sites are typically small, sloped, with minimal to fair separation; parking pads are short pull-offs or straight-ins; adequate space for a medium to large tent in most sites; special sections for campers with pets; firewood is available for gathering in the park; gathering firewood prior to reaching the campground is recommended; fireplaces; water at several faucets; restrooms; paved driveways; gas and snacks at a service station 0.15 mile west; limited supplies and services are available in Yosemite Village.

Activities & Attractions: Tuolumne and Merced Groves of Giant Sequoias are both within a few miles; nature walks, campfire programs in summer.

Natural Features: Located on a rolling slope in a dense forest of super tall conifers, plus some young timber; a small meadow is adjacent to the campground; elevation 6200'.

Season, Fees & Phone: May to October; $12.00; 14 day limit; park information (209) 372-0265 (live) or (209) 372-0264 (comprehensive recorded message).

Camp Notes: If Crane Flat and nearby Hodgdon Meadow (described elsewhere) are both filled when you arrive, you may be able to secure a spot in one of several small national forest and BLM camps along Highway 120 and Highway 140 west of the park. Also, Tamarack Flat, a 52-site, no-water, Yosemite camp area, may be available. It's located 4 miles east of Crane Flat on Tioga Pass Road, then 3 miles south on a rough park road.

RIVER
Yosemite National Park

Location: Eastern California in south-central Yosemite National Park.

Access: From any of the park entrances, follow the signs to Yosemite Valley/Yosemite Village to the one-way road (Southside Drive) through the valley, eastbound; at a point just opposite the turnoff to Curry Village, turn northerly (left) for 0.2 mile to *Upper River* on the right and *Lower River* on the left.

Facilities: 263 campsites in 2 major sections; sites are small, basically level, and closely spaced; parking pads are paved, mostly short or short+ straight-ins; adequate space for a large tent in most sites; fireplaces; gathering firewood outside the Valley prior to arrival in the campground is recommended; water at faucets; restrooms; holding tank disposal station; paved driveways; limited supplies and services are available in Yosemite Village.

Natural Features: Located in a moderately dense conifer forest on the banks of the Merced River in Yosemite Valley; the classic natural architecture, for which Yosemite is world-renowned, is in and around the valley; elevation 4000'.

Activities & Attractions: Trails; visitor center; nature center; nature walks; campfire programs; free shuttle buses.

Season, Fees & Phone: Certain sections open all year, subject to weather conditions; $14.00; 7 day limit; reservations required year 'round; please see Appendix for additional reservation information; park information (209) 372-0265 (live) or (209) 372-0264 (comprehensive recorded message).

Camp Notes: River Campground and its bigger twin, Pines, are so comparable that it really comes down to which one you're able to obtain reservations for. The shuttles are a good deal.

PINES
Yosemite National Park

Location: Eastern California in south-central Yosemite National Park.

Access: From any of the park entrances, follow the signs to Yosemite Valley/Yosemite Village to the one-way road (Southside Drive) through the valley, eastbound; continue past the Curry Village turnoff and past the turnoff to River Campground for 0.5 mile to *Upper Pines* on the right, *Lower Pines* on the left, and *North Pines* straight ahead, across the river.

Facilities: 499 campsites in 3 major sections; (a group camp is also available in this vicinity); sites are small+, essentially level, with nominal separation; parking pads are paved, mostly short+ straight-ins; adequate space for a large tent in most sites; fireplaces; gathering firewood outside the Valley prior to arrival in the campground is recommended; water at faucets; restrooms; holding tank disposal stations; paved driveways; limited supplies and services are available in Yosemite Village.

Activities & Attractions: Hiking trails; visitor center; nature center; nature walks; campfire programs; free shuttle buses.

Natural Features: Located in a moderately dense conifer forest on the banks of the Merced River in Yosemite Valley; many of Yosemite's most notable natural features are in and around the valley; elevation 4000'.

Season, Fees & Phone: Certain sections open all year, subject to weather conditions; $14.00; 7 day limit; reservations required year 'round; please see Appendix for additional reservation information; park information (209) 372-0265 (live) or (209) 372-0264 (comprehensive recorded message).

Camp Notes: Sites in Pines seem to be slightly larger or farther apart than those in its near-twin camp, River Campground. North Pines is adjacent to a large horse/mule stable complex. In addition to Yosemite Valley's huge, standard campgrounds at Pines and River, a walk-in tent camp is available at the far west end of the Valley complex. Sunnyside Campground has three dozen tent sites, water, restrooms, and is generally available all year. A 25-site backpackers' camp for campers without vehicles is available in the Valley as well. A two-night limit is imposed in the backpackers' camp.

WAWONA
Yosemite National Park

Location: Eastern California in the southwest corner of Yosemite National Park.

Access: From Wawona Road (a continuation of California State Highway 41) at a point 1 mile north of Wawona, 6 miles north of the South Entrance Station, and 26 miles south of Yosemite Village, turn west into the campground.

Facilities: 100 campsites in 3 loops; (a group camp is also available); sites are small, close together and somewhat sloped; parking pads are gravel, mostly short straight-ins or pull-offs; adequate space for a large tent in most sites; fireplaces; firewood is available for gathering in the park; water at faucets; restrooms; paved driveways; gas and camper supplies in Wawona; limited supplies and services in Yosemite Village; adequate supplies and services are available in Oakhurst, 22 miles south.

Activities & Attractions: Pioneer Yosemite History Center; trails; fishing; campfire programs; Mariposa Grove, largest of 3 sequoia groves in the park, lies several miles south.

Natural Features: Located on the east bank of the the South Fork of the Merced River; campground vegetation consists primarily of light to medium dense tall conifers; sites in the A and C sections tend to be more in the open than those in the middle B Loop; many sites are along the river or have a river view; heavily timbered hills and ridges flank the river; elevation 4000'.

Season, Fees & Phone: Open all year; $10.00; 14 day limit; park information (209) 372-0265 (live) or (209) 372-0264 (comprehensive recorded message).

Camp Notes: This campground stretches along the river for almost a mile. Toward the north end, the sites are pretty tightly packed and the driveway is narrow. As an option, Summerdale, a national forest camp just outside the park, has larger and more level sites in a creekside setting, but costs a little more as well. (See separate description.)

WHITE WOLF
Yosemite National Park

Location: Eastern California in central Yosemite National Park.

Access: From Tioga Pass Road (California State Highway 120) at a point 22 miles east of the Big Oak Flat entrance and 32 miles west of the Tioga Pass entrance, turn north onto a paved access road and proceed 1.2 miles to the campground entrance, on the right side of the road, just past the lodge.

Facilities: 87 campsites; sites are small and closely spaced, and vary from fairly level in most sites, to a little sloped in some; parking pads are gravel, mainly short straight-ins; large tent areas; fireplaces; some firewood is available for gathering in the surrounding area; water at several faucets; restrooms; paved driveways; showers at the lodge; gas and camper supplies at Tuolumne Meadows, 25 miles east.

Activities & Attractions: Trails; campfire programs and nature walks in summer.

Natural Features: Located in a moderately dense stand of tall conifers; a small creek flows past a number of sites; a meadow lies just south of the camping area; elevation 8000'.

Season, Fees & Phone: June to October; $10.00; 14 day limit; park information (209) 372-0265 (live) or (209) 372-0264 (comprehensive recorded message).

Camp Notes: Since the parking spots here are a little snug, this campground seems to be favored mostly by tenters and tent trailer campers. Another park campground that's accessible from near White Wolf is Yosemite Creek. From Tioga Pass Road at a point 0.4 mile east of the White Wolf turnoff, head south on a rough road for five miles to the campground. Yosemite Creek has 75 basically primitive sites, vaults, no drinking water and a nominal fee, near a stream. Neither the rugged road into Yosemite Creek nor the small campsites are really compatible with large vehicles or vehicles with trailers.

PORCUPINE FLAT
Yosemite National Park

Location: Eastern California in central Yosemite National Park.

Access: From Tioga Pass Road (California State Highway 120) at a point 31 miles east of the Big Oak Flat entrance and 23 miles west of the Tioga Pass entrance, turn north into the campground.

Facilities: 52 campsites; sites are small, tolerably level, with nominal to fair separation; parking surfaces are earth/gravel, mostly short to short+ straight-ins or pull-offs; small to medium-sized tent areas; fireplaces; some firewood is available for gathering in the area; no drinking water; vault facilities; narrow, gravel/earth driveways; gas and camper supplies at Tuolumne Meadows, 25 miles east.

Activities & Attractions: Forest atmosphere; roadside convenience.

Natural Features: Located on a forested flat; sites are moderately sheltered by tall conifers; elevation 8100'.

Season, Fees & Phone: May to October; $6.00; 14 day limit; park information (209) 372-0265 (live) or (209) 372-0264 (comprehensive recorded message).

Camp Notes: There's a hushed, tall timber environment here. The vehicle paths are narrow and prone to be rutty, and most of the campground can only handle smaller vehicles. The campsites are scattered throughout the forest in a complex of strings and loops, so it would pay to take your time to find all of the isolated sites here. (Finding a vacant site after dark could be a challenge.) Regardless, or because of, its undeveloped state, Porcupine Flat fills early every night in midsummer, as do all of Yosemite's campgrounds.

TUOLUMNE MEADOWS
Yosemite National Park

Location: Eastern California near the east boundary of Yosemite National Park.

Access: From Tioga Pass Road (California State Highway 120) at a point 7 miles west of the Tioga Pass entrance and 48 miles east of the Big Oak Flat entrance, turn south, proceed 0.15 mile to the campground entrance.

Facilities: 325 campsites, including about 25 backpacker sites; sites are small and closely spaced, with minimal visual separation, and slightly sloped; parking pads are short, dirt straight-ins; adequate space for a large tent in most sites; separate section for campers with pets; fireplaces or fire rings; firewood is available for gathering in the park; gathering firewood from outside the campground area, or b-y-o, is suggested; water at several faucets; restrooms; narrow, roughly paved driveway; gas, camper supplies, showers and post office nearby.

Activities & Attractions: Elizabeth Lake Trail leads off from the south end of the campground; numerous other trails in the area; campfire circles; limited fishing.

Natural Features: Located on a rolling, rocky flat in a moderately dense stand of tall conifers on the edge of Tuolumne Meadows; the Tuolumne River flows past the east end of the campground; a timbered ridge lies to the north, high peaks rise to the east and south; elevation 8600'.

Season, Fees & Phone: June to October; $12.00 for a standard site, $3.00 per person for backpackers or others without vehicles; reservations required July-August; 14 day limit; please see Appendix for additional reservation information; park information (209) 372-0265 (live) or (209) 372-0264 (comprehensive recorded message).

Camp Notes: This ancient, simple campground is a favorite with tent campers. It's a bit far to commute between here and dazzling Yosemite Valley (55 miles). Quite candidly, though, you may discover that you don't *have* to stay within striking distance of the Valley, and that Tuolumne's own natural luster is very gratifying indeed.

TIOGA LAKE
Inyo National Forest

Location: Eastern California east of Yosemite National Park.

Access: From California State Highway 120 at milepost 1 +.2 (1 mile northeast of the Tioga Pass entrance of Yosemite National Park, 12 miles west of Lee Vining), turn south into the campground.

Facilities: 12 campsites; sites are small, basically level and closely spaced; parking surfaces are gravel, short straight-ins; enough room for small to medium-sized tents; fire rings; b-y-o firewood; water at a hand pump; vault facilities; paved driveway; gas and snacks 1 mile east; adequate supplies and services are available in Lee Vining.

Activities & Attractions: Fishing; motorless boating.

Natural Features: Located on a small point on the north shore of Tioga Lake; vegetation consists mostly of grass, plus a few trees; bordered by the high, rugged peaks of the east slope of the Sierra Nevada; Tioga Pass tops out at 9945', a mile southwest; campground elevation 9700'.

Season, Fees & Phone: June to September; $8.00; 14 day limit; Mono Lake Ranger District, Lee Vining, (619) 647-3000.

Camp Notes: Excellent mountain-lake views. A highly scenic option to camping in Yosemite. Tioga Lake is just as popular as the park camps, too, especially with small-tent campers.

ELLERY LAKE
Inyo National Forest

Location: Eastern California east of Yosemite National Park.

Access: From California State Highway 120 at milepost 2 +.4 (2 miles northeast of the Tioga Pass entrance of Yosemite National Park, 11 miles west of Lee Vining), turn south into the campground.

Facilities: 12 campsites in a string and a loop; about half of the sites are park 'n walk units; sites are small, essentially level, with nominal separation; parking pads are paved, short to medium-length straight-ins; small to medium-sized areas for tents; fire rings; b-y-o firewood; water at a hand pump; vault facilities; hard-surfaced driveway; gas and snacks nearby; adequate supplies and services are available in Lee Vining.

Activities & Attractions: Fishing.

Natural Features: Located along the bank of Lee Vining Creek near the stream's exit into Ellery Lake; campsites are slightly sheltered by bushes; a thin line of tall conifers on a hillside borders the south edge of the campground; elevation 9500'.

Season, Fees & Phone: June to September; $8.00; 14 day limit; Mono Lake Ranger District, Lee Vining, (619) 647-3000.

Camp Notes: Three other camps in the area that are accessible from near the Ellery Lake turnoff are worth a look. Tioga Junction, Sawmill and Saddlebag Lake Campgrounds can be reached from milepost 2 +.1, then via a side road that leads north from the highway. Tioga Junction is just off the side road near the highway; Sawmill is 1.5 miles up the narrow road. Tioga Junction has six sites, Sawmill has five sites; both camps are on streamside flats, and have vaults but no drinking water. Saddlebag Lake is two miles up the single-lane side road at the south tip of the lake of the same name, with 18 sites, drinking water and vaults.

LEE VINING CREEK
Mono County Park

Location: Eastern California west of Lee Vining.

Access: From California State Highway 120 at milepost 8 + .6 (9 miles east of the Tioga Pass entrance of Yosemite National Park, 3 miles west of Lee Vining), turn south onto a paved access road and go 0.1 mile; turn right to the Upper section or left to the Lower section. **Alternate Access** (for Lower Lee Vining Creek): From Highway 120 at milepost 9 + .4, (0.8 mile east of the principal turnoff) turn south into the Lower unit.

Facilities: 106 campsites in 2 strings; sites are very small to small, and closely spaced; parking surfaces are gravel, mostly short straight-ins or pull-offs; small tent spaces; fire rings; limited firewood is available for gathering in the area; water at central faucets; vault facilities; adequate supplies and services are available in Lee Vining.

Activities & Attractions: Fishing.

Natural Features: Located on a narrow flat along the bank of Lee Vining Creek in a narrow valley on the east slope of the Sierra Nevada; campsites receive light to medium shade/shelter from tall conifers and aspens; elevation 7500'.

Season, Fees & Phone: May to October; $5.00; for information, call Mono Lake Ranger District, Inyo National Forest, Lee Vining, (619) 647-3000.

Camp Notes: The campground extends for about a mile and a half along the creek, and virtually all sites are streamside. As evidenced by the number of fishing rods poked out across the stream on a typical afternoon, it apparently is a good fishing camp.

ASPEN GROVE
Mono County Park

Location: Eastern California west of Lee Vining.

Access: From California State Highway 120 at milepost 8 + .6 (9 miles east of the Tioga Pass entrance of Yosemite National Park, 3 miles west of Lee Vining), turn south onto a paved access road and go 0.1 mile; turn west (right) and proceed 1.5 paved miles, then swing south (left) for 0.1 mile to the campground.

Facilities: 54 campsites; sites are small, with minimal to nominal separation; parking pads are grass/earth, short straight-ins or medium-length pull-offs; a little additional leveling may be needed on some pads; small tent areas; fire rings; some firewood is available for gathering in the area; water at several faucets; vault facilities; sandy earth driveway; adequate supplies and services are available in Lee Vining.

Activities & Attractions: Fishing.

Natural Features: Located on a short shelf above Lee Vining Creek; sites are in a grove of aspens interspersed with a few tall conifers; some open, sage-covered areas are withing the campground; bordered by steep, partially forested mountains; elevation 7600'.

Season, Fees & Phone: May to October; $5.00; for information, call Mono Lake Ranger District, Inyo National Forest, Lee Vining, (619) 647-3000.

Camp Notes: A small cascade just upstream of the campground and a pleasant meadow along the downstream bank lend added interest to this rustic spot. The campground is also called just "Aspen".

BIG BEND
Inyo National Forest

Location: Eastern California west of Lee Vining.

Access: From California State Highway 120 at milepost 8 + .6 (9 miles east of the Tioga Pass entrance of Yosemite National Park, 3 miles west of Lee Vining), turn south onto a paved access road, go 0.1 mile, then swing west (right) and proceed 1.8 miles on pavement, then another 0.6 mile on gravel to the campground.

Facilities: 17 campsites; sites are small to medium-sized, closely spaced, with fair visual separation; parking pads are gravel, short to medium-length straight-ins; a bit of additional leveling may be needed on some pads; small to medium-sized tent spots; fire rings; some firewood is available for gathering in the general area; water at several faucets; vault facilities; narrow, gravel driveway; adequate supplies and services are available in Lee Vining.

Activities & Attractions: Fishing.

Natural Features: Located along the bank of Lee Vining Creek in a valley on the east slope of the Sierra Nevada; campsites are very well shaded/sheltered by very tall conifers and aspens; dense, high bushes border many of the sites; elevation 7800'.

Season, Fees & Phone: May to September; $8.00; 14 day limit; Mono Lake Ranger District, Lee Vining, (619) 647-3000.

Camp Notes: Steep mountainsides and cliffs rise above the campround. Overall, it's probably the best of the camps along Lee Vining Creek.

Southern California

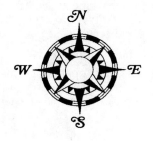

Public Campgrounds

The Southern California map is located in the Appendix.

Southern California 1

KIRK CREEK
Los Padres National Forest

Location: Central California Coast south of Monterey.

Access: From California State Highway 1 at milepost 19 (29 miles south of Big Sur, 39 miles north of San Simeon), turn west into the campground.

Facilities: 33 campsites in 2 loops; (a hike-bike site is also available); sites are generously medium-sized, and most are quite private; parking pads are gravel, medium-length straight-ins; most pads will probably require additional leveling; large, slightly sloped tent areas; fire rings; b-y-o firewood is recommended; water at several faucets; restrooms; paved driveways; gas and groceries, 3 miles south and 4 miles north; nearest sources of limited or better supplies and services are 60 miles, north or south.

Activities & Attractions: Terrific views; trailhead on the east side of the highway.

Natural Features: Located on a moderately steep, open slope just above the Pacific Ocean; campground vegetation consists of dense, ceiling-height shrubbery around most sites, plus some tall conifers; steep, brushy hills and mountains form the backdrop to the east; a coastal promontory lies a short distance to the north; elevation 100'.

Season, Fees & Phone: Open all year; $10.00; 14 day limit; Monterey Ranger District, King City, (408) 385-5434.

Camp Notes: Kirk Creek is undoubtedly a popular spot. It reportedly fills up on most nights during summer. But it might be worth a wait to get a campsite. The views up and down the coast are quite impressive. This is one of only a handful of national forest campgrounds along the entire Pacific Coast.

Southern California 2

PLASKETT CREEK
Los Padres National Forest

Location: Central California Coast south of Monterey.

Access: From California State Highway 1 at milepost 13 +.6 (34 miles north of San Simeon, 34 miles south of Big Sur), turn east into the campground.

Facilities: 43 campsites in a main loop plus a small side loop; sides are generally medium-sized, with minimal separation; parking pads are paved, short to medium-length straight-ins, and many will require a little additional leveling; plenty of room for tents, though spaces are generally slightly sloped; fire rings and barbecue grills; limited firewood is available for gathering, b-y-o is recommended; water at faucets; restrooms; paved driveways; gas and groceries, 2 miles north.

Activities & Attractions: Sand Dollar Beach and day use facility just north and west of the campground.

Natural Features: Located on a slight to moderate slope at the base of a forested hill several hundred yards from the Pacific Ocean; campground vegetation consists of a spacious, grassy infield ringed by large evergreens; elevation 200'.

Season, Fees & Phone: Open all year; $10.00; 14 day limit; Monterey Ranger District, King City, (408) 385-5434.

Camp Notes: This campground almost has the appearance of a small state park campground--it has a "landscaped" look. The sites are of typical width and spacing; but they are quite long or "deep", and consequently tents can be pitched on the expansive infield "lawn" quite a distance from the loop driveway. The sites in the small loop just to the north of the primary camping area are smaller, but a little more private. Plaskett Creek might have spaces available a little later in the day than Kirk Creek (described above), since it isn't right at the ocean's edge. Supplies are really scarce along this stretch of the coast. Morro Bay and Monterey, each about 60 miles south and north, respectively, are the only real supply points, other than a few snack and gas stops, on this section of the Coast.

SAN SIMEON CREEK
San Simeon State Beach

Location: Central California Coast northwest of San Luis Obispo.

Access: From California State Highway 1 at milepost 53 +.2 (at the north end of the San Simeon Creek Bridge), turn east onto San Simeon Creek Road and proceed 0.1 mile; turn south (right) for 0.2 mile to the park entrance station; continue ahead for 0.2 mile to a "T" intersection, then turn right into the campground

Facilities: 131 campsites (2 hike-bike sites are also available); sites are small, generally level, with minimal to fair separation; most parking pads are paved, short to short+ straight-ins, some are extra-wide; adequate space for large tents; fire rings; b-y-o firewood; water at several faucets; restrooms with showers; holding tank disposal station; paved driveways; limited+ supplies and services are available in Cambria.

Activities & Attractions: Beach access across the highway; campfire center.

Natural Features: Located on a creekside flat and on a hillside above the stream; vegetation consists mostly of large, open grassy areas, plus trees and shrubbery which provide very light to light shade/shelter for some campsites; sea level.

Season, Fees & Phone: Open all year; please see Appendix for standard California state park fees and reservation information; park info phone (805) 927-2020.

Camp Notes: At San Simeon Creek, the view you get from most campsites is a good shot of the highway. (Most of the campground is below the built-up road.) But the sea is very near.

WASHBURN
San Simeon State Beach

Location: Central California Coast northwest of San Luis Obispo.

Access: From California State Highway 1 at milepost 53 +.2 (at the north end of the San Simeon Creek Bridge), turn east onto San Simeon Creek Road and proceed 0.1 mile; turn south (right) for 0.2 mile to the park entrance station; continue ahead for 0.2 mile to a "T" intersection, then left and go up the hill for 1 mile to the campground.

Facilities: 69 (primitive) campsites; sites are small+, with nil separation; parking pads are packed gravel, medium-length straight-ins; a little additional leveling may be required; large tent areas; water at several faucets; vault facilities; packed gravel driveways; limited+ supplies and services are available in Cambria.

Activities & Attractions: Superlative vistas; beach access across the highway.

Natural Features: Located on an unsheltered, rolling hilltop on the lower west slope of the Coast Range above the Pacific Ocean; campground vegetation consists mostly of a few bushes on a grassy surface; elevation 150'.

Season, Fees & Phone: Open all year; please see Appendix for standard California state park fees and reservation information; park info phone (805) 927-2020.

Camp Notes: From this windswept hilltop are incredible, splendid views of the coastal hills and mountains and of the ocean. If you're self-contained, or a tent, pickup or van camper with an appetite for adventure, Washburn would be the way to go at San Simeon.

CERRO ALTO
Los Padres National Forest

Location: Central California coastal area north of San Luis Obispo.

Access: From California State Highway 41 (Morro Road) at milepost 7 +.2 (8 miles northeast of Morro Bay, 9 miles southwest of Atascadero), turn south onto a narrow, winding, paved access road and proceed 0.5 mile to the first group of sites; remaining sites are situated along either side of the next 0.4 mile of the campground roadway.

Facilities: 24 campsites, including 8 walk-in units; sites are mostly small to medium in size, with minimal to very good separation; parking pads are paved or gravel, mainly short to medium-length straight-ins; additional leveling will probably be required on most pads; tent areas are small to medium-sized and sloped; fireplaces or barbecue grills; some firewood is available for gathering in the vicinity; water at several faucets; vault facilities; paved roadway; turnaround at the upper end; adequate supplies in Morro Bay; complete supplies and services are available in Atascadero.

Activities & Attractions: Cerro Alto Trail, a 2-mile, 2-hour walk, leads to what are reportedly some of the best views along the Central Coast; the area has many other trails which were heavily used as major supply routes by the early settlers; foot bridge across the creek.

Natural Features: Located in a heavily vegetated canyon along the East Fork of Morro Creek, in the Santa Lucia Range; tall oaks and willows provide a substantial amount of shelter/shade for the campsites; campground signs state that there is a considerable amount of poison oak in the area, particularly along the stream; a local promontory, 2620' Cerro Alto ("High Hill"), stands just to the southeast; elev. 1000'.

Season, Fees & Phone: Open all year; $7.00; 14 day limit; Santa Lucia Ranger District, Santa Maria, (805) 925-9538.

Camp Notes: This campground has received some favorable publicity because of its environment and because of the many trails in the area. Arrive early to get a summer weekend campsite.

MORRO STRAND
Morro Strand State Beach

Location: Central California Coast northwest of San Luis Obispo.

Access: From California State Highway 1 at milepost 32 (at the north edge of the city of Morro Bay), turn west onto Yerba Buena Street and proceed 0.2 mile to the campground.

Facilities: 104 campsites in 2 rows parallel to the beach; sites are small, level, with nil separation; parking pads are paved, short straight-ins/pull-offs (depending upon how you park); enough space for very small tents in most sites (see *Camp Notes*); fire rings; firewood is usually for sale, or b-y-o; water at several faucets; restrooms with freshwater rinse showers; paved driveways; adequate supplies and services are available in Morro Bay.

Activities & Attractions: Fishing.

Natural Features: Located just above the beach and below a short bluff; campground vegetation consists primarily of tall bushes and short trees between sites that provide some shelter from the wind, plus patches of grass for the table areas; sea level.

Season, Fees & Phone: Open all year; please see Appendix for standard California state park fees and reservation information; phone c/o Morro Bay State Park (805) 772-2560 or 772-9723.

Camp Notes: There actually isn't a lot of room for a tent in most of the campsites, but the parking space could be used for a large, free-standing tent if your vehicle is small. Good views of 600' Morro Rock and the ocean from the campground.

MORRO BAY
Morro Bay State Park

Location: Central California Coast northwest of San Luis Obispo.

Access: From California State Highway 1 at milepost 27 + .8 (11 miles northwest of San Luis Obispo, 1 mile south of the city of Morro Bay), turn south onto South Bay Boulevard; proceed 0.8 mile, then bear southwest (right) onto State Park Road (which gradually curves northwest and then north) for 0.75 mile to the campground.

Facilities: 135 campsites, including 20 with partial hookups; (hike-bike sites and a reservable group camp are also available); sites are small to small+, level, with nominal to fair separation; parking pads are medium-length, gravel/dirt straight-ins in most of the sites; hookup units have paved pull-throughs; good-sized, level tent areas; storage cabinets; fireplaces or fire rings; firewood is usually for sale, or b-y-o; water at hookups and at several faucets; restrooms with showers; holding tank disposal station; paved driveways; adequate supplies and services are available in Morro Bay.

Activities & Attractions: Museum of Natural History features displays and audio-visual programs; guided nature walks and interpretive programs; fitness trail; hiking trails, including trails to viewpoints on

Black Hill; fishing; boating; public boat launch just north of the park; 18-hole public golf course and marina, operated by concessionaires; day use area.

Natural Features: Located on a large wooded flat on the east shore of Morro Bay; tall conifers and some hardwoods provide a substantial amount of shelter/shade in most campsites; Black Hill rises to 661' east of the campground; sea level.

Season, Fees & Phone: Open all year; please see Appendix for standard California state park fees and reservation information; park office (805) 772-2560 or 772-9723.

Camp Notes: There's little doubt that this is one of the nicer coastal parks. From the museum's observation room you can look out to haystack-shaped Morro Rock and across Morro Bay through an array of large windows (bay windows, so to speak). No single state park in California has it all; but if you were to take the combined facilities, activities, attractions, ease of access, and super scenery of Morro Bay and its neighboring sister park, Montana de Oro, they would probably come closest to presenting you with the whole enchilada.

Southern California 8

MONTANA DE ORO
Montana de Oro State Park

Location: Southern California coastal area west of San Luis Obispo.

Access: From U.S. Highway 101 at milepost 25 +.8 on the south edge of San Luis Obispo, take the Los Osos/Baywood Exit and travel northwest on Los Osos Valley Road for 10.5 miles into Los Osos; pass through town, then west and south on Pecho Valley Road (paved) for 2 miles to the park boundary; continue for another 2.5 miles, then turn east (left) for 0.2 mile to the campground. **Alternate Access:** From California State Highway 1 at milepost 27 +.8 (1 mile southeast of the city of Morro Bay, 11 miles northwest of San Luis Obispo), turn south onto South Bay Boulevard and travel 5 miles into Los Osos; turn west (right) onto Los Osos Valley Road/Pecho Valley Road and continue as above.

Facilities: 50 campsites; sites are medium-sized, reasonably level (considering the terrain), with fair to fairly good separation; parking pads are mostly paved, short straight-ins, some are extra wide; adequate space for medium to large tents; fire rings; b-y-o firewood; water at a central faucet; vault facilities; paved driveways; adequate supplies and services are available in Los Osos.

Activities & Attractions: 50 miles of hiking and horse trails.

Natural Features: Located on hilly terrain in the San Luis Range above seven miles of Pacific Ocean shoreline; campsites are in a forested canyon and are sheltered by tall conifers plus some hardwoods, on a grassy surface; elevation 400'.

Season, Fees & Phone: Open all year; please see Appendix for standard California state park fees and reservation information; park office (805) 528-0513.

Camp Notes: *Montana de Oro* ("Mountain of Gold") refers not to the precious metal but to the natural springtime radiance of the mountainsides in this region. While you're camping here, (or on your way in or out), a brief side trip to Los Osos Oaks State Reserve might be worthwhile. The reserve is just off the south side of Los Osos Valley Road at the east edge of the town of Los Osos. A loop trail takes you through the 85-acre plot that holds stands of weathered, intricately gnarled, centuries-old oak trees.

Southern California 9

EL CHORRO
San Luis Obispo County Regional Park

Location: Central California coastal area northwest of San Luis Obispo.

Access: From California State Highway 1 at milepost 22 +.2 (5 miles northwest of San Luis Obispo, 6 miles southeast of Morro Bay, opposite the main entrance to the Camp San Luis Obispo National Guard facility), turn north onto a paved access road, and proceed 0.3 mile to the campground.

Facilities: 25 campsites; sites are mostly small, tolerably level considering the slope, with nominal separation; parking pads are paved, medium-length straight-ins; large areas for tents; fire rings; b-y-o firewood; water at several faucets; restrooms with coin-op showers; adequate supplies in Morro Bay; complete supplies and services are available in San Luis Obispo.

Activities & Attractions: Large day use area; sports field.

Natural Features: Located on a gentle slope in a valley surrounded by low, grassy hills; landscaping consists of small hardwoods and some conifers on a grassy surface; elevation 150'.

Season, Fees & Phone: Open all year; $11.00; 15 day limit; San Luis Obispo County Parks Department (805) 549-5219.

Camp Notes: If a campsite is tough to find at the area's seaside campgrounds (Pismo State Beach and Morro State Beach), as is often the case, El Chorro might be a welcome alternative. It's only a few minutes' drive from here to the sand and the surf. Superior views of neighboring hills and rugged mountains from up here.

NORTH BEACH
Pismo State Beach

Location: Southern California Coast south of San Luis Obispo.

Access: From California State Highway 1 at a point 0.75 mile north of the intersection of Highway 1 & Grand Avenue at the south edge of the city of Pismo Beach, turn west into the campground.

Facilities: 103 campsites; (hike-bike sites are also available); sites are generally medium-sized, level, with fair to very good separation; parking pads are paved, mostly long pull-throughs; top-notch tent spots; storage cabinets; fire rings; firewood is usually for sale, or b-y-o; water at several faucets; restrooms; holding tank disposal station; paved driveways; adequate+ supplies and services are within 1 mile.

Activities & Attractions: Short trails from the campground along a creek and to the beach; campfire center; golf course and day use area nearby.

Natural Features: Located on a large, grassy flat; tall hardwoods and evergreens provide very light to medium shelter/shade in most campsites; sea level.

Season, Fees & Phone: Open all year; please see Appendix for standard California state park fees and reservation information; park office (805) 489-2684.

Camp Notes: If you want to camp at Pismo Beach, it's a tough choice between North Beach and Oceano (see info below). Both are quite nice. This one is in a more open setting, with less tall vegetation, but with large, grassy areas. Like Oceano, there are no ocean views, but the sea is only a short walk away.

OCEANO
Pismo State Beach

Location: Southern California Coast south of San Luis Obispo.

Access: From California State Highway 1 in Oceano at a point 1.1 miles south of the intersection of Highway 1 and Grand Avenue in Grover City, turn west onto Pier Avenue and proceed 0.2 mile; turn north (right) into the campground entrance.

Facilities: 82 campsites, including 42 with partial hookups, in 2 sections; sites are small to small+, level, with minimal to fair separation; hookup pads are paved, medium to long, parallel pull-throughs; standard pads are mostly short to medium-length straight-ins; excellent tent-pitching possibilities in the standard section; fire rings; firewood is usually for sale, or b-y-o; water at several faucets; restrooms with showers; paved driveways; groceries nearby; adequate+ supplies and services are within 3 miles.

Activities & Attractions: Trails from the campground along the lagoon and to the beach; lagoon interpretive trail (a guide pamphlet is available); nature programs; beach access; Pismo Dunes SVRA, adjacent.

Natural Features: Located on a moderately to densely wooded flat; campsites are lightly to moderately shaded/sheltered by large hardwoods, tall conifers, and bushes; Oceano Lagoon, adjacent to the campground, and high dunes provide added natural interest; sea level.

Season, Fees & Phone: Open all year; please see Appendix for standard California state park fees and reservation information; park office (805) 489-2684.

Camp Notes: When the tide is out, there are several square miles of sand that you can wander out onto. Don't forget to pack your clam gun. The beach is world famous for its Pismo clams and you might bag a 'keeper'. (The Pismo mollusks once were so plentiful that settlers plowed the beach to harvest them, then used the 'crop' as fertilizer and livestock feed.) Oceano Lagoon, the campground's namesake, is a man-made freshwater pond dredged from the coastal marshlands. There are a couple of disadvantages to camping in the sites adjacent to the lagoon, especially if you're easily 'bugged'. Nonetheless, those spots are some of the more naturally interesting ones in the campground. Unlike most state parks and beaches on this section of the coast, Pismo's campsites are within moderate walking distances of plenty of goods and services. They're handy if you run out of beans and wienies, or you're just "born to shop".

GAVIOTA
Gaviota State Park

Location: Southern California Coast west of Santa Barbara.

Access: From U.S Highway 101 at milepost 46 +.3 (10 miles south of Buellton, 1 mile west of Gaviota, 32 miles west of Santa Barbara) turn southwest onto Gaviota Beach Road and proceed 0.3 mile to a fork; take the left fork for 0.1 mile to the campground. (Note: if northbound on U.S. 101, you'll have to figure out an appropriate way to get into the southbound lanes on the 4-lane, undivided highway in order to get onto the park road.)

Facilities: 59 campsites; (hike-bike sites are also available); most sites are very snug rectangles, level, in basically a parking lot-type arrangement in several parallel rows; parking areas are hard-surfaced, short straight-ins or short+ pull-offs; small tent areas in some sites, none in others; fire rings or barbecue grills; b-y-o firewood; water at central faucets; (b-y-o drinking water is recommended); restrooms with showers, plus auxiliary vaults; paved driveways; limited supplies and services are available in Buellton.

Activities & Attractions: Swimming beach; fishing; boat launch; pier; hiking and equestrian trails, including a short trail to a hot springs area and a trail which leads into adjacent Los Padres National Forest and to the summit of 2400' Gaviota Peak; (trails are accessed from near the junction of U.S.101 & State Highway 1).

Natural Features: Located at the lower end of a canyon (Cañada de la Gaviota) near a small beach; rows of large hardwoods provide light to medium shade/shelter; a small creek flows past the campground; bordered by rocky, grassy hills and low mountains dotted with trees and brush; sea level.

Season, Fees & Phone: Open all year; please see Appendix for standard California state park fees and reservation information; phone c/o CDPR Gaviota District Office, Goleta, (805) 968-3294.

Camp Notes: Seeing only this close-quartered campground and its small beach might lead you to wonder if Gaviota is little more than a state beach with a state park signboard. (Glancing skyward to the railroad trestle which looms over the campground might raise a question or two, as well.) But the park's territory goes east from the beach for two miles, and flanks '101 for about a mile on either side of the highway, so there's still room for a measure of seclusion here. If you're not very deep into beach play or hiking but still want to stick around for a while, you might consider taking a side trip to the unique city of Solvang, three miles southeast of Buellton. Solvang claims the title of "Danish Capital of America", and probably is the largest of the European-motif communities in the West. The town's architectural style is pure Scandinavian gingerbread. (Or is it Danish pastry?)

REFUGIO
Refugio State Beach

Location: Southern California Coast west of Santa Barbara.

Access: From U.S. Highway 101 near milepost 36 +.5 (9 miles east of Gaviota, 22 miles west of Santa Barbara), take the Refugio Road Exit, then from the south side of the freeway, go southwest on Refugio Road for 0.4 mile to the park entrance station and the campground. (If you're northbound on U.S. 101, you'll need to take a freeway underpass to get onto the park road.)

Facilities: 85 campsites in 2 sections; (hike-bike sites and a large group camp are also available); sites are very small to small, level, with minimal to fair separation; sites in the south section are perhaps a little larger and better-separated than those in the other loop; parking pads are gravel/dirt, mostly short straight-ins; small tent areas; fire rings; firewood is usually for sale, or b-y-o; water at several faucets; restrooms with showers; paved driveways; complete supplies and services are available in Santa Barbara.

Activities & Attractions: Swimming beach; surf fishing; large day use area.

Natural Features: Located along and near a small cove on the Santa Barbara Channel; the park has lots of short and tall palms, big hardwoods, shrubbery, and open, expansive lawns; most campsites are well shaded and sheltered; bordered by the Santa Ynez Mountains to the north; sea level.

Season, Fees & Phone: Open all year; please see Appendix for standard California state park fees and reservation information; park office (805) 968-3294.

Camp Notes: Refugio's landscaping should rank near the top of all state beaches' implementations of trees, shrubs, and grass. On an off-season weekend, it would be a very nice place to spend some leisure time. All three beaches on this east-west segment of the Coast benefit from direct southerly exposure and are fairly well sheltered from heavy seas when a norther' blows down the Coast. The Channel Islands provide a measure of protection from southerly seas as well.

EL CAPITAN
El Capitan State Beach

Location: Southern California Coast west of Santa Barbara.

Access: From U.S. Highway 101 at milepost 34 (11 miles east of Gaviota, 20 miles west of Santa Barbara), turn south onto the park access road for 0.2 mile to the park entrance station; swing right into the campground.

Facilities: 142 campsites in 4 loops; (hike-bike sites, enroute sites and 3 group camps are also available); sites are small or small+, generally level, with nominal to fair separation; parking pads are paved, short straight-ins, but many are extra wide; medium to large areas for tents; fire rings; firewood is usually for sale, or b-y-o; water at several faucets; restrooms with showers; holding tank disposal station; paved driveways; complete supplies and services are available in Santa Barbara.

Activities & Attractions: Beach access; swimming areas; surf fishing for perch, bass and halibut; small interpretive center; several day use areas.

Natural Features: Located near the beach and on a bluff overlooking the Santa Barbara Channel; medium-dense to dense hardwoods provide good to excellent shelter/shade for campsites; the Santa Ynez Mountains rise just north of the park; sea level.

Season, Fees & Phone: Open all year; please see Appendix for standard California state park fees and reservation information; phone c/o CDPR Gaviota District Office, Goleta, (805) 968-3294.

Camp Notes: Like several other campgrounds along the coast, some sites are close to railroad tracks and to the highway, but you can't have everything. El Capitan State Beach was once part of *Rancho Nuestra Sonora del Refugio*, ('Our Lady of Refuge Ranch') which stretched from here westerly to near Point Conception, south of Lompoc. The 25-mile band of coastline, hills and innumerable canyons on the south slopes of the Santa Ynez Mountains was originally owned by Jose Francisco de Ortega, who was addressed as *"El Capitan"*.

CACHUMA LAKE
Santa Barbara County Recreation Area

Location: Southwest California north of Santa Barbara.

Access: From California State Highway 154 at milepost 14 +.7 (24 miles northwest of Santa Barbara, 7 miles southeast of Santa Ynez), turn northeast onto a paved access road and continue 0.2 mile to the park entrance; most campsites are straight ahead or east (right) of the entrance.

Facilities: 530 campsites (+/- a dozen or so), including a few with hookups, in 6 major areas; (hike-bike sites are also available; group camp areas are available by reservation); sites vary from small to medium+ in size, with minimal to very good separation; most parking pads are gravel/dirt, short to medium-length straight-ins; hookup pads are gravel, long straight-ins which may require additional leveling; most tent areas are large and generally level; fireplaces or fire rings; b-y-o firewood; water at several faucets; restrooms with showers; holding tank disposal station; paved driveways; gas and camper supplies and laundry in the park; limited supplies and services are available in Santa Ynez.

Activities & Attractions: Boating; fishing for bass, panfish, trout and catfish; nature trails; swimming pool; playground.

Natural Features: Located on a peninsula on the northwest shore of man-made Cachuma Lake, on the north slope of the Santa Ynez Mountains; vegetation consists of lots of oaks and a few pines throughout the park, plus sections of lawns; elevation 800'.

Season, Fees & Phone: Open all year; $11.00 for a standard site, $15.00 for a hookup site; park office (805) 688-4658.

Camp Notes: A description of this BIG campground is difficult to encapsulate. The largest and most private sites are in the Mohawk area, 0.5 mile east (right) of the entrance station. The hookup units are in the Apache area, near the entrance. The best views (and there are some really great lake/mountain views here) may be from the camping areas out along a peninsula, directly north (straight ahead) of the entrance station. Then, too, there's a small cluster of hike-bike-tent sites on Teepee Island, accessible via a footbridge adjacent to a parking area. Good luck!

FREMONT
Los Padres National Forest

Location: Southwest California north of Santa Barbara.

Access: From California State Highway 154 at milepost 21 +.6 (17 miles north of Santa Barbara, 14 miles southeast of Santa Ynez), turn east onto Paradise Road and travel 3.3 miles; turn south (right) into the campground.

Facilities: 15 campsites; sites are medium-sized, with minimal to nominal visual separation; parking pads are short, paved straight-ins; some pads may need additional leveling; some large, but sloped, tent areas; fire rings and barbecue grills; b-y-o firewood is suggested; water at several faucets; restrooms; limited supplies in Santa Ynez; complete supplies and services are available in Santa Barbara.

Activities & Attractions: Numerous foot, horse, and vehicle trails in the canyon; seasonal fishing on the Santa Ynez River.

Natural Features: Located on a hillside above the Santa Ynez River in Santa Ynez Canyon in the Santa Ynez Mountains; sites are moderately shaded/sheltered by large oaks; elevation 1000'.

Season, Fees & Phone: Open all year; $7.00; 14 day limit; Santa Barbara Ranger District (805) 967-3481.

Camp Notes: This are the first of the campgrounds in the one-way in/one-way out road in Santa Ynez Canyon. For larger vehicle combinations, Fremont's short, somewhat sloped parking areas probably make it the least desirable of the area's five campgrounds. Good views from this hillside.

PARADISE
Los Padres National Forest

Location: Southwest California north of Santa Barbara.

Access: From California State Highway 154 at milepost 21 +.6 (17 miles north of Santa Barbara, 14 miles southeast of Santa Ynez), turn east onto Paradise Road and proceed 3.9 miles; turn south (right) into the campground.

Facilities: 15 campsites; sites are medium to large, with minimal to nominal separation; parking pads are gravel/dirt, mostly level, medium to long straight-ins; excellent tent camping possibilities; fire rings and barbecue grills; b-y-o firewood is suggested; water at several faucets; restrooms; limited supplies in Santa Ynez; complete supplies and services are available in Santa Barbara.

Activities & Attractions: Many hiking, horse, and vehicle trails in the canyon; seasonal fishing on the Santa Ynez River.

Natural Features: Located on a large flat in Santa Ynez Canyon along the north slope of the Santa Ynez Mountains; the campground is moderately shaded/sheltered by large oak trees; elevation 1000'.

Season, Fees & Phone: Open all year; $7.00; 14 day limit; Santa Barbara Ranger District (805) 967-3481.

Camp Notes: Paradise is excellent for both vehicles and tents, but tends to be more populated than its relative, Fremont, just down the road. Good views of the mountains to the north, across the canyon from the campground. The river is stocked in early spring, and fishing is reportedly good then, until the river dries in April or May.

LOS PIETROS
Los Padres National Forest

Location: Southwest California north of Santa Barbara.

Access: From California State Highway 154 at milepost 21 +.6 (17 miles north of Santa Barbara, 14 miles southeast of Santa Ynez), turn east onto Paradise Road and drive 4.7 miles; turn south (right) into the campground.

Facilities: 37 campsites; sites are average-sized, with nominal separation; parking pads are paved, short to medium-length straight-ins, and many will require a little additional leveling; large, but slightly sloped, tent areas; fire rings and barbecue grills; b-y-o firewood is recommended; water at several faucets; restrooms; paved driveway; ranger station 0.8 mile east; limited supplies in Santa Ynez; complete supplies and services are available in Santa Barbara.

Activities & Attractions: Trails; early spring trout fishing on the Santa Ynez River.

Natural Features: Located on a rolling slope on the south side of Santa Ynez Canyon; most sites are quite well shaded/sheltered by large oak trees; some views of the canyon and nearby mountains from the campground area; elevation 1000'.

Season, Fees & Phone: Open all year; $7.00; 14 day limit; Santa Barbara Ranger District (805) 967-3481.

Camp Notes: Interestingly, even though this area is only 10 miles from the ocean, summer days often experience temperatures well into the 90's. The high temps are due to a regional phenomenon known as the Santa Ana, a hot, dry, easterly wind. This campground might be an excellent choice for a warm-day camp, since it has more shade than any of the other campgrounds in Santa Ynez Canyon.

Southern California 19

UPPER OSO
Los Padres National Forest

Location: Southwest California north of Santa Barbara.

Access: From California State Highway 154 at milepost 21 +.6 (17 miles north of Santa Barbara, 14 miles southeast of Santa Ynez), turn east onto Paradise Road and ride 6.7 miles; turn north (left) onto a narrow, paved road and continue for 1.1 miles to the campground.

Facilities: 27 campsites, including 14 equestrian units, and several park 'n walk sites, in 2 loops; parking pads are paved, basically level, straight-ins; primary loop has medium-length pads, equestrian loop has long pads; excellent spots for large tents in most sites; steel corrals in the equestrian area; fire rings and barbecue grills; b-y-o firewood is suggested; water at several faucets; restrooms; paved driveways; limited supplies in Santa Ynez; complete supplies and services are available in Santa Barbara.

Activities & Attractions: Trailhead for the Santa Cruz Trail, which leads north into the San Rafael Wilderness; other foot and horse trails in the area; designated two-wheeled vehicle routes; fishing for stocked trout on the Santa Ynez River in early spring; Lower Oso is a picnic area.

Natural Features: Located in a side canyon/arroyo off Santa Ynez Canyon along the north slope of the Santa Ynez Mountains; campground vegetation consists of some tall, full oak trees on a grassy surface; the campground is bordered by low, rocky hills, with high and dry mountains in the distance; signs indicate this is rattlesnake country; elevation 1200'.

Season, Fees & Phone: Open all year; $7.00; 14 day limit; Santa Barbara Ranger District (805) 967-3481.

Camp Notes: This is one of the few easily accessible forest campgrounds in the region which can accommodate horses quite handily. There are some nice views of Santa Ynez Canyon area from in and near the campground.

Southern California 20

SANTA YNEZ
Los Padres National Forest

Location: Southwest California north of Santa Barbara.

Access: From California State Highway 154 at milepost 21 +.6 (17 miles north of Santa Barbara, 14 miles southeast of Santa Ynez), turn east onto Paradise Road and travel 8.8 miles to the campground, on the south (right) side of the road.

Facilities: 34 campsites; sites are medium to medium+ in size, level, with minimal separation; parking pads are gravel, medium-length straight-ins; plenty of room for tents; fire rings and barbecue grills; limited firewood is available for gathering, b-y-o is suggested; water at several faucets; vault facilities; narrow, paved driveway; limited supplies in Santa Ynez; complete supplies and services are available in Santa Barbara.

Activities & Attractions: Fishing; hiking trails; several orv roads and trails.

Natural Features: Located near the bank of the Santa Ynez River in Santa Inez Canyon along the north slope of the Santa Ynez Mountains; campground vegetation consists of grass and some low brush, plus tall, full oak trees which provide a considerable amount of shade/shelter; somewhat dry, tree-and-brush-covered hills and high mountains surround the area; elevation 1100'.

Season, Fees & Phone: Open all year; $7.00; 14 day limit; Santa Barbara Ranger District (805) 967-3481.

Camp Notes: This is the farthest east of the five major campgrounds in the Santa Ynez Recreation area. It might be helpful for you to stop at the ranger station at Los Prietos, 4 miles west of here, on the north side of Paradise Road, on the way to the campground. Maps and detailed information about local foot trails and areas designated for orv (off-road vehicle) use are available there.

Southern California 21

SAN LORENZO
Monterey County Regional Park

Location: Western California south of Salinas.

Access: From U.S. Highway 101 at the Broadway Exit in King City near milepost 41, proceed east for 0.4 mile to the park entrance; the campground is 0.5 mile beyond the entrance.

Facilities: 125 assorted campsites, including nearly 100 with partial or full hookups; (a nice group camp area is also available); sites are small to medium-sized, level, with minimal to nominal separation; parking pads are grass, packed gravel, or hard-surfaced, long straight-ins or long parallel pull-throughs; large, sandy pads for tents in standard sites; fire rings or barbecue grills; water at central faucets and at hookup sites; restrooms with showers; holding tank disposal station; paved driveways; adequate+ supplies and services are available in King City.

Activities & Attractions: Agriculture and Rural Life Museum features exhibits of antique farm equipment; day use area; playground.

Natural Features: Located on a large flat in the Salinas River Valley; sites receive very light to light-medium shade from very large hardwoods and some evergreens on a watered and mown grass surface; bordered by agricultural land; the valley is flanked by hills and mountains in the medium distance; elevation 300'.

Season, Fees & Phone: Open all year; $10.00 for a standard site, $14.00 for a partial hookup site, $16.00 for a full hookup site, $1.00 for a pooch; weekly rates available; park office (408) 755-4899.

Camp Notes: Good mountain views east and west, particularly west toward the Coast Range. Probably one of the best freeway stops in the state.

Southern California 22

WHEELER GORGE
Los Padres National Forest

Location: Southwest California northeast of Ventura.

Access: From California State Highway 33 (Maricopa Highway) at milepost 19 +.2 (9 miles north of Ojai, 60 miles south of Maricopa) turn west into the campground.

Facilities: 72 campsites; sites are generally medium-sized, level, with good visual separation; most parking pads are paved, short to medium-length straight-ins; some pads are gravel, and a handful are long, paved pull-throughs; medium-sized tent areas; fire rings and barbecue grills; b-y-o firewood is recommended; water at several faucets; vault facilities; paved driveways; adequate+ supplies and services are available in Ojai.

Activities & Attractions: Fishing; many trails in the area; Matilija Hot Springs and Matilija Reservoir, 4 miles southwest.

Natural Features: Located on a roadside flat along the North Fork of Matilija Creek in Wheeler Gorge; vegetation in the campground consists primarily of dense, medium-high oaks and willows which provide a considerable amount of shade/shelter; small side streams flow through the campground; surrounded by dry, brushy hills and mountains; elevation 2000'.

Season, Fees & Phone: April to November; $9.00; 14 day limit; Ojai Ranger District (805) 646-4348.

Camp Notes: If you're coming from Ojai (which, chances are, you will be), you'll have to pass through several low, narrow tunnels and a slim section of road to get here. The highway is really snakey coming in from the north, as well. Information and sketched maps about the trails in the area may be available at the campground's info station, or from the ranger station in Ojai. Another local public campground is

Camp Comfort County Park, on the southwest corner of Ojai. It has close to a hundred small tent and rv sites (some with electrical-hookups), and showers.

LAKE CASITAS
Casitas Municipal Water District Recreation Area

Location: Southwest California north of Ventura.

Access: From California State Highway 150 at milepost 11 +.3 (5 miles west of Ojai, 17 miles east of Carpinteria), turn south onto Santa Ana Road, proceed 0.15 mile, then turn west (right) to the entrance station. **Alternate Access:** From California State Highway 33 at milepost 8.9 in Oak View, turn west onto Santa Ana Boulevard, drive 1 mile, then turn north onto Santa Ana Road and continue for 2.2 miles to the entrance station.

Facilities: 461 campsites in 12 areas; sites are generally small to medium-sized and closely spaced; sites vary from level to somewhat sloped; most parking pads are dirt/gravel, primarily short to medium-length, straight-ins or pull-offs; adequate space for a large tent in most sites; fire rings or fireplaces in many sites; b-y-o firewood; water at several faucets; restrooms, supplemented by vault facilities; coin-op showers; holding tank disposal station; paved driveways; 24-hour security; limited supplies in Oak View; adequate+ supplies ad services are available in Ojai.

Activities & Attractions: Boating (extra-fee permit required); no canoes, kayaks, inflatables, and other small craft permitted; fishing for trout, bass, catfish and panfish (fishing hours vary).

Natural Features: Located along the north shoreline of Lake Casitas in Santa Ana Valley; site conditions vary from open to sheltered, level to hilly; a variety of hardwoods provide varying degrees of shelter/shade; some areas have mown lawns; surrounded by low hills and mountains; elevation 600'.

Season, Fees & Phone: Open all year; $10.00; 14 day limit; park office (805) 649-2233.

Camp Notes: It might be a good idea to contact the park prior to visiting here, since there is an extensive list of do's and don'ts applicable to the use of the facilities which may affect your plans.

STECKEL
Ventura County Park

Location: Southwest California northeast of Ventura.

Access: From California State Highway 150 at milepost 29.9 (3.4 miles north of Santa Paula, 11 miles west of Ojai), turn east onto Mupu Road, cross the bridge, then turn south into the campground; the campground's loops are located along a half-mile-long section of paved road.

Facilities: 121 campsites, including some with electrical hookups, in 5 loops; sites are small, basically level, with little separation; most parking pads are paved, short straight-ins; tent-pitching in designated areas; assorted fire appliances; b-y-o firewood; water at several faucets; central restrooms; paved driveways in most loops; adequate supplies and services are available in Santa Paula.

Activities & Attractions: Playground; horseshoe pits.

Natural Features: Located on a flat on the east bank of Santa Paula Creek; several loops have small to medium-height hardwoods; the loop closest to the creek, has large, full oak trees which provide the greatest amount of shade/shelter in the campground; some grass has been planted in several loops; surrounded by semi-dry hills and mountains; elevation 600'.

Season, Fees & Phone: Open all year; $9.00 for a site, $3.00 additional for electrical hookups; Ventura County Parks Department, Ventura, (805) 654-3951.

Camp Notes: This park is located in one of the state's more productive agricultural areas. Another county park with a campground, Kenney Grove, is east of here, off State Highway 126, just northwest of Fillmore. Kenney Grove (appropriately, in a stand of oak and eucalyptus and surrounded by orange groves) has 55 campsites, including some with electrical hookups.

CARPINTERIA
Carpinteria State Beach

Location: Southern California Coast northwest of Ventura.

Access: From U.S. Highway 101 in Carpinteria, take the Casitas Pass Road/California State Highway 224 Exit at milepost 2 +.6; proceed west on Highway 224 to Carpinteria Avenue, north on Carpinteria Avenue to Palm Avenue, then west on Palm Avenue to the park entrance and the campground, for a total of 0.75 mile from the freeway.

Facilities: 262 campsites, including 86 with full hookups; (hike-bike sites are also available); sites are very small to small+, level, with zilch to nominal separation; most parking pads are paved, short to medium-length straight-ins; parking slots in the hookup section are very short, double-wide straight-ins; some pull-off/parallel parking for longer rv's; enough space for small to medium-sized tents; fire rings; firewood is usually for sale, or b-y-o; water at faucets throughout; restrooms with showers; holding tank disposal station; paved driveways; adequate+ supplies and services are available in Carpinteria.

Activities & Attractions: Beachcombing; swimming; fitness area; clamming; visitor center with displays about whale-watching, tide pools and Chumash Indians; large day use area.

Natural Features: Located on level terrain at the edge of an ocean beach; vegetation consists of very light to medium-dense, large hardwoods and conifers, a few palms, and large, grassy areas; sea level.

Season, Fees & Phone: Open all year; please see Appendix for standard California state park fees and reservation information; park office (805) 684-2811.

Camp Notes: The surroundings are generally quite nice, and thus the place is really packed most of the summer. Good views of the Channel Islands.

HOBSON BEACH
Ventura County Park

Location: Southern California Coast northwest of Ventura.

Access: From U.S. Highway 101 (northbound) near milepost 32 +.5 (3 miles northwest of Ventura), from the east side of the freeway proceed through the underpass to the west side, then go northerly (right) on Rincon Parkway (a frontage road) for 5 miles; turn west (left) into the park. **Alternate Access:** From U.S 101 at the Sea Cliff Exit (10 miles northwest of Ventura, 7 miles southeast of Carpinteria), go to the west side of the freeway, then travel south on Rincon Parkway for 0.7 mile; turn west (right) into the park and the campground.

Facilities: 28 campsites; sites are small, with minimal separation; parking slots are hard-surfaced, short straight-ins; small areas for free-standing tents; fire rings; b-y-o firewood; water at several faucets; restrooms with showers; paved driveway; camper supplies at a park store; complete supplies and services are available in Ventura

Activities & Attractions: Ocean views; shore fishing.

Natural Features: Located on a short shelf just above the Pacific Ocean; a few tall palms decorate the grounds, and provide limited shade for some sites, but most sites are unsheltered; sea level.

Season, Fees & Phone: Open all year; $14.00; 14 day limit; reservations accepted, contact Ventura County Parks Department, Ventura, (805) 654-3951.

Camp Notes: Overnight parallel parking for over 100 self-contained vehicles is also available along several miles of Rincon Parkway south of here. For several dollars less than at Hobson Beach, you get about the same amount of parking space, and vaults.

FARIA BEACH
Ventura County Park

Location: Southern California Coast northwest of Ventura.

Access: From U.S. Highway 101 (northbound) near milepost 32 +.5 (3 miles northwest of Ventura), from the east side of the freeway proceed through the underpass to the west side, then go northerly (right) on Rincon Parkway (a frontage road) for 4 miles to the park; turn west (left) into the park. **Alternate Access:** From U.S. 101 (southbound), just drive past the park and get off the freeway at the next exit, 1 mile southeast of the park; double-back northwest to the above-mentioned limited (north-off/south-on) exit, then go north on Rincon Parkway.

Facilities: 42 campsites; sites are very small, level, with zip separation; parking surfaces are paved, short straight-ins; a small, free-standing tent could be set up in the parking space; fire rings; b-y-o firewood;

water at several faucets; restrooms with showers; paved driveway; camper supplies at a park store; complete supplies and services are available in Ventura.

Activities & Attractions: Ocean views; surf fishing from the seawall.

Natural Features: Located on a short shelf just above the Pacific Ocean; campsites are essentially unsheltered; several palms and some other trees make up most of the park's landscaping; sea level.

Season, Fees & Phone: Open all year; $14.00; 14 day limit; reservations accepted contact Ventura County Parks Department, Ventura, (805) 654-3951.

Camp Notes: So you thought only the national parks held the franchises on miniscule campsites? Witnessing a medium-sized rv maneuver into one of these slots is analogous to watching a circus hippo wiggle into an easy chair.

Southern California 28

EMMA WOOD
Emma Wood State Beach

Location: Southern California Coast northwest of Ventura.

Access: From U.S. Highway 101 (northbound) near milepost 32 +.5 (3 miles northwest of Ventura), from the east side of the freeway proceed through the underpass to the west side, then go south on a frontage road for 0.7 mile to the park. **Alternate Access:** From U.S. 101 (southbound), the simplest access is just to drive past the park and get off the freeway at the next exit, 1 mile southeast of the park, then double-back northwest to the above-mentioned partial (north-off/south-on) exit. (Note: there's limited turnaround space at the south end of the park driveway.)

Facilities: 61 campsites; sites are very small, with nil separation; parking slots are paved, ultra short straight-ins; enough space for small tents; no drinking water; vault facilities; holding tank disposal station; paved driveways; complete supplies and services are available in Ventura.

Activities & Attractions: Unrestricted ocean views; fishing.

Natural Features: Located on a narrow strip of land on a short shelf above a mile-long, rocky beach; sites are unsheltered; sea level.

Season, Fees & Phone: Open all year; $10.00; operated by Ventura County; reservations accepted, contact Ventura County Parks Department, Ventura, (805) 654-3951.

Camp Notes: The camp slots are situated in a mile-long string stretched along the shore. At high tide on a windy day, your trailer tongue will be lapping sea water. The freeway is fairly close behind and above the beach, but the railroad tracks between '101 and the park would probably block any misguided vehicles from dropping into your campsite.

Southern California
L.A. Basin
Please refer to the Northern California map in the Appendix

Southern California 29

McGRATH
McGrath State Beach

Location: Southern California Coast west of Oxnard.

Access: From U.S. Highway 101 near milepost 28 +.5 in Ventura, take the Seaward Avenue Exit, then from the south/west side of the freeway, turn southeast (left) onto Harbor Boulevard and go southeast and south for 3 miles; turn west (right) onto the park access road and go 0.15 mile to the park entrance station; the first campsites are 0.15 mile beyond the entrance. **Alternate Access:** From California State Highway 1 (Oxnard Boulevard) in Oxnard, at a point 1 mile south of the junction of State Highway 1 & U.S. Highway 101 turn west onto Gonzales Road and travel 4.5 miles; turn north (right) onto Harbor Boulevard and proceed 0.6 mile; turn west (left) onto the park access road and continue as above.

Facilities: 174 campsites; (a hike-bike site is also available); sites are small to small+, level, with nominal to fairly good separation; parking pads are paved, short to medium-length straight-ins; large, grassy areas for tents; fire rings; b-y-o firewood; water at central faucets; restrooms with showers; disposal station; paved driveways; complete supplies and services are available in Ventura and Oxnard.

Activities & Attractions: Beachcombing; trail to the beach; Santa Clara River Nature Trail; small visitor center; campfire center; Channel Islands NP visitor center, 1 mile north.

Natural Features: Located near an ocean beach; the campground is on the lee side of a dune and has large expanses of grass bordered by dense bushes and medium-height trees; Santa Clara Estuary Natural Preserve, adjacent; sea level.

Season, Fees & Phone: Open all year; please see Appendix for standard California state park fees and reservation information; park office (805) 654-4744

Camp Notes: McGrath's campground is unique among California camps. The sites are situated in six clusters or pods, with three perfectly circular cul-de-sacs within each pod. The parking pads radiate outward at an angle from each cul-de-sac. The entire campground, therefore, if you were to view it from above (or on the campground map), would resemble an assemblage of gears--for an 18-speed transmission, a Rube Goldberg contraption, or maybe a cuckoo clock.

THORNHILL BROOM BEACH
Point Mugu State Park

Location: Southern California Coast southeast of Oxnard.

Access: From California State Highway 1 at milepost 5 +.9 (13 miles southeast of Oxnard, 21 miles northwest of Malibu) turn south (i.e., right, if approaching from Oxnard) into the campground.

Facilities: 102 (semi-primitive) campsites in 2 sections; sites are very small with nil separation; parking surfaces are paved, short straight-ins or medium-length pull-offs; fire rings; b-y-o firewood; water at central faucets; vault facilities; outside, freshwater rinse showers; paved driveways; complete supplies and services are available in Oxnard.

Activities & Attractions: Swimming, surfing, windsurfing; La Jolla Canyon trailhead parking area, on the north side of the highway, 0.1 mile west of the campground entrance.

Natural Features: Located along an open, ocean beach; campground vegetation consists of a small amount of brush and grass; the low, rocky and brushy Santa Monica Mountains rise just behind the beach; sea level.

Season, Fees & Phone: Open all year; phone c/o CDPR Santa Monica Mountains District Office, Newbury Park, (818) 706-1310 or (805) 499-2112.

Camp Notes: This area is also known as La Jolla Beach. Although the physical facilities in this camp area are pretty basic, the local scenery is pretty good. A large, haystack rock adds interest to the shoreline at Point Mugu itself, at the northwest edge of the park, just up the coast from this beach. The park has a total of about five miles of ocean frontage, and you can see much of it from here. In fact, *Mugu* is derived from the Chumash Indian word *muwu*, meaning "beach".

BIG SYCAMORE CANYON
Point Mugu State Park

Location: Southern California Coast southeast of Oxnard.

Access: From California State Highway 1 at milepost 4 +.4 (14 miles southeast of Oxnard, 20 miles northwest of Malibu) turn north (i.e., left if approaching from Oxnard) and proceed 0.15 mile to the campground entrance station and the campground.

Facilities: 58 campsites; (hike-bike sites in the campground, plus individual and group backcountry camps are also available); sites are small+, essentially level, with minimal to fair separation; parking pads are paved, mostly short straight-ins, some are extra wide; small to medium-sized tent areas; fire rings; b-y-o firewood; water at central faucets; restrooms with showers; holding tank disposal station; paved driveways; complete supplies and services are available in Oxnard.

Activities & Attractions: Swimming, surfing, windsurfing; more than 70 miles of hiking and equestrian trails; mountain bike travel on designated fire roads; (a large, detailed park brochure/trail map with contour lines is available); trailhead parking here for the Sycamore Canyon Trail, and also 2 miles north at the La Jolla Canyon trailhead; day use area across the highway.

Natural Features: Located at the mouth of Sycamore Canyon in the Santa Monica Mountains; campsites are on the canyon floor, several hundred yards from the beach and are lightly to moderately shaded/sheltered by bushes and trees; canyon slopes are tree-and-brush-covered; sea level.

Season, Fees & Phone: Open all year; please see Appendix for standard California state park fees and reservation information; phone c/o CDPR Santa Monica Mountains District Office, Newbury Park, (818) 706-1310 or (805) 499-2112.

Camp Notes: Sycamore Canyon's environmental conditions are nearly perfect for the wintering of monarch butterflies, and millions of the vividly marked and colored insects migrate to the lower canyon in early fall. Monarchs aren't the only noteworthy visitors to the park: California gray whales reportedly have demonstrated a certain preference for the shallow waters just offshore of the park's beaches and can often be seen during their annual December to May migration.

LEO CARRILLO
Leo Carrillo State Beach

Location: Southern California Coast west of Santa Monica.

Access: From California State Highway 1 at milepost 62 +.2 (0.6 mile south of the Los Angeles-Ventura county line, 20 miles south of Oxnard, 28 miles northwest of Santa Monica,) turn east to the park entrance; Canyon section is to the east of the entrance; Beachside section is accessible via an underpass. (Vehicles must be less than 8 feet high to use the underpass.)

Facilities: 50 campsites in the Beach section, 78 sites in the Canyon section; (hike-bike sites and a walk-in group camp are also available); sites in the Beach section are in a paved parking lot arrangement, with short, level, straight-in parking slots and fireplaces; Canyon section has conventional, small+, acceptably level, fairly well-separated sites with paved, short+ parking pads and fire rings; firewood is usually for sale, or b-y-o; water at several faucets; restrooms with showers; holding tank disposal station; paved driveways; nearest sources of adequate supplies are in Oxnard and Santa Monica.

Activities & Attractions: Swimming beach; surf fishing; several miles of hiking trails; guided nature walks.

Natural Features: Located on the beach and in a canyon a few hundred yards from the beach; very little vegetation or shelter in the beach section; large hardwoods, shrubs and grass in the canyon section; sea level to 200'.

Season, Fees & Phone: Open all year; please see Appendix for standard California state park fees and reservation information; phone c/o CDPR Santa Monica Mountains District Office, Newbury Park, (818) 706-1310 or (805) 499-2112.

Camp Notes: If you don't *have* to have a campsite with a continuous ocean view, the very nice, wooded, Canyon section might be considered the area of choice here. Leo Carrillo had many starring roles in the golden days of radio and motion pictures, and was active in civic affairs. But he may be best-known for his weekly performances, with co-star Duncan Ranaldo, in the early days of television as the jovial sidekick of the *Cisco Kid*.

MALIBU CREEK
Malibu Creek State Park

Location: Southern California northwest of Los Angeles.

Access: From U.S. Highway 101 (Ventura Freeway) at the Las Virgenes Road/Malibu Canyon Exit (7 miles east of Thousand Oaks, 6 miles west of Woodland Hills), travel south on Las Virgenes Road/L.A. County Road N1 for 3.5 miles; turn west (right) onto the park access road for 0.1 mile to the entrance station; continue past the entrance continue southwest and south for another 0.7 mile to the campground. **Alternate Access:** From California State Highway 1 at a point 2 miles west of Malibu, head north on Malibu Canyon Road/L.A. County Road N1 for 6 miles to the park access road and continue as above.

Facilities: 63 campsites; (hike-bike sites and 2 group camps are also available); sites are small+, with nominal separation; parking pads are hard-surfaced, short straight-ins; additional leveling will be required in some sites; enough space for just about any-size tent; fireplaces; charcoal fires only; water at several faucets; restrooms with showers; holding tank disposal station; paved driveways; complete supplies and services are available in Thousand Oaks and Woodland Hills.

Activities & Attractions: More than 15 miles of hike/horse trails; mountain bikes are limited to 15 miles of designated fire roads; (a large, detailed park brochure/map with contour lines is available from the park office); nature trail for visually handicapped individuals; fishing for rainbow trout (stocked in cooler seasons), bass, bluegill, sunfish, bullheads; visitor center; campfire center; day use area nearby.

Natural Features: Located in Malibu Canyon in the craggy Santa Monica Mountains; campsites are unshaded to very lightly shaded; elevation 700'.

Season, Fees & Phone: Open all year; please see Appendix for standard California state park fees; phone c/o CDPR Santa Monica Mountains District Office, Newbury Park, (818) 706-1310 or (805) 987-3303.

Camp Notes: Malibu Creek's stated role is offering outdoor recreation opportunities "on the boundary of two worlds ... the freeways, people and pressures of the Los Angeles Basin ... and within an easy walk are rugged cliffs and shady canyons, brushy fields and bedrock pools, solitude and silence". (On a visit to Malibu Creek's campground one fine Sunday afternoon, we spotted a lanky dude sprinting up a trail toting a four-cubic-foot boom box, closely shadowed by a pair of petite picnickers struggling with an eight-cubic-foot cooler. A few people never get the word. Ed.)

TOPANGA
Topanga State Park

Location: Southern California northwest of Los Angeles.

Access: From California State Highway 27 at milepost 4 +.7 (8 miles south of the junction of Highway 27 & U.S. 101 in Woodland Hills, 5 miles north of the junction of Highway 27 & State Highway 1 in Topanga Beach), turn east (i.e., left if approaching from '101) onto Entrada Road and wind steeply up for 1.1 mile to the park entrance station; continue ahead for 0.1 mile to the main parking lots and trailheads.

Facilities: Primitive trail camps for hikers, bicyclists and equestrians (register with the park office); drinking water, vaults, hitch rails and water troughs; complete supplies and services are available in Woodland Hills; nearest standard public campground is in Malibu Creek State Park.

Activities & Attractions: More than 30 miles of hiking and equestrian trails; mountain biking on designated fire roads; nature trail (a guide pamphlet is available).

Natural Features: Located in and above Topanga Canyon and in the Santa Monica Mountains east of the canyon; vegetation consists mostly of stands of hardwoods, brush and open grassy sections; majority of the park is near-wilderness; elevation 1400' to 2100'.

Season, Fees & Phone: Open all year; please see Appendix for standard California state park fees and reservation information; park office (213) 455-2465.

Camp Notes: Much of the vegetation within the park is representative of the drought-resistant ecological community known as *chaparral* which occurs extensively in Southern California. Most people come in just to have a picnic or day hike; but the park is best enjoyed by obtaining a good map of the area and hitting the trails to a campsite in the outback. There's a lot of rugged country around here.

BOLSA CHICA
Bolsa Chica State Beach

Location: Southern California Coast between Long Beach and Huntington Beach.

Access: From California State Highway 1 near its intersection with Warner Avenue (4 miles north of Huntington Beach, 10 miles south of Long Beach) turn west into the park.

Facilities: 50 enroute campsites for self-contained vehicles in a paved parking lot arrangement; parking slots are paved, short straight-ins; (no tents); water at central faucets; restrooms with freshwater rinse showers; complete supplies and services are available in Huntington Beach.

Activities & Attractions: Swimming, surfing, windsurfing; 8 miles of bicycle lanes; beach volleyball; grunion gathering and whale watching, seasonally; interpretive programs; very large day use area.

Natural Features: Located on about 1.4 miles of sandy beach; Bolsa Chica Ecological Preserve, 1000 acres of coastal wetlands set-aside for viewing and studying bird and marine life, is adjacent to the beach; sea level.

Season, Fees & Phone: Open all year; please see Appendix for standard California state park fees and reservation information; park office (714) 846-3460.

Camp Notes: This long, wide, open, windswept beach is a favorite spot of 'do-ers', but there's plenty of room for a few thousand onlookers as well.

HUNTINGTON
Huntington State Beach

Location: Southern California Coast south of Los Angeles.

Access: From California State Highway 1 at its intersection with Brookhurst Street just north of the Santa Ana River crossing (south entrance) or from Highway 1 at its intersection with Beach Boulevard/State Highway 39 (north entrance) in the city of Huntington Beach, turn west into the park.

Facilities: 60 enroute campsites for self-contained vehicles in a paved parking lot arrangement; parking slots are paved, short straight-ins; (no tents); water at central faucets; restrooms with freshwater rinse showers; holding tank disposal station; complete supplies and services are available within 3 miles.

Activities & Attractions: Swimming; surfing; fishing; beach volleyball; very large day use area.

Natural Features: Located on a 2-mile-long beach on the edge of an ocean plain; some small areas are landscaped with grass, plants and palms; sea level.

Season, Fees & Phone: Open all year; please see Appendix for standard California state park fees; park office (714) 536-1454 or (714) 536-1455.

Camp Notes: This is a 'ditto' of Bolsa Chica in most respects. Huntington is said to have "world famous" (although perhaps not truly 'world class') surfing.

CHILAO
Angeles National Forest

Location: Southwest California northeast of Pasadena.

Access: From California State Highway 2 at milepost 49 +.7 (32 miles northeast of Glendale, 34 miles west of Wrightwood), turn northwest onto Chilao Road (paved); continue for 0.15 mile to the Little Pines Loop, 0.55 mile to the Manzanita Loop, or 1.1 miles to the Meadow Loop. (Access can also be gained from milepost 50 +.6, near the Chilao Visitor Center).

Facilities: 111 campsites in 3 loops; sites are generally medium to large, with fair to very good separation; parking pads are paved, mostly medium to long straight-ins which have been fairly well leveled; adequate space for medium to large tents in most sites; many park 'n walk sites in the Meadow Loop; fire rings or barbecue grills; b-y-o firewood is recommended; water at several faucets; vault facilities; holding tank disposal station at Charlton Flat near milepost 47 +.5; paved driveways; nearest supplies (adequate+) are available in the La Canada/Flintridge area, 26 miles southwest.

Activities & Attractions: Hiking trails; national forest visitor center; amphitheater.

Natural Features: Located on 2 small, rocky, pine-and-manzanita-covered hills (Little Pines, Manzanita) and on a tree-rimmed, grassy flat (Meadow) in the heart of the San Gabriel Mountains; elevation 5300'.

Season, Fees & Phone: April to October, but may be available in winter, subject to weather conditions; $10.00; Arroyo Seco Ranger District, Flintridge, (818) 790-1151.

Camp Notes: If a good, unrestricted mountain view is important, then many of the sites in the Little Pines or the Manzanita Loops should serve well. The Meadow Loop's somewhat less-developed campsites are better sheltered/shaded than those in the other areas.

BUCKHORN
Angeles National Forest

Location: Southwest California northeast of Pasadena.

Access: From California State Highway 2 at milepost 58 +.3 (26 miles west of Wrightwood, 40 miles northeast of Glendale), turn north (right) onto a narrow, paved, steep access road and proceed 0.4 mile down to the campground.

Facilities: 39 campsites; sites are generally small to average in size, and closely spaced; parking pads are paved, short straight-ins; tent areas are small to medium-sized; some parking pads and tent spots are somewhat level, remainder are bumpy or sloped; fire rings and barbecue grills; some firewood may be available for gathering in the general vicinity, b-y-o is suggested; water at several faucets; vault facilities; narrow, paved driveway; limited supplies and services are available in Wrightwood.

Activities & Attractions: Hiking trail; the San Gabriel Wilderness lies just to the south.

Natural Features: Located in a heavily forested ravine on the north side of the San Gabriel Mountains; campground vegetation consists of a variety of tall conifers, a few hardwoods, and ferns; a small, seasonal creek flows through the center of the camping area; 1 mile east of Cloudburst Summit; elevation 6300'.

Season, Fees & Phone: April to October, but may be available with limited services in winter, subject to weather conditions; $12.00; Arroyo Seco Ranger District, Flintridge, (818) 790-1151.

Camp Notes: Buckhorn is somewhat more heavily forested than other campgrounds in this area--and therein lies much of its appeal. The vegetation reminds some visitors of camps much farther north. With 39 sites in such a small area, the campground can optimistically be described as "compact". It's a pretty tight squeeze for all but the smallest trailers. Apparently many tent and small-vehicle campers find it to be just the right spot.

Southern California 39

GRASSY HOLLOW
Angeles National Forest

Location: Southwest California northwest of San Bernardino.

Access: From California State Highway 2 at milepost 77 + .4 (0.6 mile west of Blue Ridge Summit, 6 miles northwest of Wrightwood, 59 miles northeast of Glendale), turn north onto a paved access road and proceed 0.1 mile to the campground.

Facilities: 15 campsites; (an adjacent group camp is also available); sites are basically small; about half of the sites are quite close to each other, the remainder are slightly separated; parking pads are dirt/gravel, medium to medium+ straight-ins which will require additional leveling; tent areas are medium to large and sloped; fire rings; some firewood is available for gathering in the vicinity; water at central faucets; vault facilities; paved main driveway, dirt/gravel loop driveways; limited supplies and services are available in Wrightwood.

Activities & Attractions: Angeles National Forest Visitor Center at Big Pines, 2 miles east; the Pacific Crest Trail passes right through the campground; Sheep Mountain Wilderness, directly south.

Natural Features: Located on a sloping flat on the southwest side of Blue Ridge, northeast of the San Gabriel Mountains; campground vegetation consists of a mixture of tall conifers, patchy grass and very little underbrush; elevation 7300'.

Season, Fees & Phone: May to October; $10.00; Valyermo Ranger District (805) 944-2187.

Camp Notes: Quite candidly, this campground probably isn't the first choice of most campers who travel this region. It's close to the highway, small, and most of the neighbors are in full view. On the other hand, it may serve as a convenient, and available, stop late on Friday evening in summer.

Southern California 40

TABLE MOUNTAIN
Angeles National Forest

Location: Southwest California northwest of San Bernardino.

Access: From California State Highway 2 at milepost 79 + .9, just west of the national forest visitor center at Big Pines, (4 miles northwest of Wrightwood, 61 miles northeast of Glendale) turn north onto Table Mountain Road (paved) and continue up the hill for 1.1 miles; turn left onto the campground access road, and go a final 0.15 mile to the campground.

Facilities: 118 campsites in 6 loops; sites are medium to a generous medium in size, with nominal separation; parking pads are gravel/sand, medium-length straight-ins; large tent areas; about half the sites are reasonably level, the remainder are quite sloped; fire rings, plus a few barbecue grills; some firewood may be available in the general vicinity, gather some wood before arriving to be sure; water at several faucets; vault facilities; limited supplies and services are available in Wrightwood.

Activities & Attractions: Nature trail; Big Pines Visitor Center; Sheep Mountain Wilderness lies due south of here.

Natural Features: Located on a westward-facing slope on Table Mountain, on the northwest edge of Blue Ridge, northeast of the San Gabriel Mountains; campground vegetation consists of tall pines and other conifers, some oaks, and a small amount of young growth and low-level brush; the campground lies almost directly in line with the San Andreas Rift; elevation 7000'.

Season, Fees & Phone: May to October; $10.00; Valyermo Ranger District (805) 944-2187.

Camp Notes: On a reasonably clear night, the brilliant lights in the valleys below and the dazzling galactic display overhead compete for your undivided attention. For views, you might check the Zuni Loop first.

Southern California 41

FEATHERLY
Orange County Regional Park

Location: Southwest California between Los Angeles and Riverside.

Access: From California State Highway 91 (Riverside Freeway) at the Gypsum Canyon Road Exit at milepost 16 +.4 (8 miles west of Corona, 14 miles east of Anaheim), turn north onto Gypsum Canyon Road and proceed 0.3 mile to the park entrance station and the campground.

Facilities: 126 campsites; (several rv group camps and youth group areas are also available); sites are mediums-zed, level, with nominal separation; parking pads are sandy-based, wide, medium to long straight-ins; excellent, very large, grassy tent areas; fire rings; b-y-o firewood; water at faucets throughout; restrooms with showers; coin-op laundry; holding tank disposal station; paved driveways; complete supplies and services are available in Corona.

Activities & Attractions: Trails for guided tours; unusual children's play area constructed of mostly natural materials.

Natural Features: Located on a grassy flat dotted with large, full hardwoods, along the south bank of the Santa Ana River in Santa Ana Canyon; low, barren hills and ridges border the river north and south; the park consists of 700 acres, including more than 500 of wild lands along the river; park wildlife reportedly includes mountain lions; elevation 600'.

Season, Fees & Phone: Open all year; $9.00; 15 day limit; park office (714) 637-0210.

Camp Notes: The campground is really quite nice. There are grassy lawns all over the place, and it's about as naturally level as you'll find anywhere. The sites are of average width, but are quite long (deep). The freeway is close at hand, and the traffic can be heard throughout most of the park. Nevertheless, it's still a popular spot. With its semi-arid climate and wintertime highs averaging 65° F, Featherly might make a good winter stop.

Southern California 42

PRADO
San Bernardino County Regional Park

Location: Southwest California west of Riverside.

Access: From California State Highway 83 at a point 1.2 miles northeast of the junction of Highway 83 & State Highway 71 northwest of Corona and 7 miles south of the junction of Highway 83 & State Highway 60 (Pomona Freeway) at Ontario, turn southeast onto the paved park access road; proceed 0.1 mile to the park entrance station, then 1 mile farther to the campground.

Facilities: 50 campsites with full-hookups; (rv group camping and youth group camping areas are also available, by reservation); site size is slightly above average, with little separation; parking pads are paved, level, mostly long pull-thoughs; tent areas are large and level; fireplaces, plus some barbecue grills; firewood is usually for sale, or b-y-o; water at sites; restrooms with showers; paved driveway; complete supplies and services are available within 10 miles in just about any direction.

Activities & Attractions: Fishing (extra fee); boating (no gasoline motors, 18' limit); boat ramp and courtesy dock; equestrian trail; playground; immense day use area; sports field, golf course and shooting range close by.

Natural Features: Located on a slightly rolling, grassy hill planted with shade trees; the park is surrounded primarily by flat to gently rolling agricultural land; the park's 56-acre lake is within view of many of the campsites; elevation 900'.

Season, Fees & Phone: Open all year; $16.00; 14 day limit; park office (714) 597-4260.

Camp Notes: Combine the grassy slopes dotted with hardwoods, the lake, and a couple of adjacent large-scale livestock operations, and you have a true pastoral setting for this campground. It is suggested that you arrive by noon Friday for a weekend spot in summer.

RANCHO JURUPA
Riverside County Regional Park

Location: Southwest California west of Riverside.

Access: From California State Highway 60 (Pomona Freeway) at the Rubidoux Boulevard Exit at milepost 9 +.7 northwest of Riverside, turn south onto Rubidoux Boulevard; proceed 0.7 mile to Mission Boulevard; turn southeast (right) onto Mission and continue for 0.65 mile to Crestmore Road; turn south (right) onto Crestmore, and follow it around to the southwest for 1.3 miles to the park entrance station; the campground is 0.4 mile beyond the entrance.

Facilities: 80 campsites with partial-hookups; sites are average-sized and quite level, with minimal separation; parking pads are very long pull-throughs or medium-length straight-ins; ample space for large tents on designated surfaces; fire rings; b-y-o firewood; water at sites; restrooms with showers; holding tank disposal station; gravel driveways; limited to adequate supplies are available along Mission Boulevard; complete supplies and services are available in Riverside.

Activities & Attractions: Fishing (extra fee); playground; hiking; day use area.

Natural Features: Located on a grassy flat near the south shore of a small lake; campground vegetation consists of lawns dotted with medium-sized hardwoods; surrounding countryside is comprised of lightly wooded fields and rocky hills; 1339' Mount Rubidoux rises above the east end of the park; elevation 800'.

Season, Fees & Phone: Open all year; $12.00; reservations available; Riverside County Parks Department (714) 787-2553.

Camp Notes: The park grounds are simply, but nicely, landscaped. Rancho Jurupa is just far enough off the concrete to have a rural atmosphere.

LIVE OAK GROVE
Ronald W. Caspers/Orange County Wilderness Park

Location: Southwest California southeast of Los Angeles.

Access: From California State Highway 74 (Ortega Highway) at milepost 7 +.6 (8 miles northeast of the Ortega Highway Exit on Interstate 5 at San Juan Capistrano, 24 miles southwest of the Lake Elsinore Exit on I-15), turn north into the park; proceed 0.5 mile to the park entrance station, then 0.6 mile farther (past the visitor center) to the campground.

Facilities: 42 campsites; (Starr Mesa equestrian camp is also available); sites are medium to large, level, with some separation; parking pads are gravel/dirt, short to medium-length straight-ins, some are double-wide; adequate space for large tents in most sites; barbecue grills (charcoal fires only); water at central faucets; vault facilities; holding tank disposal station; gravel driveways; adequate+ supplies and services are available in San Juan Capistrano.

Activities & Attractions: Trails for hikers and horses (restricted to parties of 2 or more adults, no children, permit required); visitor center with exhibits of local flora and fauna, geology, history, and a wildlife diorama; nature walks, evening programs.

Natural Features: Located on a large, level flat along Bell Creek in the western foothills of the Santa Ana Mountains; huge oak trees provide an ample to dense amount of shade/shelter in most sites; park wildlife includes mountain lions and rattlesnakes; elevation 600'.

Season, Fees & Phone: Open all year; $8.00; 15 day limit; camping restricted to adults, 18 years of age or older, minimum of 2 per party; park office (714) 728-0235 or (714) 831-2174.

Camp Notes: Orange County isn't all subdivisions and shopping malls. This is the county's premier wilderness park and the largest piece of public-access real estate outside of Cleveland National Forest. The 7600-acre park straddles both sides of the highway along a several-mile stretch. (The park was the scene of a mountain lion attack on two children, hence the restrictions.)

UPPER SAN JUAN
Cleveland National Forest

Location: Southwest California southeast of Los Angeles.

Access: From California State Highway 74 at milepost 2.1 (2.1 miles east of the Riverside-Orange County line, 19 miles east of San Juan Capistrano, 15 miles west of the Interstate 15 exit at Lake Elsinore), turn north into the campground.

Facilities: 18 campsites, including several walk-ins; sites are generally small to medium in size, somewhat sloped, with reasonable separation; walk-in sites tend to be smaller; parking pads are paved, short to medium-length straight-ins; most pads will need a little additional leveling; tent areas are OK for medium-sized tents, but a little sloped; fire rings and barbecue grills; b-y-o firewood is recommended; water at hand pumps; vault facilities; paved driveway; camper supplies at a small store, 1 mile east; adequate+ supplies and services are available in San Juan Capistrano and Lake Elsinore.

Activities & Attractions: Trailhead, 0.25 mile east; San Mateo Canyon Wilderness lies south of the highway.

Natural Features: Located in the somewhat dry, narrow, San Juan Canyon in the Santa Ana Mountains, in a grove of huge oak trees; other vegetation consists of tall grass and some low-level brush; intermittent water in a campside stream; elevation 1800'.

Season, Fees & Phone: May to October, may be available at other times; $8.00; 14 day limit; Trabuco Ranger District, Corona, (714) 736-1811.

Camp Notes: A few of the campsites are close to the highway, but most are sufficiently far off the road. Traffic normally goes by slowly enough on this twisty highway anyway, so noise usually shouldn't be a strong factor in deciding on staying here. This is the westernmost of three national forest camps along or near this highway.

BLUE JAY
Cleveland National Forest

Location: Southwest California southeast of Los Angeles.

Access: From California State Highway 74 near milepost 6 (6 miles east of the Riverside-Orange County line, 23 miles east of San Juan Capistrano, 11 miles west of the Interstate 15 exit for Lake Elsinore), turn north onto a paved access road (should be signed for "Los Piños Conservation Camp"); proceed 1.8 miles (the road eventually steepens considerably) to a "T" intersection; turn right onto a dirt road (very steep and rocky in spots), and continue for 0.8 mile to the campground. (A possible alternative route is via a long, rough, winding gravel road, accessible from near Highway 74 milepost 6 +.7, east of the above turnoff.)

Facilities: 50 campsites, including quite a few walk-in sites, in 3 sections; (nearby Falcon Group Camp is also available); sites are generally of ample medium size, although some are huge, and well separated; parking pads are gravel/dirt, medium to long straight-ins; some good tent-pitching opportunities; fire rings and barbecue grills in each site; some firewood may be available for gathering locally, b-y-o is suggested; water at several faucets; vault facilities; camper supplies on Highway 74 near milepost 3; adequate+ supplies are available in Lake Elsinore and San Juan Capistrano.

Activities & Attractions: Some really sweeping vistas; foot trails; self-guided orienteering course.

Natural Features: Located on sloping terrain in the Santa Ana Mountains; most sites are sheltered/shaded by large oak trees; elevation 3300'.

Season, Fees & Phone: May to October; $8.00; 14 day limit; Trabuco Ranger District, Corona, (714) 736-1811.

Camp Notes: It might be a good idea to thoroughly check out the entire campground prior to selecting a site, in order to get a good idea of the variety of "accommodations" here. For the small price of a short haul, walk-in campers can enjoy grand views of the mountains from several nice sites.

EL CARISO
Cleveland National Forest

Location: Southwest California southeast of Los Angeles.

Access: From California State Highway 74 at milepost 6.5 (6.5 miles east of the Riverside-Orange County line, 23 miles east of San Juan Capistrano, 11 miles west of the Interstate 15 exit at Lake Elsinore), turn north into the main loop of the campground; or at milepost 6 +.7, turn south into the south loop.

Facilities: 25 campsites in the main loop, 19 sites in the south loop; sites are generally small to medium-sized, with some separation; main loop parking pads are paved, short to short+ straight-ins, and most will require some additional leveling; south section pads are grave/dirt, short straight-ins; tent areas, including some rock-framed tent pads, are medium to large and somewhat level; fire rings and barbecue grills; some firewood may be available for gathering in the area, b-y-o to be sure; water at several faucets; vault facilities; paved or gravel/dirt driveways; ranger/fire station across the highway; camper supplies 3 miles west; adequate+ supplies and services are available in Lake Elsinore and San Juan Capistrano.

Activities & Attractions: Numerous foot trails and back roads in the area; amphitheater; day use area adjacent.

Natural Features: Located on a roadside flat near the southern end of the Santa Ana Mountains; campground vegetation consists primarily of large live oaks plus some pines, providing a considerable amount of shelter/shade; elevation 3000'.

Season, Fees & Phone: Open all year; $8.00; 14 day limit; Trabuco Ranger District, Corona, (714) 736-1811.

Camp Notes: This main campground has the appearance of a CCC Special. The rather elaborate rockwork in the retaining walls and framing for the tent spots adds a finished, but natural, touch. Facilities in the south section are somewhat more basic and parking space is limited.

Southern California

Southwest Corner

Please refer to the Northern California map in the Appendix

DOHENY
Doheny State Beach

Location: Southern California Coast northwest of San Clemente.

Access: From Interstate 5 in Dana Point at the exit for Beach Cities/Pacific Coast Highway/California Highway 1 (near milepost 7, 3 miles south of San Juan Capistrano, 7 miles north of San Clemente) proceed westerly on a viaduct for 1 mile and onto Pacific Coast Highway; at Del Obispo Street, turn southerly (left) onto Dana Point Harbor Drive, go 0.1 mile to Park Lantern, then swing east (left again) onto the park access road for 0.1 mile to the park entrance station; the campground is 0.4 mile farther; (Tip: try to hug the left lanes as soon as you exit the freeway and line up early for all of the left turns to the park.)

Facilities: 120 campsites; (hike-bike sites are also available); sites are small+, level, with minimal to nominal separation; parking pads are paved, short to short+ straight-ins plus some medium to long pull-throughs; generally enough room for small tents; fire rings; firewood is usually for sale, or b-y-o; water at several faucets; restrooms with showers; holding tank disposal station; paved driveways; complete supplies and services are available within 3 miles.

Activities & Attractions: Swimming; volleyball courts; hiking trail; fishing; interpretive center; day use areas.

Natural Features: Located at the edge of the sand, with large hardwoods, palms and large shrubs that provide very light to light-medium shade/shelter in the camp area; acres of mown lawns within the park; ocean views from many campsites; sea level.

Season, Fees & Phone: Open all year; please see Appendix for standard California state park fees and reservation information; park office (714) 496-6172.

Camp Notes: Getting off the Interstate might involve a minute or two of perspiration (especially if the traffic is heavy and you're hauling a big rig), but it's worth the effort. Of the trio of beach parks in the area (also see San Clemente and San Onofre), Doheny would be the one to take your friends to.

SAN CLEMENTE
San Clemente State Beach

Location: Southern California Coast in San Clemente.

Access: From Interstate 5 (northbound) in San Clemente, take the Cristianitos Road/Avenida del Presidente Exit to the west side of the freeway, then north for 0.9 mile on Avenida del Presidente; turn west onto Avenida Calafia and proceed 0.2 mile; turn south (left) onto the park access road for 0.2 mile to the park entrance station; the campground begins just beyond the entrance. **Alternate Access:** From Interstate 5 (southbound) take the Avenida Calafia Exit west onto Avenida Calafia and continue as above.

Facilities: 157 campsites, including 72 with full hookups; (several hike-bike sites and a reservable group camp are also available); sites are small to small+, essentially level, with minimal to nominal separation; parking pads are paved, short to medium-length straight-ins or long pull-throughs; some sites have small ramadas for the table area; plenty of tent space; fire rings; firewood is usually for sale, or b-y-o; water at several faucets; restrooms with showers; paved driveways; complete supplies and services are available in San Clemente.

Activities & Attractions: Swimming; fishing; trail down to the beach campfire center; day use area.

Natural Features: Located above the ocean on a bluff on a large, grassy flat dotted with hardwoods; most campsites are some distance from the edge of the bluff; some campsites receive very light to light shade from large hardwoods; elevation 100'.

Season, Fees & Phone: Open all year; please see Appendix for standard California state park fees and reservation information; park office (714) 492-3156.

Camp Notes: San Clemente was the site of a former Western White House. (No, it wasn't the actor's local address; it was the home of the *other* President from California.) The facilities at the state beach are quite good. Lots of grass (albeit, worn) and a fair number of trees. A few campsites have ocean views.

SAN MATEO
San Mateo State Park

Location: Southern California southeast of San Clemente.

Access: From Interstate 5 at the Cristianitos Road Exit on the south edge of San Clemente at the San Diego-Orange County Line, travel northeast on Cristianitos Road for 1 mile; turn southwest (right) into the campground

Facilities: 160 campsites, including 80 with partial hookups; sites are small to medium-sized, with minimal to nominal separation; parking pads are paved, medium-length straight-ins; a little additional leveling may be needed on many pads; large, slightly sloped areas for tents; fire rings; b-yo- firewood; water at hookup sites and at several faucets; restrooms with showers; holding tank disposal station; paved driveways; complete supplies and services are available in San Clemente.

Activities & Attractions: Ocean beach, 1.5 miles down the valley by foot trail or via the highway; amphitheater for interpretive programs; close to USMC Camp Pendleton.

Natural Features: Located in a wide, shallow valley on a southward facing slope above the north bank of San Mateo Creek; vegetation in the campground consists of bushes, and assorted evergreens and hardwoods on a surface of sparse grass and small plants; the valley is bordered by brushy hills; (state informational literature describes the campground as having "serene coastal scrub surroundings"); elevation 100'.

Season, Fees & Phone: Open all year; please see Appendix for standard California state park fees; park office (714) 361-2531.

Camp Notes: San Mateo Campground is an offshoot of an agreement between California citizens and the local electrical power company. Funding for construction of the campground and the trail down to Trestles Beach were exchanged for former beach access which was obstructed by development of the San Onofre atomic juice maker, just south of here. Compare this large, modern campground to the simple national forest camps in the Santa Ana Mountains, a few miles northeast. The forest camps were built by the CCC in the 1930's for a few thousand bucks apiece. San Mateo's facilities cost $4.7 million in 1990's dollars.

SAN ONOFRE
San Onofre State Beach

Location: Southern California Coast south of San Clemente.

Access: From Interstate 5 at the Basilone Road-San Onofre Exit (3 miles south of San Clemente, 17 miles north of Oceanside), turn west off the freeway, then south onto a frontage road; continue south, past the San Onofre Nuclear Generating Station, for 2.5 miles to the main park entrance and the first campsites.

Facilities: 221 enroute campsites; (a number of hike-bike sites are also available); sites are very small, level, with minimal separation, in a long line located between the lanes of the Interstate and a bluff that parallels the beach; parking slots are paved, short straight-ins; small tent areas; water at several faucets; restrooms with freshwater rinse showers; holding tank disposal station; paved driveways; complete supplies and services are available in San Clemente.

Activities & Attractions: Swimming; fishing; several trails down to the beach; nature trail.

Natural Features: Located on a bluff above the ocean; some campsites have limited ocean views; some shrubbery has been planted between sites; elevation 50'.

Season, Fees & Phone: Open all year; please see Appendix for standard California state park fees and reservation information; park phone (714) 492-3156 or (714) 492-4872.

Camp Notes: Only a chain link fence separates most of the campsites from eight-lane oblivion. Note that the acronym for the neighboring plutonium power pumper is SONGS. The campground is located right next to a 'nuke' plant, but there are no electrical hookups. Odd.

Southern California 52

GUAJOME
San Diego County Park

Location: Southwest corner of California northeast of Oceanside.

Access: From California State Highway 76 at milepost 7 +.1 (7 miles northeast of Oceanside, 11 miles southeast of the California 76 Exit on Interstate 15 near Bonsall), turn south onto Guajome Lakes Road, and proceed 0.1 mile to the park entrance, and 0.2 mile farther to the campground. (If you're traveling Interstate 5, take the Mission Road-Highway 76 Exit at Oceanside, then northeast on '76.)

Facilities: 17 campsites with partial hookups; sites are slightly above-average in size, with fairly good visual separation; parking pads are paved straight-ins, some are double-wide, and most are long and level; tent areas are medium to large and level; fire rings; firewood is usually for sale, or b-y-o; water at sites; restrooms with showers; holding tank disposal station; paved driveway; complete supplies and services are available in Oceanside.

Activities & Attractions: Children's play area; fishing; hiking and equestrian trails; large day use area; Rancho Guajome Adobe historical site nearby; famous, and very photogenic, Mission San Luis Rey, just west of the park.

Natural Features: Located on a hilltop, with short conifers, bushes, palms, and watered and mown lawns, overlooking a valley; small Guajome Lake, a pond complete with an island, is near the campground; elevation 600'.

Season, Fees & Phone: $11.00 for a site, $2.00 for an extra vehicle, $1.00 for dogs; Open all year; 14 day limit; reservations available, contact the San Diego County Parks and Recreation Department Office, 21 to 90 days in advance, at (619) 565-3600; for general information (619) 565-5928.

Camp Notes: Nice park. Subjectively speaking, this is one of the nicest-looking parks in this part of California. It fits in well with the surrounding suburban/semi-rural community. If you don't *have* to stay on the beach, this campground is well worth a look.

Southern California 53

SOUTH CARLSBAD
South Carlsbad State Beach

Location: Southern California Coast south of Oceanside.

Access: From San Diego County Highway S21/Carlsbad Boulevard at milepost 15 +.4 (4 miles south of Carlsbad, 4 miles north of Encinitas): if *southbound*, turn west into the park entrance and the campground; if *northbound* on this divided highway, watch for the signs to get you going in the right direction; you'll need to continue north on S21 past the park entrance to the Ponto Drive Exit, then swing around and double-back for 0.8 mile to the park entrance. (From Interstate 5, take the Poinsettia Lane Exit north of Encinitas, go west 0.6 mile on Poinsettia Lane to S21, then to the park entrance.)

Facilities: 226 campsites; sites are small to small+, level, with fair to fairly good separation; parking pads are sandy gravel, short to short+ straight-ins/pull-offs; generally adequate space for large tents; storage cabinets; fire rings; firewood is usually for sale, or b-y-o; water at several faucets; restrooms with showers; holding tank disposal station; paved driveways; park store; complete supplies and services are available in Carlsbad.

Activities & Attractions: Swimming; fishing; campfire center.

Natural Features: Located on a bluff just above the beach; vegetation consists mostly of large shrubs, plus a few palms; park area includes 3.5 miles of beach; sea level.

Season, Fees & Phone: Open all year; please see Appendix for standard California state park fees and reservation information; park office (619) 438-3143.

Camp Notes: South Carlsbad has twice the oceanfront property and more beachfront sites than its sister park to the south, San Elijo (see separate info). Otherwise, they are comparable. The campsites in both areas are somewhat unconventional since they really are just gravel rectangles bordered by shrubs. The sites are nearly identical in size, shape and landscaping to those in all of the campgrounds in Lake Mead National Recreation Area. Simple, practical, and cheap to construct and maintain.

SAN ELIJO
San Elijo State Beach

Location: Southern California Coast northwest of San Diego.

Access: From San Diego County Highway S21 near milepost 10 +.5 just across the railroad tracks from midtown Cardiff, turn west to the park entrance station; the campground stretches for several 10ths of a mile parallel to the highway north and south of the entrance. (From Interstate 5, take the Manchester/Cardiff by the Sea or Birmingham Drive Exit south of Encinitas, then travel a mile west to Cardiff and go across the RR tracks and onto S21.)

Facilities: 171 campsites; sites are small to small+, level to somewhat sloped, with fair to fairly good separation; parking pads are gravel, short+, straight-ins/pull-offs; adequate space for a large tent (if your vehicle doesn't take up a lot of space); fire rings; firewood is usually for sale, or b-y-o; water at several faucets; restrooms with showers; holding tank disposal station; paved driveways; adequate supplies and services are available in Cardiff.

Activities & Attractions: Beach access; bikeway/jogway; swimming; campfire center; day use area nearby.

Natural Features: Located on a short bluff or 'rise' a few feet above the beach; vegetation includes large shrubs, hardwoods and evergreens between sites, plus tall palms; sea level.

Season, Fees & Phone: Open all year; please see Appendix for standard California state park fees and reservation information; park office (619) 753-5091.

Camp Notes: Actually, there are a lot of pretty nice, visually separated, oceanfront campsites here (although the local folks in the houses up on the bluff behind the park can probably look down and see what variety of soup you're having for lunch.) Many campsites are along the edge of the bluff overlooking the ocean. The campground is very popular with tent campers.

SILVER STRAND
Silver Strand State Beach

Location: Southwest corner of California south of San Diego.

Access: From California State Highway 75 at a point 6 miles south of the Coronado Bridge and 5 miles northwest of the Interstate 5 Exit for Highway 75/Imperial Beach/Palm Avenue, turn west then north to the park entrance station; continue north on the park driveway for 0.6 mile to the camping area.

Facilities: 122 enroute campsites in a parking lot arrangement; sites are very small, level, with zip separation; parking slots are long straight-ins or pull-throughs; (no tents); vehicles must have completely self-contained facilities and must include "1 verifiable towed/towing vehicle"; complete supplies and services are available in Coronado and Imperial Beach.

Activities & Attractions: Mile-long ocean beach, plus land on San Diego Bay and bikeway on the east side of the highway; day use area adjacent.

Natural Features: Located on a long, narrow spit between the Pacific Ocean and San Diego Bay; a few palms decorate the grounds; sea level.

Season, Fees & Phone: Open all year; please see Appendix for standard California state park fees and reservation information; park office (619) 435-5184.

Camp Notes: Decades ago, as the story is told, a gentleman named Julius opened a small fast food stand on a corner in New York City. From this miniature Mac, he sold coffee, donuts, sandwiches and his specialty, fresh-squeezed orange juice, to the restive workers of Gotham. In order to speed his customers on their way (and to increase his turnover and profit), along the front of the service counter he installed a row of small, hard stools which were large enough for a quick perch, but too uncomfortable for a leisurely stop. The legend lives on in Silver Strand's camplot.

SANTEE LAKES
Padre Dam Municipal Water District Regional Park

Location: Southwest corner of California northeast of San Diego.

Access: From California State Highway 67 near milepost 3, at the Mission Gorge Road Exit in Santee, proceed west on Mission Gorge Road through midtown Santee for 2.3 miles to Carlton Hills Boulevard, then go north 0.5 mile to Carlton Oaks Drive; turn west (left) onto Carlton Oaks Drive and proceed 0.4 mile turn north into the park entrance and continue for 0.9 mile to the campground area.

Facilities: 203 campsites, majority with full hookups, in 5 loops; sites are generally small, level and very close together; parking pads are dirt/gravel or paved, straight-ins or pull-throughs, and vary from short to long; barbecue grills; b-y-o firewood; water at sites and at central faucets; restrooms with showers; holding tank disposal station; paved driveways; security patrols; small store and laundromat in the park; adequate+ supplies and services are available in Santee.

Activities & Attractions: Fishing for bass, panfish and catfish; limited boating; swimming pool; horseshoe pits; volleyball; (all activities require payment of special fees).

Natural Features: Located on or near the shores of a chain of 7 small lakes; some sections of the campground have mown lawns and a few large hardwoods; dry hills surround the immediate area; elevation 350'.

Season, Fees & Phone: Open all year; $11.00 for a primitive site, $14.00 for a full-hookup site; weekly and monthly rates available; 30 day limit; park office (619) 448-2482.

Camp Notes: In this campground, your next-door neighbors are not only other campers, but also the residents of the subdivision just on the other side of the fence. There's definitely a modern city park flavor here. The origin and use of the seven lakes' water is unique. About a million gallons a day of treated water percolates through a filtering layer of 400 feet of sand and then is fed to the uppermost of the small, man-made lakes. From there, the water flows down through each of the other six lakes in succession, then it's recycled for agricultural and industrial uses.

LAKE JENNINGS
San Diego County Park

Location: Southern California northeast of San Diego.

Access: From Interstate 8 at the Lake Jennings Park Road Exit near milepost 22 (7 miles east of El Cajon, 15 miles east of downtown San Diego), turn northwest onto Lake Jennings Park Road and proceed 1 mile to Bass Road (the turnoff comes up quickly as you round a curve); turn right, onto Bass Road, and continue for 0.3 mile to the campground.

Facilities: 100 campsites, including many with full or partial hookups, and 16 walk-in sites; sites are generally small to medium-sized and sloped; parking pads are paved straight-ins and pull-throughs, and vary from short to long; additional leveling will be needed on many pads; barbecue grills and fire rings; firewood is usually for sale, or b-y-o; water at faucets throughout; restrooms with showers; complete supplies and services are available in El Cajon.

Activities & Attractions: Fishing for trout, bass, catfish and panfish October to May, weekends only; boat launch and docks (extra fee) on the opposite side of the lake from the campground.

Natural Features: Located on a hill overlooking Lake Jennings; campground vegetation consists of natural and planted grass, conifers and hardwoods; somewhat dry, rocky mountains can be seen in the distance; elevation 800'.

Season, Fees & Phone: Open all year; $7.00 for a walk-in site, $8.00 for a standard site, $11.00 for a partial hookup site, $12.00 for a full hookup site, $1.00 for a dog; 14 day limit; reservations available, recommended for summer weekends, contact the San Diego County Parks and Recreation Department Office, 21 to 90 days in advance, at (619) 565-3600; for general information (619) 565-5928.

Camp Notes: There are some super views of the lake and the mountains to the east from this hillside. You might need a land anchor in some of the more sloped sites, though.

DOS PICOS
San Diego County Park

Location: Southwest corner of California northeast of San Diego.

Access: From California State Highway 67 at milepost 21 (3 miles southwest of Ramona, 23 miles north of El Cajon), turn southeast (i.e., a sharp, hairpin-style right turn if you're northbound) onto Mussey Grade Road; proceed 1.1 miles, then turn west (right) onto Dos Picos Park Road, and continue for 0.8 mile to the park entrance.

Facilities: 62 campsites, including many with partial hookups, in 3 loops; sites are medium-sized, level, with minimal to nominal separation; parking pads are paved, medium to long straight-ins; excellent, large tent areas; fire rings, plus some barbecue grills; firewood is usually for sale, or b-y-o; water at hookup sites and at central faucets; restrooms with showers; holding tank disposal station; paved driveways; adequate supplies and services are available in Ramona.

Activities & Attractions: Playground; jogging course; large day use area.

Natural Features: Located on a slightly rolling flat near the base of the rocky-topped, boulder-strewn, dual-peaked, saddle-backed mountain for which the park is named; sites are situated along both sides of a stream bed; most sites are well sheltered/shaded by mature hardwoods, with very little low-level vegetation; small lake/pond within walking distance of the campground; elevation 1400'.

Season, Fees & Phone: Open all year; $8.00 for a standard site, $11.00 for a partial hookup site, $1.00 for a dog; 14 day limit; reservations available, contact the San Diego County Parks and Recreation Department Office, 21 to 90 days in advance at (619) 565-3600.

Camp Notes: Since it's one of the parks closest to the city, Dos Picos tends to be quite popular on weekends. A less-populous alternative might be the campground at William Heise County Park, about a 45-minute drive east of here.

DOANE VALLEY
Palomar Mountain State Park

Location: Southwest California northeast of San Diego.

Access: From the junction of California State Highway 76 and San Diego County Highway S6 (3 miles east of Rincon Springs, 23 miles northwest of Santa Ysabel), turn north onto Highway S6 and climb 7 miles to the junction of SD County Highways S6 & S7; turn northwest (left) onto S7 and travel 2.9 miles to the park entrance; continue ahead for 0.25 mile, then swing sharply north (right) and proceed 1.5 miles on a steep, narrow, paved road to the campground.

Alternate Access: From the junction of State Highway 76 & SD County Highway S7 (8 miles southeast of Rincon Springs, 10 miles north of Santa Ysabel) head north/northwest on S7 for 11 miles to the junction of S6 & S7, and continue on S7 to the park, as above. (Note: the first access is via steep, winding, but panoramic miles from the main highway; the second access is along a much easier route, particularly if you're pumping a 10-speed, or you're driving something larger than a van or a full-size pickup with a topper.)

Facilities: 31 campsites in 2 loops (the Cedar Grove Group Camp is also available, by reservation); sites are generally small and sloped, with very little separation; parking pads are paved, short straight-ins or pull-offs; tent areas vary from small to large, and most are somewhat sloped; a few, designated, medium-sized rv and handicapped sites; storage cabinets (bear boxes); fire rings or barbecue grills; firewood is usually for sale, b-y-o is recommended; water at central faucets; restrooms with showers; paved driveways; camper supplies at the junction of Highways S6 and S7.

Activities & Attractions: A half-dozen hiking trails through several miles of forest and meadow; (a park brochure/trail map with contours is available from the park office); Doane Valley Nature Trail; fishing for stocked trout at Doane Pond; observation point; campground amphitheater; several day use areas; Palomar Observatory is 15 road miles northeast.

Natural Features: Located on moderately steep slope in a dense forest of large hardwoods intermixed with very tall conifers; some hillsides are thickly carpeted with ferns; elevation 4600'.

Season, Fees & Phone: Open all year, except during brief periods of heavy snow; please see Appendix for standard California state park fees and reservation information; park office (714) 742-3462.

Camp Notes: The park's host-mountain was named by the early Spanish for the thousands of pigeons which made it their home. (*Palomar* means "pigeon roost" or "pigeon coop"). A number of early settlers also made this land their home, and four apple orchards in the park trace their roots to the plantings of 1880's homesteaders. The campground seems to be particularly popular with campers in tents and small vehicles looking for a quiet, forest environment.

Southern California 60

OBSERVATORY
Cleveland National Forest

Location: Southeast corner of California northeast of San Diego.

Access: From the junction of San Diego County Highways S6 & S7 (8 steep, twisty, scenic miles via Highway S6 from the junction of S6 and California State Highway 79 near Rincon Springs, or 12 easier miles via Highway S7 from the junction of S7 and Highway 79 near Lake Henshaw), proceed northeast on S6 for 2.4 miles to milepost 50 +.2; turn southeast (right), and go 0.1 mile to the campground.

Facilities: 42 campsites; sites are medium to large, with some separation; parking pads are paved, medium-length straight-ins, most of which will require some additional leveling; tent areas are large and somewhat level; fire rings and barbecue grills in most sites; some firewood is available for gathering in the vicinity; water at several faucets; vault facilities; camper supplies at a small store at the junction of Highways S6 & S7, 2 miles south.

Activities & Attractions: Renowned Palomar Observatory (open for limited visitation by the public during daytime hours) can be reached via a 2.3 mile trail from the campground, or by continuing up Highway S6.

Natural Features: Located on a sloping flat just below the summit of Mount Palomar; campground vegetation consists of a wide variety of hardwoods and conifers on a grass-and-needle-covered forest floor; large, open, grassy areas within the campground; elevation 4800'.

Season, Fees & Phone: May to November, but occasionally open as late as the end of December; $7.00; 14 day limit; Palomar Ranger District, Ramona, (619) 788-0250.

Camp Notes: Cal-Tech's famous scientific institution to which the campground's name eludes is impressive enough in photographs. But to personally view that gleaming white dome encircled by rich green grass and trees, against the backdrop of a deep blue sky, is an experience.

Southern California 61

FRY CREEK
Cleveland National Forest

Location: Southeast corner of California northeast of San Diego.

Access: From the junction of San Diego County Highways S6 & S7 (8 steep, winding, but satisfyingly scenic miles via S6 from the junction of S6 and California State Highway 79 near Rincon Springs, or 12 more gentle miles via Highway S7 from the junction of S7 and Highway 79 near Lake Henshaw), proceed northeast on S6 for 2.6 miles (just past Observatory Campground) to milepost 50 +.4; turn north (left) into the campground.

Facilities: 19 campsites, including several walk-ins, in 2 sections; sites are a little on the small side, sloped, and somewhat close together; parking pads are paved, mostly short straight-ins which require additional leveling; small tent spots; fire rings and barbecue grills in most sites; some firewood is available for gathering in the vicinity; water at several faucets; vault facilities; narrow, paved driveways; camper supplies at a small store at the junction of Highways S6 and S7, 2 miles south.

Activities & Attractions: Fry Creek Nature Trail to Penny Pines Plantation; California Institute of Technology's famous Palomar Observatory, 2 miles beyond the campground, at the end of S6.

Natural Features: Located on a densely forested hilly area along Fry Creek; a great variety of large hardwoods and tall conifers, and even some ferns, shelter the campground; elevation 4900'.

Season, Fees & Phone: May to November; $7.00; 14 day limit; Palomar Ranger District, Ramona, (619) 788-0250.

Camp Notes: This campground is a bit of a surprise, considering it's in Cleveland National Forest (which is about 80 percent chaparral). It's not recommended for trailers, since the driveway is quite tight.

Fry Creek, and nearby Observatory Campground, both built in the 1960's, are two of the newer campgrounds in this national forest.

DRIPPING SPRINGS
Cleveland National Forest

Location: Southwest corner of California southeast of Riverside and northeast of San Diego.

Access: From California State Highway 79 at milepost 9.5 (7 miles west of Aguanga, 10 miles east of Temecula), turn` south onto a paved access road and continue for 0.2 mile to the campground.

Facilities: 25 campsites; sites are medium sized, with nominal separation; parking pads are paved, medium-length straight-ins, or medium to long pull-throughs, and many will require additional leveling; most tent areas are fairly good sized and reasonably level; barbecue grills and/or fireplaces; b-y-o firewood; water at faucets throughout; vault facilities; paved driveway; camper supplies in Aguanga and Temecula.

Activities & Attractions: Trailhead for the Dripping Springs Trail, which leads south into the Aqua Tibea Wilderness.

Natural Features: Located along a streambed between a pair of long, tree-and-brush-covered hills; some of the sites are on a somewhat open flat, the remainder are stretched out along a hillside; campground vegetation consists primarily of grass and large, full oaks; elevation 1600'.

Season, Fees & Phone: May to November; $7.00; 14 day limit; Palomar Ranger District, Ramona, (619) 788-0250.

Camp Notes: This campground sees quite a bit of summer weekend activity, perhaps because it's a quick and easy shot via freeway or four-lane from the San Diego or Riverside metro areas to Temecula, then only a few, easy, two-lane miles from there. If your preference runs toward campgrounds with a little less activity, you might try Oak Grove, described next.

OAK GROVE
Cleveland National Forest

Location: Southwest corner of California northeast of San Diego.

Access: From California State Highway 79 at milepost 49 +.1 (5 miles north of Sunshine Summit, 6 miles south of Aguanga), turn east into the campground (on the opposite side of the highway from the National Forest Oak Grove Work Center).

Facilities: 81 campsites in 3 loops; sites are small to medium in size, level, and generally quite private; parking pads are paved, mostly medium to very long straight-ins, plus a few pull-throughs; medium to large tent areas; fireplaces and/or barbecue grills; b-y-o firewood; water at faucets throughout; restrooms; paved driveways; camper supplies in Sunshine Summit and Aguanga.

Activities & Attractions: Pleasant surroundings; amphitheater.

Natural Features: Located on a roadside flat in a small valley ringed by the green and gold hills typical of the southern California ranch country; campground vegetation consists of oaks and other hardwoods, plus large bushes between many sites which produce a substantial amount of shelter/shade and privacy; the Palomar Divide lies to the west; temperate, fairly dry climate; elevation 2800'.

Season, Fees & Phone: May to November; $7.00; 14 day limit; Palomar Ranger District, Ramona, (619) 788-0250.

Camp Notes: This campground displays two somewhat different natural personalities: many of the sites are quite well-sheltered horizontally by tall bushes, but are lightly shaded; others are more open, but well-shaded. It's a really nice place that rarely fills up. Oak Grove was the site of one of the Butterfield Overland Mail stage stations that operated between San Francisco and St. Louis between 1858 and 1861.

WILLIAM HEISE
San Diego County Park

Location: Southwest corner of California northeast of San Diego.

Access: From California State Highway 78 at milepost 56 + .9 (1 mile west of Julian, 6 miles east of Santa Ysabel), turn south onto Pine Hills Road; proceed 2.2 miles to Frisius Drive; turn east (left) onto Frisius Drive, and continue for 2.1 miles to the park entrance and the campground just beyond.

Facilities: 102 campsites in 3 loops, including 2 loops for rv campers and 1 loop for tenters; (a large loop reserved for group use is also available); site size varies from small to large, separation from very little to good; parking pads are paved, short to long, mostly straight-ins; most pads will probably require additional leveling; tent areas are large, and vary from acceptably level to sloped; fire rings and/or barbecue grills; firewood is usually for sale, or b-y-o; water at several faucets; restrooms; central showers; holding tank disposal station; paved driveways; gas and groceries in Julian; limited supplies and services are available in Santa Ysabel.

Activities & Attractions: Many foot trails in the park; large, well-equipped, playground; horseshoe courts; nature walks and programs on weekends.

Natural Features: Located on rolling terrain in a dense forest of hardwoods and pines at the northern tip of the Laguna Mountains; mild summers, cool winters; occasional snowfall; elevation 4200'.

Season, Fees & Phone: Open all year; $9.00 for a site, $1.00 for a dog; 14 day limit; reservations available, contact the San Diego County Parks and Recreation Department Office, 21 to 90 days in advance, (the group 'caravan' loop can be booked as far as a year in advance), at (619) 565-3600.

Camp Notes: Tent campers may have a slight edge here. Even though the sites in the 42-site tent loop are a bit on the small side, the tent loop normally doesn't fill up, so the selection of campsites or the distance from the neighbors may be a little better. Nice campground.

PASO PICACHO
Cuyamaca Rancho State Park

Location: Southwest California northeast of San Diego.

Access: From California State Highway 79 at milepost 9 + .3 (12 miles north of Interstate 8 Julian/Japatul Road Exit, 11 miles south of Julian), turn west into the Paso Picacho entrance station; just inside the entrance, bear left and continue for 0.1 mile to the campground.

Facilities: 85 campsites in a complex network of loops; (2 group camps and a number of environmental campsites are also available in this area, 2 horse camps are available near the park's Stonewall Mine area); sites are small +, with nominal to fair separation; parking pads are short to medium-length straight-ins, most of which will probably require additional leveling; large, but sloped, tent areas; fire rings; firewood is usually for sale, or b-y-o; water at central faucets; restrooms with showers; narrow, paved driveways; holding tank disposal station; gas and groceries in Julian; nearest source of complete supplies and services is El Cajon, 35 miles southwest.

Activities & Attractions: Over a hundred miles of hiking and horse trails, including a 3.5 mile trail from here to the summit of 6512' Cuyamaca Peak; Paso Nature Trail; small interpretive center; campfire center; day use area.

Natural Features: Located on a densely forested slope in the Peninsular Range; campground vegetation consists of a light to medium-dense mixture of hardwoods and conifers; Cuyamaca Lake is 2 miles north; elevation 4900'.

Season, Fees & Phone: Open all year, depending upon winter weather conditions; please see Appendix for standard California state park fees and reservation information; park office (619) 765-0755.

Camp Notes: From Paso Picacho, a moderately difficult trail winds to the summit of Cuyamaca Peak. At the top you look out across this 25,000-acre park to the Pacific Ocean, Mexico, Anza-Borrego Desert and the Salton Sea.

GREEN VALLEY
Cuyamaca Rancho State Park

Location: Southwest corner of California northeast of San Diego.

Access: From California State Highway 79 at milepost 4 + .2 (7 miles north of Interstate 8 Julian/Japatul Road Exit, 16 miles south of Julian), turn west into the Green Valley entrance station; turn right and proceed 0.3 mile to a fork; take the right fork for campsites 1-22; take the left fork and go another 0.2 mile to the main camp loops.

Facilities: 81 campsites in 2 loops, plus an extension; (hike-bike campsites and a primitive camp, accessible by trail, are available nearby); sites are small+, quite sloped, with nominal to fair separation; parking pads are mostly paved, short to medium-length straight-ins; additional leveling would be needed in virtually all sites; medium to large tent areas; fire rings; b-y-o firewood; water at most sites; restrooms with showers; paved driveways; gas and groceries in Julian; nearest source of complete supplies is El Cajon, 30 miles southwest.

Activities & Attractions: Trails, trails, trails--the park has more than a hundred miles of equestrian and foot trails, several of which lead off from this area; short trail to the falls; interpretive displays; campfire center; park museum, nearby, houses exhibits and artifacts about the local Kumeya-ay Indians and the early Spanish explorers; day use areas.

Natural Features: Located on rolling slopes near the edge of a ravine in a densely forested river valley; the Sweetwater River flows past the camp loops; surrounding mountainous areas have moderately dense forestation interspersed with meadows; elevation 4000'.

Season, Fees & Phone: Open all year, subject to winter weather conditions; please see Appendix for standard California state park fees and reservation information; park office (619) 765-0755.

Camp Notes: Green Valley's campground apparently is popular mostly with pickup, van and tent campers. The handiwork of the Civilian Conservation Corps can still be identified in certain places around the park. The CCC built the park's first trails and campgrounds during the Great Depression. Don't get your expectations up too high about the deep drop of the tumbling waters at the 'falls'.

CIBBETS FLAT
Cleveland National Forest

Location: Southwest corner of California east of San Diego.

Access: From Interstate 8 at the Cameron Station-Kitchen Creek Road Exit at milepost 52 (52 miles east of San Diego, 60 miles west of El Centro), turn north onto Kitchen Creek Road (paved) and proceed 4.5 miles; turn east (right), cross a wooden bridge, and continue for 0.2 mile to the campground.

Facilities: 24 campsites, including 6 park 'n walk sites; sites are generally average-sized with little separation; parking pads are paved, medium-length straight-ins which may require a little extra leveling; adequate space for large tents in most sites; fireplaces or fire rings; b-y-o firewood is recommended; water at faucets throughout; vault facilities; paved driveways; limited supplies in Alpine, 21 miles west; complete supplies and services are available in El Cajon, 36 miles west.

Activities & Attractions: Laguna Lake Recreation Area can be reached by continuing northward on Kitchen Creek Road for about 10 miles, or via the Sunrise Highway, from I-8 at Laguna Junction, a half-dozen miles west of here; access to the Pacific Crest Trail from near the campground; designated shooting areas south of the campground, on the east side of Kitchen Creek Road.

Natural Features: Located on a gently sloping grassy flat at the base of a brush-and-tree-covered hill in the Laguna Mountains; almost all sites have a large hardwood for shelter/shade; Kitchen Creek, a trickle of a stream, flows past the campground; higher mountains rise in the surrounding area; 4055' Laguna Summit is a few miles west of the campground; elevation 3800'.

Season, Fees & Phone: Open all year; $8.00; 14 day limit; Descanso Ranger District, Alpine, (619) 445-6235.

Camp Notes: Its location upwards of 4000', easy accessibility, and fair distance from the Interstate combine to make this campground a popular summer weekend spot. Tiny, but welcome, Kitchen Creek adds the finishing touch.

BOULDER OAKS
Cleveland National Forest

Location: Southwest corner of California east of San Diego.

Access: From Interstate 8 at the Cameron Station-Kitchen Creek Road Exit at milepost 52 (52 miles east of San Diego, 60 miles west of El Centro), turn south, then west onto a paved frontage road (Old Highway 80) and proceed 1.2 miles to the campground.

Facilities: 35 campsites in 2 loops, including 19 sites in the loop for standard camping, and another 16 sites for equestrian use; majority of the sites are large, reasonably level, and moderately spaced; parking pads are gravel, medium to long straight-ins in the standard loop, and long pull-throughs in the equestrian loop; large, fairly level tent spots; steel corrals in the equestrian loop; fire rings; b-y-o firewood is recommended; water at several faucets; vault facilities; gravel driveways; limited supplies in Alpine, 21 miles west; complete supplies and services are available in El Cajon, 36 miles west.

Activities & Attractions: Access to the Pacific Crest Trail; day use area has a parking lot for trailers.

Natural Features: Located on a dry flat in the boulder-strewn, chaparral-covered Laguna Mountains; many sites are sheltered/shaded by large oak trees; elevation 3300'.

Season, Fees & Phone: Open all year; $8.00 for a standard site, $10.00 for an equestrian unit; 14 day limit; Descanso Ranger District, Alpine, (619) 445-6235.

Camp Notes: This is one of the nicer freewayside forest campgrounds in the state. Since it's several hundred yards away, the Interstate really isn't that obtrusive. Reports from here indicate that the campground virtually never fills, and the equestrian section is hardly ever used. Several miles southwest of Boulder Oaks is Lake Morena, a county park campground located just off San Diego County Highway S1, accessible from I-8 several miles west of here. Lake Morena has dozens of campsites, water, restrooms, and a lake that offers limited boating, plus fishing for good-sized bass, panfish and cat.

Southern California
South Central Inland
Please refer to the Northern California map in the Appendix

Southern California 69

BASALT
San Luis Reservoir State Recreation Area

Location: West-central California south of Modesto.

Access: From California State Highway 152 at milepost 10 +.95 (5 miles west of the Los Banos/Highway 152 Exit on Interstate 5, 36 miles east of Gilroy), turn south onto a paved access road; proceed 2.1 miles to the entrance station, then 0.3 mile to the campground. (If you're southbound on Interstate 5, you can shave 3 miles from the trip by taking the Santa Nella-Gilroy Exit, then go south for 3 miles on State Highway 33 to Highway 152, then west on 152 for 3 miles to the park turnoff.)

Facilities: 79 campsites in 2 loops; sites are medium+ in size, with nominal separation; parking pads are paved, medium to long, wide, straight-ins; pads are basically level, but those in the south loop may require a little additional leveling; excellent tent areas; fireplaces; b-y-o firewood; water at several faucets; restrooms with showers; holding tank disposal station; nearly complete supplies and services are available in Los Banos, 11 miles east.

Activities & Attractions: Fishing for black bass, shad, striped bass, channel catfish; boating; boat launch (2 miles west of the campground, launch fee); visitor center with audio-visual programs (at Highway 152 milepost 8, west of the Basalt Turnoff); interpretive programs on weekends.

Natural Features: Located in the easternmost foothills of the Coast Range, near the south shore of San Luis Reservoir, on the west edge of the San Joaquin Valley; a variety of large, full hardwoods provide a fairly generous amount of shelter/shade within the campground; ringed by grassy hills sparingly dotted with brush and small trees; higher, more forested hills lie in the near distance; hot, dry and often windy in summer, mild in winter; elevation 400'.

Season, Fees & Phone: Open all year; please see Appendix for standard California state park fees and reservation information; park office (209) 826-1196 or (209) 826-1197.

Camp Notes: Basalt is one of two developed campgrounds within the recreation area. The other is a 22-unit primitive campground with ramadas, water and vault facilities, which can also be used by picnickers. It's located at Los Banos Creek Reservoir, 10 miles southeast of San Luis Reservoir. Los Banos Creek is accessible via a roundabout route from State Highway 152 just west of the city of Los Banos, then south on Volta Road, east on Pioneer Road and south on Canyon Road (crossing over to the southwest side of I-5) for a total of eight paved miles to the campground.

Southern California 70

MADEIROS
San Luis Reservoir State Recreation Area

Location: West-central California south of Modesto.

Access: From State Highway 33 at a point 0.4 mile north of its junction with Highway 152, 2.5 miles south of Santa Nella, proceed west on a park access road for 1 mile to the camp area. (If you're southbound on I-5, see the short cut info in the *Access* section under Basalt Campground.)

Facilities: Large, open camp/picnic area, with drinking water, vault facilities and large parking area; nearly complete supplies and services are available in Los Banos, 11 miles east.

Activities & Attractions: Swimming beach; boating; boat launch and docks; fishing for striped bass, black bass, channel cat, crappie, bluegill; visitor center, 2 miles west.

Natural Features: Located on grassy slopes dotted with trees above the south shore of O'Neil Forebay, a 2000-acre secondary impoundment associated with San Luis Reservoir; bordered by grassy, tree-dotted hills and low mountains; elevation 300'.

Season, Fees & Phone: Open all year; please see Appendix for standard California state park fees; park office (209) 826-1196 or (209) 826-1197.

Camp Notes: O'Neil Forebay acts as an "hydraulic junction" (a liquid buffer zone) between the main reservoir, a local canal, and the California Aqueduct, in what is a more complex water system than first meets the eye. San Luis Reservoir SRA provides the only major picnicking and camping facilities in the San Joaquin Valley, other than the freeway rest areas, within a few easy miles of Interstate 5.

LOS ALAMOS
Angeles National Forest

Location: Southwest California northwest of Los Angeles.

Access: From Interstate 5 at the Hungry Valley Road Exit near milepost 78 (18 miles north of Castaic, 15 miles south of Lebec), go to the west side of the freeway and a "T" intersection; turn south (left) onto a paved local road and proceed 1.5 miles to the recreation area entrance station; just past the entrance, go across an aquaduct, then swing northward (right) and continue for another 2 miles north and west; turn south (left) into the campground.

Facilities: 93 campsites in 2 loops; sites are small to medium-sized, with nil separation; parking pads are gravel, medium-length straight-ins or pull-offs; most pads will require some additional leveling; adequate space for tents in most sites; fire rings; b-y-o firewood; water at faucets; restrooms; holding tank disposal station; paved driveways; limited supplies and services are available in Castaic.

Activities & Attractions: Fishing, boating and boat launch (extra charges) at Pyramid Lake, 2 miles south; Hungry Valley State Vehicular Recreation Area is to the north.

Natural Features: Located on an easy slope in Cañada de los Alamos a side canyon at the lower end of Hungry Valley; campground vegetation consists mostly of some high brush on a surface of sparse grass; b-y-o shade; bordered by brush-blanketed, juniper-dotted hills; high mountains rise to the west; elevation 3100'.

Season, Fees & Phone: Open all year; $10.00; 14 day limit; Arroyo Seco Ranger District, Angeles NF, Flintridge, (818) 790-1151.

Camp Notes: *Cañada de los Alamos* can be loosely translated as "Poplar Ravine", but the stately hardwoods are few and far between around here. Although the *Cañada* is brushy and dry, the views up the canyon to the mountains in the west/northwest are quite respectable.

OAK FLAT
Angeles National Forest

Location: Southwest California northwest of Los Angeles.

Access: From Interstate 5 near milepost 66 at the Templin Highway Exit (21 miles north of San Fernando, 22 miles south of Lebec), drive to the west side of the freeway, then turn north onto the old Golden State Highway; continue north, parallel to the Interstate for 2.9 miles to the ranger station access road; turn west, and proceed 0.2 mile to the campground.

Facilities: 26 campsites; sites are small to medium-sized, with nominal separation; parking pads are gravel/dirt, medium to long, slightly sloped straight-ins; adequate space for large tents; fireplaces, fire rings or barbecue grills; b-y-o firewood is recommended; water at several faucets; vault facilities; gravel/dirt driveway; ranger station; limited supplies and services are available in Castaic, 7 miles south.

Activities & Attractions: Oak Flat Nature Trail; small campfire circle; Piru Creek, 2 miles north (maybe some fishing).

Natural Features: Located on a flat in a grove of medium-height oak trees which form a canopy that provides shade/shelter in an otherwise open and dry canyon; the area is bordered by brush-covered hills and low mountains; elevation 2800'.

Season, Fees & Phone: April to October; $5.00; 14 day limit; Arroyo Seco Ranger District, Flintridge, (818) 790-1151.

Camp Notes: This is the most easily accessed of the very few campgrounds available to Interstate 5 travelers in the Los Angeles-Bakersfield gigalopolis. There is also a bargain-lot, primitive camping area along Piru Creek. If you're on the skids, or just prefer a simple, green, creekside setting, it might be worth a look. (Signs caution against camping on the flood plain.) Oak Flat, however has tap water and substantially more shade, two important commodities in this canyon.

CASTAIC LAKE
Castaic Lake State Recreation Area

Location: Southern California north of Los Angeles.

Access: From Interstate 5 at the Castaic Exit near milepost 59 +.5, from the east side of the freeway, proceed east on lake Hughes Road for 0.4 mile to the recreation area.

Facilities: Camping for tents and rv's is being developed (please contact the park office for current information); a reservable group camp is available.

Activities & Attractions: Swimming on a sheltered lagoon; limited boating (manual, sail, or electric power) on the lagoon; boating with some restrictions on the main lake; boat launches; fishing for stocked trout, also bass, catfish and crappie; playground; very large day use areas.

Natural Features: Located near 2000-acre Castaic Lake; developed areas are landscaped with expansive lawns well-dotted with hardwoods and some conifers; elevation 1200'.

Season, Fees & Phone: Open all year; camping fees TBA; park entry fee $5.00 per vehicle, $7.00 for an rv; park office (805) 257-4050.

Camp Notes: Castaic Lake SRA is locally called Warren M. Dorn Recreation Complex. It's operated by The County of Los Angeles Parks and Recreation Department. It is suggested that you contact the park office for current information about camping facilities.

MILLERTON LAKE
Millerton Lake State Recreation Area

Location: Central California north of Fresno.

Access: From the junction of California State Highways 41 & 145 (19 miles north of Fresno, 15 miles east of Madera, 27 miles south of Oakhurst), travel east on County Road 145 (an extension of State Highway 145) for 3.3 miles to a "Y"; bear slightly north (left) continuing on Road 145 for 1.2 miles; turn east (right, remaining on Road 145) and proceed 2.6 miles to the park entrance station (at the southwest corner of the lake); the camp areas are located over the next 2.5 miles on the north shore along the main park road.

Facilities: 160 campsites in a half-dozen areas; (2 group camps, a boat-in camp and a trail camp are also available); sites in the sections closest to the entrance (Rocky Point, Mono, Fort Miller, etc.) are medium-sized, and generally well separated; parking pads are gravel, somewhat sloped, short to medium-length straight-ins; sites in the area farthest from the entrance (the "Meadow" area), are more level and have longer pads, but less separation; some sites have storage cabinets; fire rings; b-y-o firewood; water at several faucets in the first sections; water at faucets throughout the Meadow area; restrooms with showers, supplemented by vault facilities; holding tank disposal station; paved driveways; groceries 3 miles west, on Road 145.

Activities & Attractions: Designated swimming area; fishing for the standard warm water species; boating; boat launches; marina; hiking and horse trails; relocated, original Millerton courthouse (one-time Fresno County Courthouse, moved from what is now a submerged location); numerous day use areas.

Natural Features: Located along the shore of Millerton Lake, an impoundment on the San Joaquin River in the western foothills of the Sierra Nevada; campsites in the sections closest to the entrance are on a series of tree-dotted hills and slopes; Meadow area above the north-east shore is primarily on a large hilltop, somewhat shaded by hardwoods; elevation 600'.

Season, Fees & Phone: Open all year; please see Appendix for standard California state park fees and reservation information; park office (209) 822-2332.

Camp Notes: There are some really nice campsites here, so a look around might be worthwhile. Summer weekends are busy, (reportedly, more than 30,000 people and over 1000 boats have used the park on certain holiday weekends), but early in the week the place is often nearly deserted.

SUMMERDALE
Sierra National Forest

Location: East-central California north of Fresno.

Access: From California State Highway 41 at a point 1.6 miles south of the South Entrance to Yosemite National Park, 1 mile north of Fish Camp, and 14 miles north of Oakhurst, turn west onto a paved access road and proceed down the hill for 0.3 mile to the campground.

Facilities: 30 campsites; sites are medium or better in size, level, and reasonably well separated; parking pads are paved straight-ins, and vary from short to a generous medium in length; excellent, large tent areas; fire rings; firewood is available for gathering in the vicinity; water at several faucets; vault facilities; paved driveway; gas and groceries in Fish Camp, 1 mile south; adequate supplies and services are available in Oakhurst.

Activities & Attractions: Fishing; Mariposa Grove and Wawona in Yosemite, within 6 miles north.

Natural Features: Located on a large flat along the east bank of Big Creek on the west slope of the Sierra Nevada; campground vegetation consists of large hardwoods and a few very tall conifers above tall grass; the campground is bordered by timbered, low hills; elevation 5000'.

Season, Fees & Phone: May to October; $8.00; 14 day limit; Mariposa Ranger District, Oakhurst, (209) 683-4665.

Camp Notes: If camping within Yosemite proper isn't on your Must-Do-It-At-All-Costs list, then consider staying outside of the park in a place like this. The campground fills up in summer, and on many other weekends, so an early arrival (or a wait for a vacancy) may be the order of the day. For that matter, if Summerdale is full, or you're self-contained, self-sufficient, self-deprivating, or between paychecks, an option worth exploring might be to jackcamp on national forest land. There are a number of forest roads leading to little outlying places to siwash in around here.

FORKS
Bass Lake/Sierra National Forest

Location: East-central California north of Fresno.

Access: From California State Highway 41 (Southern Yosemite Highway) at milepost 39 (3.5 miles north of Oakhurst, 10 miles south of Fish Camp), turn southeast onto Road 222 (Bass Lake Road, paved, begins as a 4-lane road) and travel 3.5 miles to a major fork; take the right fork and go 0.3 mile to a second major fork; bear right again and continue along the south-west lake shore on Road 222 for another 1.8 miles; turn southwest (right) into the campground.

Facilities: 31 campsites; sites vary from small to large, with fair separation; parking pads are hard-surfaced, mostly short straight-ins; small to large, sloped tent spots; fire rings, plus some barbecue grills; b-y-o firewood is recommended; water at several faucets; restrooms; paved driveways; holding tank disposal station nearby on Road 222; gas and camper supplies along Road 222; adequate supplies and services are available in Oakhurst.

Activities & Attractions: Goat Mountain Trail (watch out for poison oak); designated swimming beach nearby; boating; windsurfing; fishing; South Entrance of Yosemite National Park is 12 miles north of the Bass Lake Road turnoff.

Natural Features: Located on sloping terrain above a bay on the south-west shore of Bass Lake; dense oaks and tall conifers provide ample shelter for most campsites; the lake is encircled by forested hills and mountains; elevation 3400'.

Season, Fees & Phone: April to November; (Forks or one of the other Bass Lake camps may be available with limited services in winter); $10.00; 10 day limit; Mariposa Ranger District, Oakhurst, (209) 683-4665 or Bass Lake Recreation Office (209) 642-3212 (summer).

Camp Notes: Bass Lake is one of the more popular water recreation spots in this region. No matter which of the four campgrounds you choose to stay in for a while (Forks or the three described below), you can "rest assured" that a highway patrol or sheriff's car won't be far away.

LUPINE-CEDAR BLUFF
Bass Lake/Sierra National Forest

Location: East-central California north of Fresno.

Access: From California State Highway 41 at milepost 39 (3.5 miles north of Oakhurst, 10 miles south of Fish Camp), turn southeast onto Road 222 (Bass Lake Road, paved) and travel 3.5 miles to a fork; take the right fork and go 0.3 mile to a second fork; bear right again and continue on Road 222 for another 3.4 miles; turn southwest (right) into the campground.

Facilities: 113 campsites, including a number of park 'n walk tent sites, in 6 loops; most sites are small-minus to small-plus in size, with nominal to fair separation; parking pads are paved, mostly short to medium-length straight-ins; a little additional leveling may be needed on some pads; small to large areas for tents; fire rings and some barbecue grills; b-y-o firewood is recommended; water at several faucets; restrooms; paved driveways;

Activities & Attractions: Boating; windsurfing; fishing for 16 species of fish; (a fish identifier and other angling info is available at the recreation office).

Natural Features: Located on a slope about a hundred yards above the south-west shore of Bass Lake; sites are lightly to moderately shaded mostly by tall conifers above very little ground cover; elevation 3400'.

Season, Fees & Phone: April to November; $10.00; 10 day limit; Mariposa Ranger District, Oakhurst, (209) 683-4665 or Bass Lake Recreation Office (209) 642-3212 (summer).

Camp Notes: The forest atmosphere is a little more 'open' here than in the other Bass Lake camps. The driveways and pads in this area are also somewhat more 'open' (wider) than those in other campgrounds, and thus a bit easier to negotiate by slightly longer vehicles or trailer combos. As a practical matter, though, don't plan on hauling a big rig into any of the four campgrounds on the lake unless you bring an experienced flight deck officer and a slick shoehorn to help slip your outfit into a slot.

SPRING COVE
Bass Lake/Sierra National Forest

Location: East-central California north of Fresno.

Access: From California State Highway 41 at milepost 39 (3.5 miles north of Oakhurst, 10 miles south of Fish Camp), turn southeast onto Road 222 (Bass Lake Road, paved) and travel 3.5 miles to a fork; take the right fork and go 0.3 mile to a second fork; bear right again and continue on Road 222 for another 4.2 miles; turn southwest (right) into the campground.

Facilities: 63 campsites; sites are very small to small, sloped, with slight to fair separation; parking pads are packed gravel or hard-surfaced, majority are short straight-ins; small to medium-sized tent areas; fireplaces; b-y-o firewood is recommended; water at several faucets; restrooms; paved driveways; adequate supplies and services are available in Oakhurst.

Activities & Attractions: Spring Cove Trail (watch for poison oak); boating; windsurfing; fishing; picnic areas nearby.

Natural Features: Located on a moderate slope above the south-west shore of Bass Lake; campsites receive moderate shade/shelter from tall conifers; the lake lies in a basin ringed by forested hills and low mountains; elevation 3400'.

Season, Fees & Phone: April to November; $10.00; 10 day limit; Mariposa Ranger District, Oakhurst, (209) 683-4665 or Bass Lake Recreation Office (209) 642-3212 (summer).

Camp Notes: Some nice lakeshore picnic sites are within walking distance of this campground. For a longer walk, you could head up the Spring Cove Trail to the Goat Mountain Trail, then down that route to Forks Campground (see info above). The 8.5 mile trip is along moderate grades through the forest. Be sure to remember to fill your canteen at the campground before you embark.

WISHON POINT
Bass Lake/Sierra National Forest

Location: East-central California north of Fresno.

Access: From California State Highway 41 at milepost 39 (3.5 miles north of Oakhurst, 10 miles south of Fish Camp), turn southeast onto Road 222 (paved) and travel 3.5 miles to a fork; take the right fork and go 0.3 mile to a second fork; bear right again and continue on Road 222 for another 5.1 miles; turn southwest (sharply right) into the campground.

Facilities: 47 campsites; sites are very small to small, sloped, with minimal to fair separation; parking pads are hard-surfaced, narrow, short straight-ins or short+ to medium-length pull-throughs; small to medium-sized tent areas; fireplaces and some barbecue grills; b-y-o firewood is recommended; water at several faucets; restrooms; paved driveway; adequate supplies and services are available in Oakhurst.

Activities & Attractions: Boating; windsurfing; boat launch just across the main road; fishing.

Natural Features: Located on rolling, sloped terrain above the south-west shore of Bass Lake; campsites are moderately sheltered by a mixture of tall conifers, oaks and other hardwoods; the lake is rimmed by well-timbered hills; elevation 3400'.

Season, Fees & Phone: April to November; $10.00; 10 day limit; Mariposa Ranger District, Oakhurst, (209) 683-4665 or Bass Lake Recreation Office (209) 642-3212 (summer).

Camp Notes: About a third of the slim sites here have lake views through the trees. (As actor W.C. Fields once remarked: "All things considered, I'd rather be in Philadelphia". Ed.)

DORABELLE
Sierra National Forest

Location: East-central California northeast of Fresno.

Access: From California State Highway 168 at milepost 45 +.5 (in the community of Shaver Lake, 51 miles northeast of Fresno), turn east onto Dorabella Road, and proceed 0.45 mile to the campground

Facilities: 67 sites; sites are generously medium-sized and generally well separated; parking pads are paved or gravel, medium-length straight-ins which may require additional leveling; adequate, but slightly sloped, space for a large tent in most sites; fireplaces; some firewood is available for gathering in surrounding forest lands; water at several faucets; restrooms; paved driveways; large overflow camping area; limited to adequate supplies and services are available in Shaver Lake.

Activities & Attractions: Boating; trout fishing; several short trails in and around the campground.

Natural Features: Located on a densely forested, terraced hillside at the southwest corner of Shaver Lake, an impoundment on the Stevenson Creek watershed, in the Sierra Nevada; campground vegetation consists of very tall conifers and light brush; boulders and a rock ledge form a portion of the campground's backdrop; surrounded by heavily timbered hills and low ridges; elevation 5400'.

Season, Fees & Phone: Late-April to the end of October; $10.00; 14 day limit; Pineridge Ranger District, Shaver Lake, (209) 841-3311.

Camp Notes: This is one of the more attractive forest campgrounds in this area. The water level of Shaver Lake, however, may be subjected to a substantial drop during dry seasons. When the lake is at a more or less normal level, the overall environmental 'package' is very pleasing. In good times, the lake is stocked with trout every several weeks, and fishing is said to be good.

RANCHERIA
Sierra National Forest

Location: East-central California northeast of Fresno.

Access: From the northeast end of California State Highway 168 at milepost 65 +.7 (22 miles northeast of Shaver Lake, 71 miles northeast of Fresno), turn southwest (left) into the campground.

Facilities: 161 campsites; sites are small to medium-sized, with good separation; parking pads are gravel, short to medium-length straight-ins, and most will require additional leveling; enough space for a medium to large tent in most sites, but tent areas are quite sloped; fireplaces or fire rings; some firewood is available for gathering in the vicinity; water at several faucets; restrooms, plus auxiliary vaults; paved driveways; limited to adequate supplies and services are available in Shaver Lake.

Activities & Attractions: Boating; boat launch nearby; fishing; guided nature walks and campfire programs may be scheduled.

Natural Features: Located on the densely forested northeast shore of Huntington Lake; a variety of tall conifers plus light underbrush are in and around the campground; some sites have a glimpse of the lake through the forest, all are within walking distance of the lake; elevation 7000'.

Season, Fees & Phone: May to October; $12.00; 14 day limit; campground office (209) 893-2111 (seasonally) or Pineridge Ranger District, Shaver Lake, (209) 841-3311.

Camp Notes: Huntington Lake is certainly a very picturesque spot for a campout. (But if you get a tent site at Rancheria, keep your spare socks flat; if you roll them into a ball they may tumble down the steep slope and ... plop! Soggy socks. Ed.)

DEER CREEK & COLLEGE
Sierra National Forest

Location: East-central California northeast of Fresno.

Access: From the northeast end of California State Highway 168 at milepost 65 +.9 (22 miles northeast of Shaver Lake, 71 miles northeast of Fresno), turn southwest (left) onto Huntington Lake Road and continue for 0.4 mile to *College*, or 0.7 mile to *Deer Creek*; both campgrounds are on the south (left) side of the road.

Facilities: *Deer Creek*: 28 campsites in 3 small loops; *College*: 11 campsites; **both camps**: sites are small, with some visual separation in Deer Creek, and very little separation in College; parking pads are dirt/gravel, short to medium-length straight-ins; pads are fairly level in Deer Creek and somewhat sloped in College; fire rings; some firewood is available for gathering in the vicinity; water at several faucets; restrooms; semi-paved/gravel driveways; limited to adequate supplies and services are available in Shaver Lake.

Activities & Attractions: Boating; boat launch nearby; fishing; nature walks and campfire programs may be scheduled.

Natural Features: Located at the northeast corner of Huntington Lake on the west slope of the Sierra Nevada; campground vegetation consists of thin to moderately dense, tall conifers, plus some tall grass and second-growth timber; both campgrounds are very near the lakeshore; the lake is encircled by high, timbered peaks and ridges; elevation 7000'.

Season, Fees & Phone: May to October; $12.00; 14 day limit; campground office (209) 893-2111 (seasonally) or Pineridge Ranger District, Shaver Lake, (209) 841-3311.

Camp Notes: Of these two relatively similar campgrounds, Deer Creek probably takes the ribbon. Although its sites are perhaps a tad smaller than those at College, the overall forest atmosphere, and the lake views from some of the sites and from the campground area, give it an edge.

KINNIKINNICK
Sierra National Forest

Location: East-central California northeast of Fresno.

Access: From the northeast end of California State Highway 168 at milepost 65 +.9 (22 miles northeast of the town of Shaver Lake, 71 miles northeast of Fresno), turn southwest (left) onto Huntington Lake Road and proceed 1 mile; turn right into the campground.

Facilities: 32 campsites sites are generally small to medium-sized, with fairly good visual separation; parking pads are dirt/gravel, short to medium-length straight-ins which may require additional leveling; adequately sized, somewhat sloped tent areas; fireplaces or fire rings; some firewood is available for gathering in the vicinity; water at several faucets; water closets (mini restrooms); hard-surfaced, narrow driveways; limited to adequate supplies and services are available in Shaver Lake.

Activities & Attractions: Boating; boat launch nearby; fishing; guided nature walks and campfire programs may be scheduled in summer.

Natural Features: Located at the northeast corner of Huntington Lake on the upper west slope of the Sierra Nevada; campground vegetation consists of moderately dense, tall conifers, tall grass and some second-growth timber; elevation 7000'.

Season, Fees & Phone: May to October; $12.00; 14 day limit; campground office (209) 893-2111 (seasonally) or Pineridge Ranger District, Shaver Lake, (209) 841-3311.

Camp Notes: Kinnikinnick (sounds like an eastern Algonquin Indian word doesn't it?) Campground is a couple-hundred yards from the lakeshore, but without lake views. If you stay here, perhaps you could ask the campground 'ranger' about the origin of the word.

CATAVEE
Sierra National Forest

Location: East-central California northeast of Fresno.

Access: From the end of California State Highway 168 at milepost 65 +.9 (22 miles northeast of the town of Shaver Lake, 71 miles northeast of Fresno), turn southwest (left) onto Huntington Lake Road and continue for 1.2 miles to the campground, on the right side of the road.

Facilities: 26 campsites; sites are generally small to average in size, with fair separation; parking pads are dirt/gravel, short to medium-length straight-ins' some additional leveling may be required; medium to large, somewhat sloped tent areas; fireplaces or fire rings; some firewood is available for gathering in the vicinity; water at several faucets; vault facilities; hard-surfaced driveways; limited to adequate supplies and services are available in Shaver Lake.

Activities & Attractions: Boating; boat launch nearby; fishing; guided nature walks and campfire programs may be scheduled.

Natural Features: Located in the Sierra Nevada at the northeast corner of Huntington Lake; sites receive medium shade/shelter from tall conifers and some new-growth timber on a surface of tall grass; elevation 7000'.

Season, Fees & Phone: May to October; $12.00; 14 day limit; campground office (209) 893-2111 (seasonally) or Pineridge Ranger District, Shaver Lake, (209) 841-3311.

Camp Notes: Following Huntington Lake Road southwestward past Catavee for another three miles will take you to Upper and Lower Billy Creek Campgrounds at the other end of the lake. Basically, it's the same deal at Billy Creek as in the camps at this end of the lake: a total of 57 small campsites in both units, water, restrooms, straight-in pads, near the lake, etc.

AZALEA, CRYSTAL SPRINGS, SUNSET
Kings Canyon National Park

Location: East-central California east of Fresno.

Access: From California State Highway 180/Kings Canyon Road at points in the vicinity of Grant Grove Village in Kings Canyon National Park (58 miles east of Fresno, 0.2 mile south of the Kings Canyon NP Visitor Center), turn west into *Sunset*; or at a point 0.3 mile north of the visitor center, turn west into *Azalea* or east into *Crystal Springs*. (Note that the road follows a north-south line is this section.)

Facilities: *Azelea*: 118 campsites; *Crystal Springs*: 67 campsites; *Sunset*: 192 campsites; *all camps*: sites are generally small+ to medium-sized, with nominal to fair separation; parking pads are paved or gravel/dirt, short to medium-length straight-ins; although pads have been fairly well leveled, additional leveling will be needed in many sites; large, well-cleared, but sloped tent areas; fireplaces or fire rings; b-y-o firewood; water at several faucets; restrooms; holding tank disposal station in Azalea; paved driveways; gas and groceries are available in Grant Grove Village.

Activities & Attractions: Several trails in the area; national park visitor center; naturalist-guided programs; ski touring.

Natural Features: Located on moderately steep, rolling terrain in the Sierra Nevada; campground vegetation consists of a variety of moderately dense, tall conifers, plus a small amount of young growth and brush; overall, Sunset probably has the most shelter/shade, Azalea the least; some of the sites in Sunset have valley views, most other sites have limited views; elevation 6500'.

Season, Fees & Phone: One of the campgrounds is open all year, with limited services in winter; other camps are open May to October; $7.00; 14 day limit; Sequoia & Kings Canyon NPs Headquarters, Three Rivers, (209) 565-3456 (info office) or (209) 565-3351 (24-hour recording).

Camp Notes: These three campgrounds are similar enough to describe them as if they were just three sections of the same huge campground. Any one of the threesome should serve well for someone passing between Sequoia and Kings Canyon, or who desires a high, cool campsite. But the park's other camping area, 30 long but scenic miles east of here at Cedar Grove (see Sheep Creek, et.al.), is certainly worth going the extra mileage to visit and explore.

Southern California 86

PRINCESS
Sequoia National Forest

Location: East-central California east of Fresno.

Access: From California State Highway 180 (Kings Canyon Road) at milepost 116 +.6 (6 miles northeast of the Grant Grove Visitor Center in Kings Canyon NP, 64 miles east of Fresno), turn south/southwest onto a paved access road and proceed 0.2 mile to the campground.

Facilities: 90 campsites in 3 loops; sites are medium-sized, with fair to good separation; parking pads are sand/gravel straight-ins, and many may require additional leveling; tent areas are quite large, but sloped; fire rings; firewood is available for gathering in the surrounding area; water at several faucets; vault facilities; holding tank disposal station; gas and groceries are available in Grant Grove Village.

Activities & Attractions: Numerous primitive roads and 4wd trails in the area; fishing and boating on Hume Lake, 3 miles southeast; Kings Canyon National Park lies to the east and south.

Natural Features: Located in rolling terrain at the north edge of a large park (mountain meadow) in Indian Basin in the Sierra Nevada; campground vegetation consists of very tall conifers, some low-level brush and tall grass; heavily timbered ridges surround the area; elevation 5900'.

Season, Fees & Phone: May to October; $8.00; 14 day limit; Hume Lake Ranger District, Dunlap, (209) 338-2251.

Camp Notes: This is really a nice spot which doesn't appear to be overused. The origin of the name of the campground is unclear. But the camp's three loops are called Shining Cloud, Yellow Moon and Morning Star, so just use a little imagination.

Southern California 87

HUME LAKE
Sequoia National Forest

Location: East-central California east of Fresno.

Access: From California State Highway 180 (Kings Canyon Road) at milepost 116 +.8 (6 miles northeast of the Grant Grove Visitor Center in Kings Canyon NP, 64 miles east of Freezeno), bear easterly off the highway onto Hume Lake Road (paved); proceed 3.2 miles to a fork in the road; take the left fork, and continue for 0.4 mile to the campground entrance.

Alternate Access: From the Generals Highway (the north-south road between Kings Canyon and Sequoia National Parks) at a point 6 miles south-east of Grant Grove Village, head northward on Hume Lake Road (a paved, narrow, curvy forest road) for 10 miles to the campground. (Note: the *Alternate Access* is a 'scenic backway' to Hume Lake and might be useful if you're northbound from Sequoia NP; however, it probably won't save any time or more than a couple of miles.)

Facilities: 75 campsites in 4 loops; sites are medium-sized, with some separation; parking pads are sand/dirt straight-ins which will require some additional leveling; tent areas are large, but sloped; fireplaces; firewood is available for gathering in the surrounding area; water at several faucets; restrooms; paved driveways; holding tank disposal station at Princess Campground, on Highway 180; gas and groceries are available in Grant Grove Village.

Activities & Attractions: Limited boating; fishing; road continues around to the south shore and to Sandy Cove designated swimming area; Kings Canyon National Park lies to the south and east.

Natural Features: Located on a moderately steep slope in a medium-dense forest on the north shore of 87-acre Hume Lake in the Sierra Nevada; campground vegetation consists of tall conifers, and some tall grass; high, timbered peaks rise in the surrounding area; lake views through the forest from a few sites; elevation 5200'.

Season, Fees & Phone: May to October; $12.00; 14 day limit; Hume Lake Ranger District, Dunlap, (209) 338-2251.

Camp Notes: Hume Lake was formed by a dam constructed in the early 1900's to serve as a source of water for the longest lumber flume ever built. The products of a sawmill on the lake shore were dispatched on a wild, wet ride along the flume's 59-mile length all the way to Sanger, on the east edge of Fresno. Except for miscellaneous components and the manpower element, nature provided most of the raw materials and power for the harvest, the mill, the flume and the transportation. Even though the campground is full (which it often is in summer), or you're not planning to camp here, the short trip up Hume Lake Road is worth the time. One of the best mountain/canyon panoramas in the Sierra--of Kings Canyon and Monarch Wilderness, to the east--is available along the road.

SHEEP CREEK
Kings Canyon National Park

Location: East-central California east of Fresno.

Access: From California State Highway 180/Kings Canyon Road in Grant Grove Village in Kings Canyon National Park (4 miles northeast of the park's Big Stump Entrance Station, 58 miles east of Fresno) head easterly on Highway 180 for 29 miles to the end of Highway 180 at the park's Cedar Grove area; continue east on a paved park road for 1.3 miles; turn north (left), into the campground.

Facilities: 111 campsites; sites are small to medium-sized, with fair to fairly good separation; parking pads are paved, mostly short straight-ins, plus a few longer long pull-throughs; additional leveling will be needed on many pads; large, generally sloped tent areas; fireplaces; some firewood may be available for gathering in the general area; lockable storage cabinets (bear boxes); water at several faucets; restrooms; paved driveways; holding tank disposal station; gas, groceries, showers and coin-op laundry are available in Cedar Grove.

Activities & Attractions: Hiking trails to falls viewpoints and into the back country; motor nature trail; amphitheater for scheduled nature programs; short foot trails in the campground area; Boyden Caverns (Sequoia National Forest) 3 miles west.

Natural Features: Located on a slope above the South Fork of the Kings River in Kings Canyon; Sheep Creek enters the river from the south near the campground; majority of campsites are quite well sheltered/shaded by tall conifers; closely bordered by high, steep hills and mountains; elevation 4600'.

Season, Fees & Phone: May to November; $7.00; 14 day limit; Sequoia & Kings Canyon NPs Headquarters, Three Rivers, (209) 565-3456 (info office) or (209) 565-3351 (24-hour recording).

Camp Notes: It may be difficult to decide (if a decision can even be made) which is the better of the two totally different perspectives of Kings Canyon you'll encounter on your trip to this remote spot. On one hand are the commanding panoramas of the canyon you'll see from highwayside overlooks (or *outlooks*) on the way to and from the inner canyon. And then there are the very pleasing river vistas and spectacular vertical views from the canyon floor. Kings Canyon is one of the neatest places in the Sierra.

SENTINEL
Kings Canyon National Park

Location: East-central California east of Fresno.

Access: From California State Highway 180/Kings Canyon Road in Grant Grove Village in Kings Canyon National Park (4 miles northeast of the park's Big Stump Entrance Station, 58 miles east of Fresno) head easterly on Highway 180 for 29 miles to the end of Highway 180 at the park's Cedar Grove area; continue east on a paved park road for 1.7 miles; turn north (left), go 0.1 mile, then swing west (left) into the campground.

Facilities: 83 campsites; sites are small to small+, with nominal to fair separation; parking pads are hard-surfaced, mostly short straight-ins, plus a few longer long pull-throughs; a little additional leveling may be needed in some sites; large tent areas, some are a bit sloped or bumpy; fireplaces; some firewood may be available for gathering in the general vicinity; bear boxes; water at several faucets; restrooms; paved driveways; ranger station; gas and groceries in Cedar Grove.

Activities & Attractions: Hiking trails to falls viewpoints and into the back country; motor nature trail; amphitheater for scheduled nature programs.

Natural Features: Located on a rolling, gentle slope in Kings Canyon above the South Fork of the Kings River in the Sierra Nevada; campsites receive ample shelter/shade from moderately dense tall conifers; closely bordered by high, steep mountains; elevation 4600'.

Season, Fees & Phone: May to November; $7.00; 14 day limit; Sequoia & Kings Canyon NPs Headquarters, Three Rivers, (209) 565-3456 (info office) or (209) 565-3351 (24-hour recording).

Camp Notes: All things considered, Sentinel may offer best compromise of site size, separation and levelness of the trio of camps in Cedar Grove. The river is just a short walk down the slope from any campsite in all three campgrounds.

Southern California 90

MORAINE
Kings Canyon National Park

Location: East-central California east of Fresno.

Access: From California State Highway 180/Kings Canyon Road in Grant Grove Village in Kings Canyon National Park (4 miles northeast of the park's Big Stump Entrance Station, 58 miles east of Fresno) head easterly on Highway 180 for 29 miles to the end of Highway 180 at the park's Cedar Grove area; continue east on a paved park road for a final 2.4 miles to the campground, on the north (left) side of the road.

Facilities: 120 campsites; (Canyon View Group Campground, 0.4 mile west, is also available, by reservation only); sites are good-sized, with nominal to fair separation; parking pads are sandy gravel, mostly medium to long pull-offs or pull-throughs, plus some straight-ins; a little additional leveling may be needed in many sites; large, generally sloped tent areas; bear boxes; fire rings; some firewood may be available for gathering in the area; water at several faucets; restrooms; paved driveways; gas and groceries in Cedar Grove.

Activities & Attractions: Hiking trails to falls viewpoints and into the high country; motor nature trail.

Natural Features: Located on a northward-facing, forested slope deep in Kings Canyon near the South Fork of the Kings River; campsites are lightly to moderately sheltered/shaded by tall conifers and a few hardwoods on a surface of evergreen needles; closely flanked by the high, rocky, steep mountains of the west slope of the Sierra Nevada; elevation 4600'.

Season, Fees & Phone: May to November (or as needed); $7.00; 14 day limit; Sequoia & Kings Canyon NPs Headquarters, Three Rivers, (209) 565-3456 (info office) or (209) 565-3351 (24-hour recording).

Camp Notes: Once you get settled in at the campground, be sure to take the five-mile trip easterly for another four miles to the turnaround loop and parking area at Road's End. Scenic high drama unfolds from there.

Southern California 91

STONY CREEK
Sequoia National Forest

Location: East-central California east of Fresno.

Access: From the Generals Highway at a point 13.5 miles south of Grant Grove Village in Kings Canyon National Park and 15 miles north of the Lodgepole area in Sequoia National Park (1.1 miles north of the Sequoia Park-Sequoia Forest boundary), turn west (i.e., left, if northbound) into the campground.

Facilities: 49 campsites in a figure-8 loop; sites are small to medium-sized, with nominal separation; parking pads are short to medium-length, paved or gravel/sand straight-ins; about half of the pads are level, the remainder will probably require some additional leveling; good-sized, fairly level tent areas; fireplaces; firewood is available for gathering in the vicinity; water at several faucets; restrooms; paved driveways; gas and groceries at Stony Creek Village, 0.5 mile north, and at Grant Grove and Lodgepole.

Activities & Attractions: Day use area on the opposite side of the highway; limited mountain views from the area.

Natural Features: Located on a gently sloping flat in a moderately dense forest of tall conifers; surrounded by heavily timbered hills and ridges; the stream bed is filled with large, smooth rocks (hence the name for the intermittent creek which passes through the campground); elevation 6500'.

Season, Fees & Phone: May to October; $8.00; 14 day limit; Hume Lake Ranger District, Dunlap, (209) 338-2251.

Camp Notes: If the campgrounds in Sequoia National Park are filled, this one might be worth a try for a space, but it still is quite busy in summer, even on weekdays. Also, there is *usually* space available in the three Kings Canyon Campgrounds, a dozen miles north at Grant Grove.

DORST
Sequoia National Park

Location: East-central California east of Fresno.

Access: From the Generals Highway (the main north-south road between Kings Canyon and Sequoia National Parks) at a point 3.5 miles south of the north park boundary near Stony Creek Village, 18 miles south of Grant Grove Village, and 26 miles north of Lodgepole Village, turn west onto a paved access road and go down 0.2 mile into the campground.

Facilities: 238 campsites in a maze of loops; sites are small to medium-sized, with minimal to nominal separation; parking pads are gravel or paved, mostly short straight-ins; additional leveling may be needed on many pads; medium to large, generally sloped areas for tents; storage lockers; fire rings; gathering firewood on national forest lands prior to arrival is suggested; water at several faucets; restrooms; holding tank disposal station; paved driveway; gas and groceries at Stony Creek Village, 4 miles north, and at Grant Grove and Lodgepole.

Activities & Attractions: Muir Grove Trail; amphitheater.

Natural Features: Located on steep, hilly terrain near Dorst Creek on the west slope of the Sierra Nevada; sites are very well-sheltered by medium-dense, tall conifers; surrounded by dense forest; a meadow is south of the campground; elevation 6500'.

Season, Fees & Phone: May to October; $8.00; 14 day limit; Sequoia & Kings Canyon NPs Headquarters, Three Rivers, (209) 565-3456 (info office) or (209) 565-3351 (24-hour recording).

Camp Notes: Super tall trees here--some as tall as you'd ever hope to see. Some rockwork lends engineering assistance and a touch of trim to the campground.

LODGEPOLE
Sequoia National Park

Location: East-central California east of Fresno.

Access: From the Generals Highway (the main north-south road between Kings Canyon and Sequoia National Parks) at Lodgepole (14 miles south of the north park boundary near Stony Creek Village, 15 miles north of the south park boundary at Ash Mountain), turn east (i.e., right, if northbound), and proceed 0.3 mile to the campground entrance station.

Facilities: 266 campsites in 3 major complex loops; sites are typically small, with separation ranging from nil to minimal; sites in the section closest to the entrance (#'s 1-67) are the largest and most level, followed by those in the next-closest section (#'s 189-266), then the upper section (#'s 76-187, no trailers); parking pads are paved or gravel, mainly short to medium-length straight-ins, which are level, or reasonably level considering the terrain; most spaces can accommodate a large tent on a fairly level surface; storage lockers (bear boxes); fire rings; b-y-o firewood; water at several faucets; restrooms; holding tank disposal station; paved driveways; ranger station; showers, gas, coin-op laundry and a large market are available near the visitor center.

Activities & Attractions: Stands of giant sequoias; visitor center; several trails; nature center.

Natural Features: Located in a canyon along the Marble Fork of the Kaweah River; the first camp section is located on a riverside flat, the middle section is on a hilltop, and the upper section is along a rather steep, boulder-strewn hillside; moderately dense conifer forest provides ample shelter/shade in most sites; elevation 6700'.

Season, Fees & Phone: Open all year, subject to weather conditions, with limited services October to May; $8.00-$10.00; 14 day limit; reservations recommended July-August, please see Appendix for additional reservation information; Sequoia & Kings Canyon NPs Headquarters, Three Rivers, (209) 565-3456 (info office) or (209) 565-3351 (24-hour recording)..

Camp Notes: This area might remind you a little of Yosemite--both in the shape and color of the rock, and in the state of activity. (Bring your waffle-stompers and climbing gear if there's a chance you'll get a site in the upper section.)

BUCKEYE FLAT
Sequoia National Park

Location: East-central California east of Fresno.

Access: From the Generals Highway (the main north-south road between Kings Canyon and Sequoia National Parks) at a point 6 miles north of the Ash Mountain entrance station (northeast of Three Rivers) and 10 miles south of Giant Forest Village, turn east (i.e., right, if northbound) onto a narrow, paved access road and proceed 0.4 mile to the campground.

Facilities: 28 campsites; sites are small and closely spaced; parking pads are paved, short, sloped straight-ins; (no motorhomes or trailers permitted); tent areas are medium to large, and as level as can be expected under the local circumstances; storage lockers; fire rings; b-y-o firewood; water at central faucets; restrooms; paved driveway; gas and groceries near Ash Mountain; limited supplies and services are available in Three Rivers.

Activities & Attractions: Several hiking trails (a map and info sheet are available at visitor center at Ash Mountain); stream fishing.

Natural Features: Located on a sloping flat in a narrow canyon along the Middle Fork of the Kaweah River; a dense stand of hardwoods forms a leafy canopy over much of the campground and provides some visual separation between sites; surrounded by hills covered with grass, brush, and some trees; high mountains to the east; elevation 2800'.

Season, Fees & Phone: April to October; $8.00; 14 day limit; Sequoia & Kings Canyon NPs Headquarters, Three Rivers, (209) 565-3456 (info office) or (209) 565-3351 (24-hour recording).

Camp Notes: At first sight, this campground seems strangely out of place, after all the things you've heard about Sequoia National Park. It's not in the high country with the lofty cone-bearers for which the park is named. Rather, it's in the lowlands, engulfed in hardwoods. Buckeye Flat is a neat, almost cozy, little place.

POTWISHA
Sequoia National Park

Location: East-central California east of Fresno.

Access: From the Generals Highway (the main north-south road between Kings Canyon and Sequoia National Parks) at a point 4 miles north of the Ash Mountain entrance station (northeast of Three Rivers) and 12 miles south of Giant Forest Village, turn west (i.e., left, if northbound) into the campground.

Facilities: 44 campsites; sites are medium-sized, with nominal separation; parking pads are paved, medium-length, and most are pull-offs or pull-throughs which probably could accommodate most rv's; additional leveling will probably be needed on most pads; tent spaces are large but a little sloped; fire rings; b-y-o firewood; water at central faucets; restrooms; holding tank disposal station nearby; gas and groceries are available near Ash Mountain; limited supplies and services are available in Three Rivers.

Activities & Attractions: Fishing; visitor center at Ash Mountain; several hiking trails (a map is available at the visitor center).

Natural Features: Located in a canyon on a flat along the Marble Fork of the Kaweah River near its confluence with the Kaweah's Middle Fork; campsites are situated in a light to moderately dense stand of hardwoods; brushy hillsides and mountainsides border the campground; high mountains are visible from many sites; elevation 2100'.

Season, Fees & Phone: Open all year; $8.00; 14 day limit; Sequoia & Kings Canyon NPs Headquarters, Three Rivers, (209) 565-3456 (info office) or (209) 565-3351 (24-hour recording).

Camp Notes: If you're entering Sequoia from the south on California Highway 198, this would be the first campground inside the park. It's a good spot to ponder the road ahead: the next dozen miles are pretty snakey, steep and slow-going. A lot of rv travelers park their trailers or motorhomes here, and take the towing or towed vehicle (whatever works) into the high country. If you're coming down out of Sequoia from the north, it's a good place to stop and let your brakes and emotions cool.

HORSE CREEK
Lake Kaweah/Corps of Engineers Park

Location: East-central California southeast of Fresno.

Access: From California State Highway 198 at milepost 32 +.7 (5 miles southeast of Three Rivers, 23 miles northeast of Visalia), turn north into the campground entrance.

Facilities: 80 campsites; sites are small to medium-sized, with little or no separation; parking pads are mostly paved, medium to long straight-ins, some are pull-offs; most pads will require additional leveling; adequate, but sloped, spaces for large tents; small ramadas (sun shelters) over table areas in many sites; fire rings in most sites, barbecue grills in some; b-y-o firewood; water at several faucets; restrooms with showers; holding tank disposal station; gas and groceries in Lemoncove, 6 miles west; limited supplies and services are available in Three Rivers.

Activities & Attractions: Boating; lake and stream fishing for largemouth bass, panfish, white bass, catfish; scores of thousands of rainbow trout are stocked in winter; small playground; paved paths; amphitheater.

Natural Features: Located on a grassy, rolling slope on the south shore of Lake Kaweah, an impoundment on the Kaweah River; a few hardwoods provide minimal shelter/shade for campsites; surrounded by grassy, tree-dotted hillsides; the Sierra Nevada rises a few miles to the east; hot summers, cool winters; elevation 700'.

Season, Fees & Phone: Open all year, with limited services in winter; $8.00; 14 day limit; CoE Project Office (209) 597-2301.

Camp Notes: Under the right conditions, this camp could be just the ticket. Like many reservoirs, it is subject to a late summer low. But during the spring and early summer--filled to the brim, and with Sequoia National Park at the back door--it might be a really good buy.

TULE
Success Lake/Corps of Engineers Park

Location: Central California southeast of Fresno.

Access: From California State Highway 190 at milepost 24 +.4 (8 miles east of Porterville, 7 miles southwest of Springville), turn northwest onto a paved access road and proceed 0.2 mile to the campground.

Facilities: 104 campsites with water hookups; sites are larger than average, basically level, with nominal separation; parking pads are paved, mostly long straight-ins, plus a few pull-offs and pull-throughs; tent areas are very large and level; fire rings and barbecue grills; b-y-o firewood; water at sites; restrooms with showers; holding tank disposal station; paved driveways; gas and groceries at a lakeside store; limited supplies in Springville; complete supplies and services are available in Porterville.

Activities & Attractions: Boating; boat launches; marina; fishing for black bass, striped bass, panfish, catfish; rainbow trout stocked in fall; small children's play area.

Natural Features: Located on the east shore of Success Lake, an impoundment on the Tule River, against the foothills of the Sierra Nevada; campground vegetation consists of short grass, and hardwoods in various stages of development which provide some shade/shelter in many, if not most, sites.

Season, Fees & Phone: Open all year, with limited services in winter; $8.00; 14 day limit; CoE Project Office (209) 784-0215.

Camp Notes: Wind conditions on Success Lake are said to be usually very good for small sailboats. Although it gets its share of holiday weekend traffic, Tule reportedly usually doesn't fill up at other times. Spring is the busiest time. This is one of two camping areas on Success Lake. The other, Rocky Hill, is a primitive, no fee area on the southwest shore that's open April to October.

COFFEE CAMP
Sequoia National Forest

Location: East-central California southeast of Fresno.

Access: From California State Highway 190 at milepost 37 +.2 (3 miles east of Springville, 20 miles east of Porterville), turn south (0.4 mile east of Coffee Camp picnic area) swing south into the campground.

Facilities: 20 campsites, mostly park 'n walk or walk-down sites, in 2 loops; sites are small, with nominal separation; roadside parking areas; enough level space for a small to medium-sized tent in most sites; assorted fire appliances; b-y-o firewood is recommended; water at several faucets; (the water source may be unreliable, so b-y-o water to be sure); vault facilities; limited supplies and services are available in Springville.

Activities & Attractions: Fishing.

Natural Features: Located in the western high foothills of the Sierra Nevada in a canyon above the Middle Fork of the Tule River; sites are on a slope and receive light to light-medium shade/shelter from hardwoods on a tallgrass surface; closely bordered by rocky/brushy canyon walls; Coffee Canyon, a side canyon, joins the main gorge from the south, opposite the campground; elevation 2000'.

Season, Fees & Phone: Open all year; $5.00; 14 day limit; Tule Ranger District, Porterville, (209) 539-2607.

Camp Notes: Nice scenery up here. There are two other campgrounds along the river east of Coffee Camp: Wishon Campground, 7 miles east, with 33 sites; and Belknap, 12 miles east, with 15 sites. Both have water and vaults. Small trailers are OK in Wishon (assuming you can drag one up there), but trailers aren't given an admission slip for Belknap. Both camps are open May to October. Fact is, this narrow, snakey 'highway' with its double-digit grades and fishhook curves makes the going a bit dicey for anything larger than a mini-pickup, so plan accordingly.

COLONEL ALLENSWORTH
Colonel Allensworth State Historic Park

Location: South-central California north of Bakersfield.

Access: From California State Highway 43 at milepost 5 +.5 in the small community of Allensworth (19 miles north of Wasco, 18 miles south of Corcoran) turn west onto Palmer Avenue and into the park; turn north (right) and follow the road around the north side of the townsite; the campground is in the far northwest corner of the park.

Facilities: 15 campsites; sites are small+ to medium-sized, level, with nominal separation; parking pads are gravel, medium to long straight-ins; large tent areas; medium-sized, central ramadas (sun shelters); fire rings; b-y-o firewood; water at central faucets; restrooms; holding tank disposal station; gravel driveway; limited to adequate supplies in Earlimart, 9 miles east, and Delano, 13 miles southeast.

Activities & Attractions: Original townsite of a pioneer community of the early 1900's and restorations or reconstructions of some of the original buildings; small visitor center with orientation film and interpretive displays; day use area with ramada.

Natural Features: Located on a vast, semi-arid plain near the south end of the San Joaquin Valley; park vegetation consists of sections of watered lawns, natural grass, low brush and scattered hardwoods; campsites receive very light natural shade; elevation 200'.

Season, Fees & Phone: Open all year; please see Appendix for standard California state park fees and reservation information; park office (805) 849-3433.

Camp Notes: Allen Allensworth was born a slave in Louisville, Kentucky in 1842, fought for the Union during the Civil War, earned an education, and went back into the army as a chaplain in 1886. Twenty years later he retired as a lieutenant colonel--and as the highest ranking African-American in the armed forces. The small rural community here was founded by Allensworth in 1908 as a means of giving Black pioneers an opportunity to live and work free of the social and economic pressures of the era. The town flourished for a while and, according to historical accounts, life here was exemplary of pioneer life elsewhere on the American frontier. But the water supply slowly diminished and the importance of the town's railroad-side location weakened as trucks became more commonly used to transport supplies and farm products. The town of Allensworth quite literally "dried up", and most of the population of what had been hundreds moved on.

KERN RIVER
Kern County Park

Location: South-central California northeast of Bakersfield.

Access: From California State Highway 178 near milepost 11 (11 miles northeast of Bakersfield, 32 miles southeast of Lake Isabella), turn north onto Alfred Harrell Highway and proceed 1.9 miles; turn right (at the fire station) onto Lake Ming Road and continue for 0.75 to the park complex; stay on the multi-lane one-way road, continuing toward the southwest for a final 0.5 mile (past the day use areas) to the campground entrance.

Facilities: 50 campsites in single, large, oval loop; sites are medium to large, with a fair amount of spacing and visual separation between sites; parking pads are paved, quite long, basically level, pull-throughs; large, level, grassy areas for tents; fire rings and barbecue grills; b-y-o firewood; water at several faucets; restrooms with showers; holding tank disposal station; paved driveway; complete supplies and services are available in Bakersfield.

Activities & Attractions: Boating; fishing.

Natural Features: Located on the south bank of the Kern River; campground vegetation consists of watered, mown lawns and numerous hardwoods which provide some shade/shelter in virtually every site; many flowering trees and bushes decorate the grounds; surrounded by low hills and barren bluffs; a local high point known as Ant Hill rises to about 950' just south of the park; elevation 450'.

Season, Fees & Phone: Open all year; $8.00-$12.00 (depending upon the season; reservations accepted; Kern County Parks Department, Bakersfield, (805) 861-2345.

Camp Notes: There are a number of nice county park campgrounds in Southern California, and this is one of them. It's landscaping stands out in quite marked contrast to the local terrain.

PARADISE COVE
Isabella Lake/Sequoia National Forest

Location: South-central California northeast of Bakersfield.

Access: From California State Highway 178 at milepost 48 +.8 (6 miles northeast of the community of Lake Isabella, 40 miles west of the junction of California State Highways 178 and 14 near Inyokern), turn north into the campground.

Facilities: 138 campsites; majority of the sites are in a closely spaced, paved parking lot (camping lot?) arrangement, without tables; about 2-dozen standard sites have paved, medium-length, sloped, straight-in pads, grassy tent spots, tables and fire rings; b-y-o firewood; water at several faucets; restrooms with showers, plus auxiliary vaults; holding tank disposal station; gas and groceries 3 miles east of the campground; limited to adequate supplies and services are available in Lake Isabella.

Activities & Attractions: Boating; fishing for bass, catfish, bluegill, crappie all year; rainbow trout are stocked each fall.

Natural Features: Located on the south shore of Isabella Lake; hardwoods provide minimal to adequate shelter/shade for the standard sites; parking lot is unsheltered; a nearly barren hill to the south forms the backdrop for Paradise Cove; high, rugged mountains lie in most other directions; elevation 2600'.

Season, Fees & Phone: Open all year, with limited services in winter; $6.00-$12.00; 14 day limit; operated by concessionaire; Cannell Meadow Ranger District, Kernville, (619) 379-5646.

Camp Notes: It's surprising what a mile will do for the view. The panoramas here seem just a little broader and more complete than those from the campgrounds on the west shore (although both are excellent). At Paradise Cove the standard sites are close to the`highway and the parking lot camping is nearer to the lakeshore. South shore camping is also available at Auxiliary Dam, a mile east of Lake Isabella. That area has open camping, restrooms, and no fee.

PIONEER POINT
Isabella Lake/Sequoia National Forest

Location: South-central California northeast of Bakersfield.

Access: From California State Highway 155 at milepost 69 +.1 (3 miles north of the community of Lake Isabella, 2.5 miles south of Wofford Heights), turn west into the campground.

Facilities: 78 campsites; sites are medium-sized, with nominal to fair separation; parking pads are paved, medium to long pull-throughs or straight-ins; many pads will require a little additional leveling; tent areas are spacious, but sloped; fire rings; b-y-o firewood; water at several faucets; restrooms with showers;

holding tank disposal station at Main Dam Campground, 1 mile south; limited to adequate supplies and services are available in the Wofford Heights-Kernville, and Lake Isabella areas.

Activities & Attractions: Boating; fishing for warm water species all year; rainbow trout planted each fall; playground.

Natural Features: Located on a moderately steep hillside at the southwest corner of Isabella Lake; oaks and large conifers provide light to moderate shade/shelter in most sites; the lake area is surrounded by rocky hills and high mountains; elevation 2600'.

Season, Fees & Phone: Open all year, with limited services in winter; $12.00; operated by concessionaire; Cannell Meadow Ranger District, Kernville, (619) 379-5646.

Camp Notes: This is the first "full service" campground on the west shore of the lake (assuming an approach to this area from the south, typical of most visitors). Another large campground at Main Dam, 1 mile south, off the east side of the highway, has nice campsites, restrooms, but no showers, limited views, and a fee. (There are some, well, uh, formidable sights from the sites right at the base of the dam.)

HUNGRY GULCH
Isabella Lake/Sequoia National Forest

Location: South-central California northeast of Bakersfield.

Access: From California State Highway 155 at milepost 67 +.2 (2.5 miles south of Wofford Heights, 5 miles north of the community of Lake Isabella), turn west into the campground.

Facilities: 78 campsites; sites are medium-sized, with fair to good separation; parking pads are paved, mostly medium-length straight-ins, plus some medium to long pull-throughs; most pads will require a little additional leveling; large, slightly sloped, tent areas; fire rings; b-y-o firewood; water at several faucets; restrooms with showers; paved driveways; limited to adequate supplies and services are available in the Wofford Heights-Kernville, and Lake Isabella areas.

Activities & Attractions: Boating; fishing; Coso Mine Loop and Isabella Peak Vista Trail; playground.

Natural Features: Located on the west shore of Isabella Lake in the semi-arid Kern River Valley; Hungry Gulch is situated on several small hills at the mouth of the gulch; campground vegetation consists largely of conifers plus some hardwoods; most sites have some shelter/shade; elevation 2700'.

Season, Fees & Phone: April to October; $12.00; operated by concessionaire; Cannell Meadow Ranger District, Kernville, (619) 379-5646operated by contractor; Isabella Lake CoE Project Office (619) 379-2742.

Camp Notes: A lot of campers come here to fish (or the other way around, too), so here are a few tips from knowledgeable locals which might contribute to making your campout more successful: Salmon eggs and spinners seem to work consistently well on trout, but you'll need to fish the deepest holes in summer. Bassers should normally stick to the coves and use lures. (Reportedly, Isabella Lake produces good bass catches.) Bluegill and crappie can be caught in smaller coves on worms and jigs. Catnappers have found that clams, anchovies and worms work well just about anywhere on the lake.

BOULDER GULCH
Isabella Lake/Sequoia National Forest

Location: South-central California northeast of Bakersfield.

Access: From California State Highway 155 at milepost 67 +.2 (2.5 miles south of Wofford Heights, 5 miles north of the community of Lake Isabella), turn east into the campground.

Facilities: 79 campsites; sites are medium-sized, with fair to good separation; parking pads are paved, medium-length straight-ins, or medium to long pull-throughs or pull-offs; a little additional leveling may be needed on some pads; large tent areas, but some may be slightly sloped; fire rings; b-y-o firewood; water at several faucets; restrooms with showers; paved driveways; limited to adequate supplies and services are available in the Wofford Heights-Kernville, and Lake Isabella areas.

Activities & Attractions: Boating; fishing; playground.

Natural Features: Located on gently sloping terrain near the west shore of Isabella Lake; sites receive minimal to light-medium shade/shelter from conifers plus a moderate quantity of hardwoods; elevation 2600'.

Season, Fees & Phone: April to October; $12.00; operated by concessionaire; Cannell Meadow Ranger District, Kernville, (619) 379-5646.

Camp Notes: Camper's Choice: a little closer to the lake (but not actually on the shore) here in Boulder Gulch; better views from up above in Hungry Gulch, just across the road.

LIVE OAK
Isabella Lake/Sequoia National Forest

Location: South-central California northeast of Bakersfield.

Access: From California State Highway 155 at milepost 64 +.9 (0.2 mile south of Wofford Heights, 7 miles north of the community of Lake Isabella), turn west into the campground.

Facilities: 199 campsites in 2 main sections (called Live Oak North and Live Oak South), including some sites designated for small group use; sites are small to medium-sized, with some visual separation; parking pads are paved, short to medium-length straight-ins or pull-throughs; most pads will require additional leveling; medium-sized tent areas; fire rings; b-y-o firewood; water at several faucets; restrooms with showers; holding tank disposal station across the highway at Tillie Creek Campground; limited to adequate supplies and services are available in the Wofford Heights-Kernville, and Lake Isabella areas.

Activities & Attractions: Boating; boat launch nearby; fishing for bass, panfish, catfish; trout stocked in the fall.

Natural Features: Located on a gently sloping hillside above the west shore of Isabella Lake; numerous medium to large oak trees, plus a few other small hardwoods and conifers, provide ample to good shelter/shade in most sites; the entire area is encircled by fairly dry hills and high, partially forested mountains; some of the uppermost sites overlook the lake; elevation 2700'.

Season, Fees & Phone: May to October; $12.00; operated by concessionaire; Cannell Meadow Ranger District, Kernville, (619) 379-5646.

Camp Notes: Some of the sites here are quite nice. Since Live Oak isn't exactly within easy walking distance of the lake, it sees less use than some of the other campgrounds near it, notably Tillie Creek Campground, just across the highway. Residential areas are adjacent to the camping area.

TILLIE CREEK
Isabella Lake/Sequoia National Forest

Location: South-central California northeast of Bakersfield.

Access: From California State Highway 155 at milepost 64 +.9 (0.2 mile south of Wofford Heights, 7 miles north of the community of Lake Isabella), turn east into the campground entrance.

Facilities: 159 campsites; (4 large group camp areas are also available); sites are generally medium-sized, with fair to very good separation; parking pads are paved, reasonably level, primarily medium to medium+ straight-ins, plus some longer pull-throughs or pull-offs; adequate level space for a large tent in most sites; fire rings; b-y-o firewood; water at several faucets; restrooms with showers; holding tank disposal station; limited to adequate supplies and services are available in the Wofford Heights-Kernville, and Lake Isabella areas.

Activities & Attractions: Boating; boat launch nearby; fishing for bass, panfish, catfish; trout stocked in the fall; playground; fish cleaning station; amphitheater.

Natural Features: Located on the west shore of Isabella Lake in the semi-arid Kern River Valley; campground vegetation consists of oaks and other hardwoods, plus some conifers; sites closest to the lakeshore are quite "open"; sites farther from the lake are situated in more dense vegetation; the Greenhorn Mountains and the Piute Mountains lie to the west and southeast, respectively; the Sierra Nevada rises several miles to the east; elevation 2600'.

Season, Fees & Phone: Open all year, with limited services in winter; $6.00 (charged March to September only); operated by concessionaire; Cannell Meadow Ranger District, Kernville, (619) 379-5646.

Camp Notes: This is the largest, best-equipped and most-frequented of the half-dozen campgrounds on this side of the lake. All sites are within a few minutes' easy walk of the lakeshore.

HEADQUARTERS
Sequoia National Forest

Location: South-central California northeast of Bakersfield.

Access: From the intersection of Kernville Road and Sierra Way at the east end of Kernville (11 miles northeast of the community of Lake Isabella, 54 miles northeast of Bakersfield), turn north onto Sierra Way and proceed 2.9 miles to the campground, on the west (left) side of the highway.

Facilities: 37 campsites; sites are small to medium-sized, level, with separation varying from very little to very good; parking pads are paved/gravel, short to medium straight-ins; large areas for tents on a sandy base; fire rings; a scant amount of firewood is available for gathering in the vicinity, b-y-o is recommended; water at several faucets; vault facilities; paved driveways; limited to adequate supplies and services are available in the Kernville-Wofford Heights metropolitan area.

Activities & Attractions: Stream fishing for regularly stocked trout; Isabella Lake recreation area, a few miles south.

Natural Features: Located on a flat along the east bank of the Kern River; campground vegetation consists of a mixture of pines and large, full hardwoods which provide adequate to very good shelter/shade in most campsites; rocky hills and ridges border the river east and west; views of high, rocky mountains to the north; elevation 2700'.

Season, Fees & Phone: $8.00; open all year (on an alternate basis in winter with a neighboring campground, Camp 3); 14 day limit; Cannell Meadow Ranger District, Kernville, (619) 376-3781.

Camp Notes: This is one of the nicer campgrounds in the Kern River-Lake Isabella area. Its variety of mature vegetation provides welcome shelter, plus an interesting contrast to the rocky surroundings.

CAMP 3
Sequoia National Forest

Location: South-central California northeast of Bakers-field.

Access: From the intersection of Kernville Road and Sierra Way at the east end of Kernville (11 miles northeast of the community of Lake Isabella, 54 miles northeast of Bakersfield), turn north onto Sierra Way and proceed 3.9 miles to the campground entrance, on the west (left) side of the highway.

Facilities: 52 campsites; sites are small to medium-sized, with a respectable amount of separation; parking pads are gravel/sand, short to medium-length straight-ins; some pads are level, others, nearer the river's edge, are a little sloped; large, basically level, areas for tents; fire rings; a limited amount of firewood is available for gathering in the vicinity, b-y-o is recommended; water at several faucets; vault facilities; paved driveways; adequate supplies and services are in the Kernville-Wofford Heights area.

Activities & Attractions: Fishing for regularly stocked trout; Isabella Lake recreation area, several miles south.

Natural Features: Located on a rocky flat along the east bank of the Kern River; campground vegetation consists of a mixture of pines and hardwoods which provide minimal shelter/shade in some campsites; most sites are relatively open and unsheltered; dry, rocky hills and ridges border the river east and west; views of high, rocky mountains to the north; elevation 2800'.

Season, Fees & Phone: Open all year (on an alternate basis in winter with a neighboring camp, Headquarters); $8.00; 14 day limit; Cannell Meadow Ranger District, Kernville, (619) 376-3781.

Camp Notes: This campground apparently is most often used as a fishing camp. Its facilities are simple, but the riverfront setting, coupled with the near and distant views make it a good stop. The Kern River is unique among the Sierra's major streams. Beginning high in the northeast tip of Sequoia National Park, it flows north to south, rather than east to west, along most of its 165-mile length. Also unlike its sister streams, the Kern no longer has a link with the sea.

RICARDO
Red Rock Canyon State Park

Location: South-east California north of Mojave.

Access: From California State Highway 14 near milepost 40 + .5 (17 miles south of the junction of California State Highways 14 and 178 at Freeman Junction near Inyokern, 25 miles north of Mojave) turn west, then immediately north onto Abbott Drive (paved); continue for 0.75 mile, then turn southwest (left) onto a gravel access road to the park entrance station and the visitor center; the campground is 0.5 mile farther west.

Facilities: 50 campsites; sites are generally small to medium in size, with nominal to fairly good separation; parking pads are gravel, medium to long, level straight-ins; tent areas are large, somewhat level; fire rings; definitely b-y-o firewood; water at central faucets; vault facilities; gravel driveway; gas and camper supplies, 6 miles south; limited supplies in Inyokern; adequate supplies and services are available in Mojave.

Activities & Attractions: Red Cliffs Natural Preserve (open only to hiking); several miles of hiking trails; campfire center near the visitor center/ranger station.

Natural Features: Located on a Mojave Desert plain; campground vegetation consists of small Joshua trees and short, desert brush; the campground is partly encircled by eroded, low, white cliffs (locally called "White House Cliffs"); the Sierra Nevada rises a few miles to the west; elevation 2600'.

Season, Fees & Phone: Open all year; please see Appendix for standard California state park fees and reservation information; phone c/o CDPR High Desert District Office (805) 942-0662.

Camp Notes: Red Rock Canyon itself flanks about a four-mile stretch of highway within the park. You can enjoy the area to a limited extent just by taking a few extra minutes to stop at one or more of the several roadside pull-outs on your way to or from the campground. Although some visitors do take advantage of the desert tranquility here in summer, it makes a much better fall through spring park. Skywatching can be highly gratifying in these crystal clear desert skies.

SADDLEBACK BUTTE
Saddleback Butte State Park

Location: Southern California north of Los Angeles.

Access: From California State Highway 14 in Lancaster, take the Avenue J Exit and travel east on Avenue J/LA County Road N5 for 20.5 miles to the intersection of N5 & 170th Street; turn south onto 170th Street and proceed 1 mile, then turn east (left) onto a gravel access road for 0.15 mile, then turn left into the campground. (Note: There are a half dozen alternate ways to get here via paved country roads, but this is the easiest and most direct route from a major highway.)

Facilities: 50 campsites; (a reservable group camp is also available); sites are small+ to medium-sized, reasonably level, with fair to fairly good separation; parking pads are gravel, short to long straight-ins; adequate space for medium to large tents; ramadas (sun/partial wind shelters) for most sites; barbecue grills and fire rings; b-y-o firewood; water at central faucets; restrooms; holding tank disposal station; gravel driveways; gas and groceries+ in the community of Lake Los Angeles, 4 miles south.

Activities & Attractions: Saddleback Butte Trail (1.6 miles); Joshua Nature Trail (a guide pamphlet is available); (an unusual "Birdwatcher's Guide to the Antelope Valley" may also be available--check around in the campground); day use area with ramadas nearby; Antelope Valley Indian Museum, another unit operated under the park system, is a few minutes' drive from the campground.

Natural Features: Located in Antelope Valley in the Mojave Desert near the west base of 3651' Saddleback Butte; vegetation consists of Joshua Trees and desert brush; elevation 2600'.

Season, Fees & Phone: Open all year; please see Appendix for standard California state park fees and reservation information; phone c/o CDPR High Desert District Office (805) 942-0662.

Camp Notes: There are really neat views of the entire valley, of Saddleback Butte itself, and of the 10,000' San Gabriel Mountains to the south. A principal feature here are the Joshua trees which grow throughout most of the park.

OH! RIDGE
Inyo National Forest

Location: Eastern California south of Lee Vining.

Access: From U.S. Highway 395 at milepost 40 + .3 (at June Lake Junction, 11 miles south of Lee Vining, 15 miles north of Mammoth Lakes Junction, 54 miles northwest of Bishop), turn southwest onto California State Highway 158 (June Lake Loop Road) and proceed 1.1 miles; turn west onto a paved access road and continue for another 1.1 miles, around the west end of the campground, to the entrance. **Alternate Access:** From the junction of U.S. 395 & State Highway 158 (at U.S. 395 milepost 46 +.4, 6 miles south of Lee Vining) travel southwest then northeast on Highway 158 for 14 miles to the campground turnoff.

Facilities: 148 campsites; (small group camps are also available); sites are small, with very little separation; parking pads are paved, short, basically level straight-ins; framed-and-gravelled pads for table and tent areas; adequate level space for a large tent in most sites; barbecue grills; a limited amount of gatherable firewood may be available some distance from the campground, b-y-o is recommended; water at several faucets; restrooms; paved driveways; small store near the campground entrance.

Activities & Attractions: Boating; fishing; designated swimming area.

Natural Features: Located on a sage flat on a bench above the north end of June Lake; a few conifers dot the flat; timbered ridges and rugged, gray mountains surround the area; elevation 7700'.

Season, Fees & Phone: May to November; $10.00; 14 day limit; Mono Lake Ranger District, Lee Vining, (619) 647-6525.

Camp Notes: Are there some views here, or what! If there isn't a view from any given site, there certainly would be one from a short walk away. This is the first of several campgrounds along Highway 158 after you leave U.S. 395 at June Lake Junction. Two small campgrounds 2 miles south of here are Gull Lake and Reversed Creek, with 12 and 17 sites, respectively. About 6 miles southwest is Silver Lake, with 65 sites. (OH! Ridge was dubbed the "Animal Cracker Campground" by our field editor because of the names given to each of the multitude of small loops--Dove, Squirrel, Rabbit, Deer--well, you get the picture. Ed.)

JUNE LAKE
Inyo National Forest

Location: Eastern California south of Lee Vining.

Access: From the junction of U.S. Highway 395 & California State Highway 158 at U.S. 395 milepost 40 +.3 (15 miles north of Mammoth Lake Junction, 11 miles south of Lee Vining) proceed southwest on Highway 158 (June Lake Loop Road) for 2.5 miles to milepost 2 +.55 on the north edge of the town of June Lake; turn west (right) into the campground. **Alternate Access:** From the junction of U.S. 395 & State Highway 158 (at U.S. 395 milepost 46 +.4, 6 miles south of Lee Vining) travel southwest then northeast on Highway 158 for 13 miles to the campground turnoff.

Facilities: 28 campsites, including 6 tents-only sites; sites are small to medium-sized, with nominal to good separation; parking pads are gravel, tolerably level, mostly short straight-ins; tent space varies from small to large; fire rings; b-y-o firewood is recommended; water at central faucets; restrooms; paved driveway; gas and groceries in June Lake.

Activities & Attractions: Fishing; boating; boat launch; hiking trails in the area.

Natural Features: Located on a slope above the south-east shore of June Lake; most sites receive light-medium shade from aspens and a few conifers; tent spots are in the open; bordered by hills and mountains; elevation 7600'.

Season, Fees & Phone: May to November; $10.00; 14 day limit; Mono Lake Ranger District, Lee Vining, (619) 647-6525.

Camp Notes: Most campsites, except for those in the tent section, are in their own little cubby holes notched into the stand of aspens that encircles the campground's grass-and-sage infield.

GULL LAKE & REVERSED CREEK
Inyo National Forest

Location: Eastern California south of Lee Vining.

Access: From the junction of U.S. Highway 395 & California State Highway 158 at U.S. 395 milepost 40 +.3 (15 miles north of Mammoth Lake Junction, 11 miles south of Lee Vining) head southwest on Highway 158 (June Lake Loop Road) for 3.5 miles to milepost 3 +.5; turn westerly (right) into *Gull Lake* Campground, or easterly (left) into *Reversed Creek* Campground. **Alternate Access:** From the junction of U.S. 395 & State Highway 158 (at U.S. 395 milepost 46 +.4, 6 miles south of Lee Vining) travel southwest then northeast on Highway 158 for 12 miles to the campground turnoffs.

Facilities: *Gull Lake*: 11 campsites; sites are small, fairly level, with fairly good separation; parking pads are gravel, mostly short to short+ straight-ins; small tent areas, some are a bit sloped; *Reversed Creek*: 17 campsites; sites are medium-sized, somewhat sloped, with fair to very good separation; parking pads are hard surfaced, short to medium-length straight-ins or long pull-throughs; medium-sized areas for tents; *both camps*: fire rings; b-y-o firewood is recommended; water at central faucets; restrooms; paved driveways; gas and groceries in June Lake, a half mile north of the campgrounds.

Activities & Attractions: Fishing; limited boating (10 mph); small boat launch.

Natural Features: Located above the east shore of Gull Lake and on a slope along the bank of Reversed Creek; sites are generally well sheltered by aspens and some conifers; lots of tall timber on the upper slopes behind the campgrounds; bordered by the hills and mountains of the east slope of the Sierra Nevada; elevation 7600'.

Season, Fees & Phone: May to October; $10.00; 14 day limit; Mono Lake Ranger District, Lee Vining, (619) 647-6525.

Camp Notes: A handful of sites in Gull Lake are along the lake shore. But Reversed Creek may get your vote for being a better overall campground. Fine mountain views from points within and around both camps.

SILVER LAKE
Inyo National Forest

Location: Eastern California south of Lee Vining.

Access: From the junction of U.S. Highway 395 & California State Highway 158 at U.S. 395 milepost 40 +.3 (15 miles north of Mammoth Lake Junction, 12 miles south of Lee Vining) travel southwest then northwest on Highway 158 (June Lake Loop Road) for 7 miles to milepost 7 +.2; turn west (right) into the campground. **Alternate Access:** From the junction of U.S. 395 & State Highway 158 (at U.S. 395 milepost 46 +.4, 6 miles south of Lee Vining) proceed southwest on Highway 158 for 8.5 miles to the campground.

Facilities: 65 campsites; sites are small to medium-sized and level; most sites have minimal to nominal separation, some sites have very good visual separation; parking pads are paved, medium to long straight-ins; large, grassy tent areas; fire rings; b-y-o firewood; water at several faucets; restrooms; paved driveways; gas and camper supplies at a nearby resort; adequate supplies and services are available in Lee Vining.

Activities & Attractions: Rush Creek Trail; access to hiking trails that lead into the Ansel Adams Wilderness; stream and lake fishing; limited boating; boat launch.

Natural Features: Located in a valley on a grassy, creekside flat along Rush Creek at the north tip of Silver Lake; sites are minimally sheltered by a few small conifers and some high bushes on a thick carpet of grass; a waterfall is just downstream (north) of the campground; the campground is closely bordered by rocky hills and rugged mountains along its east side, the peaks of the Sierra Nevada rise to 13,000' a few miles to the west; elevation 7200'.

Season, Fees & Phone: May to November; $10.00; 14 day limit; Mono Lake Ranger District, Lee Vining, (619) 647-6525.

Camp Notes: Stupendous scenery near here! Sage slopes rise many hundreds of feet above the valley to meet the high, craggy, peaks of the Eastern Sierra. You might expect to wake up to a fresh dusting of snow on the high ridgetops even in early July. The highway passes through a very scenic canyon about two miles north of the campground. Sure, you can see most of your neighbors here; but just look at the stunning views instead!

SHADY REST
Inyo National Forest

Location: Eastern California south of Lee Vining.

Access: From the junction of U.S. Highway 395 & California State Highway 203 at Mammoth Lakes Junction (milepost 25 on U.S. 395, 26 miles south of Lee Vining, 39 miles north of Bishop), travel west on Highway 203 for 3 miles into Mammoth Lakes Village (just past the ranger station); turn north (right) onto Sawmill Road (Sawmill Cutoff) and proceed 50 yards to *New Shady Rest* (on the right); or continue for another 0.25 mile to *Old Shady Rest* (on the left).

Facilities: *New Shady Rest*: 98 campsites in 2 large, complex loops; *Old Shady Rest*: 51 campsites in a single large loop; (Pine Glen Group Camp, adjacent to New Shady Rest, is also available, by reservation only); sites are medium to large, level or nearly so, with fair to very good separation; parking pads are paved or packed gravel, medium to long straight-ins; plenty of space for tents; fireplaces, plus some barbecue grills; b-y-o firewood is recommended; water at faucets throughout; restrooms; holding tank disposal station; paved driveways; adequate supplies and services are available within walking distance.

Activities & Attractions: First-rate scenery, fishing and limited boating at nearby Mammoth Lakes; national forest visitor center next to the campground; day and evening interpretive programs and guided nature walks.

Natural Features: Located on a forested, large, rolling flat and on a knoll; campground vegetation consists mostly of light to medium-dense tall conifers, plus some low shrubbery; limited views of the Sierra Nevada, a couple miles to the west, from some sites; elevation 7900'.

Season, Fees & Phone: May to mid-September; $8.00; 14 day limit; Mammoth Ranger District (619) 934-2505.

Camp Notes: Shady Rest is really a dandy campground. It may be large and it may be close to town, but you'll probably not even notice, except, perhaps, when you tire of eating hardtack and hobo stew. Then you'll find that you can saunter just a block or two over to Little Julius, Taco Chime, or Ronnie Mac's Supper Club to pick up some pizza, burritos, or 'burgers to munch on around the campfire.

TWIN LAKES
Inyo National Forest

Location: Eastern California southeast of Lee Vining.

Access: From the junction of U.S. Highway 395 & California State Highway 203 at Mammoth Lakes Junction (milepost 25 on U.S. 395, 26 miles south of Lee Vining, 39 miles north of Bishop), travel west on Highway 203 for 4 miles (through Mammoth Lakes Village) to a major junction; continue straight ahead ('203 takes off to the right) on Lake Mary Road (Forest Road 10) for 2 miles to Tamarack Road (just after the creek bridge); turn right, and continue for 0.4 mile to the first camping area, (upper section) or to the right, for another 0.3 mile, to the main camping area.

Facilities: 97 campsites in 2 main areas; sites are small to medium-sized, basically level, with minimal to nominal separation; some sites in the upper section are sloped; parking pads are gravel or paved, short to medium-length straight-ins; adequate space for a large tent in most sites; fireplaces; some firewood may be available for gathering locally, b-y-o is suggested; water at several faucets; restrooms; holding tank disposal station; paved driveways; gas and camper supplies at a small local store; adequate supplies and services are available in Mammoth Lakes Village.

Activities & Attractions: Super scenery; national forest visitor center in Mammoth Village; fishing; limited boating.

Natural Features: Located on a moderately timbered flat (main section) and on a forested hillside (upper section) along the shore of Twin Lakes in the eastern Sierra Nevada; elevation 8700'.

Season, Fees & Phone: June to October; $10.00; 7 day limit; Mammoth Ranger District (619) 934-2505.

Camp Notes: Fantastic! Rugged mountains, clear, blue lakes, cascading waterfalls. Mammoth Lakes lives up to its reputation for scenic excellence. Twin Lakes is the largest of the campgrounds around the lakes. It also has some of the best (maybe *the* best) scenery. Incidentally, the name Mammoth Lakes refers to the district in which the lakes are located, rather than to the names of the lakes themselves.

LAKE MARY
Inyo National Forest

Location: Eastern California southeast of Lee Vining.

Access: From the junction of U.S. Highway 395 & California State Highway 203 at Mammoth Lakes Junction (milepost 25 on U.S. 395, 26 miles south of Lee Vining, 39 miles north of Bishop), travel west on Highway 203 for 4 miles (through Mammoth Lakes Village) to a major junction; continue straight ahead ('203 takes off to the right) on Lake Mary Road (Forest Road 10) southerly for another 3.3 miles (to a point 1.2 miles beyond the Twin Lakes turnoff); bear right at fork, go 0.3 mile, then swing left for a final 0.1 mile to the campground.

Facilities: 51 campsites in 2 sections; sites are small and closely spaced; parking pads are paved, sloped, short to medium-length straight-ins; adequate, but sloped, space for a medium to large tents in most sites; fireplaces or fire rings; limited firewood is available for gathering in the area, b-y-o to be sure; water at several faucets; restrooms; camper supplies at a store within walking distance; adequate supplies and services are available in Mammoth Lakes Village.

Activities & Attractions: Hiking trails; national forest visitor center near Mammoth Village; guided walks and evening programs in summer; fishing.

Natural Features: Located on a terraced slope near the shore of Lake Mary; the lake is ringed with tall conifers and closely encircled by the rocky peaks of the Sierra Nevada; elevation 8900'.

Season, Fees & Phone: June to mid-September; $10.00; 14 day limit; Mammoth Ranger District (619) 934-2505.

Camp Notes: The lake-mountain views from near the campground are really excellent. Lake Mary's camping arrangements may be a little nicer, but adjacent Lake George has slightly better views.

LAKE GEORGE
Inyo National Forest

Location: Eastern California southeast of Lee Vining.

Access: From the junction of U.S. Highway 395 & California State Highway 203 at Mammoth Lakes Junction (milepost 25 on U.S. 395, 26 miles south of Lee Vining, 39 miles north of Bishop), travel west on Highway 203 for 4 miles (through Mammoth Lakes Village) to a major junction; continue straight ahead ('203 takes off to the right) on Lake Mary Road (Forest Road 10) southerly for another 3.3 miles (to a point 1.2 miles beyond the Twin Lakes turnoff); bear right at fork, go 0.3 mile, then swing left for a final 0.7 mile, crossing the bridge over St. Mary Lake outlet, to the campground.

Facilities: 18 campsites, including a number of walk-ins; sites are small and tightly spaced; parking pads are paved, short straight-ins; additional leveling will probably be needed on most pads; enough space for a medium to large tent in most sites, but it may be sloped; fireplaces or fire rings; limited firewood is available for gathering in the area, b-y-o is recommended; water at several faucets; restrooms; camper supplies at a store within walking distance; adequate supplies and services are available in Mammoth Lakes Village.

Activities & Attractions: Hiking trails; guided nature walks and evening programs in summer; fishing; national forest visitor center near Mammoth Village.

Natural Features: Located on a hill above the shore of Lake George in the eastern Sierra Nevada; campsites are moderately sheltered/shaded by tall conifers; elevation 8900'.

Season, Fees & Phone: June to mid-September; $10.00; 7 day limit; Mammoth Ranger District (619) 934-2505.

Camp Notes: Lake George is tucked away in a pocket at the south end of the chain of lakes. There are some stunningly beautiful lake-mountain vistas from here. You may need pitons instead of tent pegs to batten down the canvas on the steep, rocky slope in Lake George. But it's sure worth the view.

COLDWATER
Inyo National Forest

Location: Eastern California southeast of Lee Vining.

Access: From the junction of U.S. Highway 395 & California State Highway 203 at Mammoth Lakes Junction (milepost 25 on U.S. 395, 26 miles south of Lee Vining, 39 miles north of Bishop), travel west on Highway 203 for 4 miles (through Mammoth Lakes Village) to a major junction; continue straight ahead ('203 takes off to the right) on Lake Mary Road (Forest Road 10) southerly for another 3.5 miles to a fork (at a point 0.2 mile beyond the turnoff to Lakes Mary and George); bear left and continue for 0.6 mile to the campground.

Facilities: 79 campsites in a series of 4 loops; sites are smallish, with nominal separation; parking pads are hard-surfaced or gravel, short to medium-length straight-ins; a little to moderate additional leveling will be needed on most pads; good sized, but sloped tent areas on sandy soil; water at several faucets; restrooms; paved driveways; adequate supplies and services are available in Mammoth Lakes Village.

Activities & Attractions: Duck Pass Trail; the Lakes of Mammoth are a short distance away.

Natural Features: Located on a moderately steep, rocky slope flanked by a pair of creeks in the eastern Sierra Nevada; sites receive light to medium-dense shelter from tall conifers; elevation 9000'.

Season, Fees & Phone: June to October; $10.00; 14 day limit; Mammoth Ranger District (619) 934-2505.

Camp Notes: Campsite shelter, separation and levelness are a little better at the upper end of the campground. Coldwater may not be the most attractive campground in the forest, but you'll have a choice of creeks for rock-plopping or whatever.

CONVICT LAKE
Inyo National Forest

Location: Eastern California southeast of Lee Vining.

Access: From U.S. Highway 395 at milepost 21 +.4 (31 miles south of Lee Vining, 35 miles north of Bishop), turn south-southwest onto a paved access road and proceed 2.4 miles to the campground.

Facilities: 88 campsites, plus an overflow area; sites are small to medium-sized, with fair to very good separation; parking pads are paved, medium+ straight-ins which will require additional leveling in most cases; tent space is slightly sloped, and varies from small to large; fire rings; some firewood may be available for gathering locally, b-y-o is suggested; water at several faucets; restrooms; holding tank disposal station; paved driveways; camper supplies at a small store at the lake; adequate supplies and services are available in Mammoth Village, 7 miles northwest.

Activities & Attractions: Lake and stream fishing for trout; boating; amphitheater; foot bridge across the creek.

Natural Features: Located on a creekside flat on the northeast corner of Convict Lake; campground vegetation consists of dense willows and aspens in most of the campground, to little more than sage and a few conifers in the remaining section; a sage flat borders the campground and a nearly barren hill lies directly east; gray peaks of the Sierra Nevada rise sharply to the south; elevation 7600'.

Season, Fees & Phone: $9.00; April to late-October; 7 day limit; Mammoth Ranger District (619) 934-2505.

Camp Notes: To paraphrase the famous advertising slogan for that well known brand of jellies and preserves, "With a name like Convict Lake, it has to be good". And it is. The mountains seem to rise right out of the lake. The brown, barren hillside behind the campground, the gray peaks, the dense, green vegetation and the deep blue lake present striking contrasts to each other.

MCGEE CREEK
Inyo National Forest

Location: Eastern California northwest of Bishop.

Access: From U.S. Highway 395 at milepost 16 +.6 (31 miles north of Bishop, 35 miles south of Lee Vining), turn south/southwest onto McGee Creek Road and proceed up this steep, paved road for 1.8 miles; turn left into the campground.

Facilities: 28 campsites; sites are small to medium-sized, with little separation; parking pads are paved, short, but extra wide, and reasonably level; framed-and-gravelled table/tent pads; fire rings; b-y-o firewood is recommended; water at several faucets; restrooms; paved driveway; gas, groceries, and laundromat are available in Crowley, 2 miles southeast.

Activities & Attractions: Terrific views of high, rugged peaks; John Muir Wilderness access, at the end of McGee Creek Road, 2 miles south; boating and fishing on Crowley Lake, 5 miles, on the north side of the main highway.

Natural Features: Located on an open sage slope bordered on the south by a stand of hardwoods and conifers; situated at the base of the eastern Sierra Nevada; elevation 7600'.

Season, Fees & Phone: June to October; $8.00; 14 day limit; White Mountain Ranger District, Bishop, (619) 873-4207.

Camp Notes: While there aren't a lot of things to do in and near the campground, this may be a great place for practicing the 'best-activity-is-the-lack-of-activity' principle. Crowley Lake, nearby, has fairly good fishing for cutthroat and rainbow trout. Crowley's 'bows tend to lose their bright coloration and become quite silvery.

FRENCH CAMP
Rock Creek/Inyo National Forest

Location: Eastern California northwest of Bishop.

Access: From U.S. Highway 395 at Toms Place at milepost 10 + .3 (24 miles north of Bishop, 41 miles south of Lee Vining), turn south onto Rock Creek Road and proceed first to the recreation area entrance station; obtain a campground permit, then continue 0.2 mile to the campground access road (on the right, opposite the dump station); turn right, and drive a final 0.15 mile to the campground.

Facilities: 86 campsites; sites are small, with good visual separation; parking pads are paved, short to medium-length straight-ins; leveling is OK in some, but most pads will require a little additional leveling; generally small to medium-sized tent areas; fireplaces or fire rings; some firewood is available for gathering in the area; water at several faucets; restrooms; holding tank disposal station; paved driveways; gas and groceries are available in Toms Place.

Activities & Attractions: John Muir Wilderness; fishing and boating on Rock Creek Lake, about a dozen miles south.

Natural Features: Located on moderately sloping, very rocky terrain along Rock Creek; campground vegetation consists primarily of medium-height, bushy pines, and sage; the Sierra Nevada is within view; elevation 7500'.

Season, Fees & Phone: May to mid-October; $8.00; 21 day limit; White Mountain Ranger District, Bishop, (619) 873-4207 or Rock Creek Entrance Station (619) 935-4253 (summer only).

Camp Notes: French Camp, because of its comparatively low altitude and proximity to the highway, potentially has one of the longer seasons and heaviest use of all the Rock Creek camps. Another forest camp near here that's worth considering is Tuff Campground. It's just off the north side of the main highway opposite the turnoff onto Rock Creek Road. Tuff has nearly three dozen sites, drinking water and vaults along a stream. Reportedly, the trout fishing is pretty good there.

HOLIDAY
Rock Creek/Inyo National Forest

Location: Eastern California northwest of Bishop.

Access: From U.S. Highway 395 at milepost 10 + .3 in Toms Place (24 miles north of Bishop, 41 miles south of Lee Vining), turn south onto Rock Creek Road (Forest Road 12, paved) and proceed 0.1 mile to the Rock Creek Recreation Area Entrance Station; obtain a camping permit, then head southerly on Rock Creek Road for 0.7 mile; turn east (left) into the campground.

Facilities: 33 campsites; sites are medium to large, with fair to good separation; parking pads are sandy gravel, mostly medium-length straight-ins; ample space for tents; fire rings; some firewood may be available for gathering in the vicinity, b-y-o firewood is suggested; water at several faucets; vault facilities; gravel driveways; gas and groceries in Toms Place.

Activities & Attractions: Scenic views.

Natural Features: Located on tilted terrain on the east slope of the Sierra Nevada; sites receive light shade/shelter from medium-height pines above a ground cover of sage; partly bordered by dry hills and mountains; elevation 7500'.

Season, Fees & Phone: Open as needed, April to October; $6.00; 14 day limit; White Mountain Ranger District, Bishop, (619) 873-4207 or Rock Creek Entrance Station (619) 935-4253 (summer only).

Camp Notes: Northward and eastward views predominate in this campground, unlike the southern scenes seen from all the camps farther up Rock Creek Canyon. From the campground's upper slopes, you can look out across the vast, semi-arid Owens River Valley to the long, lofty range of mountains beyond.

IRIS MEADOW
Rock Creek/Inyo National Forest

Location: Eastern California northwest of Bishop.

Access: From U.S. Highway 395 at milepost 10 +.3 in Toms Place (24 miles north of Bishop, 41 miles south of Lee Vining), turn south onto Rock Creek Road (Forest Road 12, paved) and proceed 0.1 mile to the Rock Creek Recreation Area Entrance Station; obtain a camping permit, then head southerly on Rock Creek Road for 4 miles; turn west (right) into the campground.

Facilities: 14 campsites; (the Aspen Group Camp. a quarter mile north of here, is available by reservation); sites are medium-sized, basically level, with minimal to nominal separation; parking pads are gravel, medium to long straight-ins; large tent spaces; fire rings; b-y-o firewood; water at a central faucet; vault facilities; gravel driveway; gas and groceries in Toms Place.

Activities & Attractions: Streamside setting.

Natural Features: Located around part of the perimeter of a large, open meadow in Rock Creek Canyon; aspens and conifers ring the meadow and provide some shelter from wind but minimal to limited shade for the campsites; closely bordered by steeply rising, tree-dotted ridges; elevation 8300'.

Season, Fees & Phone: July to September; $8.00; 7 day limit; White Mountain Ranger District, Bishop, (619) 873-4207 or Rock Creek Entrance Station (619) 935-4253 (summer only).

Camp Notes: If your camping outfit or your campmates require extra room for their bumpers, check out this camp. There's a choice of lots of sunshine or a reasonable amount of shade, and the campsites can accommodate somewhat larger appliances than those in campgrounds south of here.

Southern California 125

EAST FORK
Rock Creek/Inyo National Forest

Location: Eastern California northwest of Bishop.

Access: From U.S. Highway 395 at milepost 10 +.3 in Toms Place (24 miles north of Bishop, 41 miles south of Lee Vining), turn south onto Rock Creek Road (Forest Road 12, paved) and proceed 0.1 mile to the Rock Creek Recreation Area Entrance Station; obtain a camping permit, then head southerly on Rock Creek Road for 6 miles; turn east (left) into the campground.

Facilities: 133 campsites; sites are very small to small+, slightly sloped, with fair to good separation; parking pads are sandy gravel, short to medium-length straight-ins; many pads may require a little additional leveling; small to medium-sized areas for tents; fire rings and/or barbecue grills; limited firewood is available for gathering in the area, b-y-o is recommended; water at several faucets; restrooms; paved driveway; camper supplies at nearby resorts; gas and groceries in Toms Place.

Activities & Attractions: Trail along the creek; several other hiking trails in and around the canyon.

Natural Features: Located in Rock Creek Canyon along the banks of Rock Creek about a half mile downstream of the creek's confluence with its East Fork; sites are very lightly to moderately sheltered/shaded by short aspens and tall conifers; bordered by sage slopes and lightly timbered canyon walls that steeply rise from the canyon floor; elevation 9000'.

Season, Fees & Phone: June to September; $8.00; 14 day limit; White Mountain Ranger District, Bishop, (619) 873-4207 or Rock Creek Entrance Station (619) 935-4253 (summer only).

Camp Notes: The campground strrrretches for three-quarters of a mile along the creek. As you progress through the campground up the canyon, you'll encounter sites nestled in their own private little aspen-cordoned nooks; then there's a large group of sites on an open sage slope; finally, at the upper end, are sites which offer limited overhead shade but do provide shelter from wind and early/late sun.

Southern California 126

PINE GROVE
Rock Creek/Inyo National Forest

Location: Eastern California northwest of Bishop.

Access: From U.S. Highway 395 at milepost 10 +.3 in Toms Place (24 miles north of Bishop, 41 miles south of Lee Vining), turn south onto Rock Creek Road (Forest Road 12, paved) and proceed 0.1 mile to the Rock Creek Recreation Area Entrance Station; obtain a camping permit, then head southerly on Rock Creek Road for 7.5 miles; turn east (left) into the campground.

Facilities: 11 campsites; sites are small and closely spaced; parking pads are gravel, short to medium-length straight-ins; a bit additional leveling may be needed; medium to large tent spots; fire rings; a limited amount of firewood may be available for gathering; water at a central faucet; vault facilities; gravel driveway; camper supplies at nearby resorts; gas and groceries in Toms Place.

Activities & Attractions: Pine Grove Trailhead; numerous other trails in the general area; fishing and limited boating on Rock Creek Lake, 1 mile south.

Natural Features: Located in a canyon on a sloping flat above Rock Creek; sites receive medium shade/shelter from tall pines; adjacent to a small meadow; bordered by rocky hills and mountains; elevation 9300'.

Season, Fees & Phone: June to September; $8.00; 7 day limit; White Mountain Ranger District, Bishop, (619) 873-4207 or Rock Creek Entrance Station (619) 935-4253 (summer only).

Camp Notes: Roughcut facilities but good mountain views up the canyon. If Rock Creek Lake's camp is full (see info below), this Pine Grove would give you a place to stay within a three-minute drive of the lake. Being a Rock Creek Lake day-tripper should be an entirely tolerable role to assume. If you're into hiking, more than a dozen alpine lakes can be reached from the Pine Grove Trailhead via an interconnecting network of trails. Many are within a five-mile walk of this campground. (A trail description/map handout is available from the ranger station.)

ROCK CREEK LAKE
Rock Creek/Inyo National Forest

Location: Eastern California northwest of Bishop.

Access: From U.S. Highway 395 at milepost 10 +.3 in Toms Place (24 miles north of Bishop, 41 miles south of Lee Vining), turn south onto Rock Creek Road (Forest Road 12, paved) and proceed 0.1 mile to the Rock Creek Recreation Area Entrance Station; obtain a camping permit, then head southerly on Rock Creek Road for 8.6 miles; turn southeasterly (left, at the resort) onto a paved access road and proceed 0.3 to the northeast shore camp section; or continue around the east shore of the lake for another 0.4 mile to south shore camp area.

Facilities: 28 campsites, including a number of park 'n walk or walk-in tent sites, in 2 areas; (a group camp is available in a separate area); sites are small- to small+ in size; separation varies from none to nominal; parking surfaces are paved, short straight-ins or pull-offs; enough space for small tents in most sites, medium-sized tents in some sites; several sites have framed tent pads; fire rings; some firewood is available for gathering in the vicinity, (may have to do some clambering to get to it); b-y-o firewood to be sure; water at several faucets; restrooms; paved driveways; gas and camper supplies at nearby resorts.

Activities & Attractions: Several hiking/horse trails lead into the adjacent wilderness areas; trout fishing; limited boating; day use areas.

Natural Features: Located above the shore of Rock Creek Lake in a high-rimmed, sub-alpine basin at the head of a canyon in the Sierra Nevada; sites are unsheltered, or lightly sheltered, by some conifers and hardwoods; elevation 9600'.

Season, Fees & Phone: May to November; $8.00; 7 day limit; White Mountain Ranger District, Bishop, (619) 873-4207 or Rock Creek Entrance Station (619) 935-4253 (summer only).

Camp Notes: Tent campers are accommodated fairly well here. Some small tent sites are right along the lake shore or along a stream. The deep lake has a noticeable 'drop-off' just offshore which may be favorable to fishing from shore. On-site observations reveal that fishing for small trout can be productive.

MILLPOND
Inyo County Recreation Area

Location: Eastern California northwest of Bishop.

Access: From U.S. Highway 395 at milepost 120 +.9 (6 miles north of Bishop), turn southwest onto Ed Powers Road, drive 0.25 mile, then turn right onto Sawmill Road; proceed 1 mile on Sawmill, then turn left into the recreation complex and continue for 0.6 mile around to the south side of the recreation area and the campground. **Alternate Access:** (if *southbound* on 395, this is handier): From milepost 122 +.4, turn southwest onto Sawmill Road and continue 0.9 mile to the recreation area.

Facilities: 54 campsites; sites are small and closely spaced, in somewhat of a parking lot arrangement; parking pads are sandy gravel, level, short to medium-length, extra-wide straight-ins; adequate space for tents on the parking surface; fire rings or barbecue grills; b-y-o firewood; water at a central faucet; restrooms; sandy gravel driveways; complete supplies and services are available in Bishop.

Activities & Attractions: Fishing; motorless boating; tennis courts; ball diamonds; Mule Days annually at the end of May.

Natural Features: Located along both sides of a row of large hardwoods along a small creek in Owens Valley; the main part of the park has acres (or so it seems) of watered, mown lawns; a large pond with a small island is a short walk from the camping area; surrounded by a sage plain; the Sierra Nevada rises steeply a few miles west; elevation 4200'.

Season, Fees & Phone: Open all year, with limited services in winter; $5.00; park office (619) 872-1184 or Inyo County Parks and Recreation Department, Independence, (619) 878-2411, ext. 277.

Camp Notes: The camping is simple, but the park complex is, well, complex. The surroundings, both near and distant, are hard to beat. For more seclusion, and reportedly excellent fishing on the Owens River, another county camping area is close at hand. Pleasant Valley Campground can be reached from milepost 122 +.4 on U.S. 395: turn north onto Pleasant Valley Dam road for 1.25 miles. About 90 spaces are scattered along the river.

FOUR JEFFREY
Bishop Creek/Inyo National Forest

Location: Eastern California southwest of Bishop.

Access: From the junction of U.S. Highway 395 & California State Highway 168 in midtown Bishop, head west and southwest on Highway 168 (West Line Street) for 10 miles to the Bishop Creek Canyon Entrance Station; obtain a camping permit, then continue for another 5 miles to a major fork near milepost 3 +.3; hang a left onto a paved road and proceed southeast for 1 mile; turn easterly (left) and go 0.1 mile to the campground.

Facilities: 106 campsites; sites are small to medium-sized, with minimal to good separation; parking pads are sandy gravel, short to medium-length straight-ins; most pads will require additional leveling; small to medium-sized, generally somewhat sloped areas for tents; b-y-o shade; fire rings and barbecue grills; b-y-o firewood is recommended; water at several faucets; restrooms; holding tank disposal station; hard-surfaced driveways; camper supplies in Aspendell, on Highway 168 near mp 1; complete supplies and services are available in Bishop.

Activities & Attractions: Super Sierra Scenery.

Natural Features: Located on steeply sloped terrain in a narrow valley on the east slope of the Sierra Nevada; most sites are on an open sage slope, some sites are in among the aspens along a small stream (the South Fork of Bishop Creek); bordered by hills and mountains dotted with sage and small pines; lofty peaks rise from behind the local hills; elevation 8100'.

Season, Fees & Phone: May to October; $8.00; 14 day limit; White Mountain Ranger District, Bishop, (619) 873-4207 or Bishop Creek Entrance Station (619) 873-6829 (summer only).

Camp Notes: Shortly after you leave town, the highway crosses an enormous sage flat. The east slopes of the Sierra rise dramatically from the far end of the flat. Fabulous panoramas from along this drive. If you're lucky enough to nail down a creekside site among the aspens at Four Jeffrey, you'll have a fairly large and private site to spend your weekend, week, or whatever. Just after you angle off the main highway at the fork on the final leg up to Four Jeffrey (also spelled as "4 Jeffrey"), you'll pass a small camp on the right. Forks Campground, with nine sites and vaults, is in a small basin between the 'tines' of the 'fork'.

INTAKE 2 & BISHOP PARK
Bishop Creek/Inyo National Forest

Location: Eastern California southwest of Bishop.

Access: From the junction of U.S. Highway 395 & California State Highway 168 in midtown Bishop, cruise west and southwest on Highway 168 for 10 miles to the Bishop Creek Canyon Entrance Station; obtain a camping permit, then travel another 6 miles to milepost 1 +.5; turn southeast (left) onto a paved access road, go down 0.15 mile, then swing right into *Intake 2* Campground; or continue on the highway past the Intake 2 turnoff for 0.4 mile, (past the group camp) to milepost 2, then turn northwest into *Bishop Park* Campground.

Facilities: *Intake 2*: 12 campsites; *Bishop Park*: 20 campsites; (Bishop Park Group Camp is also available next door); *both camps*; many sites are park 'n walk tent units; sites are small, reasonably level, with minimal to fair separation; most parking surfaces are sandy gravel, short to short+ straight-ins or pull-offs; medium to large areas for tents; some sites have framed tent pads; fire rings; b-y-o firewood is highly recommended; water at central faucets; vault facilities; paved driveways; camper supplies in the hamlet of Aspendell, just up the road from the campgrounds.

Activities & Attractions: Fishing; day use area.

Natural Features: Located on a large flat along the shore of a pond and a creek bank (Intake 2); located along a narrow flat along Bishop Creek (Bishop Park); campsites receive very light shade (Intake 2) to medium shade (Bishop Park) from tall pines and hardwoods; flanked by almost-treeless sage slopes, with the majestic, gray peaks of the Sierra Nevada rising in the near distance; elevation 8100'.

Season, Fees & Phone: May to October; $8.00; 7 day limit; White Mountain Ranger District, Bishop, (619) 873-4207 or Bishop Creek Entrance Station (619) 873-6829 (summer only).

Camp Notes: Irrespective of the unorthodox moniker and location associated with a small hydroelectric project, Intake 2 is really an OK little spot. It might be a good idea to b-y-o shade if you're planning on staying at Intake 2, though. Bishop Park's campsites, most of which are beside the full, rushing stream, are very inviting.

SABRINA
Bishop Creek/Inyo National Forest

Location: Eastern California southwest of Bishop.

Access: From the junction of U.S. Highway 395 & California State Highway 168 in midtown Bishop, cruise west and southwest on Highway 168 for 10 miles to the Bishop Creek Canyon Entrance Station; obtain a camping permit, then travel another 8 miles (past the hamlet of Aspendell) to milepost 0.0; turn northwest (right) into the campground. (Note: the last mile is quite steep; at 9000', it might be a bit of a job for a heavily laden vehicle.)

Facilities: 20 campsites; sites are small to small+, slightly off-level, with minimal to fairly good separation; parking pads are sandy gravel, short to short+ straight-ins or pull-offs; medium to large tent areas on a surface of course, packed sand; fire rings; b-y-o firewood; water at central faucets; vault facilities; paved driveway; camper supplies in Aspendell, a mile north.

Activities & Attractions: Fishing for regularly stocked trout on Bishop Creek; fishing on Lake Sabrina, a mile upstream from the campground.

Natural Features: Located on a flat along the bank of Bishop Creek in a crag-rimmed canyon on the east slope of the Sierra Nevada; majority of sites are in a long, narrow clearing bordered by aspens and some pines; most campsites receive some shelter from wind, but not much midday shade; elevation 9000'.

Season, Fees & Phone: Mid-May to September; $8.00; 7 day limit; White Mountain Ranger District, Bishop, (619) 873-4207 or Bishop Creek Entrance Station (619) 873-6829 (summer only).

Camp Notes: The scenery gets better and better as you travel southwest along the one-way-in/one-way-out highway. There's a good chance that *your* campmates will also exclaim "Wow!" more than once on this trip.

TRIANGLE
Inyo County Park

Location: Eastern California south of Bishop.

Access: From U.S. Highway 395 at the north end of the community of Big Pine at milepost 100 +.9, (at the southeast corner of the junction of U.S. 395 and California State Highway 168) turn east into the campground.

Facilities: 36 campsites; sites are small, level, and closely spaced; parking pads are sandy gravel, long, extra-wide straight-ins; ample space for large, free-standing tents on the parking pads; barbecue grills; b-y-o firewood; water at several faucets; restrooms; gravel driveways; limited+ supplies and services are available in Big Pine.

Activities & Attractions: Large city park nearby; good fishing for trout on the Owens River and other local streams.

Natural Features: Located in Owens Valley; adequate to ample shelter/shade is provided by rows of hardwoods; a meadow borders the campground; the east slope of Sierra Nevada rises several miles to the west; elevation 4000'.

Season, Fees & Phone: Open all year, with limited services in winter; $6.00; Inyo County Parks and Recreation Department, Independence, (619) 878-2411, ext. 277.

Camp Notes: This is a good stop, even if it is a bit close to the highway. Although the campsites are small, the facilities are quite good for this part of the country. Also known as Big Pine Triangle, this is one of two county parks in Big Pine. The other, Baker Creek, is larger, but more rustic. To get there, turn west off the main highway onto Baker Creek Road (of course), and drive 1 mile (past the large city park) to`the campground. Baker Creek has room for about 50 campers, no water, and vault facilities. It also has at-your-tent-flap fishing on a stream which has had a couple of small impoundments added to it.

TINEMAHA CREEK
Inyo County Park

Location: Eastern California south of Bishop.

Access: From U.S. Highway 395 at milepost 92 +.9 (18 miles north of Independence, 23 miles south of Bishop), turn west onto Fish Springs Road; proceed 0.5 mile to Tinemaha Road, then turn south and continue for 2.1 miles to the campground. (The pavement ends as you turn into the campground on Fuller Road.)

Facilities: Approximately 45 campsites in a semi-open camping arrangement; parking and tent areas are large and level; a couple-dozen tables and fire facilities are available; b-y-o firewood; water at a hand pump; vault facilities; sand/gravel parking and driving surfaces; limited supplies and services are available in Big Pine, 9 miles north, or in Independence.

Activities & Attractions: Fishing for regularly stocked trout.

Natural Features: Located on a sandy flat along Tinemaha Creek in Owens Valley; large hardwoods provide adequate shelter/shade in many sites; surrounded by a sage plain; the Sierra Nevada rises a few miles west; the rugged, barren Inyo Mountains lie across the valley to the east; elevation 4000'.

Season, Fees & Phone: Open all year; $6.00; Inyo County Parks and Recreation Department, Independence, (619) 878-2411, ext. 277.

Camp Notes: This is one of a half-dozen county park campgrounds in the valley. Several of them apparently serve primarily as fishing camps, but work fine for economical regular camping as well. Another very similar county campground is Taboose Creek, just south of here. The easiest way to find it is to exit west off the main highway at milepost 87 +.7 onto Taboose Creek Road; drive 1.2 miles, then turn south (left) onto Tinemaha Road for a final 0.1 mile to the campground. Taboose Creek has facilities similar to those in Tinemaha Creek, but no drinking water, perhaps a bit more shade, and a slightly smaller stream.

OAK CREEK
Inyo National Forest

Location: Eastern California south of Bishop.

Access: From U.S. Highway 395 at milepost 75 +.7 (2 miles north of Independence, 39 miles south of Bishop), turn west onto Fish Hatchery Road; drive 1.3 miles to a fork in the road; take the right fork and continue for another 1.3 miles to the campground.

Facilities: 24 campsites; sites are small to average-sized; about a third of the sites are well separated from neighboring units, others are in several clusters; parking pads are paved or gravel, mostly short, double-wide, level straight-ins; most sites have medium to large tent spaces; fire rings; b-y-o firewood is recommended; water at several faucets; vault facilities; driveway is paved part-way, remainder is gravel; limited supplies and services are available in Independence.

Activities & Attractions: Fishing for stocked trout; fisherman's trail along the creek.

Natural Features: Located along Oak Creek on the north side of a low ridge near the base of the east slope of the Sierra Nevada; vegetation consists of tall grass, oaks, willows and other hardwoods; most sites have adequate to ample shade/shelter, a few are in the open; the campground is perched slightly above the surrounding sage plain; sweeping views of Owens Valley and the Inyo Mountains to the east; elevation 5000'.

Season, Fees & Phone: Mid-April to mid-October, but may be available at other times with limited services; $6.00; 14 day limit; Mount Whitney Ranger District, Lone Pine, (619) 876-6200.

Camp Notes: With the fish hatchery practically in the front yard, fishing ought to be good here. Most streams in this region are regularly stocked with trout throughout the summer, as long as water conditions allow.

GRAYS MEADOW
Inyo National Forest

Location: Eastern California south of Bishop.

Access: From U.S. Highway 395 in midtown Independence (41 miles south of Bishop, 69 miles north of Lone Pine) turn west onto Market Street (which shortly becomes Onion Valley Road), and proceed 5.6 miles to the Lower campground section and another 0.35 mile to the Upper camping section.

Facilities: 30 campsites in the Lower section and 22 campsites in the Upper section; sites are generally small to medium-sized, with fair to excellent separation; parking pads are paved, respectably level, short to medium-length straight-ins; some sites have good tent spots; fire rings or fireplaces; b-y-o firewood is suggested; water at several faucets; restrooms; limited supplies and services are available in Independence.

Activities & Attractions: Fishing for stocked trout.

Natural Features: Located along the bank of Independence Creek; large hardwoods, bushes and scattered, tall pines provide adequate shelter/shade in most sites; the campground is bordered by a barren hill to the north and a sage plain to the south; the east slope of the Sierra Nevada rises abruptly just west of the campground; the Inyo Mountains are in view to the east; elevation 6000'.

Season, Fees & Phone: March to mid-October; $7.00; 14 day limit; Mount Whitney Ranger District, Lone Pine, (619) 876-6200.

Camp Notes: The views from the camping area are quite extraordinary--some of the best of any campground in this region. However, if you're self-contained (or your spouse, kids, or other campmates don't mind vaults), there is a county park conveniently near here that is worth considering. Independence Creek Park is on the way to Grays Meadow, on the north side of the road, a half-mile out of Independence. It has water, vaults, big trees, a creek, and park 'em and pitch 'em where-you-will camping. The views are still terrific, and the tariff is dollars less.

LONE PINE
Inyo National Forest

Location: Eastern California south of Bishop.

Access: From U.S. Highway 395 in midtown Lone Pine (59 miles south of Bishop, 69 miles north of Inyokern), turn west onto Whitney Portal Road (paved) and proceed 6.6 miles to the campground access road; hang a left onto the paved access road and continue for 0.6 mile to the campground.

Facilities: 43 campsites, including several park 'n walk sites; (a nearby group campground is also available); sites are average in size, with minimal to fairly good visual separation; parking pads are paved, short to medium-length straight-ins which have been fairly well leveled; enough room for a medium-sized tent in most sites; fireplaces or fire rings; some firewood may be available for gathering several miles west, b-y-o is recommended; water at several faucets; vault facilities; paved driveways; adequate supplies and services are available in Lone Pine.

Activities & Attractions: Fishing; trailheads at Whitney Portal.

Natural Features: Located in a shallow stream bed along Lone Pine Creek at the eastern edge of the Sierra Nevada; campground vegetation consists of some medium-height hardwoods which provide limited shade/shelter, plus small, high desert plants; surrounded by a semi-arid, rocky, open slope; the summit of Mount Whitney is 6 miles (line of sight) west/southwest of here; elevation 6000'.

Season, Fees & Phone: April to mid-October; $7.00; 14 day limit; Mount Whitney Ranger District, Lone Pine, (619) 876-6200.

Camp Notes: What a view! From in and around the campground you can see the spire-topped peaks and razor-edged chimneys and ridges of the highest of the High Sierra. And the view of the Inyo Mountains to the east isn't too shabby either. In case this camp is full, there's a large BLM campground, Tuttle Creek, south of here, on an open plain, off of Horseshoe Meadow Road that may have some sites available. Also, don't count on getting a site in the campground at Whitney Portal, which is another six mile west of Lone Pine Campground. Reportedly, Whitney Portal usually is filled by backpackers who are either on their way into, out of, or passing through this superscenic region.

DIAZ LAKE
Inyo County Recreation Area

Location: Eastern California south of Bishop.

Access: From U.S Highway 395 at milepost 54 +.6 (2.5 miles south of Lone Pine, 67 miles north of Inyokern), turn west onto the park access road, then immediately turn south, and continue for 0.5 mile along the south shore of the lake to the campground.

Facilities: 47 individual campsites, plus a large tent-camping area; standard sites are small, level, with no separation; parking pads are sand/dirt, medium to long, parallel pull-throughs; a large tent area contains a dozen or so tables, plus fire rings and barbecue grills; b-y-o firewood; water at several faucets; restrooms; showers; sand/dirt driveways; adequate supplies and services are available in Lone Pine.

Activities & Attractions: Fishing for catfish, crappie, etc.; stocked with rainbow trout in winter; boating (extra fee); day use area; local streams also provide good trout fishing; visitor information center, 0.5 mile north, just off the east side of the highway, provides info about recreation in regional national forests and national parks.

Natural Features: Located on the southwest shore of Diaz Lake, in semi-arid Owens Valley; huge willows and other hardwoods provide a generous amount of shade/shelter in many sites, particularly in the tent area; the Sierra Nevada rises a few miles to the west, the Inyo Mountains lie to the east, across the valley; typically breezy; hot in summer, cold in winter; elevation 3700'.

Season, Fees & Phone: Open all year, with limited services in winter; $8.00; 14 day limit; Inyo County Parks and Recreation Department, Independence, (619) 878-2411, ext. 277.

Camp Notes: Here's a case where tenters may have the edge over rv'ers. The tent area not only is a little better sheltered, but it's lakeside, as well. The facilities are simple, but the place is the proverbial oasis on the high desert. Diaz Lake is a small natural lake created by an earthquake in the late 1800's. Camping is also available at a small county park, called Portagee Joe, on the southwest corner of Lone Pine.

Southern California
San Bernardino Mtns. & Mojave Desert
Please refer to the Northern California map in the Appendix

MESQUITE SPRING
Death Valley National Monument

Location: Southeast California north of Barstow.

Access: From the main north-south park road at a point 3.5 miles southwest of Scotty's Castle and 54 miles northwest of Furnace Creek, turn south onto a paved access road and proceed 1.8 miles to the campground.

Facilities: 53 campsites; (a group camping area is also available); sites are generally small, with no separation; parking pads are paved or gravel, mostly medium-length straight-ins, which may require a little additional leveling; adequate space for a large tent in most sites on a gravel/rock surface; fireplaces and barbecue grills; b-y-o firewood (gathering in the park is prohibited); water at central faucets; restrooms; holding tank disposal station; paved driveways; camper supplies at Stovepipe Wells, 43 miles south; limited to adequate supplies in Beatty, Nevada (including a half-dozen gas stations and at least that many casinos), 60 miles east.

Activities & Attractions: Scotty's Castle (Park Service tours of the interior during the winter may require a substantial wait); Ubehebe Crater, 6 miles northwest.

Natural Features: Located on a gently sloping flat at the upper end of Death Valley; campground vegetation consists of a grove of large mesquite trees that form a canopy at the entrance, plus small desert bushes and a lot of rock in the rest of the campground; the Cottonwood Mountains stand to the west, and the Grapevine Mountains are to the east; elevation 1800'.

Season, Fees & Phone: Open all year; $7.00; 30 day limit; park headquarters, Furnace Creek, (619) 786-2331.

Camp Notes: One of the mesquite trees here is believed to be over a thousand years old. Primarily because of a two thousand feet difference in elevation, it is typically 11° F cooler here than in the campgrounds farther south. This is one of only three campgrounds in the national monument that are open all year.

STOVEPIPE WELLS
Death Valley National Monument

Location: Southeast California north of Barstow.

Access: From California State Highway 190 at milepost 85 +.6 (7 miles southwest of the junction of Highway 190 & the main north-south park road, 75 miles northeast of Olancha), turn north into the camping area.

Facilities: Approximately 200 campsites in a parking lot arrangement; sites are small-, nearly level, with zero separation; parking surfaces are gravel, short to long straight-ins or pull-throughs; ample space for free-standing tents in designated sites; a few sites have fireplaces; (would it be superfluous to mention b-y-o firewood?); water at central faucets; central restrooms; ranger station; paved driveways; camper supplies and showers are available nearby.

Activities & Attractions: Unique landscape.

Natural Features: Located on a desolate plain on the floor of Death Valley; a few small desert bushes are around the perimeter of the camplot; sizeable sand dunes are in the vicinity; the valley is flanked by the barren Panamint Range a few miles to the west and the Amargosa Range to the east; sea level.

Season, Fees & Phone: October to April; $7.00; 30 day limit; park headquarters, Furnace Creek, (619) 786-2331

Camp Notes: Two other campgrounds in this section of the park are certainly worth a look. Emigrant Campground is 8 miles southwest of Stovepipe Wells at Emigrant Junction, and is also on the north side of California 190. Wildrose Campground is 21 miles south of Emigrant Junction via Wildrose Road (paved). Emigrant has 10 campsites, drinking water and restrooms nearby; Wildrose has 36 sites, vaults, no water. At an exhilarating elevation of 4000' above sea level, Wildrose is the highest standard campground in the park.

FURNACE CREEK
Death Valley National Monument

Location: Southeast California north of Barstow.

Access: From California State Highway 190 at milepost 110 +.1 (0.2 mile north of the Furnace Creek Visitor Center, 2 miles north of the junction of State Highways 190 & 178, 25 miles southeast of Stovepipe Wells), turn west, and go 0.15 mile to the campground.

Facilities: 105 campsites, plus overflow areas; sites are generally small and level, with nominal to minimal separation; parking pads are sandy gravel, medium-length straight-ins or pull-throughs; good-sized tent areas with a sandy surface; fireplaces; b-y-o firewood (gathering in the park is prohibited); water at central faucets; restrooms; holding tank disposal station; paved driveway; ranger station nearby; gas camper supplies are available at a nearby store.

Activities & Attractions: Visitor center, with exhibits and audio-visual programs; museum; interpretive trails.

Natural Features: Located on a flat in the center of Death Valley; campground vegetation consists primarily of rows of large, full trees which provide shade for some sites; barren hills surround the campground in the immediate vicinity; most sites also have quite striking views of the classic desert mountains for which the region is famous; elevation 196' below sea level.

Season, Fees & Phone: Open all year; $7.00; 30 day limit; park headquarters, Furnace Creek, (619) 786-2331.

Camp Notes: Unless you enjoy a festival atmosphere, you might consider coming here at a time other than the second weekend of November. That's when the Death Valley 49ers hold their annual rendezvous, and the park swells to capacity (and beyond). Most winter holidays and three-day weekends are also congested. Even in midsummer (midsimmer?), a surprising number of people visit the valley (although relatively few camp).

TEXAS SPRING
Death Valley National Monument

Location: Southeast California north of Barstow.

Access: From California State Highway 190 at milepost 111 (0.6 mile south of the Furnace Creek Visitor Center, 1 mile north of the junction of State Highways 190 & 178, and many miles north of nowhere else in particular), turn northeast onto a paved access road and proceed 1 mile to the campground.

Facilities: Approximately 80 campsites; (a group camp area is also available); sites vary in size, with minimal separation; parking surfaces are sandy gravel, short to medium-length straight-ins or pull-offs; adequate space for medium to large tents in most sites; fireplaces; b-y-o firewood; water at central faucets; restrooms; gravel driveway; gas and camper supplies in Furnace Creek.

Activities & Attractions: Desert panoramas; shade.

Natural Features: Located in a grove of trees on a gentle slope above the floor of Death Valley; sites are minimally to lightly shaded; sea level.

Season, Fees & Phone: October to May; $7.00; 30 day limit; park headquarters, Furnace Creek, (619) 786-2331.

Camp Notes: Texas Spring is one of three campgrounds in the Furnace Creek vicinity. Seasoned Death Valley campers prefer Texas Spring's environment and layout to Furnace Creek Campground's slightly more deluxe accommodations. The third camp area, Sunset, offers parking lot stopovers for upwards of a thousand campers during the winter months. Sunset has drinking water and restrooms on a huge, gravelly, unsheltered, gently sloping flat just across the highway from the visitor center.

CALICO GHOST TOWN
San Bernardino County Regional Park

Location: South-central California east of Barstow.

Access: From Interstate 15 at milepost 81 +.8 at the Ghost Town Road Exit (10 miles east of Barstow, 53 miles southwest of Baker), from the north side of the freeway travel 3.5 miles north then east on Ghost Town Road to Calico Road; turn north (left) and proceed 0.2 mile to the park entrance station, then a final 0.2 to the campground. **Alternate Access:** From I-15 at milepost 84 +.5 (13 miles east of Barstow), take the Yermo Exit, turn north onto Calico Road and proceed 3.9 miles to the park and continue as above. (Note: the *Access* works best for eastbound Interstate travelers; the *Alternate Access* is good for westbound traffic.)

Facilities: 174 campsites in 2 areas; 134 sites are situated in the main area east of the entrance; sites here are smallish, with minimal separation; parking pads are gravel, short straight-ins, which might require a little additional leveling; adequate space for a tent in most sites; remaining sites are located on a gravel flat west of the entrance; barbecue grills; b-y-o firewood; water at faucets throughout; restrooms with showers; holding tank disposal station; paved driveways in the main section; complete supplies and services are available in Barstow.

Activities & Attractions: Calico, a deceased mining community recently resurrected, has a group of small shops and food vendors, tours, and periodic get-togethers, including Calico Days in October and the Calico Spring Festival in May.

Natural Features: Located at the foot of the colorful Calico Mountains; main camping area is in a gently sloping draw, with quite a few small to medium-height, planted hardwoods which provide some shade/shelter; remaining sites are in somewhat of a level, parking lot arrangement, with a few small trees; elevation 2200'.

Season, Fees & Phone: Open all year; $11.00; reservations accepted, advisable for weekends, October to May, contact the park office (619) 254-2122.

Camp Notes: The main camping area is actually a little nicer than its 'mechanical' description might indicate. However, during rainy periods, it's subject to earthslides, so stay mobile.

AFTON CANYON
Public Lands/BLM Recreation Site

Location: South-central California northeast of Barstow.

Access: From Interstate 15 at milepost 111 +.5 at the Afton Road/Dunn Exit (39 miles northeast of Barstow, 24 miles southwest of Baker), from the south side of the Interstate, travel south on a gravel road for 3.4 miles to the campground. (Note that the access road is a little steep, winding and rocky in spots.)

Facilities: 19 campsites; sites are medium-sized, with some spacing but with minimal visual separation; parking pads are gravel, mostly long, level straight-ins; tent areas are large, with a sandy base; most sites have a small ramada (sun shelter); barbecue grills and fire rings; water at a hand pump; vault facilities; gravel driveway; limited supplies in Baker; complete supplies and services are available in Barstow.

Activities & Attractions: Desert environment; restricted orv use.

Natural Features: Located on a flat in a shallow desert canyon along the north bank of the Mojave River; campground vegetation consists of a few tall bushes and smaller desert plants around the sites; desert mountains north and south; .

Season, Fees & Phone: Open all year; $6.00; 14 day limit; Bureau of Land Management Barstow Resource Area Office (619) 256-3591.

Camp Notes: This simple campground provides easy access to an inexpensive public camp along Interstate 15. Though not what many campers would call spectacular, the canyon is certainly pleasant, and surprisingly green for a desert location. There's a railroad track that seems to be operational a few hundred yards from the campground, so that might be a factor affecting your decision to make a long-term camping commitment to the place.

PROVIDENCE MOUNTAINS
Providence Mountains State Recreation Area

Location: South-east California west of Needles.

Access: From Interstate 40 at the Essex Road Exit at milepost 100 (44 miles west of Needles, 100 miles east of Barstow), from the north side of the Interstate head northwest on a paved local road for 14 miles to the park boundary; here the road begins a long, moderately steep climb for the final 2 miles to the campground.

Facilities: 6 campsites; sites are very small, with minimal to nominal separation; parking surfaces are gravel, reasonably level, short straight-ins or pull-offs; enough space for small tents; fire rings and barbecue grills; firewood is usually for sale, b-y-o to be sure; water at several faucets; (b-y-o water and shade is suggested because of a limited supply of both in the park); vault facilities; gas and camper supplies in Essex, 6 miles southeast of the Interstate exit.

Activities & Attractions: Guided tours of Mitchell Caverns (1.5 miles round trip, 1 hour, it is suggested that you contact the district office for a current time and fee schedule); nature trail (a nice guide booklet is available); short hiking trails; East Mohave National Scenic Area (BLM-managed) borders the park.

Natural Features: Located on a mountainside on the east slope of the 7200' Providence Mountains; campsites are unshaded; the vast reaches of the Mojave Desert plains lie several thousand feet below the park's vantage point; elevation 4300'.

Season, Fees & Phone: Open all year; please see Appendix for standard California state park fees and reservation information; phone c/o CDPR Mojave River District Office (619) 389-2281.

Camp Notes: Most visitors are drawn here by the prospect of going deep inside the mountain to pursue stalactites and stalagmites (but no bats, at last report.) Outside in the daylight, the desert views from the campsites are first-rate.

PARK MOABI
San Bernardino County Regional Park

Location: Southeast California along the California-Arizona border east of Needles.

Access: From Interstate 40 at milepost 153 +.3 (1.3 miles west of the Arizona-California border, 11 miles east of Needles), take the Park Moabi Exit (the easternmost exit in California); turn north onto Park Moabi Road, and proceed 0.6 mile; turn left to the park entrance station and the campground.

Facilities: 664 campsites, including 31 sites with partial or complete hookups; sites are all fairly level, and vary considerably in size and separation: from small to very large, from close to quite private; hookup sites are parking-lot style, on a gravel surface; tent spots are generally large and level; tenting not permitted on the grass on weekdays (because of automatic sprinkling); some sites may lack tables and/or fire facilities; barbecue grills in most sites; b-y-o firewood; water at several faucets; restrooms, some with showers; holding tank disposal station; gravel driveways; adequate supplies and services are available in Needles.

Activities & Attractions: Boating; large boat launch area; marina nearby; fishing; small playground.

Natural Features: Located along the west bank of the Colorado River; campground vegetation consists of some watered grass and short-to-medium height, bushy trees; sandy beach; surrounded by desert mountains; elevation 600'.

Season, Fees & Phone: Open all year; $11.00 to $16.00; 14 day limit; park office (619) 326-3831.

Camp Notes: Although it often gets pretty busy at this park, they've reportedly never had to turn anyone away. The average camper here travels 250-300 miles for a weekend stay. Park Moabi's campground may prove to be very handy for I-40 travelers. For all practical purposes, the next-nearest public camps along the Interstate are more than a hundred miles from here in either direction.

MOJAVE NARROWS
San Bernardino County Regional Park

Location: Southern California north of San Bernardino.

Access: From Interstate 15 at the Lucerne Valley/Bear Valley Road Exit at milepost 37 +.6 in Victorville (32 miles north of San Bernardino, 36 miles southwest of Barstow), turn east onto Bear Valley Road (called Bear Valley Cutoff farther east); proceed 3.9 miles to Ridge Crest Drive; turn north (left) onto Ridge Crest Drive and continue for 2.6 miles, then turn left, and go 0.1 mile to the park entrance station; the campground is 0.2 mile farther.

Facilities: 87 campsites in 2 sections; some sites are in a string along a lake shore; other sites are in a parking lot arrangement; sites are small to average in size, level, with minimal separation; parking pads are paved, and vary from short straight-ins to longer pull-offs and pull-throughs; plenty of excellent tent-pitching possibilities on a grass or sandy base; fire rings and/or barbecue grills; b-y-o firewood; water at central faucets; restrooms with showers; holding tank disposal station; complete supplies and services are available on Bear Valley Road.

Activities & Attractions: Fishing (extra fee); paved, self-guided nature trail; day use area; trout derbies in winter; Roy Rogers & Dale Evans Museum in Victorville.

Natural Features: Located on the shore of Horseshoe Lake in a large valley ringed by high and dry mountains, at the southern edge of the Mojave Desert; large hardwoods provide shade/shelter in some sites; most sites are in the open; typically breezy; elevation 2700'.

Season, Fees & Phone: Open all year; $11.00; park office (619) 245-2226.

Camp Notes: You might not think that a park on the "edge of the Mojave Desert" holds much attraction, but this is actually a nice place, even in the warmer months. Reportedly, there's usually room for drop-ins, even in winter.

MESA
Silverwood Lake State Recreation Area

Location: Southern California north of San Bernardino.

Access: From California State Highway 138 at milepost 26 +.4 (10 miles north of Crestline, 11 miles east of the Palmdale/Silverwood Lake Exit on Interstate 15), turn east onto the park access road and proceed 0.6 mile to the entrance station; just beyond the entrance, turn north (left) to campsites 96-136; or continue easterly for 0.2 mile to the lower-numbered campsites. (Note that there is a "mini interchange" on Highway 138 that serves the park access road.)

Facilities: 136 campsites; (hike-bike sites and 3 group camps are also available); sites are small+ to medium-sized, with fair to good separation; at least half of the sites are basically level, remainder are slightly sloped; parking pads are paved, mostly short+ to medium+ straight-ins, and many are extra wide; also some medium+ pull-off pads; large tent areas in most sites; fire rings and barbecue grills; firewood is usually for sale, or b-y-o; water at several faucets; restrooms with showers; coin-op laundry; holding tank disposal station; paved driveways; adequate supplies and services are available in Crestline.

Activities & Attractions: Designated swimming areas; boating; boat launches; fishing for largemouth bass, striped bass, catfish, bluegill, crappie, rainbow trout; ('fish attractors' have been left at several locations around the lake); 13 miles of paved hiking and bicycling trails; campfire circle; small visitor center; several day use areas around the lake.

Natural Features: Located on the southwest shore of Silverwood Lake; the lake lies behind a dam across the West Fork of the Mojave River in a small valley in the San Bernardino Mountains; medium-high oaks and pines and shrubs provide ample shade/shelter for most campsites; wooded hills and low mountains encircle the 200'-deep lake; elevation 3400'.

Season, Fees & Phone: Open all year; please see Appendix for standard California state park fees and reservation information; park office (619) 389-2303.

Camp Notes: There are good views of the surrounding mountains from many campsites, particularly from the bike camps. Although the lake lies over the West Fork of the Mojave River and a tributary, most of the water doesn't come from local runoff, as might be expected. (But the area does get nearly 40 inches of precip annually). Most of Silverwood's contents originate nearly 700 miles from here, in the upper Feather River in northeast California. A complex system of reservoirs, rivers, aqueducts and pumping stations brings the water to Silverwood. From here, gravity takes the water through a four-mile tunnel and finally into Lake Perris, spinning a set of electric generating turbines on the way for good measure.

Southern California 148

YUCAIPA
San Bernardino County Regional Park

Location: Southwest California southeast of San Bernardino.

Access: From Interstate 10 at the Yucaipa Boulevard Exit near milepost 36 (4 miles east of Redlands, 15 miles northeast of Beaumont), from the north side of the freeway, travel east on Yucaipa Boulevard for 2.7 miles to Oak Glen Road; turn northeast (left) onto Oak Glen Road, and continue for 1.85 miles, then turn left into the park entrance and the camping areas.

Facilities: 35 campsites, including 26 rv sites and 9 individual tent/small group units, in two areas; sites in the rv section are large, mostly level, with some separation; parking pads are paved, mostly long pull-throughs, some spacious enough for the longest rv's, plus a few long straight-ins; sites in the tent/group area are park 'n walk units, situated on a level, sandy gravel pavilion; tent units have ramadas (sun shelters); barbecue grills; b-y-o firewood; water at several faucets; restrooms with showers in both areas; adequate supplies in Yucaipa; complete supplies and services are available in Redlands.

Activities & Attractions: Fishing (extra fee); playgrounds; swimming lagoon, waterslide (extra fee).

Natural Features: Located on a pair of hillsides which flank a chain of 3 lakes; watered, mown lawns planted with hardwoods surround most of the sites; the entire area is surrounded by dry hills and mountains; elevation 2900'.

Season, Fees & Phone: Open all year; $11.00; 14 day limit; reservations accepted, advisable for weekends, contact the park office (714) 790-1818.

Camp Notes: There are golf courses and there are campgrounds, and then there are campgrounds that resemble golf courses. And this is one of them. You could slip a freight train into some of the rv sites (or, more likely, a Presidential Special.) If you prefer to camp dressed in an old plaid shirt and faded jeans, sitting by a fire of buffalo chips, eating beans from a soot-blackened can, sleeping in an old bedroll stretched out on the sod 14 miles from the nearest blacktop, then this deluxe camp probably isn't the spot for you. (Well, pardon me! Ed.) A very nice park.

Southern California 149

DOGWOOD
San Bernardino National Forest

Location: Southwest California northeast of San Bernardino.

Access: From California State Highway 18 at milepost 23 +.3 (3 miles southwest of Lake Arrowhead, 6 miles east of Crestline) turn north (a very sharp right turn if you're westbound) and proceed 0.4 mile to the campground.

Facilities: 93 campsites, including quite a few park 'n walk sites, in 5 loops; sites are medium-sized, with fair to very good separation; parking pads are paved, short to short+, sloped straight-ins; a sleeping vehicle would require some (if not a lot) of additional leveling; tent areas vary from small to large and most are not very level; fireplaces; a small amount of firewood may be available for gathering, b-y-o is recommended; water at several faucets; restrooms; holding tank disposal station; paved driveways; gas and groceries 0.5 mile west; adequate supplies are available in Lake Arrowhead.

Activities & Attractions: Enchanted Loop Nature Trail; Dogwood Trail; Lake Arrowhead; uncommonly scenic drive along Highway 18 (also known as Rim of the World Drive).

Natural Features: Located in the San Bernardino Mountains in a dense forest of tall conifers, oaks, brush and ferns on a thick carpet of evergreen needles; a number of sites have tent spaces and/or tables tucked away among the trees; elevation 5600'.

Season, Fees & Phone: May to October; $12.00 for a standard site, $16.00 for a double site; 14 day limit; Arrowhead Ranger District, Rimforest, (714) 337-2444).

Camp Notes: This is a really nice, wooded setting, albeit a rather slanted one. (At the risk of sounding overly critical of the campground's designers, our field editor remarked that, in a lot of the sites here, "your macaroni and cheese would slide off the plate". Ed.)

Southern California 150

NORTH SHORE
San Bernardino National Forest

Location: Southwest California northeast of San Bernardino.

Access: From California State Highway 173 at milepost 18.6 (3 miles northeast of the community of Lake Arrowhead), turn east onto Hospital Road; go 0.15 mile, then bear left (just opposite the hospital) onto a paved access road and continue up the hill for 0.3 mile to the campground.

Facilities: 27 campsites, including a number of park 'n walk sites; sites are small to medium in size, and a little close together, although some are scattered in separate locations; parking pads are paved, mostly short to short+ straight-ins which are slightly sloped; tent areas are spacious, and slightly sloped also; fire rings; b-y-o firewood; water at several faucets; restrooms; paved driveways; adequate supplies and services are available in the Lake Arrowhead area.

Activities & Attractions: Boating; (the majority of Lake Arrowhead's shoreline is privately owned).

Natural Features: Located on a hilltop on the northeast corner of Lake Arrowhead in the San Bernardino Mountains; campground vegetation consists of moderately dense, large oaks, tall pines, and manzanitas on a surface of tall grass; elevation 5200'.

Season, Fees & Phone: April to November, limited to weekends only; $10.00; Arrowhead Ranger District, Rimforest, (714) 337-2444).

Camp Notes: There are some very commanding views of the mountains, particularly to the east, just a short walk away from any of the campsites. Lake views, however, are generally quite limited. Some of the park 'n walk sites would make good choices for tent campers.

Southern California 151

HANNA FLAT
San Bernardino National Forest

Location: Southwest California east of San Bernardino.

Access: From California State Highway 38 at milepost 56 in midtown Fawnskin (6 miles west of Big Bear City, 41 miles east of San Bernardino), turn northwest onto Forest Road 3N14 (at the east end of the Grout Creek bridge, should be signed for "Holcomb Valley") and proceed 2.4 miles to the campground, on the left side of the road. (Note: at 1.8 miles, continue straight ahead on Road 3N14, rather than turning right toward Holcomb Valley.)

Facilities: 88 campsites; sites are medium-sized, with fair to good separation; parking pads are paved, mostly medium-length straight-ins which may require some additional leveling; tent areas are medium to large and many are sloped; fire rings; very little firewood is available for gathering, b-y-o is recommended; water at several faucets; restrooms, supplemented by vault facilities; gas and groceries in Fawnskin; adequate supplies and services are available in the Big Bear City-Big Bear Lake area.

Activities & Attractions: Forest environment; Big Bear Lake, 2.5 miles (down by the main highway).

Natural Features: Located on a sloping, rolling flat in a forest of pines and oaks in the San Bernardino Mountains; an intermittent stream passes through the campground area; elevation 7000'.

Season, Fees & Phone: May to September; $10.00; 14 day limit; Big Bear Ranger District, Fawnskin, (714) 866-3437.

Camp Notes: Judging by the *Access* description, you'd think that "just getting here is half the fun", but it isn't as tricky as it may seem. The toughest part is finding the correct road off the main highway, since the highway signs at Fawnskin may be a bit unreliable. The campground setting is very pleasant, although lacking in distant views. The area around the campground is favored by local atv/orv/dirt bike enthusiasts.

COLDBROOK
San Bernardino National Forest

Location: Southwest California east of San Bernardino.

Access: From California State Highway 18 at milepost 48 (just west of midtown Big Bear Lake, turn south onto Mill Creek Road and go 0.45 mile to Tulip Lane; bear right onto Tulip Lane for a final 0.15 mile to the campground.

Facilities: 36 campsites; sites are medium-sized, with nominal to fair separation; parking pads are gravel/dirt, mostly short to medium-length straight-ins; a little additional leveling will be needed on most pads; tent areas are generally large, but somewhat sloped; barbecue grills and fire rings; b-y-o firewood is recommended; water at several faucets; restrooms; adequate+ supplies and services are available in the Big Bear Lake-Big Bear City metropolitan area.

Activities & Attractions: Fishing and boating on nearby Big Bear Lake.

Natural Features: Located on a hillside in the San Bernardino Mountains; campsites are shaded by medium-dense, tall conifers and oaks; elevation 6800'.

Season, Fees & Phone: Late May to late September; $11.00; 14 day limit; Big Bear Ranger District, Fawnskin, (714) 866-3437.

Camp Notes: Campsites here are in a bit more open forest setting than those at neighboring Pineknot.

PINEKNOT
San Bernardino National Forest

Location: Southwest California east of San Bernardino.

Access: From California State Highway 18 (Big Bear Boulevard) in midtown Big Bear Lake, turn south onto Summit Boulevard; proceed south 0.5 mile to the ski area; turn east (left) onto a paved road and continue for 0.15 mile, then turn right into the campground.

Facilities: 52 campsites in 2 loops; sites are about average in size and separation for a forest camp; parking pads are gravel, short to medium-length straight-ins; most pads will require additional leveling; tent areas are large, but quite sloped; barbecue grills and fire rings; b-y-o firewood is recommended; water at several faucets; restrooms; adequate+ supplies and services are available in the Big Bear Lake-Big Bear City comfort zone.

Activities & Attractions: Boating, boat launch, fishing on Big Bear Lake.

Natural Features: Located on a northward-facing slope in a moderately dense forest of medium to tall conifers, plus some oaks; elevation 6800'.

Season, Fees & Phone: Late May to late September; $11.00; 14 day limit; Big Bear Ranger District, Fawnskin, (714) 866-3437.

Camp Notes: Since it's right on the south edge of town, this campground isn't exactly in the pristine wilderness. It hasn't much in the way of scenic views. But it's really handy if you're planning to participate in the area's recreational activities and don't desire to pay the duty at the local motel.

BARTON FLATS
San Bernardino National Forest

Location: Southwest California east of San Bernardino.

Access: From California State Highway 38 at milepost 27 +.6 (28 miles east of Redlands, 22 miles southwest of Big Bear City), turn north into the campground.

Facilities: 47 campsites, including some double sites; sites are average-sized, with nominal to fairly good separation; parking pads are paved, mostly medium-length straight-ins which probably will require additional leveling; adequate space for a large tent in most sites, but it may be sloped; fire rings and barbecue grills; some firewood may be available for gathering in the surrounding area; water at several faucets; vault facilities; paved driveways; gas and groceries are available in Angeles Oaks, 6 miles west.

Activities & Attractions: Small national forest visitor center a half mile west; short hiking trails; viewpoint.

Natural Features: Located on a forested flat in the San Bernardino Mountains; sites receive light to light-medium shade/shelter from vegetation consisting of very tall pines and cedars, plus some oaks on a tall grass/conifer surface; a timbered ridge lies to the south; elevation 6300'.

Season, Fees & Phone: May to October; $7.00 for a single site, $14.00 for a double site; 14 day limit; San Gorgonio Ranger District, Mentone, (909) 794-1123.

Camp Notes: Campsites toward the west end of the campground are a bit more level than the others.

SAN GORGONIO
San Bernardino National Forest

Location: Southwest California east of San Bernardino.

Access: From California State Highway 38 at milepost 28 +.1 (28 miles east of Redlands, 22 miles southwest of Big Bear City), turn north into the campground.

Facilities: 60 campsites; sites are medium-sized, with fair separation; most parking pads are paved, short+ to medium-length straight-ins; some additional leveling will probably be needed on most pads; adequate, but sloped, space for large tents; fire rings and barbecue grills; some gatherable firewood may be available in the surrounding area; water at several faucets; vault facilities; paved driveways; gas and groceries are available in Angeles Oaks, 6 miles west.

Activities & Attractions: Small national forest visitor center just west of the campground; short hiking trails; viewpoint.

Natural Features: Located on a light to moderately forested flat in the San Bernardino Mountains; campground vegetation consists of very tall pines, cedars and oaks on a forest floor of tall grass and evergreen needles; a timbered ridge lies to the south; elevation 6400'.

Season, Fees & Phone: May to October; $7.00; 14 day limit; San Gorgonio Ranger District, Mentone, (909) 794-1123.

Camp Notes: San Gorgonio's campsites are a little farther from the highway and a bit better sheltered than those at Barton Flats Campground, just down the road from here. Its forest is perhaps more varied, including noticeably more oaks, as well.

SOUTH FORK
San Bernardino National Forest

Location: Southwest California east of San Bernardino.

Access: From California State Highway 38 at milepost 30 +.8 (31 miles east of Redlands, 19 miles south of Big Bear City), turn south into the campground.

Facilities: 24 campsites in 2 loops; sites are of ample size, and fairly well separated; parking pads are paved, mostly short to medium-length straight-ins; most pads will probably require a little additional leveling; most tent areas are large, and either level or on a slight slope; fire rings and/or barbecue grills; some firewood may be available for gathering in the vicinity, b-y-o is suggested; water at several faucets; vault facilities; paved driveways; gas and groceries in Angeles Oaks, 9 miles west.

Activities & Attractions: Santa Ana River Trail; fishing.

Natural Features: Located on a flat along the South Fork of the Santa Ana River, where the South Fork enters the main stream; another small side stream flows past the east end of the campground; moderately dense, tall conifers on a base of grass and evergreen needles shelter the campsites; several sites are riverside; high mountains rise to the north and are visible from some sites; San Gorgonio Wilderness lies directly south of here; elevation 6400'.

Season, Fees & Phone: May to October; $7.00; 14 day limit; San Gorgonio Ranger District, Mentone, (909) 794-1123.

Camp Notes: This is a good campground, and a popular one, because of the riverfront location. Although some sites are close to the highway, others are a couple-hundred yards off the road. Campsites here also tend to be a bit more private than those in other nearby campgrounds due to the denser forest and low-level branches which provide better visual separation between sites.

HEART BAR
San Bernardino National Forest

Location: Southwest California east of San Bernardino.

Access: From California State Highway 38 at milepost 33 +.5 (34 miles east of Redlands, 16 miles south of Big Bear City), turn south onto a hard-surfaced road and proceed 0.25 mile to the campground, on the west (right) side of the access road.

Facilities: 94 campsites, including a number of double sites, in 2 sections; sites are small to medium in size, with nominal to fairly good separation; parking areas are paved, medium-length straight-ins; tent areas are large and acceptably level; fire rings; a limited amount of firewood may be available for gathering in the area, b-y-o is suggested; water at central faucets; vault facilities; paved driveways; gas and groceries in Angeles Oaks, 13 miles west; adequate+ supplies and services are available in the Big Bear City-Big Bear Lake area.

Activities & Attractions: Campfire circle; weekend nature walks and campfire programs may be scheduled.

Natural Features: Located in an open forest setting in the San Bernardino Mountains; campground vegetation consists of tall conifers and short grass; Onyx Summit, at 8443', is 6 miles east; campground elevation 6900'.

Season, Fees & Phone: May to October; $7.00 for a standard site, $14.00 for a double site; 14 day limit; San Gorgonio Ranger District, Mentone, (909) 794-1123.

Camp Notes: Campsites in the west section are entitled to some of the best scenic views of all sites in all the campgrounds along this highway. (Not long ago, the Forest Service invested a million buckaroos in facility renovations and aesthetic enhancements in order to offer the type of camping opportunities this location merits.) A solid forest camp.

CHINO HILLS
Chino Hills State Park

Location: Southern California west of Riverside.

Access: From California State Highway 71 (northwestbound) at a point 5.5 miles northwest of the junction of State Highways 71 & 91 west of Corona, 9 miles southeast of Pomona, jog left, then right onto Pomona-Rincon Road and travel northwest (parallel to Highway 71) for 0.9 mile; turn southwest (left) onto Soquel Canyon Parkway and proceed 1 mile, then turn left onto Elinvar Drive, go 0.2 mile, turn left onto Sapphire Drive for another 0.2 mile, then turn southwest (right) onto the park access road (gravel/dirt) and continue southwest then southeast for 3.5 miles to the campground.

Alternate Access: From State Highway 71 (southeastbound) at a point 8 miles southeast of Pomona, turn southwest (right) onto Los Serranos Avenue (Los Serranos is a continuation of Central Avenue from Chino), go 50 yards, then swing southeast (left) onto Pomona-Rincon Road, travel 0.2 mile, then turn southwest onto Soquel Canyon Road and continue as above. (Note: the park access road may be closed during and just after rainy periods.)

Facilities: Small, primitive camping area with drinking water and vault facilities; trail camps are also available.

Activities & Attractions: Over 30 miles of hiking, horse, and bike trails (some restrictions apply).

Natural Features: Located on the grass-coated, nearly treeless Chino Hills; short to medium-high grass comprises most of the vegetation, plus stands of hardwoods in some draws and pockets; elevation 1200'.

Season, Fees & Phone: Open all year, subject to weather conditions; please see Appendix for standard California state park fees and reservation information; phone c/o CDPR Chino Hills District Office, Riverside, (714) 780-6222.

Camp Notes: From a moderate distance, these smooth-to-moderately contoured hills seem to have a surface that's painted on: Kelly green in late winter and spring cycling to tawny yellow in summer and fall. Actually, these "hills" could qualify as "mountains" in just about anybody's lexicon.

LAKE PERRIS
Lake Perris State Recreation Area

Location: Southern California southeast of Riverside.

Access: From California State Highway 60 near milepost 19 (11 miles west of the junction of Highway 60 & Interstate 10 near Beaumont, 6 miles east of the junction of Highway 60 & Interstate 215 east of Riverside) take the Moreno Beach Drive Exit and travel south on Moreno Beach Drive for 3.2 miles, then southwest (right) on Via Del Lago for 1.2 miles to the Moreno (north) park entrance station; just beyond the entrance, turn southwest (right) and follow the well-marked route for 1.4 miles to the main campground entrance station.

Alternate Access: From California State Highway 215 (Escondido Freeway) in Val Verde (4 miles northwest of the city of Perris, 4 miles southeast of the junction of Highway 215 & California State Highway 60 east of Riverside), head east on Pomona Expressway for 2.3 miles; turn north (left) onto Lake Perris Drive and proceed 1.2 miles to the Perris (southwest) entrance station; continue northeast for 0.7 mile to the day use areas or for another 1.2 miles to the campground. (There are at least a dozen other possible routes to the park, but the above accesses should serve the majority of campers.)

Facilities: 431 campsites, including 264 with partial hookups; (several group camp areas and a primitive equestrian camp are also available); sites are small- to small+, with minimal to nominal separation; hookup sites are clustered in small 'parking lot' arrangements; most parking pads are paved, short straight-ins; about half of the pads will require a little additional leveling; enough space for medium to large tents in most sites; fireplaces and/or fire rings; b-y-o firewood; storage cabinets (bear boxes); water at several faucets; restrooms with showers; waste water receptacles; holding tank disposal station; paved driveways; complete supplies and services are available within 5 miles west/northwest.

Activities & Attractions: Boating; several boat launches; marina; fishing for bass, also stocked trout, catfish, bluegill, sunfish; fishing piers; designated swimming beaches; water slide; playground; hiking/biking trail (mostly paved) around the lake; hiking trails to overlook points; Regional Indian Museum; nature walks, evening campfire programs, fishing clinics and other outdoor-related activities, scheduled seasonally; large day use areas with ramadas.

Natural Features: Located on rolling, sloping terrain above the north shore of Lake Perris; campsites are very lightly to lightly shaded by scattered hardwoods and conifers on a surface of sparse grass; sandy beach; bordered by dry, boulder-strewn rolling hills and low mountains; elevation 1600'.

Season, Fees & Phone: Open all year; campsite reservations definitely recommended for weekends, spring through fall; please see Appendix for standard California state park fees and reservation information; park office (714) 657-0676.

Camp Notes: Just about all camp spots have good lake and mountain views. Alessandro Island, a massive, solitary mound, rises from the lake just offshore of the campground. Tent campers have much better sites than rv'ers here. Lake Perris has the largest developed campground in the California state park system. Another lake park with a large campground in the general vicinity is Lake Elsinore State Recreation Area, located at the northwest end of Lake Elsinore, near the city of the same name, a dozen miles southwest of Lake Perris. Recreational facilities on the state land are operated under a long-term lease by a concessionaire. Lake Elsinore SRA is located on State Highway 74, two miles southwest of 74's junction with Interstate 5.

MARION MOUNTAIN
San Bernardino National Forest

Location: South-central California southeast of Riverside.

Access: From California State Highway 243 at milepost 9 +.85 (200 yards south of the Forest Service Alandale Fire Station, 19 miles southeast of Banning, 5 miles northwest of Idyllwild) turn northeast onto a paved road and go 0.15 mile; turn left onto a sandy gravel road, and proceed 1.6 miles to the campground.

Facilities: 24 campsites in 2 loops; sites are generally small to medium-sized, with a little bit of separation; parking pads are paved or gravel, short to medium-length straight-ins; most pads will require additional leveling; medium to large, sloped tent spaces; fireplaces or barbecue grills; some firewood is available for gathering locally; water at central faucets; vault facilities; paved driveways; gas and groceries at Pine Cove, 2 miles southeast; limited+ supplies in Idyllwild; nearest source of complete supplies and services is Banning.

Activities & Attractions: Some really commanding views of the mountain tops, ridges and valleys in the San Jacinto Mountains; Marion Mountain Trail.

Natural Features: Located on a sloping flat partway up (or down) the mountain; campground vegetation is comprised of light to moderately dense, very tall pines and cedars, plus some oaks; elevation 6400'.

Season, Fees & Phone: Mid-April to October; $7.00; 14 day limit; San Jacinto Ranger District, Idyllwild, (714) 659-2117.

Camp Notes: Of the three national forest campgrounds in this area, Marion Mountain is the highest and has the best views. Although it's quite possible to shoehorn a larger trailer or motorhome into some of these sites, it seems to be more suitable for pickups, vans, and other small rigs.

Fern Basin
San Bernardino National Forest

Location: South-central California southeast of Riverside.

Access: From California State Highway 243 at milepost 9 +.85 (200 yards south of the Forest Service Alandale Fire Station, 19 miles southeast of Banning, 5 miles northwest of Idyllwild) turn northeast onto a paved road and proceed 0.15 mile; turn left onto a sandy gravel road, and go 1.1 mile; turn left again for a final 0.1 mile to the campground.

Facilities: 22 campsites; sites vary from small to large, with fair to good separation; parking pads are paved or sandy gravel, short straight-ins; additional leveling will be needed on most pads; tent areas are medium to large, but sloped; barbecue grills or fire rings; some firewood is available for gathering in the vicinity; water at central faucets; vault facilities; paved driveway; gas and groceries at Pine Cove, 2 miles southeast; limited+ supplies and services are available in Idyllwild.

Activities & Attractions: Trailhead; some views of the mountains and across a valley from the campground area.

Natural Features: Located on a forested slope in the San Jacinto Mountains; campground vegetation consists of oaks, pines and cedars, and only a small amount of low-level brush and new growth; elevation 6300.

Season, Fees & Phone: May to October; $7.00; 14 day limit; San Jacinto Ranger District, Idyllwild, (714) 659-2117.

Camp Notes: While this campground doesn't have either the tiny creek or the good views of the other two forest camps in this area, it tends to fill up a little less quickly on summer weekends. Nonetheless, it does usually fill. If you're running late on Friday afternoon, it might pay to check this one first.

Dark Canyon
San Bernardino National Forest

Location: South-central California southeast of Riverside.

Access: From California State Highway 243 at milepost 9 +.85, (200 yards south of the Forest Service Alandale Fire Station, 19 miles southeast of Banning, 5 miles northwest of Idyllwild) turn northeast onto a paved road and proceed 0.15 mile; turn left onto a sandy gravel road, and go 0.75 mi; turn left again onto another gravel road, and continue for 1.5 miles to the campground. (The road crosses a small creek just before reaching the campground.)

Facilities: 22 campsites; sites are generally small, with little separation; parking pads are paved or sandy gravel, mostly short straight-ins which will require additional leveling; tent areas vary, but are basically medium-sized and sloped; fireplaces or barbecue grills; some firewood is available for gathering in the area; water at several faucets; vault facilities; paved driveway; gas and groceries at Pine Cove, 3 miles southeast; limited+ supplies and services are available in Idyllwild.

Activities & Attractions: Seven Pines Trail; trail to Black Mountain.

Natural Features: Located on a moderate to steep slope in the San Jacinto Mountains; campground vegetation consists of large oaks and very tall conifers; a trickle of a rocky creek tumbles past the campground; elevation 5800'.

Season, Fees & Phone: Mid-April to mid-October; $7.00; 14 day limit; San Jacinto Ranger District, Idyllwild, (714) 659-2117.

Camp Notes: Signs and literature indicate that the road into the campground and the campground itself are not suitable for trailers. Most visitors concur with those sentiments. (Someone does occasionally manage to wriggle a tent trailer along the one-lane path into the campground.) Pleasant surroundings, though.

Southern California 163

STONE CREEK
Mount San Jacinto State Park

Location: South-central California southeast of Riverside.

Access: From California State Highway 243 at milepost 9 +.85, (200 yards south of the Forest Service Alandale Fire Station, 19 miles southeast of Banning, 5 miles northwest of Idyllwild), turn northeast onto a paved access road and proceed 0.2 mile to the campground.

Facilities: 50 campsites; sites are small+ to medium-sized, with fair to good separation; parking pads are gravel/dirt, short straight-ins, including several extra-wides; good-sized, but somewhat sloped, tent spots; fire rings; some firewood may be available for gathering on adjacent national forest lands, or b-y-o; water at several faucets; vault facilities; hard-surfaced driveway; gas and groceries at Pine Cove, 2 miles southeast; limited+ supplies and services are available in Idyllwild.

Activities & Attractions: Quite respectable mountain views to the east and north from the campground area.

Natural Features: Located in a lightly forested area of tall conifers, brushy hardwoods, and lower level mountain shrubbery in the San Jacinto Mountains; elevation 6100'.

Season, Fees & Phone: Principal season is April to November; may be available at other times, subject to weather conditions; please see Appendix for standard California state park fees and reservation information; park office (714) 659-2607.

Camp Notes: There are some really good to excellent campsites here. This is one of the comparatively few state park campgrounds that normally (emphasis on *normally*) isn't booked solid every weekend. Overall, the sites here are touch nicer than those in the local national forest campgrounds.

Southern California 164

IDYLLWILD
Mount San Jacinto State Park

Location: South-central California southeast of Riverside.

Access: From California State Highway 243 at milepost 5 (on the north edge of the community of Idyllwild, 24 miles southeast of Banning), turn west, go past the ranger station, and into the campground.

Facilities: 33 campsites; (4 trail camps in the State Wilderness are also available, by reservation only); sites are small+ to medium-sized, with some separation provided by vegetation; parking pads are sand/dirt, mostly short straight-ins, many are extra wide; additional leveling will probably be required in most sites; medium to large tent areas, about half are fairly level; fire rings; some firewood may be available for gathering on nearby national forest lands, or b-y-o; water at several faucets; restrooms with showers; limited+ supplies and services are available within walking distance in Idyllwild.

Activities & Attractions: Campfire center for evening programs in summer; trails into the San Jacinto Wilderness; cross-country skiing.

Natural Features: Located near the heart of the high, rugged, San Jacinto Mountains; vegetation consists of tall conifers, large oaks, and some low-level, bushy hardwoods; 10,800' San Jacinto Peak rises a half-dozen miles north of here; elevation 5400'.

Season, Fees & Phone: Open all year; please see Appendix for standard California state park fees and reservation information; park office (714) 659-2607.

Camp Notes: This park has somewhat of a dual personality: in summer, it's popular with Southern Californians who find it's a convenient place to come to escape the sizzle in the lowlands; and snow-

189

campers and x-c skiers find it's a convenient place to escape the midwinter blahs. This is also known as Headquarters Campground.

IDYLLWILD
Riverside County Park

Location: South-central California southeast of Riverside.

Access: From California State Highway 243 at milepost 4 +.3 (on the south side of the community of Idyllwild, 24 miles southeast of Banning), turn west onto Riverside County Playground Road (not very well marked), and proceed west 0.3 mile (after the stop sign, continue past the intersection of Playground and Pinecrest) to the campground; **Alternate Access:** From the north edge of Idyllwild, turn west onto Maranatha Drive, then immediately left onto Pinecrest, and proceed 0.4 mile to Playground Road; turn right onto Playground Road and continue for 0.2 mile to the campground entrance.

Facilities: 96 campsites; sites are generally small, with minimal separation; parking pads are sandy, mostly short to medium-length straight-ins, which probably will require additional leveling; small to medium-sized, quite sloped tent areas; fireplaces or fire rings at each site; firewood is usually for sale, b-y-o is recommended; water at several faucets; restrooms; coin-op showers; paved or sandy gravel driveways; limited+ supplies and services are within walking distance in Idyllwild;

Activities & Attractions: Trail to the visitor center; 2-hour loop trail; amphitheater.

Natural Features: Located in a moderately dense forest of tall conifers and a few hardwoods, at the edge of a deep, narrow ravine; most sites are situated along a hillside; elevation 5400'.

Season, Fees & Phone: Open all year, subject to weather conditions, with limited services in winter; $10.00; 14 day limit; reservations accepted May to September, contact Riverside County Parks Department (714) 787-2553.

Camp Notes: The Idyllwild area might remind you of certain places in the Sierra, just not quite as busy.

HURKEY CREEK
Riverside County Regional Park

Location: South-central California southeast of Riverside.

Access: From California State Highway 74 at milepost 62 +.7 (3.4 miles southeast of the junction of State Highways 74 & 243 southeast of Idyllwild, 33 miles northeast of Palm Desert), turn east onto a paved access road and proceed 0.1 mile to the campground.

Facilities: 105 campsites, including 9 walk-ins; sites are medium-sized, perhaps slightly longer (deeper) than typical park sites; parking pads are sandy/dirt, mostly medium-length straight-ins; many pads will require additional leveling; large, sandy earth tent areas; fire rings; b-y-o firewood is recommended; water at several faucets; restrooms with coin-op showers; paved driveways; limited+ supplies in Idyllwild, 8 miles northwest; nearest sources of complete supplies and services are Banning or Palm Desert, each about 33 miles.

Activities & Attractions: Foot trails, including a nature trail; lots of opportunities for just strolling across the grassy flat; fishing and boating at Lake Hemet, 1 mile south.

Natural Features: Located on a large, light to moderately forested, gently sloping flat in Fern Valley; campground vegetation consists of tall pines, some young pines, and a grassy forest floor of; an intermittent stream flows past he camp area; elevation 4400'.

Season, Fees & Phone: Open all year; $10.00; 14 day limit; reservations accepted May to September, and suggested for summer weekends, contact Riverside County Parks Department (714) 787-2553.

Camp Notes: Some literature and maps spell the name of this campground, and it's associated creek, Herkey. The people in the Idyllwild area seem to be making a concerted effort to promote and develop this region's scenic and recreational resources.

PINYON FLATS
San Bernardino National Forest

Location: South-central California south of Palm Springs.

Access: From California State Highway 74 at milepost 80 +.5 (0.5 mile west of Riverside County Fire Station #30, 15 miles south of Palm Desert, 26 miles southeast of Idyllwild), turn north onto Pinyon Drive and proceed 0.2 mile to the campground, on the west (left) side of the road. (Note that the curving highway follows basically an east-west line in this section; also note that the mileposts may be a little inconsistent in their placement.)

Facilities: 19 campsites; sites are generally large and level, with good separation; parking pads are gravel/dirt, medium to long straight-ins; large, sandy or grassy tent areas; barbecue grills; b-y-o firewood; water at several faucets; vault facilities; complete supplies and services are available in Palm Desert.

Activities & Attractions: High desert atmosphere; Bighorn Sheep Overlook on Highway 74, 2 miles east at milepost 82 +.3, from which desert bighorn can often be viewed.

Natural Features: Located on a flat in the high desert near the southeast base of the San Jacinto Mountains; campground vegetation consists of dry grass, pinyon pines, yuccas, century plants and junipers, and a wide assortment of other small, bushy plants; most sites have some shelter/shade; the lofty San Jacinto Mountains stand to the west, the Santa Rosa Mountains are to the south; elevation 4000'.

Season, Fees & Phone: Open all year; $7.00; 14 day limit; San Jacinto Ranger District, Idyllwild, (714) 659-2117.

Camp Notes: Actually, this is perhaps the highest of the high desert--from here on west along this highway the landscape becomes considerably more forested. Northerly, the elevation drops very rapidly-- nearly 4000' in the 15 miles to Palm Desert. It's surprisingly green and mild around here, even in midsummer. Pleasant place.

BLACK ROCK CANYON
Joshua Tree National Monument

Location: South-central California east of San Bernardino.

Access: From the junction of California State Highways 62 & 247 in the city of Yucca Valley, (21 miles north of Interstate 10, 54 miles, as the crow flies, due east of San Bernardino), turn south onto Joshua Lane; proceed south, then east, for 4.5 miles to a "T" intersection at San Marino Drive; turn right (south again) and go a final 0.35 mile (following a short jog in the road) to the campground.

Facilities: 100 campsites in a complex of loops; sites are small to medium-sized, with fair to good separation; parking pads are gravel, short to medium-length straight-ins, pads are level to slightly sloped; adequate space for a large tent in most sites; fire rings; b-y-o firewood; water at several faucets; restrooms; holding tank disposal station; paved/gravel driveways; ranger station; complete supplies and services are available in Yucca Valley.

Activities & Attractions: Trails to Black Rock Spring (1.5 miles), Eureka Peak (5 miles), and other, more distant, points in the park; equestrian facilities.

Natural Features: Located on a gentle slope at the mouth of Black Rock Canyon near the northwest end of the Little San Bernardino Mountains; the campground is situated within a veritable forest of Joshua trees, junipers, cholla cactus, and desert bushes; elevation 4000'.

Season, Fees & Phone: November to April; $7.00; 14 day limit; park headquarters, Twentynine Palms, (619) 367-7511.

Camp Notes: Joshua trees are interesting in that each has its own individual shape or character. Look around, and you'll rarely, if ever, find two adult trees that are alike. This campground contains a classic assortment of high desert plant life. It almost certainly ranks near the top of the tally of desert campgrounds.

INDIAN COVE
Joshua Tree National Monument

Location: South-central California east of San Bernardino.

Access: From California State Highway 62 at milepost 27 +.4 (6 miles west of Twentynine Palms, 15 miles east of the junction of State Highways 62 & 247 at Yucca Valley), turn south onto Indian Cove Road (paved), and proceed 3.2 miles (continuing past the ranger station) to the campground.

Facilities: 110 campsites in 2 loops; (a reservable) group camp is also available); sites vary in size, but many are large and well separated; parking pads are sandy, short to medium-length straight-ins and pull-offs; some pads will require additional leveling; tent areas are medium to large, and many are acceptably level; fire rings; b-y-o firewood; water is available at the ranger station, 1.8 miles north; vault facilities; paved driveways; adequate supplies and services are available in Twentynine Palms.

Activities & Attractions: Unique setting; campfire circle; foot trail; park visitor center in Twentynine Palms.

Natural Features: Located among a large cluster of interestingly eroded rock formations at the base of the hills along the northern edge of Joshua Tree National Monument; many sites are situated in their own little rock alcoves; campground vegetation consists of a sparse population of Joshua trees and small desert plants; elevation 3200'.

Season, Fees & Phone: Open all year; $7.00; 14 day limit in winter, 30 day limit in summer; park headquarters, Twentynine Palms, (619) 367-7511.

Camp Notes: In addition to being in a really distinctive setting, the campground offers some really terrific vistas out across a wide valley to the north. Indian Cove is on the north edge of the national monument's Wonderland of Rocks. Summer temps throughout the monument can be expected to be well into the 100's by day and may cool into the low 70's at night.

JUMBO ROCKS
Joshua Tree National Monument

Location: South-central California between Riverside and Blythe

Access: From the park's main north-south highway (called Pinto Basin Road by some sources) at a major junction 8.5 miles south of the park's visitor center near Twentynine Palms and 32 miles north of the Mecca/Twentynine Palms Exit on Interstate 10, turn west onto a paved park road (listed as Quail Springs Road on some maps); proceed 3.8 miles, then turn south (left) for 0.2 mile to the campground. **Alternate Access:** From California State Highway 62 in the town of Joshua Tree (near the west edge of Twentynine Palms), head south/southeast on Park Boulevard (which soon becomes Quail Springs Road) for 22 miles (passing Hidden Valley, Ryan and Sheep Pass Campgrounds along the way) to the Jumbo Rocks Campground turnoff; turn south and continue as above.

Facilities: 128 campsites; sites are small and closely spaced; parking surfaces are sandy, short straight-ins or pull-offs; small to medium-sized areas for tents; fire rings; b-y-o firewood; no drinking water; vault facilities; sandy driveways; adequate supplies and services are available in Twentynine Palms.

Activities & Attractions: Scenic drives; rock climbing; hiking.

Natural Features: Located amongst a massive rock formation on the high desert east of the Little San Bernardino Mountains; vegetation consists of Joshua trees and small desert plants; elevation 4400'.

Season, Fees & Phone: Open all year; $7.00; 14 day limit in winter, 30 day limit in summer; park headquarters, Twentynine Palms, (619) 367-7511.

Camp Notes: The campground is named for the humungous heap of stones among which the campsites are sequestered. Jumbo Rocks is the largest of a cluster of a half dozen camps in the central park area. The others: Belle, Hidden Valley, Ryan, Sheep Pass, and White Tank, are within 7 miles east or west of Jumbo Rocks and offer a total of some 130 sites. All have similar facilities in essentially comparable surroundings. (According to reliable local reports, several of these campgrounds are solidly in the Land of the Site Savers. Rock climbers, hikers and others eager to help their fellow recreationers often manage to pass good campsites along to an unbroken succession of friends and acquaintances over an extended period.)

COTTONWOOD
Joshua Tree National Monument

Location: South-central California between Riverside and Blythe.

Access: From the park's main north-south highway (called Cottonwood Springs Road in this section), at a point a few yards south of the Cottonwood Visitor Center (7 miles north of the Mecca/Twentynine Palms Exit on Interstate 10, 39 miles south of Twentynine Palms), turn east onto the paved campground access road; continue for 0.7 mile to the campground.

Facilities: 62 campsites in 2 loops; (a reservable group camp is also available); sites are small, with minimal to nominal separation; parking pads are paved, short to medium-length straight-ins, or narrow, medium-length pull-offs; tent areas are medium to large, level, with a sandy base; fireplaces; b-y-o firewood; water at central faucets; restrooms; holding tank disposal station; paved driveways; ranger station; gas and minimal supplies at Chiriaco Summit, 7 miles south, then 4 miles east on I-10; adequate supplies and services are available in Indio, 25 miles west.

Activities & Attractions: Visitor center; hiking trails; 4wd trail to Pinkham Canyon; amphitheater.

Natural Features: Located on a high desert plain, with dry, high mountains to the east and to the distant west, and low hills directly south of the campground; a profusion of low-level, brushy plants, (but no Joshua trees) occupy the campground area; elevation 3000'.

Season, Fees & Phone: Open all year; $7.00; 14 day limit in winter, 30 day limit in summer; park headquarters, Twentynine Palms, (619) 367-7511.

Camp Notes: Oddly enough, the Joshua tree is botanically classified as a distant relative of the lily and not as a tree at all. It is actually a large yucca, and it does bloom in spring. The armed plant supposedly was named by the early Mormons to whom its outstretched extremities fancifully resembled the biblical character Joshua pointing toward the Promised Land. Cottonwood Campground looks like an excellent place for tent camping. This region seems to be a favorite of European visitors (German, Dutch, Scandinavian), even in summer. The 'word' here is that arrival on or before Thursday is practically mandatory on winter weekends.

LAKE CAHUILLA
Riverside County Park

Location: South-central California south of Indio.

Access: From the intersection of California State Highway 86 & 58th Avenue (6 miles south of midtown Indio, 3 miles south of Coachella and 10 miles northwest of the junction of State Highways 86 & 195), turn west onto 58th Avenue and travel 5.7 miles to the park. (A less-straightforward access is from California State Highway 111 on the west end of Indio, then south via Jefferson Street along a zigzag route.)

Facilities: 140 campsites, including 60 with partial hookups; sites are small, level, and closely spaced, with some visual separation; parking pads are gravel, short to medium-length straight-ins or pull-throughs; small to medium sized sandy gravel or sparse grass tent areas; water at faucets throughout; restrooms with showers; holding tank disposal station; security fence; paved driveway; adequate supplies and services are available in Indio.

Activities & Attractions: Fishing for striped bass, bluegill, catfish, plus stocked trout in winter; interpretive trail.

Natural Features: Located on the south shore of 135-acre Lake Cahuilla on the southwest edge of the Coachella Valley; campground vegetation consists of some grass, and planted hardwoods which provide a reasonable amount of shelter/shade, and a modicum of separation between campsites; long, gravel/earth beach around the lakeshore; stark, barren, desert mountains lie directly west and south, and north, across the valley; sea level.

Season, Fees & Phone: Open all year; $7.00 for a standard (primitive) site, $12.00 for a partial hookup site; 14 day limit; reservations recommended in winter, contact Riverside County Parks Department (714) 787-2553; park office (619) 564-4712.

Camp Notes: It may very well be open for business in summer, but, gosh, is it *HOT*. They seem to be making a real effort to turn this park into a camper's oasis.

HEADQUARTERS
Salton Sea State Recreation Area

Location: Southeast California between Indio and El Centro.

Access: From California State Highway 111 at milepost 7 +.6 (21 miles southeast of Indio, 67 miles northwest of El Centro) turn west, go 0.1 mile to the park entrance station, then south (left) for 0.4 mile to the campground.

Facilities: 40 campsites, including 15 with full hookups, in 2 areas; hookup sites are medium-sized, parallel pull-throughs in a paved, semi-parking lot arrangement; standard sites are in a separate section, with short, straight-in parking pads and large, sandy tent spots; standard sites have ramadas (sun shelters); all sites are level; fire rings; b-y-o firewood; water at hookup sites and at central faucets; restrooms with showers; holding tank disposal station; limited supplies and services are available in Mecca, 11 miles north.

Activities & Attractions: Boating; boat launch, dock, and boat wash; fishing for sargo, tilapia, gulf croaker, and orangemouth corvina; self-guided nature trail; visitor center.

Natural Features: Located on the northeast shore of the Salton Sea; a few palm trees and hardwoods are planted in the separators between the hookup sites; a fair amount of shade/shelter is provided by planted hardwoods in the standard campsite section; the west shore of the sea is lined by high and dry desert mountains; annual rainfall is 2.5 inches; elevation 220' below sea level.

Season, Fees & Phone: Open all year; please see Appendix for standard California state park fees and reservation information; park office (619) 393-3052 or 393-3059.

Camp Notes: Locals often refer to the Salton Sea as the "ocean", since it is an inland sea, of sorts. Millennia ago, the sink (basin) in which it lies was part of the Gulf of California. During the spring floods of 1905, a levee on a Colorado River canal burst and river water flooded the Salton Sink. During the two years it took to bring the rampaging waters under control a new 700-square mile inland sea was formed. Like several other inland oceans, including the Great Salt Lake, the Salton Sea has no outlet. Depending upon the season, the specific location, and your own sense of smell, you may faintly detect (or be clobbered by) the briny fragrance of this region.

MECCA BEACH
Salton Sea State Recreation Area

Location: Southeast California between Indio and El Centro.

Access: From California State Highway 111 at milepost 6 +.2 (23 miles southeast of Indio, 65 miles northwest of El Centro), turn west, go 0.1 mile to the entrance station, then 0.2 mile farther to the campground.

Facilities: 108 campsites; sites are small, level, with virtually no separation, in what is basically a large parking lot; parking slots are paved, short straight-ins; small, gravel, table and tent area behind each site; fire rings; b-y-o firewood; water at central faucets; restrooms with showers; holding tank disposal station; limited supplies in Mecca, 12 miles north; adequate supplies and services are available in Indio.

Activities & Attractions: Boating; boat launch, dock, and boat wash accessible from 1.5 miles north, near park headquarters; fishing; visitor center near park headquarters.

Natural Features: Located on the northeast shore of the Salton Sea; the table/tent areas in the campground are somewhat shaded by small hardwoods and a few palm trees; the west shore of the sea is bordered by the Santa Rosa Mountains; the Chocolate Mountains serve as the backdrop for the east shore; some peaks reach to 10,000'; elevation 220' below sea level.

Season, Fees & Phone: Open all year; please see Appendix for standard California state park fees and reservation information; park office (619) 393-3052 or 393-3059.

Camp Notes: Great fishing for sargo, tilapia, gulf croaker, and the ever-elusive orangemouth corvina is what brings most people to the Salton Sea. Depending upon which of the seagoing transplants you're going after, you'll need jigs, spoons, spinners, live bait or canned corn. (Whole kernel corn, not the creamed variety; and if the fish aren't cooperating, you can always dine on the corn. Ed.) Mecca Beach, and Headquarters next door, are the only two developed campgrounds in the park. Three other areas south of Mecca can provide undeveloped ("beach") camping for several hundred campers for several bucks a night.

MAYFLOWER
Riverside County Regional Park

Location: Southeast California along the California-Arizona border north of Blythe.

Access: From U.S. Highway 95 at milepost 3.5 (3.5 miles north of the Intake Boulevard Exit on Interstate 10 on the east end of Blythe, and many miles south of nowhere), turn east onto 6th Avenue and proceed 2.4 miles; turn north (left) and continue for another 0.6 mile to the campground.

Facilities: 177 campsites, including 152 with electrical hookups, in 3 sections; the standard section contains 25 average-sized, sites with tables and barbecue grills, a few with ramadas (sun shelters); the hookup sites are in a parking lot arrangement; all sites are essentially level, with very little separation; by-o firewood; water at faucets throughout; restrooms with showers; paved driveway; holding tank disposal station; adequate to complete supplies and services are available in Blythe.

Activities & Attractions: Boating; large, paved, boat launch; fishing; day use area.

Natural Features: Located on a large, grassy flat along the west bank of the Colorado River; the standard section has watered lawns, and large hardwoods that provide a substantial amount of shade/shelter; the remainder of the campground has watered lawns planted with a few young hardwoods; elevation 250'.

Season, Fees & Phone: Open all year; $10.00 for a standard site. $12.00 for a partial hookup site; monthly rates are available in winter; 14 day limit April-October; reservations recommended in winter, contact Riverside County Parks Department (714) 787-2553.

Camp Notes: The facilities here are quite simple, but this is a pleasantly green park that contrasts sharply with the surrounding desert-mountain terrain. The campground is something of a haven for river rats in summer, since it has fairly good put-in/take-out facilities. Some of the sites have river views.

BORREGO PALM CANYON
Anza-Borrego Desert State Park

Location: Southwest California northeast of San Diego.

Access: From San Diego County Highway S22 at milepost 17 +.5, at the intersection of Palm Canyon Drive and Montezuma Valley Road, (1.4 miles west of the town circle, called "Christmas Circle", in the city of Borrego Springs) proceed 0.2 mile west on the park access road; turn north onto the campground access road and continue for 1 mile to the campground entrance station. (Note: From the west boundary of the park for 11 miles down to Borrego Palm Canyon, County Highway S22 is steep and twisty, so if you're driving something--or someone--which doesn't take well to curves and grades, a better route might be via County Highway S3 over Yaqui Pass; but the vast views from the highwayside pull-outs along S22 are incredible.)

Facilities: 117 campsites, including 52 with full hookups, in 3 sections; (an equestrian camp and a number of group camps are also available, by reservation); sites are generally medium-sized, with fair to fairly good separation; hookup sites tend to be larger; parking pads are paved, level, long pull-throughs in the hookup section; parking pads in the tent section are gravel/earth and tend to be slightly sloped; adequate space for large tents; ramadas (sun shelters) in many of the tent sites; fire rings; b-y-o firewood; water in the hookup units and at central faucets; restrooms with showers; paved driveways; limited+ to adequate supplies and services are available in Borrego Springs.

Activities & Attractions: Visitor center with a large botanical garden and interpretive exhibits and slide programs about desert vegetation, wildlife and geology; Borrego Palm Canyon Nature Trail (an excellent guide pamphlet is available); hiking trails; campfire center.

Natural Features: Located at the east edge of the San Ysidro Mountains overlooking the vast Borrego Valley to the east; campground vegetation includes large, desert bushes and a few palms; the park is highly regarded for its spectacular early spring wildflower bloom; elevation 1200'.

Season, Fees & Phone: Open all year; please see Appendix for standard California state park fees and reservation information; park office (619) 767-4684 or (619) 767-5311.

Camp Notes: Try to plan your itinerary so the visitor center is one of your first stops after settling-in at your campsite. The visitor center is an underground operation. (Well it really *is*--the earth berming helps to keep the place cool.) Borrego Palm Canyon is the largest and most highly developed area in the park. There are some tremendous daytime and nighttime vistas of the valley from here. Some of the palms look like characters from Sesame Street.

TAMARISK GROVE
Anza-Borrego Desert State Park

Location: Southwest California northeast of San Diego.

Access: From San Diego County Highway S3 at a point 0.3 mile northeast of the junction of Highway S3 with California State Highway 78, 18 miles northeast of Julian and 12 miles south of Borrego Springs, turn south into the campground.

Facilities: 27 campsites; (small, primitive camp areas are available nearby at Yaqui Well, 0.3 mile southwest, and just north of the summit of Yaqui Pass, 2 miles northeast) sites about average in size, level, with fair to fairly good separation; parking pads are paved, short, but extra wide straight-ins; adequate space for a medium to large tent in most sites; ramadas (sun shelters) for all sites; fire rings; b-y-o firewood; water at central faucets; restrooms with showers; paved driveway; limited+ to adequate supplies and services are available in Borrego Springs.

Activities & Attractions: Cactus Loop Trail; campfire center; interpretive garden; small visitor center/ranger station.

Natural Features: Located in a desert canyon flanked by Pinyon Ridge to the west and Yaqui Ridge to the east; most campsites are fairly well shaded/sheltered by huge Tamarisk trees; other local vegetation consists of a good cross-section of typical desert plants; elevation 1400'.

Season, Fees & Phone: Open all year; reservations available October to May, and advised for holidays and weekends; please see Appendix for standard California state park fees and reservation information; park office (619) 767-4684 or (619) 767-5311.

Camp Notes: Anza-Borrego's 600,000 acres make it the largest state park in the contiguous United States. (It's almost the size of Rhode Island.) Although a lot of people may not think so, it can even be thoroughly enjoyed in summer, provided you bring your sense of adventure (and, of course, your standard complement of hot-weather supplies as well). While summer camping in the desert isn't for everyone, you might consider doing it at least once. (There won't be any crowds.)

VALLECITO
San Diego County Park

Location: Southwest corner of California northeast of San Diego.

Access: From San Diego County Highway S2 at milepost 34 +.8 (30 miles north of Ocotillo, 18 miles south of the junction of Highway S2 & California State Highway 78 west of Julian), turn south into the campground.

Facilities: 44 campsites in 2 loops; sites are generally quite spacious, level, with fair to good separation; parking pads have a sandy gravel surface, and are medium to long straight-ins, pull-offs or pull-throughs; large, good to excellent tent spots; fire rings, plus barbecue grills; b-y-o firewood; water at faucets throughout; restrooms; gravel driveways; camper supplies and gas at a small store near Aqua Caliente County Park, 3.5 miles southeast; gas and groceries in Julian; limited supplies and services are available in Ocotillo.

Activities & Attractions: Site of the Vallecito stage station; reconstruction of the Butterfield station building; playground.

Natural Features: Located on a desert flat with medium-height, full, desert shade trees throughout the campground; the Vallecito Mountains lie to the north and the Tierra Blanca Mountains are to the south; summer average daytime high temps typically are above 100° F; elevation 1500'.

Season, Fees & Phone: October to June, but may also be open during the summer; $7.00 for a site, $1.00 for a dog; discounts available for weekday use by disabled persons and senior citizens; 14 day limit; San Diego County Parks Department, San Diego, (619) 565-5928.

Camp Notes: This is a really attractive desert campground. There's a surprising amount of greenery in here. Certainly worth checking out.

AQUA CALIENTE SPRINGS
San Diego County Park

Location: Southwest corner of California northeast of San Diego.

Access: From San Diego County Highway S2 at milepost 38 +.3 (26 miles north of Ocotillo, 21 miles south of the junction of Highway S2 & California State Highway 78 west of Julian), turn south onto Aqua Caliente Hot Springs Road (paved), and proceed 0.4 mile to the campground.

Facilities: 126 campsites, including many with partial or full hookups, in 2 sections; (group camping is also available); sites are medium-sized, with nominal to fair visual separation; parking pads are sandy gravel, fairly level, medium-length straight-ins; adequate space for tents in most sites; fire rings, plus a barbecue grills; b-y-o firewood; water at faucets throughout; central restrooms; paved driveways; gas and camper supplies at a nearby store; gas and groceries in Julian; limited supplies and services are available in Ocotillo.

Activities & Attractions: Very popular hot springs and mineral pools; bathhouse; recreation building; numerous trails and scenic views within surrounding Anza-Borrego Desert State Park.

Natural Features: Located at the foot of the Tierra Blanca Mountains in the Anza-Borrego desert area; some sites are on open hilltop, others are on a sloping flat among small to medium-height bushes and trees which provide some shelter/shade; Aqua Caliente Hot Springs are a few yards from the camping area; elevation 800.

Season, Fees & Phone: October to May; $8.00 for a standard site, $11.00 for a partial-hookup site, $12.00 for a full-hookup site; 14 day limit; reservations recommended for holiday weekends, contact San Diego County Parks Department, San Diego, at (619) 565-3600; for general information (619) 565-5928.

Camp Notes: Four natural springs--one cool and fresh, the others warm and sulphurous--are the center of attention here. People from all over come to soak up some warmth and minerals in the reportedly therapeutic hot springs.

Bow Willow
Anza-Borrego Desert State Park

Location: South-central California northeast of San Diego.

Access: From San Diego County Highway S2 at milepost 48.3 (14 miles northwest of the Ocotillo Exit on Interstate 8, 31 miles southeast of the junction of Highway S2 & California State Highway 78) turn south onto a gravel access road and proceed 1.5 miles to the campground.

Facilities: 15 campsites; sites are medium-sized, somewhat sloped, with minimal separation; parking pads are medium-length, sloped, with a sandy gravel surface; tent areas are fairly large, with a sandy base, best for free-standing tents, or tents with sand anchors; ramadas (sun shelters) for most sites; no fires allowed; limited water at a central faucet, for drinking and cooking only; vault facilities; sandy gravel driveway; gas and groceries during the winter at a small store 10 miles northwest on S2 near Aqua Caliente Park; limited supplies in Ocotillo.

Activities & Attractions: A half-dozen foot trails lead off from the campground into the hills and mountains; desert flora and fauna exhibit; Carrizo Badlands Overlook on Highway S2, 3 miles southeast.

Natural Features: Located on a sandy slope at the base of a rocky hillside near the southern boundary of the state park; local vegetation consists of an extensive variety of typical desert plants; barren mountains lie in most directions, particularly northeast across the badlands; elevation 1000'.

Season, Fees & Phone: Principal season is October to May, available for limited use remainder of the year; please see Appendix for standard California state park fees; park office (619) 767-4684 or (619) 767-5311.

Camp Notes: This camp has a nice, simple, natural ambience about it. Another state park primitive camping area (dry camp), Mountain Palm Springs, is located 1.2 miles northwest of here, and a half mile west of the highway on a sandy track.

Wiest Lake
Imperial County Park

Location: Southeast corner of California north of El Centro.

Access: From the junction of California State Highway 111 & Imperial County Road S26 (Rutherford Road) at a point 5 miles north of Brawley, 5 miles south of Calipatria, proceed east on Rutherford Road; for 2.2 miles to Dietrich Road (just at the west end of the Alamo River Bridge), then turn south into the park and the campground.

Facilities: 38 campsites, including some with electrical hookups, in several groups; sites are small, and vary from level to slightly sloped; parking pads are gravel, short to medium-length straight-ins; some nice, medium-sized tent areas; barbecue grills in some sites; b-y-o firewood; water at faucets throughout; restrooms with showers; gravel driveways; limited supplies in Brawley; complete supplies and services are available in El Centro.

Activities & Attractions: Fishing for bass, bluegill, catfish; limited boating; small boat launch; day use area.

Natural Features: Located on the east and south shore of small, shallow Wiest Lake in the Imperial Valley; some campsites are in the open, others are sheltered by large hardwoods; some sites have grassy areas; the stark Chocolate Mountains stand to the northeast, and the southern tip of the Salton Sea lies several miles northwest; elevation 100' below sea level.

Season, Fees & Phone: Open all year; $7.00 for a standard site, $10.00 for an electrical hookup site; Imperial County Parks and Recreation Department, El Centro, (619) 339-4384 or park manager (619) 344-3712.

Camp Notes: By all accounts, this is just about the only bona fide public camping area in the agricultural phenomenon known as the Imperial Valley. According to local sources, there's almost always a camp spot to be had here, except for a few holiday weekends.

Southern California 182

HOT SPRING
Long Term Visitor Area/BLM

Location: Southeast corner of California east of El Centro.

Access: From Interstate 8 near milepost 53 (5 miles east of Holtville, 18 miles east of El Centro, 44 miles west of Yuma), take the easternmost exit for Holtville to the north side of the Interstate; proceed east (right) on a north frontage road (Evan Hewes Highway) for 1 mile; turn north (left) and go 0.1 mile to the camping area.

Facilities: A virtually unlimited number of level spaces in which to park a self-contained recreation vehicle on the desert sand; holding tank disposal station; limited+ supplies and services are available in Holtville; complete supplies and services are available in El Centro.

Activities & Attractions: Economical, months-long, winter camping opportunities.

Natural Features: Located on a desert plain in the Imperial Valley on the Mojave Desert; vegetation consists of the standard spectrum of desert plants and brush; the Algodones Dunes (also known as the Sand Hills) are a few miles to the east; the Chocolate Mountains, an extensive range of desert peaks, rise farther north and northeast; harsh summers, with high temps that commonly approach 120° F; temperate winters; elevation 50' below sea level.

Season, Fees & Phone: Available all year; principal season of use is October to April; $50.00 for a 7-month permit (required for overnight camping between September 15 and April 15); 7 month limit; Bureau of Land Management California Desert District Office, Riverside, (714) 697-5200.

Camp Notes: This is one of four LTVA's on public lands along or near I-8 in the Mojave Desert. The others--Tamarisk, Dunes Vista and Pilot Knob--are east of here and farther from commerce. The LTVA's were organized by the BLM to offer elementary, no-frills, secure camping opportunities in established zones. The areas are used principally by retirees looking for an economical spot to anchor an rv that's close to supplies and services during the winter months. This LTVA is situated just outside the southeast edge of the Imperial Valley's extensive metropolitan area, between a power plant and the freeway. It's "just off the map", so to speak. The local terrain is as flat as a pancake griddle and, in summer, twice as hot. But it's the mild winter temperatures that draw as many as several hundred campers to each of these convenient, cheap locations.

Southern California 183

PICACHO
Picacho State Recreation Area

Location: Southeast California north of Yuma, Arizona.

Access: From Interstate 8 at the Winterhaven/4th Avenue Exit on the *east* edge of Winterhaven, (the easternmost exit in California, 1 mile west of Yuma), drive northwest on a local road for 0.3 mile; swing east (a sharp right) onto Picacho Road/Imperial County Road S24 (paved) and proceed east for 0.3 mile, pass under the railroad tracks, and head north out of town; after 3.5 miles, S24 takes off to the east, but continue north on Picacho Road for another 0.6 mile, then the pavement ends and the trip begins; press on in a generally northerly direction along a gravel/dirt/sand/dust road; (soon you'll zigzag across a canal, pass the city dump, drive under some high-voltage power lines, then bear slightly right at a fork, and that's the last evidence of civilization you'll probably encounter); keep heading northwest toward and then past a prominent group of peaks for another 19.5 miles to the park and the campground.

Facilities: 50 campsites; (2 group camps, 1 of them for boat-in use, plus 2 individual boat-in camps, are also available; group camps are reservable); sites are small, with nominal separation; parking pads are gravel straight-ins; adequate space for tents; fire rings; b-y-o firewood; water at faucets; vault facilities; showers; gravel driveways; gas and groceries+ in Winterhaven; complete supplies and services are available in Yuma.

Activities & Attractions: Boating (more than 50 miles of open river are accessible from here); boat launch; fishing; Picacho Mills Historic Trail.

Natural Features: Located along the west bank of the Colorado River in the Mojave Desert; the Chocolate Mountains and Picacho Peak, a 2000-foot volcanic 'plug', dominate the landscape; several backwater lakes lie on both sides of the river; some riverside and lakeshore areas are lined with canes, reeds and stands of Tamarisk; (mosquitos can be quite bothersome in spring and early summer); elevation 200'.

Season, Fees & Phone: Open all year; please see Appendix for standard California state park fees; phone c/o CDPR Picacho District Office, Winterhaven, (619) 339-5110.

Camp Notes: This isn't just a trip--it's a genuine adventure. Note that, although some maps depict other roads and jeep trails in the region, the access described above is really the *only* way to get into this place without a boat or a 'copter--unless you can get the *Enterprise* to beam you in.

IMPERIAL DAM
Long Term Visitor Area/BLM

Location: Southeast corner of California north of Yuma, Arizona.

Access: From U.S. Highway 95 at milepost 44 +.1 (20 miles north of Yuma, 60 miles south of the junction of U.S. 95 and Interstate 10), turn northwest onto Imperial Road, pass between a pair of artillery pieces, and travel 7.4 miles through the U.S. Army Yuma Proving Grounds, to Senator Wash Road; turn north (right) onto Senator Wash Road, and turn west (left) into any of six camping areas.

Facilities: A virtually unlimited number of level spaces in which to park a self-contained recreation vehicle on the desert sand; drinking water; vault facilities in some areas; holding tank disposal station; nearest sources of complete supplies and services are in Yuma.

Activities & Attractions: Low-cost camping; fishing and boating on nearby impoundments; Imperial Dam.

Natural Features: Located on a valley plain near the west bank of the Colorado River in the Mojave Desert; vegetation consists of an assortment of common desert plants and brush; the valley is flanked by the Chocolate Mountains to the west and the rugged Castle Dome Mountains to the east; winter weather is pleasantly desert-mild; summer highs are typically in the range of 100° F to 120° F, with some local humidity courtesy of Imperial Dam; elevation 200'.

Season, Fees & Phone: Available all year; principal season of use is October to April; $50.00 for a 7-month permit (required for overnight camping between September 15 and April 15); 7 month limit; Bureau of Land Management Yuma District Office (602) 726-6300.

Camp Notes: Like other LTVA's (see Hot Spring LTVA in this volume, also La Posa LTVA in *Volume IV Desert Southwest* of this series), Imperial Dam offers bargain-basement winter camping. (Since this is the desert, perhaps we should say they offer "rock-bottom prices".) A casual tourist who unknowingly encountered an LTVA during the summer 'off season' might at first believe it to be the remains of an ancient Indian culture, or perhaps the remnants of an impromptu desert subdivision that never got off the ground. If you shun posh rv parks carpeted with astro turf and decorated with plastic palms, and instead prefer camping served *au naturel* with plenty of company, this might be the place for you.

SQUAW LAKE
Public Lands/BLM Recreation Site

Location: Southeast corner of California north of Yuma, Arizona.

Access: From U.S. Highway 95 at milepost 44 +.1 (20 miles north of Yuma, 60 miles south of the junction of U.S. 95 and Interstate 10), turn northwest onto Imperial Road, pass between a pair of artillery pieces, and continue 7.4 miles through the U.S. Army Yuma Proving Grounds, to Senator Wash Road; turn north onto Senator Wash Road, and proceed 3.9 miles (the road curves to the east after about 3 miles) to the road's end), and the campground.

Facilities: 139 campsites in a large, level, paved, parking lot arrangement; sites/spaces are small to small+ in size, with no separation; space for a few tents adjacent to some sites; fire rings at many sites; b-y-o firewood; water at central faucets; restrooms with freshwater rinse showers; holding tank disposal station nearby; nearest source of supplies and services (complete) is Yuma.

Season, Fees & Phone: Open all year; $6.00; 14 day limit; Bureau of Land Management Yuma District Office (602) 726-6300.

Natural Features: Located on the north shore of Squaw Lake; local vegetation consists of some grass and a few planted trees; the campground is situated just west of the Colorado River; desert plains and barren hills and mountains surround the area; Senator Wash, another sizeable impoundment, is nearby; elevation 200'.

Activities & Attractions: Fishing; boating; designated swimming area; Imperial Dam.

Camp Notes: Access to this area is also possible from Interstate 8 at Winterhaven, via Imperial County Road S24, on the California side of the Colorado River. But the above access information will put you here with fewer directional problems, (i.e., you won't get lost as easily).

Nevada

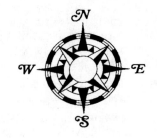

Public Campgrounds

The Nevada map is located in the Appendix.

Nevada 1

MOUNT ROSE
Toiyabe National Forest

Location: Western Nevada southwest of Reno.

Access: From Nevada State Highway 431 at milepost 8 +.1 (8 miles northeast of Incline Village on Lake Tahoe, 16.7 miles southwest of the junction of Nevada State Highway 431 & U.S. Highway 395), turn east onto a paved access road; proceed 0.4 mile to the campground.

Facilities: 24 campsites in a loop and a string; sites are small to medium-sized, with fair separation; parking pads are paved, medium-length, most are straight-ins; many pads have been cut into the hillside and will require some additional leveling; tent spots are somewhat sloped and sandy/rocky; most sites will accommodate large tents; fireplaces; limited firewood is available for gathering in the area, b-y-o is recommended; water at several faucets; restrooms, plus auxiliary vaults; paved driveways; adequate supplies and services are available in Incline Village.

Activities & Attractions: Views from near here are spectacular; Lake Tahoe to the west, and Reno and Carson City to the east; several hiking trails meander through these peaks to small mountain lakes.

Natural Features: Located in the Sierra Nevada near a rocky ridge overlooking the Tahoe Basin; vegetation consists of some junipers and pines; several sites are situated along the edge of a large meadow; barren, rocky-topped mountains in the area include Mount Rose at 10,778'; vast panoramas of the Washoe Valley from just east of the summit of Mount Rose Pass; elevation 8900'.

Season, Fees & Phone: May to September; $7.00; 14 day limit; Carson Ranger District, Carson City, (702) 882-2766 (office) or (702) 882-9211 (recorded information).

Camp Notes: Even if you can't spend the night at Mount Rose Campground, try to approach the Lake Tahoe Basin from this direction, i.e., from the north. If weather conditions are normal or better, the sight is one you'll not soon forget.

Nevada 2

LAKE TAHOE NEVADA
Lake Tahoe Nevada State Park

Location: Western Nevada west of Carson City.

Access: From Nevada State Highway 28 at milepost 2 +.5, (5.5 miles south of the junction of Highway 28 & State Highway 431 in Incline Village, 2.5 miles north of the Washoe County-Carson City line) turn west into the park's Sand Harbor unit (day use) to the park office for information, maps and permits.

Facilities: Primitive camping in 2 backcountry campgrounds, 1 at the north end of the park, one approximately in the center of the park; (a backcountry pamphlet/map with contour lines is available, along with backcountry permits, at the park office).

Activities & Attractions: Hiking on the Tahoe Rim Trail; hiking, horseback riding and mountain biking on more than 20 miles of old logging roads; cross-country skiing.

Natural Features: Located in the mountains above the east shore of Lake Tahoe in the Sierra Nevada; moderately dense conifers are the predominant forms of vegetation; campground elevation 7200'.

Season, Fees & Phone: Principal backcountry camping season is May to October; please see Appendix for standard Nevada state park fees; park office (702) 831-0494.

Camp Notes: In his classic *Roughing It*, Mark Twain said of Lake Tahoe: "I thought it must surely be the fairest picture the whole earth affords". Right on. The park holds much, much more land than even the sizeable chunk which most visitors see as they drive Highway 28. The backcountry is what could be called "reclaimed near-wilderness". Most of it was logged off during the mining boom of the 1800's, but much of it has re-grown to a freshly forested state. (Although we normally don't include detailed information on camping in the boonies, the park's backcountry campgrounds may be your only source of refuge on a busy Tahoe weekend.)

NEVADA BEACH
Lake Tahoe Basin Management Unit

Location: Western Nevada on the southeast shore of Lake Tahoe.

Access: From U.S. Highway 50 at milepost 1 +.9 (1.9 miles north of the Nevada-California border, 10.7 miles south of Spooner Junction at U.S. 50 & Nevada State Highway 28), turn west onto Elks Point Road (paved); proceed 0.5 mile to a fork in the road; bear left into the campground.

Facilities: 54 campsites in 2 loops; sites are quite spacious, with fair separation; parking pads are paved, level, medium to long straight-ins; most sites have level grassy areas adequate for large tents; fire rings and barbecue grills; limited firewood is available for gathering in the area, b-y-o to be sure; water at faucets; restrooms; paved driveways; adequate+ supplies and services are available in the city of South Lake Tahoe, 4 miles south.

Activities & Attractions: Boating; boat launch; sailing; fishing; swimming; 4wd trails lead east of here into the Daggett Pass area; Spooner Lake, 11 miles north, offers picnicking and hiking; the drive along the east shore of Lake Tahoe northward toward Incline Village is through some beautiful, relatively undeveloped country.

Natural Features: Located in the Sierra Nevada on the southeast shore of Lake Tahoe; campground vegetation consists of tall conifers and very little underbrush over a forest floor of grass and pine needles; high, forested peaks of the Sierra are visible across the lake as they rise sharply from the the lake shore; elevation 6200'.

Season, Fees & Phone: May to September; $12.00; 7 day limit; Lake Tahoe Basin Management Unit, South Lake Tahoe, CA (916) 573-2600 or (916) 544-5994.

Camp Notes: Nevada Beach is the only highway-accessible public campground on the Nevada side of Lake Tahoe. The entire atmosphere here, on the east shore of Lake Tahoe, is very different from that of the 'developed' atmosphere on the west (California) shore.

DAVIS CREEK
Washoe County Park

Location: Western Nevada south of Reno.

Access: From U.S. Highway 395 at milepost 7 +.6 (18 miles south of Reno, 12 miles north of Carson City), turn west onto Nevada State Highway 429; proceed 0.4 mile west and southwest; turn northwest (right) onto a park access road and continue for 0.25 mile to the campground.

Facilities: 44 campsites, including 19 designated for trailers (no hookups), in 2 loops; sites are medium-sized, with fair to good separation; parking pads are mostly short to medium-length straight-ins, plus some long pull-throughs; many pads may require additional leveling; some good, large tent spots, but they may be a bit sloped; fireplaces; firewood is usually for sale, or b-y-o; water at several faucets; restrooms with showers; holding tank disposal station; paved driveways; gas and groceries in Washoe City, 3 miles north; complete supplies and services are available in Reno and Carson City.

Activities & Attractions: Discovery Hiking Trail; separate day use area; access to Davis Creek; fishing; swimming; hang gliding.

Natural Features: Located on a sage slope at the edge of an open forest area and tucked up against forested hills; campground vegetation consists of conifers, sage, light underbrush and sparse grass on sandy soil; some views of Washoe Lake and the surrounding valley; elevation 5100'.

Season, Fees & Phone: Open all year, with limited services in winter; $8.00 for a site, $1.00 for a pet; 7 day limit; park office (702) 849-0684.

Camp Notes: This is a really nice park in a pleasant, forest environment on the western edge of the Great Basin. Reportedly, there are a good number of people who make this a comfortable base of operations for exploration of the many notable Western Nevada landmarks.

WASHOE LAKE
Washoe Lake State Recreation Area

Location: Western Nevada north of Carson City.

Access: From U.S. Highway 395 (*northbound*) at Exit 42 (4 miles north of Carson City, 26 miles south of Reno), turn northeast onto East Lake Boulevard and travel 3.25 miles; turn west (left) into the park entrance; turn south (left) and go 0.4 mile to the day use area; or turn north (right) and proceed 0.2 mile, then turn west (left) into the campground. **Alternate Access:** From U.S. 395 (*southbound*) at milepost 10 +.25 (16 miles south of Reno, 14 miles north of Carson City), turn southeast onto East Lake Boulevard; proceed 7 miles south; turn west (right) into the park entrance and continue as above.

Facilities: 49 campsites in 2 loops; (a group camp and an equestrian area are also available); sites are generally large, with nominal separation; parking pads are paved, level, long pull-throughs or straight-ins; tent spots are large and level; some pads for tent/table areas; several sites have ramadas (sun shelters); fire rings; b-y-o firewood; water at several faucets; restrooms with showers; holding tank disposal station; paved driveways; gas and groceries in New Washoe City, 4 miles north; complete supplies and services are available in Carson City.

Activities & Attractions: Boating; sailing; windsurfing; boat launch; fishing for perch and catfish; sandy beach in the day use area; short hiking and equestrian trails.

Natural Features: Located on a sage plain in Washoe Valley on the southeast shore Washoe Lake; vegetation in the campground consists of large sagebrush, sparse grass and some trees; the lake is 6 miles long, 5000-acres in area, and 6 to 15 feet deep; the lake is ringed by low dry hills to the north, high dry mountains to the east, higher barren peaks to the south, and forested mountains to the west; typically breezy; elevation 5000'.

Season, Fees & Phone: Open all year, with limited services November to April; please see Appendix for standard Nevada state park fees; park office (702) 687-4319.

Camp Notes: This is a good, high desert campground. The sagebrush around here is so huge that it provides more shade than most of the trees. (If you desire shade trees, you could take a walk over to the park's day use area.) Very good to excellent views in all directions. There's a lot of recreation potential here.

DAYTON
Dayton State Park

Location: Western Nevada northeast of Carson City.

Access: From U.S. Highway 50 at milepost 6 +.5 (1.4 miles east of Dayton, 22 miles west of Silver Springs), turn south into the south unit of the park; proceed 0.1 mile to the entrance station; turn west (right) into the campground.

Facilities: 10 campsites; sites are smallish, level, with nominal to fair separation; parking pads are gravel, medium-length straight-ins or pull-offs; sandy/gravel, framed tent/table pads are adequate for large tents; fire rings; b-y-o firewood; water at several faucets; restrooms; holding tank disposal station; gravel driveways; limited supplies in Dayton; complete supplies and services are available in Carson City.

Activities & Attractions: Hiking along the Carson River Trail; fishing; horseback riding; historical exhibits nearby.

Natural Features: Located on a desert plain bordered by low hills dotted with a few trees; the Carson River flows past the southern edge of the park; large hardwoods provide very light shade for several campsites; the Sierra Nevada rises a few miles west; elevation 4400'.

Season, Fees & Phone: Open all year, with limited services November to April; please see Appendix for standard Nevada state park fees; park office (702) 885-5678.

Camp Notes: Dayton is the first known site where gold was discovered in Nevada, and it became an early gold mining tent city. With the discovery of the Comstock Lode and the advent of the Silver Rush, the first ore-crushing stamp mill was constructed here and the town served as an important silver ore processing site. Like so many others in the Far West, the boom was short-lived.

FORT CHURCHILL
Fort Churchill State Historic Park

Location: Western Nevada east of Carson City.

Access: From U.S. Highway 95A at milepost 36 +.1 (8 miles south of Silver Springs, 24 miles north of Yerington), turn west onto Fort Churchill Road (paved); proceed westerly for 0.9 mile; angle southwest into the park entrance; at a 3-way intersection just inside the entrance continue southwest (past the museum turnoff) for another 0.7 mile to a fork; take the right fork onto a gravel road for 0.2 mile to the campground.

Facilities: 20 campsites; (a group camp/picnic area is also available); sites are generally quite spacious, fairly level and well-separated; parking pads are gravel, medium to very long, straight-ins or pull-throughs; ample space for large tents; fire rings and fireplaces; firewood is usually for sale, or b-y-o; water at several faucets; vault facilities; holding tank disposal station; gravel driveways; gas and groceries in Silver Springs.

Activities & Attractions: Ruins of Fort Churchill, a U.S. Army post established in 1860 and left to the desert 10 years later; museum/visitor center has historical exhibits; trail from the campground to the ruins.

Natural Features: Located along or near the north bank of the Carson River; very tall cottonwoods provide a substantial amount of shade for campsites; a small stream trickles past the campground; surrounding desert plains and hills are rocky and sage-covered; distinctive purple mountains are visible on the horizon; elevation 4300'.

Season, Fees & Phone: Open all year, with limited services November to April; please see Appendix for standard Nevada state park fees; park office (702) 577-2345.

Camp Notes: Fort Churchill is located along the pioneer route, the Carson Route of the California Trail. The fort served as a desert outpost to protect the Pony Express and other travelers during the years of the Indian Wars. All that remains of the fort are the adobe walls of some of its buildings. The park's tall cottonwoods are part of a long, continuous line of trees which stretch along the river for many miles through the otherwise harsh desert terrain.

SILVER SPRINGS BEACH 7
Lahontan State Recreation Area

Location: Western Nevada east of Carson City.

Access: From U.S. Highway 95A at milepost 41 +.4 (2.8 miles south of Silver Springs, 29 miles north of Yerington), turn east onto Fir Avenue and travel 1.6 miles to a 3-way intersection; turn north (left) and proceed 0.35 mile to the park entrance station; continue ahead for 1.8 miles, then turn east (right) into the campground. (Note: the above directions will take you to Beach 7; by continuing east on Fir Avenue at the 3-way intersection, then south on a dirt road, you can reach the primitive camp areas on Beaches 4, 6, 8, and 10.)

Facilities: 27 campsites; sites are small to medium-sized, with nominal to fair separation; parking pads are paved, level, medium to very long straight-ins; tent spots are grassy or sandy, mostly level, and adequate for large tents; barbecue grills and fire rings; b-y-o firewood is recommended; water at several faucets; restrooms with showers (nearby); holding tank disposal station; paved driveways; (primitive, 'dispersed' camping is also permitted along most of the shore of the reservoir); gas and groceries+ in Silver Springs; nearest source of complete supplies and services is Carson City, 45 miles west.

Activities & Attractions: Boating; sailing; boat launch; designated swimming beach; fishing for channel catfish, white bass, crappie; (a detailed boating and fishing guide is available); swimming; hiking; campfire circle for scheduled summer evening programs; day use areas.

Natural Features: Located on the west shore of Lahontan Reservoir, an impoundment on the Carson River; campsites receive light to light-medium shade from tall cottonwoods; desert hills and mountains surround the lake; the reservoir is 16 miles long and has upwards of 60 miles of shoreline; dozens of small bays and coves provide shelter and add interest to the shoreline; elevation 4200'.

Season, Fees & Phone: Open all year, with limited services November to April; please see Appendix for standard Nevada state park fees; park office (702) 577-2226.

Camp Notes: Silver Springs Beach is a desert park but, since it is situated in groves of trees on the shore of this large reservoir, it offers good choices of sun or shade. The recreation area is available year 'round, but if you venture here in winter, keep in mind that this is a *high* desert park--it consistently drops below freezing at night and there's occasional snow, too.

Nevada 9

RIVERSIDE & CHURCHILL BEACH
Lahontan State Recreation Area

Location: Western Nevada east of Carson City.

Access: From U.S. Highway 50 near milepost 5 (0.5 mile northwest of the dam, 10.5 miles northeast of Silver Springs, 15 miles southwest of Fallon), turn south onto a park access road and proceed 0.6 mile to the Riverside camp area; or continue for an additional 0.2 mile to the Churchill Beach camp areas (just south of the dam.)

Facilities: Primitive (open) camping along the river (also on beaches, unless otherwise designated); gas and groceries+ in Silver Springs; nearest source of adequate supplies and services is Fallon, 16 miles northeast.

Activities & Attractions: Boating, sailing; boat launch, 1 mile southwest in the Cove area, just off U.S. 50; designated swimming beach; fishing for catfish, white bass, crappie, plus some walleye; swimming; day use area.

Natural Features: Located along the east shore of Lahontan Reservoir and along the Carson River just downstream of Lahontan Dam; predominant vegetation is desert brush, plus some hardwoods along the lake shore; bordered by a desert plain, with desert hills and mountains in most directions; elevation 4200'.

Season, Fees & Phone: Open all year, with limited services November to April; please see Appendix for standard Nevada state park fees; park office (702) 867-3500.

Camp Notes: Lahontan is named for the Ice-Age Lake Lahontan which once covered nearly 9000 square miles of the Great Basin to a depth of hundreds of feet. If you look closely, you may be able to distinguish a portion of the ancient lake's former shoreline around the nearby mountainsides. The new Lahontan is a bit smaller. When the reservoir is full it has about 10,000 surface acres of water, but the average area is probably closer to half of that figure. It's still a good-sized body of water, considering the present-day desert climate.

Nevada 10

SPORTSMAN'S BEACH
Walker Lake/BLM Recreation Site

Location: West-central Nevada southeast of Reno.

Access: From U.S. Highway 95 at milepost 65 (16 miles north of Hawthorne, 57 miles south of Fallon), turn east into the campground.

Facilities: 17 campsites; sites are small, with virtually no separation; parking pads are medium to long straight-ins, and most will require additional leveling; tent areas are large, but sloped and rocky; ramada (arched sun/wind shelter) in each site; fire rings; b-y-o firewood, (absolutely b-y-o firewood); no drinking water; vault facilities; paved driveways; gas and groceries, 2 miles south; adequate supplies and services are available in Hawthorne.

Activities & Attractions: Boating; small, paved boat launch; state recreation area (day use) 2.6 miles south.

Natural Features: Located on a rocky sage slope on the west shore of Walker Lake, a natural, freshwater lake; campground vegetation consists of desert brush and sage; some small trees have been planted between sites; the mostly barren Wassuk Range, directly west, has some vegetation at higher levels; elevation 4100'.

Season, Fees & Phone: Open all year; no fee (subject to change); 14 day limit; Bureau of Land Management Office, Carson City NV, (702) 882-1631.

Camp Notes: Don't let the objective description of this spot turn you off. It's really a unique place. To find such an immense body of water in this starkly naked terrain is an undeniably curious encounter. That intrepid frontiersman, legendary mountain man and western good guy, Jedediah Smith, was the first American to pass by here, in 1828. But it wasn't until some years later that another famous explorer, John Fremont, named the lake after his number two scout and tour guide, Joseph Walker. If the planet Mars had a lake, it would look like this.

RYE PATCH
Rye Patch State Recreation Area

Location: Northwest Nevada northeast of Reno.

Access: From Interstate 80 Exit 129 (120 miles northeast of Reno, 22 miles northeast of Lovelock, 45 miles southwest of Winnemucca), turn west (I-80 runs north/south in this section) onto Nevada State Highway 401 (Ryepatch Road, paved); proceed 1.1 miles to the park entrance station; continue 0.3 mile west (across the dam); turn south (left) and proceed 0.1 mile down a paved driveway to the *River* camping area; or continue west then north beyond the River camp area turnoff for another 0.8 mile to the *Westside* camping area.

Facilities: *River*: 31 campsites; sites are medium to large, level, with nominal to fair separation; parking pads are paved, mostly medium to long straight-ins; tent spots are grassy, and roomy enough for large tents; *Westside*: 12 campsites; sites are around the edge of a paved parking lot; parking pads are short straight-ins; small tent spots; small ramadas (sun shelters) for a few sites; *both areas*: fire rings and barbecue grills; b-y-o firewood; water at several faucets; restrooms with showers in Riverside, vaults in Westside; holding tank disposal station; paved driveways; gas and groceries at the Interstate; adequate supplies and services are available in Lovelock and Winnemucca.

Activities & Attractions: Boating; boat launch at Westside; fishing for channel cat, crappie, white bass, black bass; designated swimming beach.

Natural Features: Located on the southwest shore of Rye Patch Reservoir (Westside area) and on the banks of the Humboldt River (River area); Westside sites are near the lake shore and have a few small trees between them; River area sites are on a grassy shelf slightly above the river; some River sites are located alongside a grove of hardwoods; the reservoir is bordered by chalk-colored, sage-dotted bluffs and hills and distant mountains; elevation 4100'.

Season, Fees & Phone: Open all year, with limited services November to April; please see Appendix for standard Nevada state park fees; park office (702) 538-7321.

Camp Notes: This is a welcome stop along an otherwise barren 500-mile stretch of high desert 'tween Reno and Salt Lake City. (There are also a couple of good freewayside rest areas in Nevada; but for all practical purposes, the only other greenery along I-80 is in the Nevada casinos, or inside the cash registers at the fuel stops in Utah.)

Nevada
East
Please refer to the Nevada map in the Appendix

BOB SCOTT
Toiyabe National Forest

Location: Central Nevada east of Austin.

Access: From U.S. Highway 50 at milepost 30 +.7 (7 miles east of Austin, 63 miles west of Eureka), turn north into the campground.

Facilities: 10 campsites, including a multiple family/group unit; sites are medium-sized, with fairly good separation; parking pads are paved, short to medium-length straight-ins or pull-offs, and most will probably require additional leveling; medium to large, fairly level, tent areas; fire rings; a small amount of firewood is available for gathering in the general area; water at central faucets; restrooms; paved driveways; limited supplies and services are available in Austin.

Activities & Attractions: Remoteness coupled with convenience (of sorts); historic silver mining district in the Austin area; some fishing at Birch Creek, 8 miles.

Natural Features: Located on a slight slope just east of Austin Summit in the Toiyabe Range; campground vegetation is mostly sage and moderately dense, short to medium-height pines and junipers that provide some shelter/shade in most sites; hills and mountains covered with sage and dotted with trees make up the surrounding countryside; elevation 7200'.

Season, Fees & Phone: May to October; $6.00; 14 day limit; Austin Ranger District (702) 964-2671.

Camp Notes: *Toiyabe* is a Shoshone word that means "black mountains". Highway signs along U.S. 50 proudly proclaim it to be "The Loneliest Road in America". Few travelers would dispute its claim to that title. Drive Highway 50 late at night, and you'll believe you're motoring along on the dark side of the moon.

BERLIN
Berlin-Ichthyosaur State Park

Location: Central Nevada southwest of Austin.

Access: From Nevada State Highway 361 at a point 1 mile north of the community of Gabbs (34 miles north of the junction of Highway 361 & U.S. 95 east of Hawthorne, 28 miles south of the junction of Highway 361 & U.S. 50 between Austin and Fallon), head east on a paved local road for 22 miles to the Berlin unit of the state park and the campground.

Facilities: 14 campsites; sites are small, with minimal separation; parking pads are gravel, short to short+ straight-ins; adequate space for medium to large tents; fireplaces; b-y-o firewood; water at central faucets; vault facilities; holding tank disposal station; limited to adequate supplies and services are available in Hawthorne, Fallon, Austin, and Tonopah.

Activities & Attractions: Mining ghost town of Berlin, preserved in a state of 'arrested decay'; exhibits of the fossils of ancient fish-lizards; ranger-naturalist talks scheduled in summer.

Natural Features: Located on the west slope of the Shoshone Mountains on the east edge of the high desert plain of Ione Valley; elevation 6500'.

Season, Fees & Phone: Open all year, subject to winter weather conditions, with limited services in winter; please see Appendix for standard Nevada state park fees; park office (702) 867-3001.

Camp Notes: Berlin is a bit hard to reach from civilization. (For that matter, what place in Nevada *isn't* hard to reach from civilization--and perhaps that's the whole point in coming here.) Poking around the residential/commercial district and the old mill can consume a couple of hours. The nearby ichthyosaur exhibit contains the fossilized remains of a trio of large sea serpents caught on the beach when the tide went out on a primordial sea about 100 million years ago. The threesome were members of the largest species of animals of their time. The biggest of the critters were 70 feet long and weighed-in (on the fish scale) at up to 60 tons.

WILD HORSE CROSSING
Humboldt National Forest

Location: Northeast Nevada north of Elko.

Access: From Nevada State Highway 225 at milepost 100 +.3 (11 miles south of Mountain City, 27 miles south of the Nevada-Idaho Border, 73 miles north of Elko), turn west and cross the bridge into the campground.

Facilities: 20 campsites; sites are medium-sized, reasonably level, with fair separation; parking pads are gravel, medium-length straight-ins or long pull-throughs; adequate space for a large tent in most sites; fire rings and barbecue grills; b-y-o firewood; water at hand pumps; vault facilities; gravel driveway; gas and groceries (and, of course, a casino) in Mountain City; adequate supplies and services are in Elko.

Activities & Attractions: Stream fishing for small trout; also fishing and boating at Owyhee Reservoir, 10 miles south.

Natural Features: Located on an open, grassy flat along the west bank of the Owyhee River at the north end of the Independence Mountains; North Wild Horse Creek enters the river at this point; campground vegetation consists of tall grass and sage within the center of the loop, plus junipers and hardwoods which provide limited shade/shelter in some sites; hills and low mountains covered with sage and grass and dotted with a few evergreens and hardwoods surround the area; elevation 5900'.

Season, Fees & Phone: May to October; $5.00; 14 day limit; Mountain City Ranger District (702) 763-6691.

Camp Notes: This seems to be one of those oft-forgotten little places in a not-too-frequently-visited part of Nevada. The drive through Owyhee Canyon, between the reservoir and the small community of Owyhee, is worth the trip. It's an unexpectedly pleasant scenic drive. Mountain City is an early mining town that has gradually transformed itself into a local sportsmen's center. Wild Horse Crossing probably primarily serves as a hunters' and fishermen's camp, but it makes a good stop for anyone.

NORTH WILD HORSE
Public Lands/BLM Recreation Site

Location: Northeast Nevada north of Elko.

Access: From Nevada State Highway 225 at milepost 94 +.1 (17 miles south of Mountain City, 33 miles south of the Nevada-Idaho Border, 67 miles north of Elko), turn northeast onto a gravel access road and proceed 0.2 mile to the campground.

Facilities: 18 campsites; sites are medium-sized, with adequate to good separation; parking pads are gravel, short to medium-length straight-ins, some of which will require additional leveling; adequate, but sloped, space for tents in most sites; small ramadas (arched sun/wind shelters) in most sites; fire rings and barbecue grills; b-y-o firewood; water at a hand pump; vault facilities; gas and groceries in Mountain City; adequate supplies and services are available in Elko.

Activities & Attractions: Fishing and boating on Wild Horse Reservoir.

Natural Features: Located on a southward-facing sage slope overlooking a large valley and Wild Horse Reservoir, an impoundment on the Owyhee River; campground vegetation consists of sage and tall grass, plus a number of large hardwoods that provide natural shade/shelter in several sites; the valley is nearly completely ringed by the dry, almost treeless, hills and mountains of the high desert environment here; elevation 6400'.

Season, Fees & Phone: May to October; $4.00; 14 day limit; managed and operated by the State of Nevada; phone c/o Wild Horse SRA (702) 758-6493.

Camp Notes: Most of the sites have a really terrific view of the valley and the reservoir. The facilities are a little weathered, but for a few bucks it certainly is useable.

WILD HORSE
Wild Horse State Recreation Area

Location: Northeast Nevada north of Elko.

Access: From Nevada State Highway 225 at milepost 92 +.1 (19 miles south of Mountain City, 35 miles south of the Nevada-Idaho Border, 65 miles north of Elko), turn west onto a paved park access road and proceed 0.2 mile to the entrance station and another 0.3 mile to the campground.

Facilities: 33 campsites in 2 loops; sites are small+ to medium-sized with minimal separation; parking pads are gravel, medium to long straight-ins or pull-throughs and most are level; some sites have good, level tent spots; a few sites are extra-large, with very long parking pads; fire rings; b-y-o firewood; water at central faucets; restrooms, plus auxiliary vault facilities; showers; holding tank disposal station; gravel driveways; gas and groceries in Mountain City; adequate supplies and services are available in Elko.

Activities & Attractions: Fishing for rainbow trout, plus some kokanee salmon, brown trout and largemouth bass; boating; boat launch; weekend interpretive programs in summer.

Natural Features: Located on a pair of windswept hills overlooking Wild Horse Reservoir; campground vegetation consists mostly of tall grass and sage; the park is above the northeast shore of the 3000-acre reservoir, in a broad, high desert valley ringed by nearly treeless hills and mountains; elevation 6200'.

Season, Fees & Phone: Open all year, subject to winter weather conditions; please see Appendix for standard Nevada state park fees; park office (702) 758-6493.

Camp Notes: Most campsites have an almost totally unrestricted, 360° panoramic view of this high desert region. Tent campers do stay here, but the campground is probably much better suited to pickup, van and rv camping because of the total lack of shelter (unless you seek out shade under a big sage bush or in the shower). The reservoir was built to provide irrigation water for hay meadows on the Duck Valley Indian Reservation. Water levels are variable.

SOUTH FORK
South Fork State Recreation Area

Location: Northeast Nevada southwest of Elko.

Access: From Interstate 80 (westbound) Exit 303 at the east edge of Elko, travel into midtown Elko to the intersection of Idaho Street (the main drag) & 12th Street; turn south (left) onto 12th Street and go 0.8 mile; turn southeast (left) onto Nevada State Highway 227 (Lamoille Road) and travel 5.3 miles; turn south (right) onto Nevada State Highway 228 (Jiggs Highway) and proceed 5.5 miles to milepost 12 +.4; turn west (right) onto a local road and proceed west and south for 3.8 miles; turn west (right) onto the park access road and proceed 0.5 mile into the park and then to the camping areas around the lake shore.

Alternate Access: From Interstate 80 (eastbound) Exit 301 at the west edge of Elko, travel into midtown Elko to the intersection of Idaho & 5th Streets; turn south (right) onto 5th Street and go 0.8 mile; the road will then curve easterly (left) and become State Highway 227; continue for 6 miles to the junction of Highways 227 & 228 and continue as above. (The above routings should help you to minimize the time spent in Elko's traffic jams.)

Facilities: Open camping along the shore of the lake; vault facilities; (see *Camp Notes* section); adequate+ supplies and services are available in Elko.

Activities & Attractions: Fishing (including ice fishing); boating; boat launch.

Natural Features: Located along the shore of a reservoir on the South Fork of the Humboldt River; vegetation consists mostly of sparse grass and brush; bordered by low hills, plus the lofty Ruby Mountains to the east; elevation 5200'.

Season, Fees & Phone: Open all year, subject to winter weather conditions; please see Appendix for standard Nevada state park fees; park office (702) 744-4346.

Camp Notes: Some of the scenic views are so-so, but others, especially toward the 11,300' mountains to the east, are excellent. Improvements in facilities are said to be "in the works", so by the time you arrive, there could be more creature comforts here.

Nevada 18

Thomas Canyon
Humboldt National Forest

Location: Northeast Nevada southeast of Elko.

Access: From Interstate 80 (westbound) Exit 303 at the east edge of Elko, travel into midtown Elko to the intersection of Idaho Street (the main thoroughfare) & 12th Street; turn south (left) onto 12th Street and go 0.8 mile; turn southeast (left) onto Nevada State Highway 227 (Lamoille Road) and travel 18 miles to Lamoille Canyon Road (road may not be signed) just west of milepost 19 on Lamoille Highway; turn south onto Lamoille Canyon Road, and continue for 7.3 miles, then turn right, into the campground.

Alternate Access: From Interstate 80 (eastbound) Exit 301 at the west edge of Elko, travel into midtown Elko to the intersection of Idaho & 5th Streets; turn south (right) onto 5th Street and go 0.8 mile; the road then curves easterly (left) and becomes State Highway 227/Lamoille Road; continue southeast on '227 for 18 miles, etc., as above.

Facilities: 42 campsites in 3 loops; sites are small to medium in size, mostly level, with good to excellent separation; parking pads are paved, short to medium-length straight-ins; adequate space for at least a medium-sized tent in most sites; many sites have large framed-and-gravelled tent pads; fire rings and barbecue grills; a limited quantity of firewood is available for gathering in the area; water at several faucets; vault facilities; paved driveways; pack-it-in/pack-it-out system of trash removal; general store in Lamoille; adequate+ supplies and services are available in Elko.

Activities & Attractions: Trails; paved foot paths; possible fishing for small trout in spring and early summer.

Natural Features: Located on a flat at the point where Thomas Canyon meets Lamoille Canyon; small streams flow past the campground; vegetation consists of rather dense, medium-height conifers and aspens, and tall grass; the Ruby Mountains, including 11,300' Ruby Dome, rise directly to the east; elevation 7600'.

Season, Fees & Phone: May to October; $5.00; 14 day limit; Ruby Mountain Ranger District, Wells, (702) 752-3357.

Camp Notes: This area is incredibly beautiful. When you see these glacially formed canyons with their lofty, rock walls rising above square miles of pine and aspen, you'll believe you've suddenly been time-and-space-warped to Glacier Park or the Canadian Rockies. It's *that* great here.

ANGEL CREEK
Humboldt National Forest

Location: Northeast Nevada southwest of Wells.

Access: From Interstate 80 Exit 351 for West Wells, at the south side of the freeway, proceed west on a frontage road which becomes Nevada State Highway 231 (paved) for 7.4 miles to the campground access road; turn left and continue for 0.8 mile to the campground.

Facilities: 18 campsites in 2 loops; sites are about average in size, with fair separation; parking pads are paved/gravel, medium to long straight-ins, plus a few pull-throughs; most pads will require a bit of additional leveling; many sites have good tent areas; fire rings and barbecue grills; a very limited amount of firewood is available for gathering in the vicinity, b-y-o is suggested; water at hand pumps; vault facilities; paved driveways; pack-it-in/pack-it-out system of trash removal; limited+ supplies and services are available in Wells.

Activities & Attractions: Angel Lake, 4 miles, has fishing for stocked trout.

Natural Features: Located in a grove of medium-tall aspens in a wide, shallow draw, surrounded by sage slopes; most sites have some shelter/shade; the East Humboldt Range rises to over 11,000' directly west of the campground; elevation 6800'.

Season, Fees & Phone: May to September; $5.00; 14 day limit; Ruby Mountain Ranger District, Wells, (702) 752-3357.

Camp Notes: There are some terrific views of the peaks immediately west of the campground, and to the east, across a broad valley. This is one of only two public campgrounds along Interstate 80 in Nevada which are handy enough to the freeway for a quick overnight stop. (The other is at Rye Patch Reservoir State Recreation Area, in western Nevada.)

ANGEL LAKE
Humboldt National Forest

Location: Northeast Nevada southwest of Wells.

Access: From Interstate 80 Exit 351 for West Wells, at the south side of the freeway, proceed west on a frontage road which becomes Nevada State Highway 231 (paved) for 12 miles (steep and winding, particularly on the last 4 miles) to the campground.

Facilities: 26 campsites; sites are small to medium-sized, with nominal separation; parking pads are paved, short to medium-length straight-ins; some pads will probably require additional leveling; mostly medium-sized, sloped tent areas; some sites have framed-and-graveled tent pads; fireplaces and barbecue grills; b-y-o firewood (some gatherable firewood might be found at lower altitudes); water at faucets (the water supply is unreliable, b-y-o water to be sure); vault facilities; paved driveways; pack-it-in/pack-it-out system of trash removal; limited+ supplies and services are available in Wells.

Activities & Attractions: Fishing for stocked trout; foot trails.

Natural Features: Located in a high, rocky basin on a slope near the shore of small Angel Lake, at the north end of the East Humboldt Range; local vegetation consists primarily of dense, low bushes, tall grass, and a few short aspens; Hole in the Mountains Peak rises to 11,300' a couple of miles south of the lake; elevation 8500'.

Season, Fees & Phone: June to September; $5.00; 14 day limit; Ruby Mountain Ranger District, Wells, (702) 752-3357.

Camp Notes: Whew! What a climb. The road has steep grades and switchbacks, so bring antacids, aspirin, and a dry towel. The trip down isn't really a whole lot of fun for the old buggy, either. If you're towing a trailer, it might be worth considering setting up camp at Angel Creek campground, along the road up, and then sightseeing solo. Lake views are unavailable from most sites at Angel Lake, but it's "right over there".

WARD MOUNTAIN
Humboldt National Forest

Location: East-central Nevada southwest of Ely.

Access: From U.S. Highway 6 at milepost 31 +.5 (6 miles southwest of Ely, 45 miles northeast of Currant, turn east-southeast onto a gravel access road and proceed 0.25 mile to the campground, on the right.

Facilities: 22 campsites in 2 loops; (group camping areas are also available); sites are medium+ to large in the A Loop, and average-sized in the B Loop; most sites are well-separated, more so in the B Loop; parking pads are gravel, mostly long pull-throughs in the A Loop, and medium-length straight-ins in the B Loop; some pads might require a little additional leveling; medium to large, level tent areas; fireplaces and barbecue grills; some firewood may be available for gathering in the general area, b-y-o to be certain; water at central faucets; vault facilities; gravel driveways; adequate supplies and services are available in Ely.

Activities & Attractions: Hiking trails; amphitheater; ball diamond and volleyball courts in the adjacent day use area.

Natural Features: Located on a slightly rolling flat hilltop in light to medium-dense piñon pines and junipers; located at Murry Summit, elevation 7316'; Ward Mountain, at 10,936', in the center of the long, north-south Egan Range, is in full view to the southeast; elevation 7400'.

Season, Fees & Phone: May to October; $5.00; 14 day limit; Ely Ranger District (702) 289-3031.

Camp Notes: There are some really nice campsites here. In fact, many are more than just nice. The sites in the A Loop are larger, and (subjectively) a little better than those in the B Loop. But there's more shelter/shade in the B area. This campground seems to combine the best of two worlds: a forested setting merged with a high desert climate. A good stop.

CAVE LAKE
Cave Lake State Recreation Area

Location: Eastern Nevada east of Ely.

Access: From U.S. Highways 6/50/93 at a point 6 miles southeast of Ely, turn east onto Steptoe Creek Road (also called Success Summit Road, gravel) and travel 5.5 miles east and northeast; turn east (right) into the park and the campground.

Facilities: 20 camp/picnic sites; sites are small, with nominal separation; parking surfaces are gravel, medium-length straight-ins or pull-offs; adequate space for tents; fire rings; b-y-o firewood; water at central faucets; vault facilities; gravel driveways; adequate supplies and services are available in Ely.

Activities & Attractions: Fishing for stocked rainbow and brown trout; limited boating; boat launch; ice fishing, snowmobiling, x-c skiing (if you have a vehicle that'll make it up the road to the park).

Natural Features: Located on the north shore of Cave Lake, a 32-acre reservoir on Cave Creek, in the Schell Creek Range; closely bordered by rocky, evergreen-dotted hills and mountains; elevation 7300'.

Season, Fees & Phone: Open all year, subject to weather conditions; principal season is May to October; please see Appendix for standard Nevada state park fees; park office, Ely, (702) 728-4467.

Camp Notes: Cave Lake has the reputation of being one of the better trout fishing spots in the state. Besides that, its a really pretty spot.

LEHMAN CREEK
Great Basin National Park

Location: Eastern Nevada east of Ely near the Nevada-Utah international border.

Access: From Nevada State Highway 487 in midtown Baker (5 miles south of the junction of Highway 487 & U.S. Highways 6/50, 7 miles north of Garrison, Utah), turn west onto Nevada State Highway 488 and travel 5.5 miles to the park boundary, then 0.05 mile farther to Wheeler Peak Road; turn northwest (right) and proceed 1.9 miles to the Lower Lehman Creek unit, or another 0.55 mile or 0.65 mile to the Upper Lehman Creek unit; (there are 2 entrances for the Upper section).

Facilities: 11 campsites in the Lower unit, 24 campsites in 2 sections in the Upper unit; Lower sites are medium to large and well-separated, with paved, long pull-throughs or medium-length straight-ins; Upper sites are small and well separated, with paved, short straight-ins; trailers are not advised in the Upper section due to snug driveways and pads; fireplaces; firewood is available for gathering in the area; water at several faucets; vault facilities; holding tank disposal station near the park visitor center; pack-it-in/pack-it-out system of trash removal; paved driveways; gas, groceries and slots in Baker.

Activities & Attractions: Lehman Caves (fee charged for Park Service tours); Wheeler Peak Scenic Drive; visitor center.

Natural Features: Located in a wide canyon along the gently sloping north bank of Lehman Creek, on the east slope of the Snake Range; dense hardwoods, timber and brush provide substantial shelter in both units; nearby mountains include Wheeler Peak, 13,063', plus several others in the 12,000' category; campground elevation 7700'.

Season, Fees & Phone: General season is May to October; Lower section is open all year, subject to brief closures during inclement weather, with limited services in winter; $7.00; 14 day limit; park headquarters (702) 234-7331.

Camp Notes: Like the other park campgrounds, the views from this one are excellent. There are a number of creekside sites here. The world's largest mountain mahogany is in the Upper section.

Nevada 24

WHEELER PEAK
Great Basin National Park

Location: Eastern Nevada east of Ely near the Nevada-Utah border.

Access: From Nevada State Highway 487 in midtown Baker (5 miles south of the junction of Highway 487 with U.S. Highways 6/50, 7 miles north of Garrison, Utah), turn west onto Nevada State Highway 488 and proceed 5.5 miles to the park boundary, then an additional 0.05 mile to Wheeler Peak Road; turn northwest (right) and proceed 9.8 miles on Wheeler Peak Road to the campground. (Note: the road is paved, but steep and winding; larger vehicles and trailers may have a tough time beyond Lehman Creek Campground, 3 miles up the road.)

Facilities: 37 campsites in 3 loops; sites are average in size, with reasonably good separation; parking pads are paved, mostly short to medium-length straight-ins, plus a few pull-throughs; many pads may require additional leveling; most tent spots are small to medium-sized and less than level; fireplaces and barbecue grills; some firewood is available for gathering in the surrounding area; water at several faucets; vault facilities; holding tank disposal station near the park visitor center; pack-it-in/pack-it-out system of trash removal; paved driveways; gas and groceries in Baker.

Activities & Attractions: Lehman Caves (fee charged for tours); trails to Wheeler Peak, several small alpine lakes and a bristlecone pine forest; Wheeler Peak Scenic Drive (which you'll use to get to the campground); park visitor center.

Natural Features: Located in a medium to dense stand of a variety of tall conifers and aspens high in the Snake Range; 13,000' Wheeler Peak and its icefield, 2 miles south, are plainly visible across a wide canyon; elevation 10,000'.

Season, Fees & Phone: May to September; $7.00; 14 day limit; park headquarters (702) 234-7331.

Camp Notes: The scenery seen from along the road and from the campground is absolutely superb. What else is there to say?

Nevada 25

BAKER CREEK
Great Basin National Park

Location: Eastern Nevada east of Ely near the Nevada-Utah border.

Access: From Nevada State Highway 487 in midtown Baker (5 miles south of the intersection of Highway 487 & U.S. Highways 6/50, 7 miles north of Garrison, Utah), turn west onto Nevada State Highway 488 and drive 5.5 miles to the park boundary, then an additional 0.2 mile to Baker Creek Road (gravel); turn south (right) onto Baker Creek Road and continue for 3 miles to the campground, on the southeast (left) side of the road.

Facilities: 20 campsites; sites are small, with good separation; parking pads are gravel, mostly short straight-ins, plus a few medium-length pull-throughs and pull-offs; most pads will probably require some extra leveling; tent areas are medium to large; fire rings and barbecue grills; firewood is available for gathering in the area; water at several faucets; vault facilities; holding tank disposal station near the visitor center; pack-it-in/pack-it-out system of trash removal; gravel driveways; gas and groceries in Baker.

Activities & Attractions: Lehman Caves (fee charged); trails to small Baker Lake and Johnson Lake; possible trout fishing on the creek; Wheeler Peak Scenic Drive; visitor center.

Natural Features: Located on a rocky, sage-dotted flat along Baker Creek; some shelter/shade is provided by medium-height conifers and some aspens; several 10,000' to 13,000' peaks stand 4 miles west; campground elevation 8000'.

Season, Fees & Phone: May to September; $7.00; 14 day limit; park headquarters (702) 234-7331.

Camp Notes: About a third of Baker Creek's campsites are streamside. The panoramas in this fairly wide creek canyon are quite excellent--both toward the lofty peaks to the west, and a hundred miles (or so it appears) out across the great valley to the east. Great Basin National Park's territory includes the former Lehman Caves National Monument and the Wheeler Peak Scenic Area of Humboldt National Forest.

Nevada 26

SPRING VALLEY
Spring Valley State Park

Location: Southeast Nevada northeast of Las Vegas near the Nevada-Utah border.

Access: From U.S. Highway 93 at milepost 119 at the east edge of the community of Pioche, turn east onto Nevada State Highway 322 and proceed east, then northeast, for 19 miles to the park entrance; turn north (left) into the campground. (Note: many maps are somewhat ambiguous in their numbering of the state highways around Pioche; best thing to do is to head for, then past the settlement of Ursine, to Eagle Valley Dam and reservoir.)

Facilities: 37 campsites in 2 loops; (a group camp area is also available); site size is slightly larger than average, with fairly good separation; parking pads are gravel, and most are medium to long straight-ins which may require a little additional leveling; medium to large, fairly level, tent areas; small ramadas (sun shelters) over table areas; fireplaces or barbecue grills; firewood is usually for sale, or b-y-o; water at several faucets; restrooms with showers; holding tank disposal station; gravel driveways; limited+ to adequate supplies and services are available in Pioche.

Activities & Attractions: Fishing for trout and bass on the reservoir; stream fishing for trout below the dam; limited boating; boat launch and dock; fish cleaning station; small amphitheater.

Natural Features: Located in a canyon on the west shore of small Eagle Valley Reservoir; the campground is in a small side canyon; vegetation consists of some junipers and piñon pines, plus sparse grass and sage, in a semi-arid, high desert environment; surrounded by low hills dotted with evergreens and brush; elevation 5800'.

Season, Fees & Phone: Open all year, with limited services November to April; please see Appendix for standard Nevada state park fees; park office, Pioche, (702) 962-5102.

Camp Notes: All in all, this is a nice place to spend some time. The surroundings, while not spectacular, are interesting. In the mid-1860's, a group of pioneers named the area Spring Valley after they had counted more than 150 springs in a single day.

Nevada 27

ECHO CANYON
Echo Canyon State Recreation Area

Location: Southeast Nevada northeast of Las Vegas near the Nevada-Utah border.

Access: From U.S. Highway 93 at milepost 119 at the east edge of the community of Pioche, turn east onto Nevada State Highway 322 and drive east for 4 miles to milepost 4 +.76; turn south onto a paved local road signed (hopefully, still) for "Echo Dam"; proceed 7.6 miles to the park boundary and continue straight ahead for another 0.4 mile to the campground, on the north (left) side of the road. (Note: road signs around here tend to be a little vague; best thing to remember might be that, if you find yourself in Utah, you missed it.)

Facilities: 34 campsites; (a group camp area is also available); sites are small+ to medium-sized, with nominal to fair separation; parking pads are gravel, medium to long straight-ins, which may require a slight amount of additional leveling; small to medium-sized, gravel pads for tents; ramadas (sun shelters) over table areas; fire rings and barbecue grills; b-y-o firewood; water at faucets throughout; restrooms; holding tank disposal station; gravel driveways; limited+ to adequate supplies and services are available in Pioche.

Activities & Attractions: Fishing for trout and panfish; boating; boat launch; Ash Canyon Nature Trail.

Natural Features: Located on a sage slope above the shore of small Echo Canyon Reservoir; some hardwoods and evergreens provide a small amount of natural shade; surrounded by dry, low hills; some views of distant mountains; elevation 5500'.

Season, Fees & Phone: Open all year, with limited services November to April; please see Appendix for standard Nevada state park fees; park office, Pioche, (702) 962-5103.

Camp Notes: The reservoir is subject to drastic decreases in water level by midsummer, so fishing, boating and the lake view might not be in their prime then. But, really, it's worth staying here regardless of the water level. You might very well have this park nearly all to yourself.

Nevada 28

CATHEDRAL GORGE
Cathedral Gorge State Park

Location: Southeast Nevada northeast of Las Vegas.

Access: From U.S. Highway 93 at milepost 108 + .9 (9 miles south of Pioche, 15 miles north of Caliente), turn west onto a paved access road and proceed west and north for 0.8 mile; turn west (left) and proceed west and north again for another 0.7 mile to the campground, on the west (left) side of the park road.

Facilities: 22 campsites; sites are small to medium in size, level, with nominal separation; parking pads are gravel, extra wide straight-ins; good, large tent areas; some sites have small ramadas (sun shelters); waste water disposal basins; fireplaces or barbecue grills; b-y-o firewood; water at several faucets; restrooms with showers; holding tank disposal station; limited+ to adequate supplies and services are available in Pioche and Caliente.

Activities & Attractions: Unusual, pastel rock formations; nature trail; small amphitheater; scenic overlook.

Natural Features: Located in a shallow canyon bordered by rocky bluffs and spire-shaped rock formations; medium to large hardwoods provide very light to light-medium shade/shelter in most campsites; canyon floor has tall grass and brush; high mountains in the near distance; elevation 4500'.

Season, Fees & Phone: Open all year, with limited services November to April; please see Appendix for standard Nevada state park fees; phone c/o Nevada State Parks District Office, Panaca, (702) 728-4467.

Camp Notes: Cathedral Gorge is closest to the main highway of the five state parks and recreation areas which offer virtually all of the public camping opportunities in this sparsely populated region. Overall, it may be the most scenically interesting of the quintet as well. Besides Cathedral Gorge and the three other campgrounds described under their own headings (Spring Valley, Echo Canyon and Kershaw-Ryan), a fifth park is available, at a price. The cost to reach the small reservoir at Beaver Dam State Park is a grueling trip from near milepost 100 on U.S. 93 (6.5 miles north of Caliente). From that point, head easterly on a gravel road across the desert hills and plains for 29 miles almost to the Nevada-Utah border. There are about 50 campsites, drinking water and vaults at Beaver Dam.

Nevada 29

McWILLIAMS
Toiyabe National Forest

Location: Southeast Nevada northwest of Las Vegas.

Access: From Nevada State Highway 156 at milepost 0 + .9 (near the southwest terminus of the highway, 2.5 miles west of the junction of State Highways 156 & 158, 42 miles northwest of Las Vegas), turn northwest (right) into the campground.

Facilities: 40 campsites, including 9 multiple-occupancy sites; sites are mostly average in size, with fair separation; parking pads are paved, short to long, mostly straight-ins, plus some pull-throughs; many pads may require additional leveling; tent spots are a bit rocky and sloped but adequate for medium to large tents; (some campers prefer tenting on the widened parking pads); fire rings and barbecue grills; b-y-o firewood is recommended; water at faucets throughout; vault facilities; paved driveways; nearest sources of supplies and services (complete) are in Las Vegas.

Activities & Attractions: Hiking; Bristlecone Loop Trail nearby; several picnic areas in the canyon, including Fox Tail and Old Mill; scenic drive from Lee Canyon to Kyle Canyon on the 9-mile Deer Creek Highway (State Highway 158).

Natural Features: Located on a lightly forested slope in Lee Canyon in the Spring Mountains; vegetation in the campground consists of short to tall timber with very little underbrush; Lee Canyon is a box canyon bordered by timbered ridges and rocky peaks; elevation 8500'.

Season, Fees & Phone: May to October; $8.00; 5 day limit; Las Vegas Ranger District (702) 477-7782.

Camp Notes: The Spring Mountains provide a forest environment smack in the midst of the desert. Perhaps this is an inland version of a 'desert island'.

Nevada 30

DOLOMITE
Toiyabe National Forest

Location: Southeast Nevada northwest of Las Vegas.

Access: From Nevada State Highway 156 at milepost 0 +.7 (0.2 mile past the turnoff to McWilliams Campground, 3 miles west of the junction of Nevada State Highways 156 & 158, 42 miles northwest of Las Vegas), turn northwest (right) into the campground.

Facilities: 31 campsites; sites are mostly medium-sized, with fair separation; parking pads are paved, short to long, mostly straight-ins, plus a few pull-throughs; additional leveling may be needed on many pads; medium to large areas for tents, though they are somewhat rocky and sloped; fire rings and barbecue grills; b-y-o firewood is recommended; water at faucets throughout; restrooms; paved driveways; complete supplies and services are available in Las Vegas.

Activities & Attractions: Hiking; Bristlecone Loop Trail nearby; 9-mile scenic drive from Lee Canyon to Kyle Canyon on the Deer Creek Highway (State Highway 158).

Natural Features: Located in Lee Canyon in the Spring Mountains; sites are situated on a lightly forested slope; vegetation in the campground is short to tall timber with very little underbrush; the canyon is flanked by forested slopes and rocky peaks; elevation 8500'.

Season, Fees & Phone: May to October; $8.00; 5 day limit; Las Vegas Ranger District (702) 477-7782.

Camp Notes: The campgrounds in Lee Canyon provide a really convenient retreat from the summer simmer in the valley far below. They're over 6000' higher (and typically 30° F cooler) than Las Vegas. (How many campers just whiz through 'Vegas on the Interstate, unaware of what the Spring Mountains hold?)

Nevada 31

HILLTOP
Toiyabe National Forest

Location: Southeast Nevada northwest of Las Vegas.

Access: From Nevada State Highway 158 (Deer Creek Highway) at milepost 4 +.5 (4.5 miles north of the junction of Nevada State Highways 157 & 158, 4.5 miles south of the junction of State Highways 158 & 156, 36 miles west of Las Vegas, 22 miles west of U.S. Highway 95), turn east onto a paved access road; proceed 0.1 mile to a fork in the road; take the left fork and continue for a few yards to the campground entrance.

Facilities: 32 campsites; sites are small to medium-sized, and fairly well separated; parking pads are paved, mostly short to medium-length straight-ins; many pads may require additional leveling; tent spots are typically for smaller tents and may be a bit sloped; fire rings and barbecue grills; b-y-o firewood is recommended; water at several faucets; vault facilities; paved driveway; complete supplies and services are available in Las Vegas.

Activities & Attractions: Hiking; nearby Desert View Interpretive Trail; access to Charleston Peak Loop Trail 0.3 mile north; scenic drive along Deer Creek Highway.

Natural Features: Located on a forested hill in the Spring Mountains; sites are situated in a terraced arrangement on the hillside; predominant vegetation in the campground is medium-height, medium dense, piñon pines and junipers; elevation 8600'.

Season, Fees & Phone: May to October; $8.00; 5 day limit; Las Vegas Ranger District (702) 477-7782.

Camp Notes: Trailers are not recommended because room for maneuvering is quite limited. Hilltop is a very popular place on summer weekends. Lots of Las Vegas area residents and visitors prefer cool, breezy 80° temperatures to the hot, dry 110° daytime highs at home. A panoramic superview is available from some of the sites closest to the top of the hill.

Nevada 32

KYLE CANYON
Toiyabe National Forest

Location: Southeast Nevada northwest of Las Vegas.

Access: From Nevada State Highway 157 at milepost 2 +.9 (33 miles west of Las Vegas, 18 miles west of the junction of Nevada State Highway 157 with U.S. 95), turn south into the campground.

Facilities: 22 campsites; sites are small to medium-sized, with pretty good separation; parking pads are paved, short to a generous medium-length, mostly straight-ins, plus a few pull-throughs; a few nice tent spots, but many are small and sloped; barbecue grills and fire rings; a little firewood is available for gathering in the area, b-y-o is recommended; water at several faucets; vault facilities; paved driveways; complete supplies and services are available in Las Vegas.

Activities & Attractions: Hiking; Cathedral Rock foot trail from nearby Cathedral Rock Picnic Area; Charleston Peak, at almost 13,000', is accessible via the 17-mile Mt. Charleston National Recreation Trail; scenic drive along Deer Creek to Lee Canyon.

Natural Features: Located on a forested slope in Kyle Canyon in the Spring Mountains; a small stream (sometimes) flows by many of the sites; campground vegetation consists of tall conifers and considerable underbrush; elevation 7100'.

Season, Fees & Phone: May to October; $8.00; 5 day limit; Las Vegas Ranger District (702) 477-7782.

Camp Notes: Just a half hour from the desert environment of Las Vegas you can hide away in cool, forested mountain surroundings here. An additional campground, Fletchers View, is less than a half mile west of Kyle Canyon Campground. It has 12 similar sites and is open as needed. There is also a parking area in the canyon which can accommodate as many as 10 self-contained units. Kyle Canyon RV Camp is available by reservation only.

Nevada 33

VALLEY OF FIRE
Valley of Fire State Park

Location: Southeast Nevada northeast of Las Vegas.

Access: From Interstate 15 Exit 75 for Valley of Fire (34 miles northeast of Las Vegas, 46 miles southwest of Mesquite) travel east on Nevada State Highway 169 for 14 miles to the west park boundary; proceed easterly for another 2 miles, then turn northwest (left) onto the campground access road for 0.3 mile to the first camp loop, or go another 0.7 mile (around the large 'island' of rock) to the second camp loop. **Alternate Access:** From Lake Mead North Shore Road at milepost 46 +.1 (9 miles south of Overton, 46 miles northeast of Henderson), turn west onto Nevada State Highway 169 and travel 7 miles to the campground turnoff.

Facilities: 59 campsites, including 12 walk-ins, in 2 loops; (a group area is also available); sites are small+ to large, reasonably level, with nominal to good separation; parking pads are gravel, short to medium-length straight-ins; a number of sites have framed-and-graveled tent/table pads and small ramadas (sun shelters); adequate space for medium to large tents; barbecue grills; b-y-o firewood; water at several faucets; restrooms with showers, plus auxiliary vaults; holding tank disposal station; gravel driveways; gas and groceries+ in Overton.

Activities & Attractions: Hiking and equestrian trails; nature trail; Indian Petroglyphs and petrified wood exhibits; visitor center; Lake Mead National Recreation Area (Overton Beach area), 7 miles east.

Natural Features: Located on 46,000 acres of desert, with red sandstone rock formations and darker hills and mountains visible in every direction; a few creosote bushes and yucca plants dot the sandy desert floor; a number of campsites are separated by huge, colorful boulders; elevation 1500'.

Season, Fees & Phone: Open all year; please see Appendix for standard Nevada state park fees; park office (702) 397-2088.

Camp Notes: Valley of Fire resembles places like Canyonlands, Monument Valley or Arches, only on a smaller, less-overwhelming scale. In midsummer, it quite regularly reaches 120° F around here; but in spring and fall the temps are nearly ideal (depending upon your individual preferences). There's plenty of water at Valley of Fire (although it all comes from spigots, unless a flash flood occurs). The camping facilities are on par with (or better than) those in the national recreation area. If you hit the Lake Mead region on a busy weekend, the valley's campgrounds could be your salvation. They should provide a somewhat more tranquility than the big rec areas south of here along Lake Mead's shore, which the locals call the "war zone".

ECHO BAY
Lake Mead National Recreation Area

Location: Southeast Nevada east of Las Vegas.

Access: From Lake Mead North Shore Road at Echo Bay Junction (20 miles southwest of the town of Overton, 42 miles northeast of Henderson), turn southeast onto Echo Bay Road (paved) and proceed 3.8 miles to the upper camp loop or another 0.7 mile to the lower camp loop.

Facilities: 153 campsites in 2 loops; sites are average-sized, level, with nominal separation; most parking pads are gravel, short, double-wide straight-ins; tent areas are sandy, and adequate for large tents; fireplaces and/or barbecue grills; b-y-o firewood; water at central faucets; restrooms; holding tank disposal station; paved driveways; gas and groceries at the marina; complete supplies and services are available in Las Vegas, 55 miles southwest.

Activities & Attractions: Boating; sailing; public boat launch; marina; fishing; hiking; lagoon near the lower loop.

Natural Features: Located on the west shore of Overton Arm of Lake Mead overlooking Echo Bay and the barren Black Mountains beyond; campground vegetation consists of a few shade trees and medium-sized oleander bushes; sites in the upper section are situated on a blufftop above the bay; sites in the lower loop are on a peninsula extending into the bay; typically breezy; elevation 1200'.

Season, Fees & Phone: Open all year; $8.00; 90 day limit; Lake Mead NRA Headquarters, Boulder City, (702) 293-8906 or (702) 293-8947.

Camp Notes: Avid anglers are lured to Lake Mead like high rollers to Las Vegas. ("...anglers...lured..." Ugh! Ed.) Echo Bay reportedly offers some of the best fishing on the lake. One of Lake Mead's heftiest and most prolific sport fish is striped bass. Reportedly, some stripers tipping the scales at half a hundredweight have been boated. Black bass, 'bows, channel cat and crappie can also be found in fishable quantities.

CALLVILLE BAY
Lake Mead National Recreation Area

Location: Southeast Nevada east of Las Vegas.

Access: From Lake Mead North Shore Road (formerly Nevada State Highway 167) at Callville Bay Junction (47 miles southwest of Overton, 24 miles southwest of Echo Bay Junction, 18 miles northeast of Henderson), turn southeast onto Callville Bay Road (paved) and drive 3.7 miles; turn southwest (right) into the campground.

Facilities: 157 campsites in 4 loops; sites are medium--sized with fair separation; parking/tent areas are rectangular in shape and will accommodate a vehicle and a tent on a fairly level, medium to large, sandy gravel surface; most sites have fire rings or barbecue grills; b-y-o firewood is recommended; water at faucets throughout; restrooms; holding tank disposal station; paved driveways; camper supplies at the marina; complete supplies and services are available in Las Vegas.

Activities & Attractions: Boating; sailing; public boat launch; marina; fishing; hiking.

Natural Features: Located on the west shore of Lake Mead on Callville Bay; sites are situated on a very slight, breezy slope above the bay; campground vegetation consists of planted palm trees and oleander bushes; some sites have great views of the bay and the barren Black Mountains across the lake to the east; summer high temperatures commonly exceed 100° F; elevation 1200'.

Season, Fees & Phone: Open all year; $8.00; 90 day limit; Lake Mead NRA Headquarters, Boulder City, (702) 293-8906 or (702) 293-8947.

Camp Notes: The historically significant community of Callville stood near this site in the 1800's, but was submerged when Lake Mead was created by Hoover Dam. Callville Bay Campground reportedly is seldom filled to capacity.

LAS VEGAS WASH
Lake Mead National Recreation Area

Location: Southeast Nevada southeast of Las Vegas.

Access: From the junction of U.S. Highway 93 & Nevada State Highway 147 (Lake Mead Drive) in midtown Henderson, travel northeast on Highway 147 for 7 miles to a junction; continue northeast and east on Lakeshore Road for another 1.9 miles to the Las Vegas Wash ranger station; turn northerly (left) onto a paved campground access road and go north for 0.1 mile, then northwest for a final 0.8 mile to the campground. **Alternate Access:** From U.S. Highway 93 at milepost 4 near the Lake Mead NRA Visitor Center (3 miles northeast of Boulder City), turn northwest onto Lakeshore Road; proceed northwest for 9 miles to the ranger station and continue as above.

Facilities: 89 campsites; sites are average-sized, with fair to good separation; parking/tent areas are rectangular in shape and will accommodate vehicle and tent on a fairly level, medium to large, sandy gravel surface; fire rings and barbecue grills; b-y-o firewood is recommended; water at several faucets; restrooms; disposal station; paved driveways; adequate supplies and services are available in Henderson.

Activities & Attractions: Boating; sailing; public boat launch; marina; very good fishing; visitor center and guided tours of Hoover Dam, 10 miles southeast.

Natural Features: Located on the west shore of Lake Mead on a short, flat ridge overlooking the lake; oleander bushes and tall palms in the campground provide the most significant shelter/shade in the vicinity; Lake Mead, with 550 miles of desert shoreline, was formed on the Colorado River by the construction of Hoover Dam in 1935; elevation 1200'.

Season, Fees & Phone: Open all year; $8.00; 30 day limit; Lake Mead NRA Headquarters, Boulder City, (702) 293-8906 or (702) 293-8947.

Camp Notes: Though open year 'round, the Lake Mead area, and Las Vegas Wash Campground specifically, are most enjoyable during the mild winter months. (However, just try to convince the thousands of enthusiastic summer holiday weekend visitors of that.)

BOULDER BEACH
Lake Mead National Recreation Area

Location: Southeast Nevada southeast of Las Vegas.

Access: From U.S. Highway 93 at milepost 4 near the Lake Mead NRA Visitor Center (3 miles northeast of Boulder City, 3 miles west of Hoover Dam), turn northwest onto Lakeshore Road; proceed northwest for 2 miles; turn northeast (right) and continue for 0.2 mile to the campground.

Facilities: 145 campsites in 2 sections; sites are small+ to medium-sized, with fair to good separation; sites in the western loops tend to be more private, those toward the east are more level; parking pads are gravel, medium to long, straight-ins or pull-offs; some pads may require minor additional leveling; tent spots are reasonably level, sandy, and adequate for large tents; fire rings; fireplaces or barbecue grills; b-y-o firewood; water at central faucets; restrooms; holding tank disposal station; camper supplies at the marina; limited supplies and services are available in Boulder City.

Activities & Attractions: Boating; sailing; public boat launch; marina; fishing; designated swimming beach adjacent; amphitheater; large visitor center with interpretive displays and audio-visual presentations.

Natural Features: Located on the southwest shore of Lake Mead above the lake's Boulder Basin area; vegetation in the campground consists of fairly tall tamarisks and palm trees, with a profusion of bushy oleanders; some sites have views of the lake, the barren desert and the surrounding rocky mountains; summer daytime temperatures rise consistently above 100° F; elevation 1200'.

Season, Fees & Phone: Open all year; $8.00; 30 day limit; Lake Mead NRA Headquarters, Boulder City, (702) 293-8906 or (702) 293-8947.

Camp Notes: Summer waters that reach upwards of 80° F (or a tad cooler) lap the Boulder Beach swim area. In the hot, (100°+) dry summer air it takes only seconds for water to evaporate off bare skin after a swim, and only a few minutes longer for a swimsuit to regain its crispness.

HEMENWAY
Lake Mead National Recreation Area

Location: Southeast Nevada southeast of Las Vegas.

Access: From U.S. Highway 93 at milepost 4 near the Lake Mead NRA Visitor Center (3 miles northeast of Boulder City, 3 miles west of Hoover Dam), turn northwest onto Lakeshore Road; proceed northwest for 0.8 mile; turn northeast (right) onto a paved access road and continue for 0.6 mile, then turn northwest (left) and go 0.1 mile to the campground.

Facilities: 180 campsites; sites are small, respectably level, with fair to good separation; parking pads are hard-surfaced, short+ to medium-length straight-ins or pull-offs; enough room for small to medium-sized tents; fireplaces; b-y-o firewood; water at central faucets; restrooms; paved driveways; limited supplies and services are available in Boulder City.

Activities & Attractions: Boating; sailing; boat launch; fishing; large visitor center with interpretive displays and audio-visual presentations.

Natural Features: Located on a moderate slope above the south shore of Lake Mead; oleander bushes border most sites; about a dozen palms plus a few other desert trees round out the landscaping; the campground is bordered by an open, brushy, rocky slope; the lake is encircled by barren hills and mountains; elevation 1200'.

Season, Fees & Phone: Open all year; $8.00; 30 day limit; Lake Mead NRA Hq, Boulder City, (702) 293-8906 or (702) 293-8947.

Camp Notes: Hemenway is named for an escarpment, known as Hemenway Wall, that rises from the lake shore about a mile east of the campground. Just below the campground is Horsepower Cove--a reflection of one of the principal pastimes at Lake Mead, recreational boating. Hemenway serves principally as a "backup" campground during peak periods.

COTTONWOOD COVE
Lake Mead National Recreation Area

Location: Southeast corner of Nevada south of Las Vegas.

Access: From U.S. Highway 95 at milepost 20 +.4 in the town of Searchlight (35 miles south of Boulder City, 20 miles north of the Nevada-California border), head east on Cottonwood Cove Road (paved) for 13 miles to the ranger station; just past the ranger station, turn south (right) into the upper camp section; or continue down the hill for another 0.8 mile, passing along the north (far left) side of the large parking lot, to the lower section. (Note: the somewhat curvy road into Cottonwood Cove descends continuously as it drops down 2300 vertical feet to lake level; climbing back out could put the pressure on your radiator and tranny cooler on a hot afternoon.)

Facilities: 145 campsites, including 45 in the lower section and 100 in the upper section; sites are small or small+, with nominal to fairly good separation; parking pads are hard-surfaced or gravel, short to medium-length straight-ins or pull-offs; some additional leveling may be needed on many pads, especially in the upper sites; enough space for a tent, contingent upon the size of your vehicle; barbecue grills; b-y-o firewood; water at central faucets; restrooms; holding tank disposal stations; paved driveways; gas and camper supplies nearby; gas and groceries+ in Searchlight. (The "+" consists mostly of casinos and freelance 'slots'.)

Activities & Attractions: Fishing; boating; large boat launch and courtesy dock; marina; designated swimming beach; amphitheater for evening programs; day use area.

Natural Features: Located on a hillside (upper section), and in a small pocket near the lake (lower section), near the west shore of Lake Mojave; vegetation consists of a variety of large hardwoods, some palms, plus oleander and other large bushes; the lake is an impoundment created by Davis Dam on the Colorado River below Lake Mead; bordered by high, desert bluffs and mountains; elevation 700'.

Season, Fees & Phone: Open all year; $8.00; 30 day limit; Lake Mead NRA Headquarters, Boulder City, (702) 293-8906.

Camp Notes: Despite the 100°+ F summer high temps, this is a popular July-August vacation spot. It is (subjectively) a much more pleasant and relaxing place in October and March. Of course, the lower section, with its ample shade and near-the-shore setting, is the *primo* camp area here; but the upper section is a bit breezier and has better views.

Jackcamping and Backpacking
in the West's Parks and Forests

In addition to camping in established campgrounds, as do the majority of visitors, thousands of campers opt for simpler places to spend a night or a week or more in the West's magnificent parks and forests.

Jackcamping

"Jackcamping", "roadsiding", "dispersed camping", or "siwashing" are several of the assorted terms describing the simplest type of camp there is: just pulling a vehicle a few yards off the main drag, or heading up a gravel or dirt forest road to an out-of-the-way spot which looks good to you. Sometimes, especially when the "Campground Full" plank is hung out to dry in front of all the nearby public campgrounds, or there *aren't* any nearby public campgrounds, it might be the only way to travel.

From what we can determine "jackcamping" is an extension of the Medieval English slang word "jacke", meaning "common", "serviceable" or "ordinary". The explanations of "roadsiding" and "dispersed camping" are self-evident. "Siwashing" is an old term from the Southwest. It apparently refers to the practice of cowboys and other travelers making a late camp by just hunkering-down in an *arroyo* or 'dry wash'. After hobbling your horse, the saddle is propped-up against the *side* of the *wash*, (hence *si'wash* or *siwash*), forming a leather 'recliner' of sorts in which to pass the night out of the wind and cold. It may not be the most comfortable way to spend the night, but by two or three a.m. you get used to the smell of the saddle anyway.

As a general rule-of-thumb, jackcamping isn't allowed in local, state and national parks. In those areas, you'll have to stay in established campgrounds or sign-up for a backcountry site.

However, jackcamping is *usually* permitted anywhere on the millions of road-accessible acres of national forest and BLM-managed federal public lands, subject to a few exceptions. In some high-traffic areas it's not allowed, and roadside signs are *usually* posted telling you so. ("Camp Only in Designated Campgrounds" signs are becoming more common with each passing year.) In certain high fire risk zones or during the general fire season it may not be permitted. For the majority of areas in which jackcamping is legal, small campfires, suitably sized and contained, are ordinarily OK. All of the rules of good manners, trash-removal, and hygiene which apply to camping anywhere, regardless of location, are enforced. (Would *you* want to camp where someone else had left their "sign"?) For off-highway travel, the "Shovel, Axe and Bucket" rule is usually in effect (see below).

Since you don't want the law coming down on you for an unintentional impropriety, it's highly advisable to stop in or call a local Forest Service ranger station or BLM office to determine the status of jackcamping in your region of choice, plus any special requirements (spark arrestors, the length of the shovel needed under the "Shovel, Axe and Bucket" rule, campfires, stay limit, etc.) Local ranchers who have leased grazing rights on federal lands are sensitive about their livestock sharing the meadows and rangelands with campers. So it's probably best to jackcamp in "open" areas, thus avoiding leaseholder vs taxpayer rights confrontations altogether. (Legalities notwithstanding, the barrel of a 12-gauge or an '06 looks especially awesome when it's poked inside your tent at midnight.) Be sure to get the name of the individual in the local public office who provided the information "just in case".

If you're reasonably self-sufficient or self-contained, jackcamping can save you *beaucoups* bucks--perhaps hundreds of dollars--over a lifetime of camping. (We know.)

Backpacking

Take all of the open acres readily available to jackcampers, then multiply that figure by a factor of 100,000 (or thereabouts) and you'll have some idea of the wilderness and near-wilderness camping opportunities that are only accessible to backpackers (or horsepackers).

Backpackers usually invest a lot of time, and usually a lot of money, into their preferred camping method, and perhaps rightfully so (timewise, anyway).

Planning an overnight or week-long foot trip into the boondocks is half the work (and half the fun too!). Hours, days, even *weeks*, can be spent pouring over highway maps, topographic maps, public lands/BLM maps, and forest maps looking for likely places to pack into. (We know!)

Backpacking in Western National Forests

To be editorially above-board about this: Of all the possible federal and state recreation areas, your best opportunities for backpack camping are in the national forest wilderness, primitive, and wild areas. Prime backpacking areas in most state parks and many national park units are measured in acres or perhaps square miles; but the back country in the national forests is measured in tens and hundreds and thousands of square miles. Here's where planning really becomes fun.

Backpacking in Western National and State Parks

Finding a backpack campsite in the West's *parks* is relatively straightforward: much of the work has been done for you by the park people. Most state and many national parks which are large enough to provide opportunities for backcountry travel have established backcountry camps which are the *only* places to camp out in the toolies. Yes, that indeed restricts your overnight choices to a few small areas in many cases; but you can still enjoy walking through and looking at the rest of the back country.

Throughout this series, designated backpack campsites and other backpacking opportunities are occasionally mentioned in conjunction with nearby established campgrounds.

Backpacking in Far West National Forests

Tens of millions of acres of incredibly beautiful backcountry can be explored in the Far West, and you probably couldn't go wrong in selecting any national forest wilderness or primitive area. The obvious choice is the High Sierra. There are hundreds and hundreds of miles of trails to explore and as many lakes and streams along which to sightsee, camp and fish. Elsewhere, the best places? The superlative *Trinity Alps Wilderness* northwest of Redding gets the blue ribbon from many backpackers. In northeast Nevada, small, relatively unknown, highly scenic *Jarbridge Wilderness* offers jagged mountain peaks in the 11,000' category. About 75 miles due south of Jarbridge is the Ruby Mountains Scenic Area, topped by 11,300' Ruby Dome.

Backpacking in Far West National Parks

Throughout most of California, the opportunities for backcountry exploration are maintained at a less liberal level than in most other regions in the West. Principally because of the population explosion and subsequent demand for room to roam, backpacking has exceeded its potential in the most popular national parks. *Yosemite, Sequoia, Kings Canyon, Lassen Volcanic, Redwood, Great Basin* National Parks, and *Whiskeytown-Shasta-Trinity* National Recreation Area all list a "limited" number of hike-in camps.

(Incidentally, the beautiful mountain country which is now encompassed by Great Basin NP's boundaries was formerly--and very appropriately--known as the "Wheeler Peak Scenic Area" of Humboldt National Forest.)

Elsewhere, *Death Valley* National Monument, *Golden Gate* National Recreation Area, and *Point Reyes* National Seashore define specific, small numbers of backcountry sites. Conversely, *Joshua Tree* National Monument lists "various locations" with "open" camping.

A permit is mandatory for backcountry camping in all the foregoing areas. In some areas it is possible, or even necessary, to reserve a backcountry campsite. Backcountry reservation information and other 'regs' are highly subject to change. We therefore suggest that you use the *Phone* information in the text to contact your selected park's headquarters and ask for the "backcountry office" or "backcountry ranger" to initialize your trip planning. In virtually every case, they'll be able to provide detailed information and maps--at no charge, or at most a couple of bucks for first-rate maps. The majority of the backcountry people are enthusiastic boondockers themselves, and they'll generally provide sound, albeit conservative, suggestions. Let's face it: they don't want to have to bail anybody out of a tough spot by extracting them on foot, in a dusty green government-issue jeep, or a 'chopper'. (Try living *that one* down when you get home, dude!)

Flatwater Boat Camping in Far West National Forests

Whiskeytown-Shasta-Trinity National Recreation Area provides specified boat-in camps along the shores of its lakes. However, *Lake Mead* National Recreation Area liberally allows "open" camping at "various locations". The same suggestion to ring the backcountry office for information applies to boat travel.

At the risk of demagoguery: We can vouch that it really pays to start planning months in advance for a backcountry trip. Besides, planning *is* half the fun.

Creative Camping

In their most elementary forms, outdoor recreation in general, and camping in particular, require very little in the way of extensive planning or highly specialized and sophisticated equipment. A stout knife, some matches, a few blankets, a free road map, a water jug, and a big sack of p.b. & j. sandwiches, all tossed onto the seat of an old beater pickup, will get you started on the way to a lifetime of outdoor adventures.

Idyllic and nostalgic as that scenario may seem, most of the individuals reading this *Double Eagle*™ Guide (and those *writing* it) probably desire (and deserve) at least a few granules of comfort sprinkled over their tent or around their rv.

There are enough books already on the market or in libraries which will provide you with plenty of advice on *how* to camp. One of the oldest and best is the *Fieldbook*, published by the Boy Scouts of America. Really. It is a widely accepted, profusely illustrated (not to mention comparatively inexpensive) outdoor reference which has few true rivals. It presents plenty of information on setting up camp, first aid, safety, woodlore, flora and fauna identification, weather, and a host of other items. Although recreational vehicle camping isn't specifically covered in detail, many of the general camping principles it does cover apply equally well to rv's.

So rather than re-invent the wheel, we've concentrated your hard-earned *dinero* into finding out *where* to camp. However, there are still a few items that aren't widely known which might be of interest to you, or which bear repeating, so we've included them in the following paragraphs.

Resourcefulness. When putting together your equipment, it's both challenging and a lot of fun to make the ordinary stuff you have around the house, especially in the kitchen, do double duty. Offer an "early retirement" to servicable utensils, pans, plastic cups, etc. to a "gear box".

Resource-fullness. Empty plastic peanut butter jars, pancake syrup and milk jugs, ketchup bottles, also aluminum pie plates and styrofoam trays, can be washed, re-labeled and used again. (The syrup jugs, with their handles and pop-up spouts, make terrific "canteens" for kids.) The lightweight, break-resistant plastic stuff is more practical on a camping trip than glass containers, anyway. *El Cheapo* plastic shopping bags, which have become *de rigueur* in supermarkets, can be saved and re-used to hold travel litter and campground trash. When they're full, tie them tightly closed using the "handles". In the words of a college-age camper from Holland while he was refilling a plastic, two-liter soft drink bottle at the single water faucet in a desert national park campground: "Why waste?".

Redundancy. Whether you're camping in a tent, pickup, van, boat, motorhome or fifth-wheel trailer, it pays to think and plan like a backpacker. Can you make-do with fewer changes of clothes for a short weekend trip? How about getting-by with half as much diet cola, and drink more cool, campground spring water instead? Do you really *need* that third curling iron? Real backpackers (like the guy who trimmed the margins off his maps) are relentless in their quest for the light load.

Water. No matter where you travel, *always* carry a couple of gallons of drinking water. Campground water sources may be out of order (e.g., someone broke the handle off the hydrant or the well went dry), and you probably won't want to fool around with boiling lake or stream water. (Because of the possibility of encountering the widespread "beaver fever" (*Giardia*) parasite and other diseases in lakes and streams, if treated or tested H₂O isn't available, boil the surface water for a full five minutes.)

(Reports from the field indicate that extremely tough health and environmental standards may force the closure of natural drinking water supplies from wells and springs in many campgrounds. The upside to this situation is that, if the camp itself remains open, chances are that no fees will be charged.)

Juice. If you're a tent or small vehicle camper who normally doesn't need electrical hookups, carry a hotplate, coffee pot, or hair dryer when traveling in regions where hookup campsites are available. The trend in public campground management is toward charging the full rate for a hookup site whether or not you have an rv, even though there are no standard sites available for you to occupy. In many popular state parks and Corps of Engineers recreation areas, hookup sites far outnumber standard sites. At least you'll have some use for the juice.

Fire. Charcoal lighter fluid makes a good "starter" for campfires, and is especially handy if the wood is damp. In a pinch, that spare bottle of motor oil in the trunk can be pressed into service for the same purpose. Let two ounces soak in for several minutes. Practice the same safety precautions you would use in lighting a home barbecue so you can keep your curly locks and eyebrows from being scorched by the flames. Obviously use extreme caution--and don't even *think* about using gasoline. A really handy option to using wood is to carry a couple of synthetic "fire logs". The sawdust-and-paraffin logs are made from byproducts of the lumber and petroleum industries and burn about three hours in the outdoors. The fire logs can also be used to start and maintain a regular campfire if the locally gathered firewood is wet.

Mosquitoes. The winged demons aren't usually mentioned in the text because you just have to *expect* them almost anywhere except perhaps in the dryest desert areas. Soggy times, like late spring and early summer, are the worst times. If you're one of us who's always the first to be strafed by the local mosquito squadron, keep plenty of anti-aircraft ammo on hand. The most versatile skin stuff is the spray-on variety. Spray it all over your clothes to keep the varmints from poking their proboscis through the seat of your jeans. A room spray comes in handy for blasting any bugs which might have infiltrated your tent or rv. Fortunately, in most areas the peak of the mosquito season lasts only a couple of weeks, and you can enjoy yourself the rest of the time. Autumn camping is great!

Rattlers. Anywhere you go in the Desert Southwest, expect to find rattlesnakes, so place your hands and feet and other vital parts accordingly. (While preparing the *Double Eagle*™ series, one of the publishers inadvertently poked her zoom lens to within a yard of a coiled rattler's snout. The photographer's anxieties were vocally, albeit shakily, expressed; the level of stress which the incident induced on the snake is unknown.)

Bumps in the night. When you retire for the night, put all your valuables, especially your cooler, inside your vehicle to protect them against campground burglars and bruins. While camping at Canyon Campground in Yellowstone National Park more than two decades ago, a pair of young brothers unwittingly left their stocked cooler out on the picnic table so they had more room to sleep inside their ancient station wagon. Sometime after midnight, they were awakened by a clatter in the darkness behind the wagon. After they had groggily dressed and crept out to investigate, the sleepy siblings discovered that a bear had broken into their impenetrable ice chest. Taking inventory, the dauntless duo determined that the brazen backwoods *bandito* had wolfed-down three pounds of baked chicken breasts, a meatloaf, one pound of pineapple cottage cheese, four quarters of margarine, and had chomped through two cans of *Coors*--presumably to wash it all down. The soft drinks were untouched. (We dined sumptuously on Spam and pork 'n beans for the rest of the trip. Ed.)

Horsepower. Your camping vehicle will lose about four percent of its power for each 1000′ gain in altitude above sea level (unless it's turbocharged). Keep that in mind in relation to the "pack like a backpacker" item mentioned previously. You might also keep it in mind when you embark on a foot trip. The factory-original human machine loses about the same amount of efficiency at higher elevations.

Air. To estimate the temperature at a campground in the mountains while you're still down in the valley or on the plains, subtract about three degrees Fahrenheit for each 1000′ difference in elevation between the valley and the campground. Use the same method to estimate nighttime lows in the mountains by using weather forecasts for valley cities.

Timing. Try staying an hour ahead of everyone else. While traveling in the Pacific Time Zone, keep your timepiece ticking on Mountain Time. That way you'll naturally set up camp an hour earlier, and likewise break camp an hour prior to other travelers. You might be amazed at how much that 60 minutes will do for campsite availability in the late afternoon, or for restrooms, showers, uncrowded roads and sightseeing in the morning.

Reptile repellant. Here's a sensitive subject. With the rise in crimes perpetrated against travelers and campers in the nation's parks and forests and on its highways and byways, it's become increasingly common for legitimate campers to pack a 'heater'--the type that's measured by caliber or gauge, not in volts and amps. To quote a respected Wyoming peace officer: "Half the pickups and campers in Wyoming and Montana have a .45 automatic under the seat or a 12-gauge pump behind the bunk". If personal safety is a concern to you, check all applicable laws, get competent instruction, practice a lot, and join the NRA.

Vaporhavens. Be skeptical when you scan highway and forest maps and see hundreds of little symbols which indicate the locations of alleged campsites; or when you glance through listings published by governmental agencies or promotional interests. A high percentage of those 'recreation areas' are as vaporous as the mist rising from a warm lake into chilled autumn air. Many, many of the listed spots are actually picnic areas, fishing access sites, and even highway rest stops; dozens of camps are ill-maintained remnants of their former greatness, located at the end of rocky jeep trails; many others no longer exist; still others *never* existed, but are merely a mapmaker's or planner's notion of where a campground *might* or *should* be. In summation: Make certain that a campground exists and what it offers before you embark on 20 miles of washboard gravel travel in the never-ending quest for your own personal Eden.

We hope the foregoing items, and information throughout this series, help you conserve your own valuable time, money, fuel and other irreplaceable resources. ***Good Camping !***

Appendix

State Maps

Far West Standard State Park Fees

California State Parks

Primitive/semi-developed campsite	$7.00
Standard/developed/enroute campsite................................	$8.00-$14.00

(The fee varies with the level of amenities, niceties, and creature comforts provided in the campground. A substantial majority of campsites throughout the state park system are priced near the top end of the range.)

Hookup campsite	$16.00-$20.00
Additional for peak season use in most parks	$2.00
Additional for "premium" & south coast camps	$2.00-$13.00
Additional for an extra vehicle in campsite...........................	$5.00-$6.00
Backcountry campsite (per person)	$3.00
Group campsite	$36.00-$187.50
Daily park entry fee (per vehicle)....................................	$5.00-$6.00
Walk-in fee (per person)...	$1.00-$2.00
Additional for a dog (Doggie Dollar).................................	$1.00

Nevada State Parks:

Primitive/semi-developed campsite	$4.00
Standard/developed campsite	$5.00
Daily park entry fee (per vehicle)....................................	$2.00-$4.00

Both states offer annual permits and discount permits for handicapped individuals, disabled veterans, and seniors. Annual park entry permits offer substantial savings for frequent park users.

The above list covers fee information needed by most campers.

It is recommended that you call your selected park a few days prior to arrival to determine the exact campsite fees you'll be charged.

Please remember that fees are subject to change without notice.

Campsite Reservations

Reservations may be made for certain individual and group campsites in national forests, national parks, and state parks in California and Nevada. As a general rule-of-thumb, reservations for midsummer weekends should be initiated at least several weeks in advance.

A fee of $6.00-$7.50 is charged for a campsite reservation. In addition to the reservation charge, the standard campground user fees for all nights which are reserved also need to be paid at the time the reservation is made. (Reservations for consecutive nights at the same campground are covered under the same fee.) If you cancel, you lose the reservation fee, plus you're charged a $5.00 cancellation fee. Any remainder is refunded. They'll take checks, money orders, VISA or MasterCard. (VISA/MC for telephone reservations).

The USDA Forest Service has established a reservation system which affects hundreds of national forest campgrounds nationwide. Continuous changes can be expected in such a large system as campgrounds with reservable sites are added or removed from the list. For additional information about campgrounds with reservable sites, and to make reservations, you may call (toll-free) the independent agent handling the reservation system:

1-800-280-CAMP   (1-800-280-2267)

Reservations for national forest camps can be made from 10 days to 120 days in advance. It is suggested that you take advantage of the full 120-day period for any medium-sized or large forest camp associated with a lake or sizeable stream, or near a national park, if you want to be assured of a campsite there on a summer holiday weekend.

For information about campsite availability and reservations at certain campgrounds in *Joshua Tree National Monument*, *Sequoia National Park*, *Whiskeytown National Recreation Area* and *Yosemite National Park*, you may call (toll-free):

1-800-365-CAMP   (1-800-365-2267)

Reservations for national park campgrounds are available from 10 to 56 days in advance. (Campsites in some national park campgrounds, particularly in *Yosemite NP*, are available *only* by reservation during spring through fall.)

Reservations for individual and group campsites in most *California state parks* may be obtained 10 to 56 days in advance by calling:

1-800-444-PARK   (1-800-444-7275)

(In summer, it is recommended that you make reservations for most California state parks well in advance; for southern coastal parks, reservations are recommended for weekends year 'round. If you're running on a loose schedule, or you prefer not to plunk down your hard-earned greenbacks for a reservation fee, your best bet might be to plan to arrive at a park between 10:00 a.m and 2:00 p.m., as the previous night's campers are checking out.)

When making a reservation by telephone, having a touch-tone phone in your slightly sweaty palms will help speed your way through the "decision tree" of verbal "menus" along the info/rez primrose path.

Reservable campsites are assigned, but you can request an rv or a tent site; rv sites are generally a little larger and most will accommodate tents. When making a reservation, be prepared to tell the reservation agent about the major camping equipment you plan to use, (size and number of tents, type and length of rv, additional vehicles, boat trailers, etc.). Be generous in your estimate. In most cases, a national forest campground's *best sites* are also those which are *reservable*. Most of the national forest campgrounds which have reservable sites still can accommodate a limited number of drop-ins on a first-come, first-served basis.

* * *

For additional information about campsite reservations, availability, current conditions, or regulations about the use of campgrounds, we suggest that you directly contact the park or forest office in charge of your selected campground, using the *Phone* information in the text.

Please remember that all reservation information is subject to change without notice.

INDEX

Important Note:

In the following listing, the number to the right of the campground name refers to the Key Number in boldface in the upper left corner of each campground description in the text.

(E.G. **Northern California 155** is **Acorn**. The number does *not* indicate the page number; page numbers are printed in the text only as secondary references.)

* A thumbnail description of a campground marked with an asterisk is found in the *Camp Notes* section of the principal numbered campground.

NORTHERN CALIFORNIA

SOUTHERN CALIFORNIA

NEVADA

Other volumes in the *Camping* series:

The Double Eagle Guide to
CAMPING *in* WESTERN PARKS *and* FORESTS

__Volume I   Pacific Northwest   ISBN 0-929760-27-1
Washington*Oregon*Idaho   Hardcover 8 1/2x11 $18.95^
(Also in paper cover   6x9   (C) 1992 $12.95)

__Volume II   Rocky Mountains   ISBN 0-929760-22-0
Colorado*Montana*Wyoming   Hardcover 8 1/2x11 $17.95^

__Volume III Far West   ISBN 0-929760-23-9
California*Nevada   Hardcover 8 1/2x11 $18.95^

__Volume IV   Desert Southwest   ISBN 0-929760-29-8
Arizona*New Mexico*Utah   Hardcover 8 1/2x11 $17.95^
(Also in paper cover   6x9   (C) 1992 $12.95)

__Volume V   Northern Plains   ISBN 0-929760-25-5
The Dakotas*Nebraska*Kansas   Hardcover 8 1/2x11 $16.95^

__Volume VI Southwest Plains   ISBN 0-929760-26-3
Texas*Oklahoma   Hard cover 8 1/2x11) $17.95^

^^^ Softcover, spiral-bound editions are also available. Recommended for light-duty, personal use only.
   Subtract $3.00 from standard hardcover price and check here _____ for *Special Binding*.

Available exclusively from: *Double Eagle* camping guides are regularly updated.

Discovery Publishing

P.O. Box 50545   Billings, MT 59105   Phone 1-406-245-8292

Please add $3.00 for shipping the first volume, and $1.50 for each additional volume.
Same-day shipping for most orders.

Please include your check/money order, or complete the VISA/MasterCard
information in the indicated space below.

Name_____

Address_____

City_____ State_____ Zip_____

For credit card orders:

VISA/MC #_____ Exp.Date_____

Prices, shipping charges, and specifications subject to change.

Thank You Very Much For Your Order!

(A photocopy or other reproduction may be substituted for this original form.)